D1246762

Essays in Jewish Intellectual History

Published for Brandeis University Press

by University Press of New England

Hanover, New Hampshire and London, England 1981

Essays in

Jewish Intellectual History

Alexander Altmann

UNIVERSITY PRESS OF NEW ENGLAND
Sponsoring Institutions
Brandeis University
Brown University
Clark University
Dartmouth College
University of New Hampshire
University of Rhode Island
Tufts University
University of Vermont

Copyright © 1981 by Trustees of Brandeis University
All Rights Reserved

Library of Congress Catalog Card Number 80-54471
International Standard Book Number 0-87451-192-5

Printed in the United States of America

Library of Congress Cataloging in Publication data
will be found on the last printed page of this book.

"The Gnostic Background of the Rabbinic Adam Legends," © *The Jewish Quarterly Review*

"Creation and Emanation in Isaac Israeli: A Reappraisal," © 1979 by the President and Fellows of Harvard College

"Free Will and Predestination in Saadia, Bahya, and Maimonides," © 1974 by the Association for Jewish Studies, Cambridge, Mass.

"Maimonides's 'Four Perfections,'" © 1972 by Tel Aviv University

"Maimonides and Thomas Aquinas: Natural or Divine Prophecy?" © 1978 by Association for Jewish Studies, Cambridge, Mass.

"Moses Mendelssohn's Proofs for the Existence of God," © 1975 by Duncker & Humblot, Berlin.

"Moses Mendelssohn on Miracles," © 1980 by Société des Études juives, Paris

"The Philosophical Roots of Mendelssohn's Plea for Emancipation," © 1974 by Jewish Social Studies, New York, N.Y.

"Mendelssohn on Excommunication: The Ecclesiastical Law Background," © 1980 by Magnes Press, The Hebrew University

"The New Style of Preaching in Nineteenth-Century German Jewry," © 1964 by the President and Fellows of Harvard College

"Franz Rosenzweig and Eugen Rosenstock-Huessy: An Introduction to Their 'Letters on Judaism & Christianity,'" © 1944 by University of Chicago Press

"Theology in Twentieth-Century German Jewry," © 1956 by Leo Baeck Institute, London

"Leo Baeck and the Jewish Mystical Tradition," © 1973 by Leo Baeck Institute, Inc., New York

For my dear brother Erwin

Contents

Preface

The fourteen essays collected in this volume span a wide area of Jewish intellectual history, one that extends from the Hellenistic period down to the twentieth century. Each of the pieces selected may be said to deal with a theme characteristic of the period concerned.

The rabbinic mind as it evolved around the beginning of the Christian era was barely touched by the Greek philosophical movement, but it confronted Gnosticism fairly and squarely. The phenomenon of the Jewish response to the Gnostic religion captivated me with particular intensity during the early years of my scholarly interests, when—in the thirties—I came under the spell of Hans Jonas's then brand-new, yet largely ignored book *Gnosis und spätantiker Geist* (1934) and wrote, in German, a volume on the rabbinic *gnosis* which, however, I never published except for some chapters that appeared as articles in German ("*'Olam und Aion*" in the *Jakob Freimann Festschrift*, Berlin 1937; "*Gnostische Motive im rabbinischen Schrifttum*" in the last volume of *MGWJ*, 1939, reprinted Tübingen, 1963), and in English ("Gnostic Themes in Rabbinic Cosmology" in *Essays Presented to J. H. Hertz*, London, 1943; "The Gnostic Background of the Rabbinic Adam Legends" in *JQR*, 1945). The last-mentioned article is reproduced in this volume in a revised form as a specimen of my research in this by now vastly enriched field. It should convey the significance of the Gnostic impact upon rabbinic Aggada.

The following four essays discuss their several topics as related, in each case, to the intellectual climate of a specific phase of medieval Jewish philosophy. Thus, creation and emanation are subjects dealt with in the context of Neoplatonism; free will and predestination are viewed against the doctrinal debates in Islamic Kalām; and human "perfections," including the gift of prophecy, are analyzed from the vantage ground of Aristotelianism. There is a close interconnection between the centrality of a particular theme and the emphases cultivated by a certain philosophical trend. This observation applies also to the next theme, that of *ars rhetorica*, which is clearly inseparable from the Italian Renaissance. With Moses Mendelssohn we move into the eighteenth-century Enlightenment and thereby into an area in which much of the philosophical and political outlook of modern Judaism was nurtured. By studying Mendelssohn's reaffirmation of the time-honored proofs for the existence of God as well as his novel proof in the teeth of Kant's disavowal of all proofs; moreover, by taking cognizance of his ambivalent doctrine of miracle, we catch a glimpse of the stirrings of a new age. The other two essays on Mendelssohn alert us to the incipient struggle for civil admission and the concomitant sociopolitical interpretation of Judaism that rejects the notion of ecclesiastical power ("excommunication"). Finally, the last four essays highlight the changes in spiritual fiber that characterize modern Judaism in the pre-Zionist German sector: the new tonality of preaching that owed a great deal to the romantic spirit; the dialog with Christianity; novel paths in the formulation of theological concepts or modes of experience; and the groping effort of reinterpreting the discarded mystical tradition.

It is hoped that the selection of essays offered in this volume will help to put into focus the openness of the Jewish mind as it traversed the various periods and managed to assimilate to its own substance what suited its purposes and thereby created and articulated new modes of human thought. In a previous collection of mine (*Studies in Religious Philosophy and Mysticism*, Ithaca, N.Y. and London, 1969; reissue Plainview, N.Y.), the emphasis was on *motif* research, tracing the development of certain key notions in Jewish philosophy and Kabbala, whereas here a variety of topics is treated as a documentation of specific phases in Jewish intellectual history.

On the technical side, it may be pointed out that the manner of transliteration of Hebrew and Arabic terms as used according to the slightly varying standards of the journals in which these essays first appeared has been left unchanged. It would have been pointless to attempt a complete uniformity.

My sincere thanks are rendered to the publishers (listed in the Acknowledgments) who kindly gave permission for the reproduction of the articles first published under their auspices.

ALEXANDER ALTMANN

Essays in Jewish Intellectual History

1 The Gnostic Background of the Rabbinic Adam Legends

THE ANGELS OPPOSE THE CREATION OF ADAM

The enmity of the angels toward man is a *topos* frequently found in haggadic and midrashic sources.[1] The angels object to the creation of man, to the giving of the Torah to Israel, and to God's desire to "dwell" in the Sanctuary. In all these instances they express their protest in the words, "What is man that Thou art mindful of him?" (Ps. 8:5).[2] The present study seeks to elucidate the Gnostic background of this motif and of some of its ramifications.

In *Genesis Rabba* (8:5) the theme is artfully treated in homiletical fashion, without, however, obliterating its relatedness to Gnostic material. The angels are described as divided on the issue of man's creation. The angels of love and of righteousness approve of God's plan, and the angels of truth and of peace object to it. The first group argues that man will perform acts of love and righteousness, while the second predicts that he will be full of falsehood and strife. What did God do? He took Truth and cast it to the ground. In dismay the angels exclaimed, "Master of the world, why dost Thou despise thy seal?" God replied, "Let truth spring from the earth" (Ps. 85:12). The reference to Truth (which has replaced the angel of truth mentioned before) as "thy seal" is easily explained. According to R. Ḥanina bar Ḥama, "Truth is the seal of God," a view exegetically expounded by Resh Laḳish and R. Reuben, a Palestinian Amora of the third generation.[3] Yet it is not difficult either to recognize in the angel of truth the figure of Satan, the "Accuser," and to perceive in the casting down of the angel of truth from heaven a homiletical variation of a motif familiar from the apocryphal Adam Books (viz., that of the Fall of Satan and the rebellious angels). It provides a clue to the whole theme of the angels' enmity toward man. In the Adam Books, Adam is said to have been created by God with the purpose of counteracting Satan and his associates among the angels. Since the sole reason of Adam's creation is God's design to oppose Satan, the latter's hostility to Adam is fully explained. One of the Gnostic Adam legends edited by Preuschen elaborates this theme: After the world's creation the angels praised God. Only the "impure Satan" (who is also called Sada'el and Beliar) did not want God to be praised because he wished to be God's equal and his own throne to be like God's. Therefore, at God's command, he was cast down from heaven by Gabriel, Michael, and nine groups of angels. He fell down "like hail from the clouds." God, then, desired to replace Satan, who had been the ruler of the lower world, by another created being of similar rank but without a similar conceit. For this reason man was made of earth: "But the benign God created man out of earth because of the conceit of Satan." Thus immediately after Satan's Fall from heaven, Adam was created. His creation took place above Jerusalem, "the place of the fallen angels," in order further to humiliate Satan.[4] Hence Satan's enmity toward Adam, which subsequently expressed itself in his desire to seduce Adam into disobedience to God, is clearly motivated.

According to such sources as *Vita Adae* (11–17)[5] and *Schatzhöhle*,[6] the ejection of Satan happened not before but after Adam's creation, being due to Satan's refusal to adore Adam. According to this version of the legend, Michael commanded the angels in the name of God to pay homage to Adam, who had been created in the image of God. Satan refused to heed this command. In *Vita Adae* he says: "I was created before Adam. He should worship me." In *Schatzhöhle* he tells his associates: "Do not adore or praise him with the [other] angels. It behooves him to adore me, seeing that I am fire and spirit, while he is only dust formed from a lump of dust." Satan is punished for his disobedience by being expelled from heaven.

> He was cast down and fell to the ground, he and all his associates. His Fall took place on the sixth day, in the second hour.[7] And they were stripped of their garments of glory, and his name was called Saṭana because he had "turned away" [from Hebr. *saṭah*] from God, and Sheda because he had been "cast down" [from Aram. *sheda'*] and Daiwa [from Hebr. *dawa*, to grieve] because he had lost the garment of glory.

Again, Satan's hatred of Adam is well explained. In *Vita Adae* (12) he explains to Adam the reason of his having seduced Eve to disobey God's command: "Adam, all my enmity, envy and pain is directed against you because it was on account of you that I was expelled and divested of my glory which I once enjoyed among the angels in heaven, and was cast down to the ground." A third group of sources[8] omits most of this legendary material and motivates Satan's enmity toward Adam simply by his envy of Adam's glory. Yet here too Adam and Satan are diametrically opposed to one another, as appears from the eschatological notion that in the end Adam will be placed upon the throne of his erstwhile seducer.[9]

As we have seen, Satan's hostility to Adam is a dominant feature of the apocryphal Adam Books. The same motif is reflected, albeit in an attenuated and homiletically varied form, in the midrashic passage quoted. In place of Satan and his associates, it is now simply the angels or certain groups of angels who oppose Adam's creation. As mentioned before, in the angel of truth we recognize Satan. Like Satan in the Adam legends, Truth is cast down from heaven. The quotation from Ps. 85:12 ("Let truth spring from the earth") may allude to man, who is made of earth and is destined to rise and replace Satan.[10] In another passage, *Tosefta Soṭah* 6:5, the angel opposing Adam's creation is called "Accuser" (*meḳaṭreg*), a rabbinic quasi-synonym of Satan. There the Accuser is said to have been fettered. The enmity of the angels is thus a remnant of the full-blown motif found in the Adam Books.

The interpretation seems complete. There is however, a Gnostic background to the Adam legends to which we wish to call attention. A clue to it may be seen in the motif of the fettering of the accusing angel that occurs in the *Tosefta* passage. It has a parallel in *Ethiop. Enoch* (10:4–5), where God commands the angel Raphael to fetter 'Azazel (Satan) and to cast him down into the darkness. This passage combines the two motifs of the fettering and casting down. It also contains the motif of darkness: "Make a hole in the desert in Duda'el and throw him into it. Put beneath him sharp and pointed stones and cover him with darkness. He shall dwell there for ever, and cover his face so that he may behold no light."[11] The fettering of Satan-'Azazel is reminiscent of the fettering of the King of Darkness, a theme that appears frequently in Mandaean literature.[12] It may be assumed that the figure of Satan in both the Book of Enoch and the Adam Books is related to the figure of the Mandaean Ur and, generally, to the Gnostic principle of evil and darkness. A pointer in this direction is the identification of the fallen angels with the "seven stars" in *Ethiop. Enoch* (18:11–21:10). Thus 'Azazel and the fallen angels may be said to bear a relation to Ur (or Rūhā) and the Seven (the seven planets). The demonic character of the planets is a constant feature in all Gnostic systems.[13] In *Ethiop. Enoch* 1:8 the fallen angels are said to be a source of all evil in the world. Whatever its ultimate mythological antecedents—the Iranian Ahriman, the Babylonian Tiāmat, or the Egyptian Seth[14]—the figure of Satan in the Adam legends bears some kinship with the Gnostic principle of evil.

We may go a step further. The motif of the enmity of Satan and his group of angels toward Adam is a reflection, however dim, of the enmity that in Gnostic literature is assumed to exist between the principle of evil and primordial man. This notion goes back to the Iranian Gayomard myth according to which the "Evil Spirit" (Ahriman) is deadly opposed to Gayomard, the primordial man, who was created as the exponent of the light in its struggle against darkness.[15] In the *Poimandres* it is the Demiurge who is opposed to the First Man (*prōtos anthropos*). The Demiurge creates the seven spirits of the planets, whereupon the Intellect (*Nous*) gives birth to his favorite son, the First Man, whom he creates in his own image. This *anthropos* also wants to be creative and he enters the sphere of the Demiurge. According to one tradition, the *Nous* gives him dominion over everything he has created. The seven planetary powers endow him each with part of their own evil nature (falsehood, avarice, audacity, pride, desire, guile, and the power of growth).[16] As a result, the Demiurge becomes his enemy. He increasingly assumes the role of a demonic power turning against *Nous* and the First Man. Reitzenstein has endeavored to show that throughout the *Poimandres* this motif of the enmity of the Demiurge toward the First Man is of vital significance.[17] In Mandaean literature Ptahil represents the typical figure of Demiurge. He has been misled into creating a world in conjunction with Rūhā and the Seven, but they have deprived him of his power as ruler of this world. He therefore decides to create Adam in order to frustrate the evil designs of Rūhā. Adam is to be the ruler of the world.[18] Here the biblical theme of man as lord of creation (Gen. i:28; Ps. 8:6–7), which we saw used in the *Poimandres*, appears in a radically Gnostic adaptation which, like other Gnostic perversions of biblical motifs, is most impressive. Man is created with the purpose of counteracting the evil powers that govern the world. Consequently, Rūhā and her helpers do all they can to destroy Adam. They plan to capture and imprison him in their world. They plot to kill him and to "cast confusion into his party." "Let him have no share in the world, let the whole world belong to us."[19] It is unnecessary to pursue the parallels in other Gnostic writings. It should have become clear that in Gnostic mythology the enmity shown to man by the forces of darkness is an organic and natural part of the system. It grows out of the basic Gnostic idea; Man is a stranger in the world of darkness that he is destined to destroy and whose forces are out to destroy him. The sharp contrasts of the Gnostic myth have been blurred in the monotheistic system of the Adam Books, but the outline is still there. The motif of Satan's enmity toward Adam has its source in the Gnostic myth.

We have traveled some distance in order to interpret the rabbinic theme of the angels' opposition to the creation of Adam. Yet there can be no doubt that behind these midrashic homilies there lies not merely a vague reminiscence of a Gnostic doctrine but a clear awareness and a definite purpose. As in so many similar instances, the midrashic or haggadic story serves the aim of combatting the Gnostic myth through the subtle employment of its very features. The intent is theological and as radically serious as is the Gnostic *Vorlage*. It concerns nothing less than man's role in the Divine scheme of things. Louis Ginzberg suggested that the *midrashim* describing the angels' opposition to man's creation meant to combat the "Philo-Gnostic opinion, according to which man was, wholly or partly, created by the lower powers, not by God Himself." It was in opposition to this particular doctrine, he maintained, that the *midrashim* stressed the angels' effort to prevent man's creation. Far from participating in it, they rather tried to sabotage it.[20] It seems to me that this interpretation fails to take account of the enmity of the angels as such. Nor does it explain the fact that this motif occurs not only in connection with the theme of creation (to which alone Ginzberg's theory would apply) but in connection with other themes as well. There is a common thread that runs through all the topics concerned with this motif, and it is of clearly Gnostic origin: The angels resist the transmission of the pneumatic force to the lower world, be it the bestowal of the Divine image upon man, the giving of the Torah, or the descent of the Shekhina. It recalls the familiar Gnostic theme of the evil planetary powers seeking to prevent the downward passage of the forces of light. It clearly shows that the angels' protests have a decidedly Gnostic background. By playing in homiletical fashion upon this motif the rabbis managed to take the Gnostic sting out of it.

THE ANGELS ADORE ADAM

The motif of the adoration of Adam by the angels in rabbinic literature takes three different forms. The first appears in *Genesis Rabba* 8:12,[21] where R. Hosha'ya describes the angels as having "mistaken" Adam for God. They wished to exclaim "Holy" before him, but God caused sleep to fall upon Adam and so they knew that he was not divine. A simile is used by R. Hosha'ya to illustrate the angels' mistake:

> What does this resemble? A king and a governor who sat in a chariot. The people wished to call out *domine*![22] before the king but did not know which of the two was the king. What did the king do? He pushed the governor out of the chariot, and so all knew which was the king. Similarly, when God created Adam, the angels mistook him [for a divine being]. What did God do? He caused sleep to fall upon him, and so all knew that he was [but] a man.

The simile has an analogy in a passage in *Mekhilta*, Shirata 3 on Ex. 15:2, where the situation at the Red Sea is thus described:

> This resembles a king who visits a province and is surrounded by a multitude of high-ranking people, warriors from right and left, in front and at the back of him. Everyone asks: Which is the king? Because he is of flesh and blood like themselves. When, however, God revealed Himself at the Red Sea, no one asked: Which is the King? When the people saw Him, they recognized Him and opened their mouth and exclaimed: "This is my God, I will glorify Him."

The similarity of the two parables suggests that they depict a familiar situation. The particular reference to the pushing out of the governor seems to be borrowed from an actual incident of which the chroniclers of the time made frequent mention and which must have stirred the imagination of the people in the East. When Galerius, co-emperor under Diocletian, returned from his hapless expedition into Armenia, Diocletian did not permit him to sit at his side in the chariot but bade him walk a mile beside him.[23] R. Hosha'ya's simile bears a striking resemblance to this story. His homily thus consists of three parts: I. The angels wish to adore Adam. II. The simile of the king and the governor. III. God causes sleep to fall upon Adam.

The second form of the *midrash* is found in *Pirḳe de-R. Eliezer*, ch. 11: Such was the impression made by Adam upon all creatures that they were seized with fear, believing that he had created them. "And they came and bowed before him." Adam, however, taught them to give all honor and glory to God, who was their Creator. This version of the *midrash* consists of two parts: I. The creatures adore Adam. II. Adam and the creatures worship God.[24]

The third variation of the theme occurs in the *Midrash Oti'ot de R. 'Aḳiba*, from which *Yalḳut Shime'oni* adopted it:

> When the angels saw him [Adam], they trembled and were taken aback before him. Then they all placed themselves before the Holy One, blessed be He, and said before Him: Master of the world, are there two powers (*shetey reshuyot*) in the world, one in heaven and one upon earth? What did God do? He put His hand upon him and reduced his stature [which had reached from earth to heaven] to a thousand cubits.[25]

The angels' question, "Are there two powers in the world?," is another way of saying "The angels wished to adore Adam." A *midrash* found in *Sefer Ḥasidim*[26] says distinctly, "The ministering angels desired to exclaim 'Holy' before him" (as in type 1), and then states that God reduced Adam's size (as in type 3). This latter variant consists, then, of two parts: I. The angels are inclined to see a divine power in Adam or wish to adore him. II. God reduces Adam's size. All three variations of the theme have, as we may note, part I more or less in common. They differ only with regard to the remedy of the angels' mistake and mention Adam's sleep, his admonition to the angels, and his reduction in size respectively. All three recensions drew obviously on an older common source that spoke of the adoration of Adam by the angels.

What was the source that underlies all variants of this homily? The adoration motif hardly stems from a biblical background, notwithstanding the fact that passages such as Ps. 8:6 and Ez. 28:12ff. raise the stature of man (Adam) far above the human level. Ps. 8:6 ("Yet Thou hast made him but little lower than *elohim* and hast crowned him with glory and honor") is interpreted in all ancient versions (Septuagint, Peshiṭṭa, Targumim) in the sense that man is but little lower than the angels (*elohim*). This could not have given rise to the idea that man was worshipped by the angels. Nor could the mythical description of Adam in Ez. 28:12ff. have led to the midrashic motif of the adoration of Adam by the angels. Adam is pictured here as a cherub, full of wisdom and perfect in beauty, but he is not elevated above angelic rank. Rabbinic exegesis of Ez. 28 (e.g., *Baba Bathra* 75a; *Pesiḳta R. Kahana*, ed. Buber, 36b) furnishes no grounds for the adoration motif.

A late midrashic work (viz., Midrash Bereshit Rabbati of R. Moses Ha-Darshan of Narbonne, first half of the eleventh century) contains the homily in its original form. The Prague manuscript of this work, on which Hanokh Albeck based his edition (1940), preserves the following passage:

> The Holy One, blessed be He, said to the ministering angels, Come and bow before him [Adam]. The ministering angels came [and acted] according to the wish of the Holy One, blessed be He. Satan was the greatest of all the angels in heaven. He said to the Holy One, blessed be He: Lord of the universe, Thou hast formed us from the splendor of the Shekhina and Thou commandest us to bow to him that Thou hast formed from the dust of the earth? The Holy One, blessed be He, answered him, This one who is dust of the earth possesses wisdom and understanding such as is not found in thee.

Satan then proposed a test, and the rest of the passage elaborates this theme (Albeck, pp. 24–26). The learned Dominican Raymond Martini (thirteenth century) quotes this passage in his *Pugio Fidei* (p. 563), adding the postscript: "And it came to pass that he [Satan] did not wish to bow before him and did not listen to the voice of God, whereupon he was cast down from heaven." [27] Louis Ginzberg's suggestion that the entire passage in *Pugio Fidei* was fabricated by Raymond Martini[28] is refuted by Albeck's edition of *Bereshit Rabbati*, which contains the *Vorlage*. It is not too surprising that a passage of this nature should have found its place in this rabbinic work. For *Midrash Bereshit Rabbati* is known to harbor a great deal of heretical extra-rabbinic material from a variety of sources.[29] As it frequently happens, a late apocryphal recension of a motif either preserves it in its original heretical form or adopts it from a foreign source that contains the original form.[30] The second of these two alternatives seems to be the case here.

This apocryphal recension of the motif unmistakably shows both the original form and the ultimate source of the idea. In the Adam Books, God himself demands that Adam be adored by the angels. In *Schatzhöhle* (ed. Bezold, p. 4), the angels hear the voice of God speak to Adam: "Behold, I have made thee king, priest, prophet, master, head and guide of all creatures. They shall serve thee and belong to thee. I have given thee dominion over everything which I have created." "When the angels heard these words," the passage continues, "they all bent their knees and adored him." In the Slavonic *Book of Adam* (ed. Jagič, p. 47), God tells the angels to proceed to Adam and pay homage to him, each with his hosts (seventy altogether). The motif goes through the whole of the apocryphal Adam Books.[31] Some passages in the Mandaean *Ginza* have been recognized as interpolations from an Adam Book.[32] They read: "After Ptahil had created that world . . . he summoned the angels of the house in order that they pay homage to the corporal Adam and his wife Ḥawa in that world of darkness." "Of the angels of fire some shall serve Adam . . . The angels of fire came and submitted to Adam. They came and bowed before him, and did not deviate from his words. Only he, the wicked, . . . deviated from the word of his master, whereupon his master laid him in fetters."[33]

The motif has a clear and definite purpose in the Adam literature. Troje has seen this purpose in an attempt to answer the problem: What place does man occupy in the hierarchy of the Hellenistic cosmos with its abundance of mediatory beings?[34] We suggest that what underlies the Adam legends in general and the motif of Adam's adoration in particular is not the Hellenistic notion of the cosmos but the Gnostic one. The tension between Adam and Satan is but a reflex of the duality of the worlds of light and darkness, of Primordial Man and Rūhā, Ur, the Seven or whatever their names may be in the various systems of Gnostic mythology. In Mandaean Gnosis we hear that the hymns that Adam sings in honor of his father Adakas-Ẓīwā (the Primordial Man) cause the world of darkness to be alarmed. The fact that Adam recognizes his counterpart and his origin in the world of light sets the process of his deliverance in motion.[35] The adoration of Primordial Man has here a significance that arises out of the very character of the Gnosis we hear that the hymns that Adam sings in honor of his father Adakas-Ẓīwā (the Primordial Man) cause the world of essential and organic feature of the myth. In the Adam literature, which is under the spell of the Gnostic world view, the motif of the adoration of Adam has, likewise, a natural place within the pattern of thought encountered there. Yet the function of the motif has changed according to the prevalent monotheistic background. Adam, who takes the place of the Gnostic Primordial Man, is no longer a divine being but the king of all creatures, including the angels, and as such not very far from being deified.

Under Gnostic influence, rabbinic thought too conceived of Adam as a being of almost divine character. The verse Gen. 3:22 ("Behold, the man is become as one of us") was interpreted by R. Judah ben R. Simon by the paraphrase: "Like the Unique One of the universe" (*Genesis Rabba* 21:5). In *Pesiḳta Rabbati* (ed. Friedmann, 192a), this view is described as a "difficult one" (*da'at ḳashah*) and is explained in the sense that Adam was destined to be immortal (*ḥay we-ḳayyam le-'olamim*) like God. The passage continues: "God intended to make him the ruler in his world and king over all his creatures. Said God, I am King in the upper worlds, let Adam be king in the worlds below." The analogy to the corresponding passages in the Adam Books is striking. The only difference is that Adam's kingship is not to be extended over the angels, since they belong to the upper worlds. In the view of R. Pappus (*Mekhilta* on Ex. 14:29; *Genesis Rabba* 21:5; *Canticles Rabba* 1:9), the verse Gen. 3:22 means to say that Adam was like one of the ministering angels. Thereupon R. Akiba protested: "Let that suffice thee, Pappus."[36] The reason for this stern disapproval is plain. R. Akiba sought to obviate the Gnostic interpretation of Adam as a divine being. In *Pesiḳta Rabbati* (192a), the interpretation offered by R. Pappus is recorded anonymously. It is there explained as an indication that Adam was like the angels only insofar as he was to be immortal.

The tendency to counteract interpretations betraying a Gnostic flavor is at work also in the different variants of the adoration motif we have traced. In fact, this motif as developed in midrashic sources can be fully understood only if viewed as a polemic against the Gnostic conception of Adam in general and the adoration motif as it occurs in the Adam Books in particular. There is a subtle irony in the rabbinic statement that the angels "mistook" Adam for God (*ṭa'u bo*) and wished to adore him. The point of describing this desire as due to a mistake can be understood and appreciated only if held against the background of the Adam Books. While the latter say that the angels were commanded to worship Adam, the *midrashim* change the character of the story by declaring that due to a mistake the angels wished to adore Adam. It is true, they imply, that the angels wanted to worship man, but it is not true that God commanded them to do so. Their desire was prompted by an error. This error, the *midrashim* continue, was corrected, and it became manifest that Adam was but a man. The adroitness of the polemical counterstroke is missed if the background of the motif is ignored. By adopting the outline of the story from the Adam Books and by altering it at the same time, in one vital respect the *midrashim* are engaged in an artful polemic. It is surprising to find that their polemical intent has not been noticed before.[37] Bacher only vaguely suggested that R. Hosha'ya's *midrash* was a protest either "against the deification of man in the Christian dogma" or "more probably against the bestowal of divine honors upon the Roman emperors."[38] Our interpretation has shown that the adoration motif goes back to the Adam literature and is used by the rabbis as a weapon against the Gnostic implications of the Adam myth.

ADAM'S SLEEP

R. Hosha'ya's *midrash* (*Genesis Rabba* 8:9) concludes, "What did God do? He caused sleep to fall upon Adam, and all knew that he was man." Why does Adam, by falling into sleep, betray his human nature? Explanations are, of course, readily at hand. Sleep is a sign of mortality, the likeness of death.[39] Troje referred to the Pythagorean conception of Superman, whose divine nature expressed itself in freedom from sleep and want.[40] By sleeping Adam exhibits his human nature. It seems, however, that there is more behind this motif than meets the eye. The simile of the king and of the governor who was pushed out of the chariot suggests that Adam's sleep has a meaning analogous to the governor's being pushed out of the chariot. Otherwise, the simile would not fit the story. We believe that both the simile and the motif of Adam's sleep convey the same idea: Adam ceased to be the *Adam Qadmon*, Primordial Man, in his glory, and became the fallen, earthly Adam. The *midrash*, accordingly, refers to Adam after his sin. In the passage of *Sefer Ḥasidim* quoted above, God is said to have reduced Adam's size and thereby brought home to the angels that Adam was no divine being. According to all rabbinic sources the reduction of Adam's stature took place after his sin and was intended as a punishment. It is, then, obvious that both in the passage of *Sefer Ḥasidim* and in R. Hosha'ya's *midrash* God's action is meant to indicate to the angels that Adam, whom they had mistaken for God, was now revealed as man fallen from his high estate. Whereas before his sin Adam's stature had filled the earth up to the heaven, he was now reduced in size and confined to the earth (according to *Sefer Ḥasidim*) or (according to R. Hosha'ya) pushed out of the chariot (the chariot may be used here as a symbol of the Divine chariot, the *Merkabah*), and cast to the ground where he now lay asleep.

To be asleep thus means being in the state of the fallen Adam, entangled in the net of this world. This, exactly, is the idea of sleep in Gnostic symbolism, and it seems to go back to Iranian mythology. Ohrmuzd causes sleep to fall upon Gayomard, the primordial man. "Before the adversary [Ahriman] came to Gayomard [and killed him], Ohrmuzd caused sleep to fall upon Gayomard. . . . When he woke up from his sleep, he saw the corporeal world as dark as the night, and of the earth not as much as the point of a needle was free from the inroad of harmful animals."[41] "Sleep" denotes here the impotence of man in the face of evil. Even assuming that Ohrmuzd brings sleep upon Gayomard only in order to make death easier for him, as Schaeder interpreted the passage, the fact remains that during Gayomard's sleep he and the world become the victims of evil and darkness. In Gnosis, sleep definitely becomes synonymous with the entanglement of man in the world of evil and his intoxication with the poison of darkness. The soul is sunk into sleep. Adam, the head and symbol of mankind, is asleep.[42] In this sense, sleep is not merely symbolical of, but identical with, spiritual death, the death of the soul, namely forgetfulness, on man's part, of his divine origin. Gnosis, therefore, endeavors to arouse man from his sleep. "Do not slumber nor sleep, and do not forget that thy Master hath commanded thee" (*Ginza*, p. 387; *John*, ed. Lidzbarski, p. 57). "Life knew about me: Adam who was asleep awoke" (*Ginza*, p. 571). "At the call of the Messenger Adam awoke" (*John*, p. 57). "He awakened the master of the mysteries, Adam whom he had sown among the bodies. He awakened me from the sleep which life had caused to fall upon my mind. He cast the seven mysteries [the evil powers of the planets] into confusion" (*Ginza*, p. 577). We have another instance of the use of this motif in a Gnostic sense in midrashic literature. The passage concerned has a direct bearing upon R. Hosha'ya's *midrash* and supports the interpretation we have offered. In *Genesis Rabba* 68 : 12, R. Ḥiyya the Elder or R. Yannai (the passage leaves it undecided which of the two)[43]—both were contemporaries of R. Hosha'ya—explains Gen. 28 : 12 ("And behold the angels of God ascending and descending on it") in the sense that the angels ascended and descended on Jacob.[44]

Some were exalting him and others degrading him, dancing, leaping, and maligning (*ofsim bo qofṣim bo soṭnim bo*). Is it thou, they said, whose features are engraved on High?[45] They ascended on High and [there] saw his features, and they descended below and found him asleep. He may be compared to a king, who sat and administered judgment in the judges' chamber; people ascend to the basilica and find him asleep; they go out to the judges' chamber and find him acting as a judge.

The same *midrash* appears also in a condensed form in a Talmudic passage (Ḥullin 91b), where it is said that the angels compared Jacob's image above with the one below and they wanted to attack him while he was asleep, but that God protected him. To understand these rabbinic passages one must bear in mind that Jacob represents here the figure of Adam, the Primordial Man.[46] The place where Jacob's dream occurred is the place where Adam was created, viz., the site of the future Temple and the center of the earth.[47] The image (*iqonin*; *eikonion*) of Man engraved upon the *Merkabah*, the Divine chariot, (Ez. 1 : 27) bears the features of Jacob.[48] Yet in his earthly existence Jacob, who stands for Man, is sunk into sleep, which means that he has become forgetful of his image upon the Divine Throne. He is entangled in sin and in darkness. Hence the angels accuse him before God. The word *soṭnim* in *Genesis Rabba* 68:12 is a clear allusion to Satan, the accusing angel. Other angels exalt him. In these two groups we easily recognize the protesting and the adoring angels mentioned in the preceding sections of this essay. The motifs of Adam's being pushed out from the chariot and of his being asleep, which occur in R. Hosha'ya's *midrash*, are now seen to correspond to the dual aspect of Jacob, who is asleep while his image appears on the *Merkabah*. Both variants of the motif have the same ultimate meaning: Adam who has forgotten his image on High is pushed out from the Chariot of the King. He is asleep down below.[49]

NOTES

1. See the synoptic presentation in *Midrash Tehillim* 8:2. For other texts, see *Tosefta Soṭah* 6:5; *Sanhedrin* 38b; *Genesis Rabba* 8:5; *Pesiḳta R. Kahana*, ed. Buber, 34a; *Numbers Rabba* 19:3.

2. For a treatment of this theme, see Louis Ginzberg, *The Legends of the Jews* V (1947), p. 69f., n. 12. The rabbinic passages dealing with the angels' opposition to the giving of the Torah have been analyzed by Joseph Schultz, "Angelic Opposition to the Ascension of Moses and the Revelation of the Law," *JQR*, N.S. LXI 4 (1971): 282–307.

3. See Shabbat 55a; Sanhedrin 64a; *Canticles Rabba* 1:9.

4. E. Preuschen, *Die apokryphen gnostischen Adamschriften aus dem Armenischen übersetzt und erläutert* (1900), p. 27ff. (no. 3). The designation of Jerusalem as "the place of the fallen angels" illustrates the anti-Jewish tendency of this source in which Preuschen sees a document of Sethian Gnosis. It bears a striking resemblance to the description of Jerusalem as the place of Rūhā and the Seven in the Mandaean *Ginza* (ed. Lidzbarski, p. 338). This contrasts with a passage in *Schatzhöhle* ("Book of the Cave of Treasures" from the school of Ephraem the Syrian), ed. Bezold, p. 4, where Jerusalem is said to be the "blessed place of the creation and elevation of Adam." Cf. Louis Ginzberg, Die Haggada bei den Kirchenvätern . . . (Berlin, 1900), pp. 25–30. The anti-Jewish attitude of the Adam legends edited by Preuschen corroborates the view that they are of Gnostic origin. Jean Doresse, *The Secret Books of the Egyptian Gnosis* (New York, 1960), p. 184, n. 64, doubted their Gnostic character.

5. The Latin version is based on a Greek text that goes back to a Hebrew source. See E. Kautzsch, *Die Apokryphen und Pseudepigraphen des Alten Testaments* II (1900): 506–12; R. H. Charles, *Apocrypha and Pseudepigrapha* I (1913): 23ff.

6. C. Bezold (tr.), *Die Schatzhöhle übersetzt* (1883): 4. Doresse (ibid.) accepts A. Götze's suggestion that the first part of this book is of Sethian origin.

7. According to the rabbinic timetable of the sixth day of creation, in the second hour God consulted with the angels whether or not Adam was to be created. See *Sanhedrin* 38a and *Leviticus Rabba* 29:1. Cf. Ginzberg, *Die Haggada bei den Kirchenvätern*, 48f.

8. *Apocalypse of Moses* 15:16; Preuschen, op. cit., p. 6ff. (no. 1).

9. *Apocalypse of Moses* 39; Preuschen, op. cit., p. 21.

10. The strange conception of Adam growing out of the earth has a parallel in Iranian mythology, where Mahryag and Marvānag, the first pair, grow out of the earth like plants. Between them the divine power of light, which originates from Gayomard, likewise sprouts from the earth. See M. H. Schaeder, *Studien zum antiken Synkretismus aus Iran und Griechenland*, Studien der Bibliothek Warburg, VII (1926): 214.

11. The motif of the fettering occurs also in *Ethiop. Enoch* 10:11.

12. See *Ginza* (ed. Lidzbarski), p. 84ff.; 507 and passim. On the chronology of the Mandaean writings, see now the summary view in Carl Andresen (ed.), *Die Gnosis II* (1971): 178–9.

13. See Hans Jonas, *Gnosis und spätantiker Geist* I (Göttingen, 1934), p. 161ff.; idem, *The Gnostic Religion*, 2nd ed. (1963), p. 260ff.

14. See L. Troje, *Adam und Zoe*, Sitzungsberichte der Heidelberger Akademie der Wissenschaften, Phil.-hist. Klasse (1916).17: 39.

15. See Schaeder, op. cit., p. 214ff.

16. The description of the power of growth as evil has its parallel in Plotinus, *Enneads* 5.2.1 19ff., where the power of production in the world of plants is said to result from the Soul's sinful move away from the contemplation of its source (Intellect and the One). See J. M. Rist, *Plotinus: The Road to Reality* (Cambridge, 1967), p. 122f.

17. See R. Reitzenstein, *Poimandres* (1904), p. 46ff. This interpretation is rejected by C. H. Dodd, *The Bible and the Greeks* (London, 1935), p. 154, n. 1. Dodd's argument does not sound convincing.

18. *Ginza*, p. 107ff.

19. *Ginza*, p. 113ff., p. 121f.

20. *Legends of the Jews*, V, p. 69, n. 12.

21. For midrashic parallels, see Theodor-Albeck, *Bereshit Rabba*, p. 63.

22. *Yalkut Shime'oni*, Gen. 23 and Isa. 394: "to recite a hymn (*himnon*) before him."

23. See Jacob Burckhardt, *Gesammelte Werke*, I (Basle, 1955), p. 81.

24. *Midrash Tanḥuma*, Pekude 3, end has a (rather corrupt) text that is based on the Pirke de-R. Eliezer passage.

25. *Oti'ot de-R. 'Akiba*, 2nd version (*Bate Midrashot*, ed. Abraham Wertheimer, II: 412); *Yalkut Shime'oni*, Gen. 20.

26. *Sefer Ḥasidim*, ed. J. Wistinetzki and J. Freimann (1924), p. 290; Louis Ginzberg, *Legends of the Jews* V, p. 86, n. 37.

27. For references to the extensive literature on Moses Ha-Darshan and Raymond Martini's use of the work *Bereshit Rabbati* see now Salo W. Baron, *A Social and Religious History of the Jews* VI (1958): 171ff.; 410ff.

28. See Louis Ginzberg, *Die Haggada bei den Kirchenvätern*, p. 44f.

29. See Baron, op. cit., p. 171.

30. See A. Geiger, *Was hat Mohammed aus dem Judenthume aufgenommen?* 2nd ed. (1902), p. 100; A. Epstein, *Eldad ha Dani* (1891), p. 78; idem, *Magazin für die Wissenschaft des Judenthums*, ed. A. Berliner and D. Hoffmann, XX (1893): 251.

31. See Troje, op. cit., p. 31; B. Murmelstein, "Adam, ein Beitrag zur Messiaslehre," *Wiener Zeitschrift für die Kunde des Morgenlande*; XXXV (1928): 269; W. Bousset, Hauptprobleme der Gnosis (1907), p. 174.

32. See R. Reitzenstein, *Das mandäische Buch des Herrn der Größe und die Evangelienüberlieferung* (1910), p. 10. As for Mani's acquaintance with the Adam Books, see M. H. Schaeder, *Urform und Fortbildungen des manichäischen Systems*, Vorträge der Bibliothek Warburg IV, p. 72.

33. *Ginza*, pp. 242; 15–16=33–34.

34. Troje, op. cit., p. 26.

35. *Ginza*, p. 113.

36. *Mekhilta* on Ex. 14:29 and *Genesis Rabba* 21:5 have the correct reading, while *Canticles Rabba* 1:9 is corrupt, as a comparison with the other Pappus passages clearly shows. Cf. A. Geiger, *Urschrift* . . . (1857), p. 329; W. Bacher, *Die Agada der Tannaiten* I (1884), p. 318ff; Theodor-Albeck (ed.), *Bereshit Rabba*, p. 200. On Pappus, see Bacher, op. cit., I:281ff, p. 317. All exegetical comments of Pappus recorded in the *Mekhilta* and in *Genesis Rabba* betray a Gnostic tendency, as has been shown by A. Marmorstein, *Religionsgeschichtliche Studien* I (1910).

37. Cf. Geiger, *Was hat Mohammed*, p. 98ff; Max Grünbaum, *Gesammelte Aufsätze zur Sprach- und Sagenkunde* (1901), p. 69ff.; idem, *Neue Beiträge zur semitischen Sagenkunde* (1893), p. 65.

38. Bacher, *Die Agada der palästinensischen Amoräer* I (1892): 102.

39. See Ginzberg, *Legends of the Jews* V, p. 80, note 25; p. 86, n. 37.

40. Troje, op. cit., p. 26. Troje recalls that according to Reitzenstein, *Historia monachorum* . . . (1916), p. 91ff. and passim, Christian asceticism has its roots in the tendency to achieve deification through freedom from bodily wants.

41. See Reitzenstein-Schaeder, *Studien zum antiken Synkretismus*, pp. 217, 221. Schaeder discovered the meaning of the word *chuāb* in the above-quoted passage to be "sleep" (op. cit., p. 217, n. 1; 351ff.; see also Schaeder's article in *Zeitschrift der Deutsch-Morgenländischen Gesellschaft* 79:205).

42. See Jonas, *Gnosis und spätantiker Geist*, p. 113ff. (*The Gnostic Religion*, p. 68ff.).

43. See Theodor's remark on the terms *ḥad* and *ḥarana* (one; the other) used here, *Bereshit Rabba*, p. 787.

44. The *Gospel According to St. John* (1:51) adopted this midrashic exegesis. See H. Odeberg, *The Fourth Gospel*, p. 35. The Septuagint renders *bo* by *epi autēs* "on it," namely the ladder. See. C. F. Burney, *The Aramaic Origin of the Fourth Gospel* (1922), pp. 115f.

45. The notion that the image (*iḳonin*) of Jacob is engraved on the throne of glory is a well-established rabbinic motif and is presupposed here. See *Genesis Rabba* 78:3; 82:2; *Numbers Rabba* 4:1; Targum Jonathan and Targum Yerushalmi on Gen. 28:12. For further references, see Ginzberg, *Legends* V:290.

46. On the midrashic notion of Jacob as the perfect man, see Ginzberg, ibid.; Johann Maier, *Vom Kultus zur Gnosis* (Salzburg, 1964), p. 129.

47. See Ginzberg, *Legends* V:73; idem, *Die Haggada bei den Kirchenvätern*, 25–30; Troje, op. cit., p. 28.

48. See n. 45. In the Mandaean *Ginza* (p. 559) occurs the notion that the soul is to meet its image on high: "I am going to meet my Image, and my Image is going to meet me; it caresses me and embraces me as if I returned from captivity." Reitzenstein, *Die hellenistischen Mysterienreligionen* (1927; 1956), p. 178ff.

49. Odeberg, op. cit., p. 36 sees in the motif of the ascending and descending angels as found in John 1:51 a symbol of the connection of earthly man with his celestial counterpart. On the influence of the Gnostic symbol of sleep on medieval Jewish thought, see Isaac Heinemann, *Die Lehre von der Zweckbestimmung* . . . (Breslau, 1926), p. 42ff.; Alexander Altmann, *Studies in Religious Philosophy and Mysticism* (Ithaca, N.Y. and London, 1969; New York, 1975), p. 36f. M. Steinschneider, *Magazin* (ed. Berliner and Hoffmann) XIX (1892): 258ff. has collected passages from the *Rasā'il Ikhwān al-Ṣafā'* and from Hebrew sources in which the motif occurs.

2 Creation and Emanation in Isaac Israeli: *A Reappraisal*

In my account of Isaac Israeli's Neoplatonic doctrine,[1] I suggested that his cosmological scheme knew of three kinds of causality by which the world came into being. Interpreting the pseudo-Aristotelian source[2] on which he drew, I distinguished between (1) creation, by which first matter and first form (wisdom), the first two simple substances, are produced "from (by) the power and the will," thereby giving rise to the hypostasis of intellect as the combination of the two; (2) emanation, which denotes the process of the coming into being of the lower hypostases (the three souls and nature, i.e., the spheric power); and (3) natural causality, viz., the production of the corporeal substances through the operation of the sphere. It is the purpose of this paper to reëxamine the validity of this differentiation, which has been challenged so far as the distinction between creation and emanation is concerned.[3] The procedure I shall follow amounts to a rewriting of the chapter on "Creation, Emanation, and Natural Causality" in the light of the critical points raised and with due regard to the progress made in Neoplatonic research during the intervening period of more than twenty years.[4]

Israeli draws a clear line between the way in which intellect comes into being from first matter and first form (wisdom), and the manner in which the subsequent hypostases originate. The difference is, in brief, one between creation "by the power and the will," on the one hand, and emanation on the other. Wherein the difference lies is explained by him in the *Book of Substances* (III, 3r–v)[5] in a passage of considerable weight. Refuting an imaginary opponent, Israeli tries to account for the way in which he had outlined the series of hypostases from intellect down to nature. Each higher hypostasis, he said, produces by its emanation (by its "ray and shade"),[6] the specific nature ("specificality" or "substantiality") of the next lower. Intellect is "the specificality of all substances, and the form which establishes their essence, since its ray and light, which emanate from its shade, are the fountain of their substantiality and the root of their forms and specificality."[7] Having thus placed intellect as the *summum genus* at the very top of the series of emanations and having left out of account the still higher two simple substances (first matter and first form or wisdom), which originate from the power and will, Israeli rightly anticipates this objection: "Why do you not add that the power and the will are the fountain of the specificality of all substances, since it is the power and the will that bring into being wisdom, which is the form and specificality of the intellect and that which perfects its essence?" In other words, why do you differentiate between the function of intellect as an emanative source and the function of power and will?

Israeli's answer is:

> You have made an absurd objection, because you have compared an influencing and acting thing (*shay' aṯarī fi'lī*) to one essential (*ḏātī*). The light of wisdom is brought into being from the power and the will (*min al-ḳudra wa-l-irāda*) by way of influence and action (*'alā sabīl al-ta'ṯīr wa-l-fi'l*), while the light which emanates (*al-munbi'a*) from intellect is essential and substantial (*ḏātī jauharī*), like the light and shining of the sun, which emanate from its essence and substantiality. Specific form is not brought into being from an influencing and acting thing, but from an essential one—like reason which establishes the essence of man, and which does not come from the soul in the way of influence and action, but is essential.

The salient point of this distinction must be seen in the difference between essential causality and causality by action. As an illustration of what is meant by essential causality, the "causes" of a definition, and more especially, the specific difference, e.g., rationality (reason) in the definition of man (rational animal), are quoted.[8] This would seem to indicate that Israeli regards the procession of the simple substances from intellect as constituting a logically necessary order in contrast to the coming into being of intellect, which is due to an act of power and will. As for causality by way of influence and action, it can denote only creation out of nothing. In his *Book of Definitions* (§42–44),[9] Israeli distinguishes between two kinds of action (causation; creation): (1) innovation and making-anew (*al-ibdāʿ wa'l-ikhtirāʿ*), which is defined as "making existent existences from the non-existent" (*ta'yīs al-aysāt min lays*); and (2) the action of "bringing into being existences from the existing." The first kind of action belongs to none except the Creator. The second is performed by the spheric power that is "appointed" by the Creator "for the action of coming-to-be and passing-away; e.g., the causing-to-be of animals and plants." Occasionally, Israeli calls the action of the spheric power also one of "influencing" coming-to-be and passing-away,"[10] which clearly shows that the two terms "acting" and "influencing" are synonymous. The same is true of "innovation" and "making-anew." Since the emanation of the substances from intellect is said to represent essential causality and not the causality of action and influencing, it is obvious that Israeli wishes to differentiate between *creatio ex nihilo* and emanation as two distinct stages in the genesis of the spiritual world.

He had, we believe, good reasons for combining an emanationist metaphysic with the concept of creation out of nothing. In so doing he followed a precedent set in certain circles of early Islamic Neoplatonism. Ammonius's book *On the Opinions of the Philosophers*, which was discovered by Stern, attributes Neoplatonic doctrines to the ancient Greek philosophers.[11] It opens with a discussion of the problem of creation: did the Creator create (*abdaʿa*) this world and the form contained in it from something or from nothing (*min shay'in am min lā shay'*)? The two alternatives are explained in these terms: if from something, then that thing is coeternal with the Creator, which is not permissible; if from nothing, the question arises whether the form of the thing was with Him, or whether He created things without having their forms with Him in essence. We may interpret the two options posed as *creatio ex nihilo* in the sense of an emanation of forms out of God's essence and as *creatio ex nihilo* in the more orthodox sense of a Divine fiat. Using Israeli's terminology, we might describe the two meanings of creation out of nothing as essential causation and causation by way of influence and action from power and will. Ammonius states in the name of Thales: "As He is the one who brings the existents into being, and 'bringing into existence' means from no preexistent thing and from nothing, yet bringing it into existence, it follows that He who brings the existent into existence need not have the form of the existents with Him in order to bring them into existence . . . As the first Creator has the utmost excellence, He cannot have forms with Him." This view clearly corresponds to the orthodox doctrine of *creatio ex nihilo*. Ammonius rejects Plutarch's opinion to the contrary: the Creator had infinite forms present with Him in his foreknowledge. He finally records in Xenophanes's name the view that is similar to Thales's: the Creator created what He desired and as He willed; He was He, and nothing existed together with Him. This view, it is explained, denies the eternity of form and matter, and of everything else besides God.[12] Israeli could well have followed this trend in Islamic Neoplatonism.

What probably clinched his adoption of the concept of *creatio ex nihilo* and his interpretation of it as "action" rather than emanative and "essential" was the very text of his pseudo-Aristotelian source, which called for an exegesis along the lines followed by him. The text[13] commences its account of the coming-into-being of the spiritual substances with a description of the first stage, which contains no reference whatsoever to emanation: "The first of created things (*awwal al-mukhtar'āt*) are two simple substances: the first matter . . . and the form which precedes that which is found with it, i.e. the perfect wisdom, by the conjunction of which with matter the nature of intellect came into being with the result that intellect, being composed of it and matter, is a species of it."[14] The first mention of emanation occurs only after intellect has appeared: "After the nature of intellect had been established,[15] a flame went forth from it and a light like the flame which goes forth from the sun and falls upon glass in a dark house. From this flame arose the rational soul." It seems, therefore, that emanation plays no part in the genesis of first matter and first form. Hence the need for assuming an act of creation *ex nihilo* from the power and the will.

One further consideration could have motivated Israeli's positing of creation *ex nihilo* prior to the series of emanations. In all Neoplatonic systems the principle prevails that from the One only one substance can proceed. As Aenesidemus put it, two cannot arise out of the One.[16] In Plotinus's *Enneads* and the Arabic texts based on it (the vulgate version of the *Theology of Aristotle*; the *Epistle on Divine Knowledge*; the *Dicta of the Greek Sage*),[17] it is intellect that immediately follows the One. In the pseudo-Empedoclean *Five Substances*, matter alone is interposed between God and the intellect: "When the Creator, blessed be He, created the world, He created the world of matter, alive with eternal intellectual life. Matter draws this life from the Creator . . . and in that matter are all forms of that world in the most subtle, simple, glorious, and beautiful manner possible . . . After He had created this matter, He created intellect."[18] The description of matter as containing "all forms" does not indicate a dual hypostasis of matter of form, let alone two distinct substances such as we meet in the Israeli source. It merely characterizes the nature of matter as the matrix of all forms.[19] There is a clear distinction between the position of two simple substances (first matter and first form or wisdom) in the Israeli source and the positing of matter in Pseudo-Empedocles. Here the unitary character of the first emanation is upheld, irrespective of whether or not the presence of "all forms" in matter is consistent with the principle that from the One only one substance can emanate. The fact that Israeli's Neoplatonic source places two simple substances at the very top of the series of emanations must have presented a problem to him. This fact obviously precluded the assumption that the two first substances owed their existence to a process of emanation. Creation *ex nihilo* as an act by power and will must have suggested itself as the only sensible interpretation. The adoption of such a theory was not altogether a novelty in a Neoplatonic context, as we have seen. It is doubtful, however, whether the combination of a creationist and an emanationist doctrine within one system had any precedent.

Israeli's positing of two simple substances as "the first of created things" may be considered as the most potent argument against any attempt of interpreting his use of the term creation *ex nihilo* in an emanationist sense. A valiant attempt of this kind was made by the late Harry A. Wolfson.[20] The identification of creation *ex nihilo* with emanation, he pointed out, was not unknown in the history of philosophy. Examples cited by him are John Scotus Erigena in Christianity, al-Fārābī and Ibn Miskawaih in Islam, and *Sefer Yeṣirah*, Ibn Gabirol, and Crescas in Judaism.[21] He could have added the long Arabic recension of the *Theology of Aristotle*, which describes the Word (*kalima*) as *nihil* (*laysa*) on account of its being neither at rest nor moving, and which designates the Word as the "Cause of Causes" and as the "First Creator."[22] Creation *ex nihilo* here undoubtedly means creation out of the Word, i.e., emanation. In Wolfson's view Israeli should be counted among those who identified *ex nihilo* with emanation. There was no need of attributing to Israeli "an unheard-of hybrid theory—creation *ex nihilo* of the two first substances constituting the intellect and emanation of the spiritual substances below the intellect." The contrast drawn by Israeli between the causality of action and essential causality was not necessarily a contrast between creation *ex nihilo* and emanation. "It may be a contrast between two kinds of emanation, one an emanation immediately from God, which follows directly from the will and power, and the other an emanation from intermediaries, which on the part of those intermediaries is an unconscious act, like the shining of the sun."[23] Wolfson further outlines his view of Israeli's position: "What we have here in Israeli is a theory of a volitional and presumably also noneternal process of emanation in which the first emanated being is described as having been created *ex nihilo* on the ground that it was not created from a pre-existent eternal matter or in the likeness of a pre-existent eternal ideal pattern."[24] We may sum up Wolfson's interpretation of Israeli as a two-stage theory of emanation: at the first stage the "emanated being"—Wolfson ignores the two first substances—arises directly from the power and the will, without any pre-existent matter or form being involved; hence the designation "creation ex nihilo"; at the second stage emanation proceeds as an unconscious act, unlike the "volitional" character of the first stage. Both emanations are a noneternal process, that is, they occur in time. What is not explained here is how by way of emanation two simple substances could have arisen simultaneously.

Ibn Gabirol, who followed Israeli in positing universal matter and universal form at the top of the series of spiritual substances, was confronted with the same problem. He did identify creation *ex nihilo* with emanation, as Wolfson pointed out,[25] and he had therefore to account for the duality of the two uppermost principles in the hierarchy of emanations. He solved the problem by deriving form from the will, and matter from the essence of God, a solution bristling with difficulties.[26] There are no grounds for assuming that Israeli linked form with the will, and matter with the power of God in order to resolve the problem presented by the emanation of these two first substances. Such a problem simply did not exist for him. He eliminated it by drawing a line between creation *ex nihilo* and emanation.

The deliberate manner in which Israeli explains this distinction can leave no doubt as to the seriousness with which he viewed it. It is important to bear this in mind so as not to be misled by occasional lapses in his terminology, which may be due to his familiarity with the usual type of purely emanationist Neoplatonic sources. Thus, when discussing the reasons for the difference in the degree of light between the various substances, he says:

> Regarding the quality of the emanation of the light from the power and the will (*inbiʿāt al-nūr min al-ḳudra wa-l-irāda*), we have already made it clear that its beginning is different from its end, and the middle from both extremes, and this for the following reason: when its beginning emanated from the power and the will, it met no shade or darkness to make it dim and coarse—while its end met various imperfections and obscurities which made it dim and coarse; the middle partook of both extremes.[27]

In this passage the "beginning" of the series can only mean what is referred to earlier in the same context as "the first of created things [which] are two simple substances," and yet this "beginning" is said to have "emanated" from the power and the will. In another sentence prior to the one quoted, Israeli speaks of "the quality of the emanation of the light which is created from the power and the will." He obviously applies here the terms "created" and "emanated" indiscriminately.

Israeli's distinction between creation and emanation calls for some closer analysis of the meaning of these two terms. The remaining part of this paper shall be devoted to such an analysis.

The creating of first matter and first form, which constitute the intellect, is described as an action "by power and will." This phrase presents a combination of terms that is at variance with what we find in the Arabic Plotinus texts, with the sole exception of the Long Recension of the *Theology* where, however, power and will, like "commandment" (*amr*), are but synonyms of the Word (*kalima*).[28] In the other texts power is opposed rather than allied to will. It is associated with utter repose, motionlessness, and necessity.

> The First Agent must be in repose (*sākin*) and motionless (*ghair mutaḥarrik*), if it is necessary that some thing is secondary to Him. His action must be without reflection (*rawīya*), motion (*ḥaraka*), and volition (*irāda*) which would be inclined toward the action product. The first action product—that is, the intellect—emanated (*inbajasa*) from the high-degree potency of the repose of the Agent (*min shiddati sukūn al-fāʿil wa-ḳūwatihi*).[29]

The element of necessity is expressed by the simile of heat emanating from fire and of cold emanating from snow. The "high-degree potency" of the first Agent is said to operate in a similar fashion.[30] A parallel to this text from the *Dicta of the Greek Sage* is found in the *Epistle on Divine Knowledge*:[31] "The First Agent acts while in repose and in stability. . . . From his perfection an act is produced . . . out of a very mighty power. The First Agent . . . is the power of all things." The simile of fire-heat, which comes from Plotinus, is reproduced here in greater detail. "Fire is a heat which completes the essence of fire; then from that heat there is born in some object another heat, resembling the heat which completes the essence of fire." The first heat is produced by an act which is the very substance of fire, whereas the second heat is by an act *from* the substance, a distinction which exemplifies the twofold nature of the act of the First Agent. As Plotinus explained it: "There is in everything the act of the essence and the act going out from the essence: the first act is the thing itself in its realized identity, the second act is an *inevitably* following outgo from the first, an emanation distinct from the thing itself."[32]

Here necessity relates to the second phase of the creative process rather than to the first, which is seen as the very substance of the Agent. Only insofar as a distinct being emerges is there any necessity. This kind of distinction opens up a possibility of interpreting Plotinus as by no means excluding will from the creative act. The nature of the One itself might be regarded as its will, and ultimately even necessity could be identified with the One's own will, as has been suggested by J. M. Rist.[33] Yet any such view was obviously far removed from the way Plotinus was understood by those who compiled the Arabic texts with which we are dealing. Thus, another passage in the *Epistle* clearly states that precisely because the First Agent "acts solely by the fact of His being," His action cannot be attributed to volition.[34] The Plotinian simile of the sun's radiation suggested a supreme Being in utter repose and acting without an exercise of will:

> It is not that He wished to originate intellect, and then intellect came into being, after the volition . . . He makes and originates things all at one go, being fixed and stable in one state . . . without motion of any kind. . . . The first action of the First Agent is intellect. Intellect is light flowing from the noble substance as sunlight flows over things from the sun."[35]

The absence of will in creation is also implied in the negation of all attributes in the One, who, in a passage of the *Theology*, is referred to as "the first light":[36] The first light is not a light in anything but is light alone, self-existing. Therefore that light comes to illumine the soul by means of intellect, without attributes like the attributes of fire or anything else of active things. All active things perform their activities by virtue of attributes within them, not by their own self, but the First Agent makes things not by any attribute, for in Him there is no attribute at all, but He makes them by His own self." The corollary of this view is, again, the exclusion of will. Power is the only term admissible to denote the activity of God.

Israeli's phrase "by power and will" has an almost polemical ring when held against the background just described. It asserts that creation, as distinct from emanation, is not a necessary process following from the very essence of God and being expressive of his power alone, but declares it to derive from both power and will. As he puts it in the passage answering an imaginary opponent, "The light of wisdom is brought into being from the power and the will by way of influence and action, while the light which emanates from the intellect is essential and substantial, like the light and shining of the sun, which emanates from its essence and substantiality."[37] In the Arabic Plotinus passage quoted above the shining of the sun is the simile characteristic of necessary, essential emanation. It is highly significant that Israeli applies it to the emanative activity of the intellect and contrasts it with the action by the power and the will. It should also be noted that the term for power (potency) found in the Arabic sources is *ḳūwa*, which reflects the Greek *dynamis*, is no longer used by Israeli with respect to God. He substitutes for it the term *ḳudra* which, in Kalām, denotes the power to act and in the long recension of the *Theology* signifies the Divine power. Israeli retains *ḳūwa* when speaking of the "light and powers" of the hypostases below God.[38] His change of terminology indicates his deviation from a purely emanationist form of Neoplatonism.

The creation of the two first substances by power and will is described by Israeli as an act performed "without mediation" (*bi-lā wasiṭa*) or "without the mediation of another substance" (*min ghair tawassuṭ jauhar ākhar*). The meaning of this phrase requires some elucidation. One is tempted to suggest that this formula implies the rejection of a school of thought that interposes a mediating power between God and the two first substances. Thus the Logos doctrine of al-Nasafī and the Ismā'īlī sect postulates the Word (*amr*) as such an intermediary, and the long version of the *Theology*, probably reflecting the Ismā'īlī doctrine, as Pines suggested,[39] describes the first intellect as "united with the word of the Creator." Israeli's repeated emphasis on the unmediated character of the creation of first matter and first form could therefore be said to carry a polemical significance. Yet it can easily be shown that this interpretation is not correct. The simple meaning of the phrase is that the first substances are more perfect than the subsequent ones because nothing stands between them and the Creator. Intellect, too, is said to "receive the light from the power and will without mediation" because it "receives the light of wisdom without the mediation of any other substance between itself and wisdom,"[40] whereas the rational soul receives it through the intermediacy of intellect, the animal soul through the intermediacy of intellect and rational soul, and so on. The term "mediation" is therefore equivalent to "intervening stage," and the phrase "without mediation" simply means without intervening, light-obscuring stages. Only occasionally does it signify the sole agency of God, as in the statement that "the sphere and the substances above . . . are generated by the power and will without the mediation of any agent except the Creator, while the compound and sensible bodies under the sphere are made by nature."[41]

The vulgate version of the *Theology* uses the phrase in exactly the same sense in which it is generally employed by Israeli. We quote a few passages that will show this clearly.

> Although all the things gush forth from It [the One], the first being, by which I mean the being of intellect, gushes forth from It first, without intermediary. Thereafter there gush forth from It all the beings of the things that are in the upper world and the lower world, through the medium of the being of the intellect and the intelligible world."

The passage goes on to explain that everything mediated and remote from the source is deficient, and that only the unmediated is perfect.[42] Only intellect is unmediated in an absolute sense. In a relative sense, that is, compared with the lower world, the entire spiritual world may be called unmediated.

> You must understand that intellect and soul and the other intelligible things are from the first originator, not passing away or disappearing, on account of their originating from the first cause without intermediary, whereas nature and sense perception and the other natural things perish and fall under corruption because they are effects of causes that are caused, that is, of intellect through the medium of the soul.[43]

As we have seen, Israeli too applies the term "without mediation" in its relative sense to all spiritual substances. In the Hebrew fragments of the pseudo-Empedoclean *Five Substances*,[44] the term "without mediation" (*belī 'emṣa'uth*) is used in the same sense.

In discussing Israeli's concept of creation, we have already noted some contrasting features of his view of emanation. Israeli defines emanation as an "essential" causality distinct from "influence and action," and he regards the spiritual substances as each emanating from the light or "essence and substantiality" of the preceding one. Essential causality implies necessity and is illustrated by the similes of fire-heat and the sun's radiation. The metaphor of "radiance" and the comparison with the sun are frequently employed by Israeli.[45] The view of emanation underlying this imagery (which, as we shall see, is not consistently maintained) accords with the account of the series of emanations in the pseudo-Aristotelian source quoted in the Mantua Text,[46] where emanation is described in terms of a "radiance and splendor" going forth in turn from intellect and the three souls. At each successive stage the radiance becomes "less and dimmer" because of the growing distance from the source.

We meet with an entirely different conception of emanation in writings of Israeli other than the Mantua Text, namely the assumption that each successive hypostasis acquires not only light but also "shadow" (*ẓill*) and "darkness" (*ẓalām*) from the preceding one, and that the shadow and darkness grow more dense at each stage, thus accounting for the progressive lessening of the spiritual force. The *Book of Definitions* uses the formula describing the lower substance as coming into being "in the horizon (*ufḳ*) and shadow" or "in the horizon and out of the shadow" of the higher one.[47] The use of the term "horizon" in this connection is familiar from the vulgate version of the *Theology*, which describes the soul as placed "within the horizon" of the intelligible world,[48] and from the *Liber de causis* (§2).[49] The motifs of "shadow" and "darkness" as concomitants of emanation may have been known to Israeli from the pseudo-Aristotelian source, although the text quoted in the Mantua Text omits all reference to them. They occur, however, in Abraham ibn Ḥasday's parallel passage[50] and in the Long Version of the *Theology*,[51] both of which are based on pseudo-Aristotle,[52] and also in Israeli's own quotation from the pseudo-Aristotelian source in his *Book on Spirit and Soul* (§9),[53] where the terms used are "shadow" and "exhaustion," that is, darkness. The metaphor of "shadow" is found also in the *al-Mudkhal al-Saghīr* (attributed to al-Rāzī the physician), where it is stated that intellect projected a shadow, from which God created the rational soul; that the latter projected a shadow from which God created the animal soul, and so on.[54] The frequent use he made of it was noted by Albert the Great, who describes it as an "elegant" saying and quotes it in many places.[55]

In the *Book of Substances* Israeli makes an interesting attempt at combining the two metaphors of light and shadow by introducing the formula "ray and shade": the form of nature is brought into being "from the shade of the vegetative soul and its ray" (*min fai al-nafs al-nabātiya wa-shu'a'hā*); the latter "from the shade of the animal soul and its ray," and so on. "Thus it is evident that the ray and shade of the intellect are the specificality of the rational soul; the ray and shade of the rational soul are the specificality of the animal soul."[56]

How does Israeli conceive the nature of emanation under the aspects of "shadow" and "ray and shade" respectively? The only text offering something like a conceptual analysis of the imagery used is a passage in the *Book of Definitions* (§6), where the difference between the higher and the lower substances is discussed. The passage explains why the former remain unaffected by what issues from them, that is, by the emanant substance, while the latter, the elements and composite bodies, are changed by what derives from them. The answer given is that "the lights . . . of the higher substances, the three souls, are not increased or decreased by the issue of what is derived from them, as these come from the shadow of their light, not from their light itself in its essence and substantiality."[57] The elements and bodies, on the other hand, are themselves changed, increased, and decreased. The point that interests us here is Israeli's theory that emanation is not really an efflux of the very light or substance of the source but the casting of a shadow by the light, and the coming-to-be of a new substance out of the shadow. More precisely, the shadow *is* the new substance. In a less radical sense, the lower substance is said to originate from both the light and the shadow, or "in the horizon and shadow," or "from the ray and shade" of the higher one. The radical interpretation, is, however, borne out by Israeli's statement: "it is clear that in every brilliant thing the light in its essence and substantiality is brighter and has a greater splendor than the light of its shadow; thus it is clear that the brilliance of the vegetative soul is greater and stronger than that of the sphere which is derived from its shadow."[58] This view might seem to imply that emanation is no longer viewed as an "essential" causality "like the light and shining of the sun, which emanates from its essence and substantiality." For it distinctly affirms that emanation is but the casting of a shadow and that the emanant substance originates in the shadow cast, not in the substance or essence of the source. Yet Israeli does not appear to have noticed any contradiction since in the same treatise in which he describes emanation as "essential" causality he also speaks of emanation in terms of "light which issues from the shadow of a substance."[59] In fact, the two metaphors of light and shade or "ray and shade," as Israeli's formula has it, designates two aspects of the emanative process, and both derive ultimately from Plotinus.

As noted before,[60] Plotinus distinguishes between two kinds of essential act, one of the essence and one resulting, as a by-product as it were, from the essence. The analogy adduced by him is heat as the very act of fire, and heat produced in something else by the first heat.[61] The very same distinction is repeated in *Enneads* II.6.3, where the heat produced from the essence is said to be a mere quality and likened to "a trace, a shadow, an image" (*ichnos, skia, eikōn*). In *Enneads* V.1.7 intellect is called an "image" (*eidōlon*) of the Originator, which in turn produces a "light and trace" (*phōs kai ichnos*). Since elsewhere Plotinus equates "trace and shadow," the formula "light and trace" might also be read as "light and shade," which would give Israeli's phrase a very respectable ancestry. Plotinus uses the term "shadow" in yet another passage (IV.3.9) where he speaks of the "shadow" projected by the soul. In *Enneads* V.2.1, intellect is said to have produced a "form" (*eidos*) of itself, that is, the soul, and soul to have made an "image" (*eidōlon*) of itself. *Enneads* V.4.2 speaks of the product of intellect as something resembling it and as an "imitation" *(mimēma)* and "image" (*eidōlon*). Thus it is obvious that in Plotinus the terms "image," "imitation," "trace," and "shadow" are synonyms expressive of what is considered to be the second phase of emanation, the act resulting from the essence. In a less specific and more general sense these terms simply denote the inferior status of the copy or "imprint" (*typos*) compared with the "original" (*archetypos*),[62] a contrast that has Philonic overtones.[63] Israeli seems to have caught the more sophisticated Plotinian nuances of these terms and to have used the simile of "shadow" accordingly.

Israeli's insistence that emanation does not imply any change, decrease, or increase in the source likewise reflects the Plotinian doctrine.[64] In Plotinus it is one of the functions of the simile of radiation (*perilampsis*) to illustrate the fact that emanation leaves the source unaffected.[65] It also entails a more or less pantheistic metaphysics.[66] Israeli, we have seen, obviates any such interpretation by introducing the idea of an act of creation *ex nihilo* prior to the stage of emanation.

The progressive reduction of the light in the course of emanation is made the subject of a special discussion in the *Book of Substances.*[67] The question posed concerns "the reasons for the difference of the substances, and the precedence of one substance to another." Israeli suggests three reasons. (1) The light—in this instance the reference is not to intellect but to the light created by power and will, that is, wisdom, also described here as "caused to emanate from the power and will"[68]—met no shadow at the beginning, while its end met various imperfections and obscurities. This represents a certain variation of the motif of "shadow," since it is no longer maintained that the light is unaffected by the issue of what derives from it. Instead, it is suggested that the light itself is vitiated by what it meets on its way, that is, by being mixed with darkness. (2) The reception of the light by one substance from the other varies according the degree of "mediation," that is, the intervening stages. Only intellect receives the light without the mediation of another substance; the others receive it through one, two, three, or more intermediaries.[69] This adds yet another motif in explaining the progressive lessening of the light. In the *Book on Spirit and Soul* (§9),[70] it appears jointly with that of "shadow and exhaustion": the splendor and brilliance of the rational soul "are less than the splendor and brilliance of intellect; the reason being that the degree of intellect is intermediate between the soul and its Creator, so that the soul acquired shadow and exhaustion, that is, darkness, as the intellect intervened between it and the light of the Creator." The two motifs of "shadow" and "mediation" are joined also in the *Book of Definitions* (§5),[71] where it is said that "the animal soul . . . comes into being from the shadow of the rational soul, on account of which it is removed from the light of the intellect and acquires shadow." (3) A third reason is "the difference between that which bestows and that which is bestowed, the bestowing and the reception of the bestowal." This reason is not further explained, however, in the text, as our fragment breaks off before the discussion of this point is reached.

One of the most significant traits of Plotinus's concept of emanation is the doctrine of the two moments of the generative process in its completeness. Unlike the two phases discussed earlier, those designated as act of the essence and act from the essence, the two moments refer (a) to the emergence of the emanant and (b) to its stabilization and completion. Even though brought into being from the essence as a separate entity, the emanant attains to permanency and creative power only after it has turned its gaze back to its source and beheld it in an act of contemplation. In A. H. Armstrong's appraisal: "Here we meet another of the great principles of the philosophy of Plotinus; that all derived beings depend for their existence, their activity, and their power to produce in their turn, on their contemplation of their source."[72] This doctrine has been preserved, however fragmentarily, in the Arabic Plotinus. It appears in the *Dicta of the Greek Sage* ("After its emanation from the First Agent, it turned to its cause and looked at it according to its potency; it thus became intellect and substance"),[73] in the vulgate version of the *Theology*,[74] and in the Hebrew fragments of the *Book of the Five Substances* attributed to Empedocles.[75] No trace of this doctrine can be found in Israeli. It may well be that his interposition of a Divine creative act between the Creator and the process of emanation thwarted the employment of this motif.

NOTES

1. A. Altmann and S. M. Stern, *Isaac Israeli: A Neoplatonic Philosopher of the Early Tenth Century* (Oxford, 1958; reprinted in 1979 by Greenwood Press, Westport, Connecticut), Part II, pp. 147–217. See in particular chapter 4 ("Creation, Emanation and Natural Causality"), pp. 171–180. The work is subsequently referred to as Altmann-Stern.

2. The distinctive features of what I called "the Israeli source" and its difference from other known types of Neoplatonism, including the Long Version of the *Theology of Aristotle*, were pointed out by me in my article "Isaac Israeli's 'Chapter on the Elements' (MS. Mantua)," *The Journal of Jewish Studies*, VII.1–2 (1956), pp. 31–57. S. M. Stern elaborated the subject in his article "Ibn Ḥasdāy's Neoplatonist: A Neoplatonic Treatise and Its Influence on Isaac Israeli and the Longer Version of the Theology of Aristotle," *Oriens*, 13–14 (1961):58–120. This article will be referred to as Stern, "Ibn Ḥasdāy's Neoplatonist."

3. See Harry A. Wolfson, "The Meaning of *Ex Nihilo* in Isaac Israeli," *The Jewish Quarterly Review*, N.S. 50 (1959):1–12; reprinted in: Harry Austryn Wolfson, *Studies in the History of Philosophy and Religion*, ed. Isadore Twersky and Georg H. Williams, I (Cambridge, Mass., 1973), pp. 222–233; see pp. 229–233 (to be referred to as Wolfson, "The Meaning").

4. See Josef van Ess, "Jüngere orientalistische Literatur zur neuplatonischen Überlieferung im Bereich des Islam," in: Kurt Flasch, ed., *Parusia . . . Festgabe für Johannes Hirschberger* (Frankfurt a.M., 1965), pp. 333–350.

5. Arabic text: S.M. Stern, "The Fragments of Isaac Israeli's 'Book of Substances,'" *The Journal of Jewish Studies*, VII. 1–2 (1956): 20–21; English translation by Stern: Altmann-Stern, p. 84.

6. For the meaning of these terms, see pp. 28–29.

7. *Book of Substances*, III, 3r; Stern, *JJS*, VII: 20; Altmann-Stern, pp. 83f.

8. On the Aristotelian "causes" of a definition, see Harry A. Wolfson, *The Philosophy of Spinoza* (New York, 1969), I, 321f.

9. Altmann-Stern, pp. 66f. The distinction offered here is indebted to al-Kindī's *Book of Definitions*; see pp. 68ff. and S. M. Stern, "Notes on al-Kindī's Treatise on Definitions," *Journal of the Royal Asiatic Society* (April, 1959): 33, 42. On al-Kindī's concept of "innovation" (*ibdāʿ*), see also Alfred L. Ivry, *Al-Kindi's Metaphysics* (Albany, N.Y., 1975), p. 166.

10. *Book of Substances*, III, 2v; Stern, *JJS*, VII: 20; Altmann-Stern, p. 83.

11. Altmann-Stern, pp. 70f.

12. Ibid.

13. See the reconstructed text in Stern, "Ibn Ḥasdāy's Neoplatonist," pp. 104f.

14. It should be noted that despite his disavowal of power and will as the *summum*

genus, Israeli admits that intellect is a species of the genus "wisdom." Yet he does not admit an emanation of intellect from wisdom. It is the conjunction of first matter and wisdom that brings about intellect.

15. According to Plotinus, the hypostases attain to creative power only after they are fully established by virtue of their contemplation of the source. This aspect of the Plotinian doctrine is absent in Israeli (see p. 32). The word "established" (*ḳāmat*) in the text quoted may, nevertheless, be a faint remnant of the Plotinian concept.

16. See Simon van den Bergh, *Averroes' Tahafut Al-Tahafut* (London, 1954), I, 63.

17. All these texts are assembled in Paul Henry and Hans-Rudolf Schwyzer, *Plotini Opera*, II (Paris & Brussels, 1959). For the literature on these texts, see Josef van Ess, op. cit.

18. Hebrew text in David Kaufmann, *Studien über Salomon Ibn Gabirol* (Budapest, 1899), p. 19; quoted by me in English in Altmann-Stern, p. 162.

19. The position is somewhat confused in the *Ghayāt al-Ḥakīm* passage quoted by me (Altmann-Stern, pp. 162f.), which seems to reflect the Israeli source. In his review of the book (*Kiryat Sefer* 35.4 [1960]: 457–9), the late Martin Plessner suggested that ps.-Empedocles's matter containing all forms was rather identical with the two first substances of the Israeli source, a view that does not seem tenable to me. In Abenmasarra's system, which follows ps.-Empedocles, prime matter as symbolized by the Divine throne is prior to intellect, as we know from Ibn 'Arabi's report. See Miguel Asín Palacios, *Abenmasarra y su Escuela* (Madrid, 1914), p. 75. The late Samuel M. Stern and I planned a joint annotated re-edition of the pseudo-Empedoclean Fragments published by Kaufmann. The project, unfortunately, came to grief owing the premature death of Dr. Stern.

20. See n. 3.

21. Wolfson, "The Meaning," pp. 231f.

22. See S. Pines, "La Longue Recension de la Théologie d'Aristote dans ses Rapports avec la doctrine Ismaélienne," *Revue des Études Islamiques* (1954), p. 10; also Gershom Scholem, "Schöpfung aus Nichts und Selbstverschränkung Gottes," *Eranos-Jahrbuch*, XXV (1957): 101ff.

23. Wolfson, "The Meaning," p. 230.

24. Ibid., p. 233.

25. Wolfson (p. 232) quotes *Fons Vitae* V.41, ed. Clemens Baeumker, p. 330 (ll. 17–20): "The creation of things by the Creator, that is, the going out (*exitus*) of forms from the prime source, that is, from the will (*voluntate*) . . . is like the going out (*exitus*) of water emanating (*emanantis*) from its source."

26. See Julius Guttmann, *Philosophies of Judaism*, trans. by David W. Silverman (New York, 1964), pp. 101f.; Jacques Schlanger, *La Philosophie de Salomon Ibn Gabirol* (Leiden, 1968), pp. 288ff.

27. *Book of Substances*, IV, 8v; Stern, *JJS*, VII: 24; Altmann-Stern, p. 88.

28. See Pines, loc. cit., p. 10.

29. Franz Rosenthal, "Ash-Shaykh al-Yūnānī and the Arabic Plotinus Source," *Orientalia* (Rome) 21 (1952): 476–7; reproduced in Henry and Schwyzer, *Plotini Opera*, II, 275; *Enneads* V. 1. 6. 25–37.

30. Ibid.

31. See Henry and Schwyzer, *Plotini Opera*, II, 337; *Enneads*, V. 4. 2. 26–38.

32. Quoted from *Enneads*, V. 4. 2. in MacKenna's translation and discussed by J. M. Rist, *Plotinus: The Road to Reality* (Cambridge, 1967), p. 70.

33. Rist, op. cit., pp. 81ff. See also Klaus Kremer, "Das 'Warum' der Schöpfung: 'quia bonus' vel / et 'quia voluit' . . . ," in: Kurt Flasch, ed., *Parusia* (see n. 4), pp. 241–264.

34. *Plotini Opera*, II, 321.

35. Ibid.; *Enneads*, V. 3. 12. 40. For the simile of the sun in Plotinus, see also V. 1. 6; V. 3. 16.

36. *Plotini Opera*, II, 383. Ibn Sīnā, commenting on this passage, identified the first light with God. See G. Vajda, "Les Notes d'Avicenne sur la Théologie d'Aristote," *Revue Thomiste* (1952, no. 2): 379ff. This interpretation must be considered correct. The objection ventured by me in Altmann-Stern, p. 173, cannot be upheld.

37. See n. 7.

38. *Book of Substances*, III, 2r; *JJS*, VII: 20; Altmann-Stern, p. 83.
39. Pines, op. cit., p. 156, n. 1.
40. *Book of Substances*, IV, 9v; *JJS*, VII: 25; Altmann-Stern, p. 89.
41. *Book of Substances*, V, 12v; *JJS*, VII: 27; Altmann-Stern, p. 91.
42. *Plotini Opera*, II, 291; see also 441.
43. *Plotini Opera*, II, 297; see also 245.
44. David Kaufmann, op. cit., p. 19.
45. See Altmann-Stern, pp. 40f. (lines 36–42); 110f.; 119.
46. See Altmann-Stern, p. 119; Stern, "Ibn Ḥasdāy's Neoplatonist," pp. 104–5.
47. Altmann-Stern, p. 41 (line 49); 45 (lines 6–7).
48. *Plotini Opera*, II, 67.
49. See Jacob Guttmann, *Die philosophischen Lehren des Isaak b. Salomon Israeli* (Münster, 1911), p. 18.
50. Abraham ben Ḥasday, *Ben Ha-Melekh We-Ha-Nazir*, ed. A.M. Haberman (Tel-Aviv, 1951), p. 202; Stern, "Ibn Ḥasdāy's Neoplatonist," p. 67.
51. See Stern, "Ibn Ḥasdāy's Neoplatonist," pp. 84, 88.
52. Ibid., pp. 64, 79–81.
53. Altmann-Stern, p. 111.
54. Quoted by Vajda, *Revue des Études Juives*, N. S., XII (1935): 30, n. 1 from a manuscript in the Bibliothèque Nationale, Paris.
55. See Jacob Guttmann, *Die Scholastik des dreizehnten Jahrhunderts* (Breslau, 1902), p. 57; idem, *Israeli*, p. 42.
56. *Book of Substances*, III, 3r; *JJS*, VII: 20; Altmann-Stern, pp. 83f.
57. Altmann-Stern, 45f. Ibn Gabirol (*Fons Vitae*, III.52) makes the point that what emanates from the source is not the essences (*essentiae*) but powers (*virtutes*) and rays (*radii*) or qualities (*qualitates*).
58. *Book of Definitions*, #6; Altmann-Stern, p. 46, lines 28–33.
59. *Book of Substances*, IV, 9r; *JJS*, VII: 25; Altmann-Stern, p. 88.
60. See n. 32.
61. Cf. *Enneads*, V. 4. 2. 28ff.; *Epistola de Scientia Divina*, nos. 169–179 in *Plotini Opera*, II, 337.
62. *Enneads*, V. 9. 5; *Epistola*, #22 in *Plotini Opera*, II, 419.
63. See Philo, *Legum Allegoria*, III, 33. 99–104, where the world is said to be but the "shadow" of the "archetype," and Beṣal'el (lit., "in the shadow of God") is described as an artificer working from mere "images" (*mimēta*) of the archetypes. Cf. Harry A. Wolfson, *Philo* (Cambridge, Mass., 1962), II, 85f.
64. *Enneads*, VI. 9. 9. For further references, see Kremer, op. cit., pp. 246f. (notes 24–25). See *Dicta Sapientis Graeci*, II, 10 in *Plotini Opera*, II, 267.
65. See A. H. Armstrong, *The Architecture of the Intelligible Universe in the Philosophy of Plotinus* (Cambridge, 1940), p. 52.
66. Ibid., p. 62.
67. IV, 8rff.; *JJS*, VII: 23–26; Altmann-Stern, pp. 88–90.
68. Concerning this inconsistency, see above, p. 23.
69. See n. 40.
70. Altmann-Stern, p. 111.
71. Altmann-Stern, p. 41, lines 55–58.
72. A. H. Armstrong, *Plotinus* (London, 1953), p. 34.
73. *Plotini Opera*, II, 275; *Enneads*, V. 1. 7. 5–6.
74. *Plotini Opera*, II, 291f.; *Enneads*, V. 2. 1. 9–11.
75. David Kaufmann, op. cit., pp. 20f.

3 Free Will and Predestination in Saadia, Baḥya, and Maimonides

In his interesting paper on "Religion in Everyday Life as Reflected in the Letters and Documents of the Cairo Geniza," Professor Goitein presented a type of Jewish piety characterized by a total submission to the all-powerful will of God that amounted in radical predestinarianism and to a denial of man's freedom of choice. To what degree, Professor Goitein asked, did this "popular religion," which bears all the marks of Ash'arite theology, find support in the "religion of the thinkers"?[1] It is the purpose of this paper to seek an answer to this question and, thereby, to shed some light on the thinkers' type of piety, a subject too vast to be treated from more than one angle in a single paper. The philosophers whose views are to be analyzed—Saadia, Baḥya and Maimonides—represent the three main streams of Jewish thought in the period with which the theme of the conference is concerned. Of the three trends—Kalām, Neoplatonism, and Aristotelianism—the first was no doubt closest to popular religion. A few introductory remarks about Jewish Kalām will therefore be in place.

In the late-Geonic period and beyond it, the Mu'tazilite Kalām exercised a formative influence not only on the Karaites but also on the Rabbanites, notwithstanding the fact that, because of their rootedness in the rich halakhic and haggadic tradition, the latter were somewhat less open to the intrusion of alien modes of thought. There are indications that a considerable part of Rabbanite Kalām literature must have gotten lost.[2] Abraham ibn Ezra's reference to a Geonic *Sefer Ha-Yiḥud*, a treatise written "in the fashion of the theologians" (*'al da'at anshey ha-meḥqar*[3]), is a case in point. The work is known only from Ibn Ezra's casual citation of a cryptic statement by the anonymous author who has been shown to reflect the teaching of the Mu'tazilite Mu'ammar (d. 830 C.E.).[4] Another instance is provided by a Geniza fragment from a *Sefer Ha-Miṣvot* published by Schreiner many years ago.[5] It probably dates from the Geonic period and clearly indicates the impact of Mu'tazilite Kalām. The extent to which Kalām notions penetrated into medieval Jewish thought has been demonstrated in Martin Schreiner's classical study, *Der Kalām in der jüdischen Literatur* (1895). The list of known Mu'tazilites among the Geonim includes Samuel ben Ḥofni and Hai Gaon, apart from Saadia. To these should be added the important figure of Rabbenu Nissim ben Jacob of Qairawān to whose Mu'tazilite orientation Ignaz Goldziher was the first to draw attention,[6] and whose *oeuvre* is now available in Shraga Abramson's excellent edition.[7] As for the impact of Kalām upon the Karaites, we are, of late, well informed, thanks to a series of analytical studies by Georges Vajda dealing with Qirqisānī, Dawūd al-Marwān al-Muqammiṣ, and Yūsuf al-Baṣīr.[8] Schreiner was the first to notice al-Baṣīr's dependence on the Baṣra Mu'tazilite 'Abd al-Jabbār,[9] and Vajda has defined this relationship more precisely.[10] It is in the aggregate of all these investigations that a picture of the role of Kalām within Judaism begins to emerge. A most penetrating synthesis of many strands of research is now provided by the late Professor Harry A. Wolfson's long-awaited "Repercussions of the Kalām in Jewish Philosophy" (Cambridge, Mass. & London, 1979).[11]

The type of piety peculiar to Jewish Kalām, as far as we can judge, is a form of enlightenment that drew its strength, and also imbibed its weakness, from a totally rationalistic, nonmystical stance. Its basic attitude is strikingly similar to that of the eighteenth-century Enlightenment. Here and there we encounter the same stress on the demonstrability of metaphysical truths; on the autonomy of ethics; the essential dispensability of relevation; the goodness of God; and the ultimate rationality of things. The two fundamental doctrines of Mu'tazilite Kalām, that is, those of *tawḥīd* and *'adl* (the unity and justice of God), predominate also in Jewish Kalām. It is hardly the result of mere historical chance, as Maimonides suggested,[12] that Jews were attracted to the rationalism of the Mu'tazila and shunned the fierce realism of the Ash'ariyya. As will be shown in the main section of this paper, the Jewish philosophers did not consider the Ash'ariyya's predestinarianism and denial of free will a live option. Mysticism, on the other hand, did hold sway among the Rabbanites—Hai Gaon is an impressive example[13]—and it is all the more remarkable that some thinkers in the Geonic period, notably Saadia Gaon, tried to give it a rational connotation. Saadia's *Commentary on the Sefer Yeṣira*[14] tends to minimize the mystical import of the combinations of letters and the Divine names, as Vajda's analysis has shown.[15] His notion of the will of God as found in the *Yeṣira* commentary probably reflects Stoic influence, and it is somewhat ironical that it had considerable repercussions in the development of Kabbala.[16] There is no difference between the *Yeṣira* commentary and the *Amānāt* as far as epistemology is concerned. Both treatises describe the process of cognition as one comprising three stages that culminate in an act of belief (*i'tiqād*) free from doubt.[17]

The transformation of traditionally accepted doctrines (*amānāt*) into rationally demonstrated beliefs (*i'tiqādāt*) is the avowed object of Saadia's philosophical treatise. Yet the stress put on rational demonstration is not meant to devalue the simple, unsophisticated faith of the untutored who rely on unquestioning acceptance of authority (*taqlīd*). Whereas the Ash'arites tended to deprecate the mere passive stance of *taqlīd*),[18] Saadia upheld what Professor Wolfson has called the "double faith theory": undemonstrated faith and demonstrated faith are of equal perfection. Full validity attaches to both types of faith, viz., to belief by tradition and to belief by speculation and understanding.[19] Certain tenets of belief such as the future redemption of Israel and the resurrection of the dead, though capable of rational explication, are not amenable to verification on purely logical grounds and hence must rest on prophetic revelation alone.[20] Kalām is not a philosophical system of autonomous reason after all but an exercise in theology anchored in a religious tradition. It makes little difference whether, with Louis Gardet, we see in the "science of Kalām" (*'ilm al-kalām*) a mere "defensive apologetic,"[21] or, with Richard M. Frank, a "systematically coherent and disciplined speculative order" of theological discourse.[22] By establishing "true tradition" (*khabar ṣādiq*) as an independent source of knowledge,[24] Saadia not only validated undemonstrated belief (*taqlīd*); he also thereby circumscribed the areas of belief to be verified by the rational method.

A case in point is the doctrine of transmigration of souls (*tanāsukh*), which Saadia ascribed to "certain people who call themselves Jews."[25] He may have had in mind contemporary oriental Jews who had adopted this belief from some Islamic sects, as we know from al-Baghdādī's *Moslem Schisms and Sects*,[26] or followers of 'Anan, the founder of Karaism, who had taught this doctrine, as Qirqisānī reports in his Kitāb al-Anwār.[27] The Mu'tazilite 'Abd al-Jabbār devoted a chapter of his *Mughni* to a refutation of the transmigrationists who had based their view on arguments related to God's justice: the sufferings of animals, little children, and the righteous could best be explained as merited by misdeeds in a previous life. In 'Abd al-Jabbār's opinion there was no need for such a theory. The suffering of the innocent could be understood as trials or as manifestations of God's grace (*luṭf*) since, according to unanimous Mu'tazilite doctrine, they served to establish a claim to compensation in the hereafter.[28] 'Abd al-Jabbār's discussion of this theme reappears in Yūsuf al-Baṣīr's *Kitāb al-Manṣūrī*, wherefrom Joseph ibn Ṣaddiq quotes and rejects it in his *Sefer 'Olam Qatan*.[29] Saadia, on the other hand, faithfully echoes the Mu'tazilite view after recording the transmigrationists' argument mentioned by 'Abd al-Jabbār: "Inasmuch as the Creator is just, it is inconceivable that He should occasion suffering to little children, unless it be for sins committed by their souls during the time that they were lodged in their former bodies."[30] In reply Saadia points out that completely guiltless individuals may be subjected to trials in order to be compensated for them afterwards, "for I find that children are made to suffer pain, and I have no doubt about their eventual compensation for these sufferings."[31] Saadia also affirms the Mu'tazilite notion that God compensates animals for any "excess of pain."[32] It was probably Saadia whom Maimonides had in mind when referring to "some of the latter-day Geonim" who had "heard it [namely, the doctrine of reward for animals] from the Mu'tazila and had approved and believed it."[33]

The notion of Divine justice, which lies at the root of the theory of compensation, also informs the Mu'tazilite concept of "merit" (*istiḥqāq*) which is rejected by the Ash'ariyya[34] but, not surprisingly, plays a dominant role in Jewish Kalām. Saadia's discussion of "merits and demerits"[35] is strongly flavored not only by the Talmudic dicta on the subject found in Qiddushin 40a-b but also by the Mu'tazilites' debate.[36] The extent to which Jewish Kalām concerned itself with the rationale for merit is evident from a variety of sources. The Leningrad fragment of Saadia's *Sefer Ha-Miṣvot* contains the following passage:

In case wisdom had made it necessary to regard as equals a benefaction by grace (*ni'ma l-tafaḍḍul*) and a benefaction by merit (*ni'ma l-istiḥqāq*) the Wise, be He exalted and praised, would have placed men straight in paradise, and would have kept them free from obligations and works. Wisdom having necessitated, however, a difference between a grant by grace and a grant by merit (investing the latter with greater happiness and a more exalted portion than the former), there now obtains a more complete fulfillment of the Divine intention. For He, be He blessed and exalted, intended by the precepts and prohibitions that they acquire greater happiness and a more exalted portion.[37]

In the Exordium to treatise 3 of his *Amānāt*,[38] Saadia expressed the very same idea: God could not have bestowed upon his creatures complete bliss and permanent happiness without giving them commandments and prohibitions. For, according to the judgment of reason, a person that achieves some good by dint of an effort obtains double the benefit that is gained by one who achieves the same good without any effort and merely through the kindness shown him by God. This being the case, Saadia declares, God preferred to assign to us the ampler portion.

Saadia's two statements seem to imply that even in the absence of any revealed commandments the performance of good deeds would be requited by God, though not in a "double" portion nor in the same "ample" manner. Put in Talmudic terms: "One who is commanded and performs is greater than one who is not commanded and performs,"[39] yet the latter is of no mean rank either. Saadia says, however, in another place[40] that if a man "were to serve God without having been commanded to do so, he would not receive any reward for it."[41] Nissim Gaon dealt with this subject in answer to the question why the Tora prescribed "rational commandments" (*miṣvot sikhliyot*), which were readily observed anyhow on grounds of reason. In the brief fragment extant he explained that the Tora made rational precepts into Divine commandments in order to establish our claim for reward, seeing that "One who is commanded and performs is greater than one who is not commanded and performs." He qualified this reply by pointing out that, truly speaking, there can be no claim to reward on our part, for we are obligated to obey God, our Creator, in the way servants obey their master, while God is under no obligation to us. The reward that He pays is in the nature of pure grace (*ḥesed*).[42] Viewed from this perspective, the well-known distinction between rational and purely revelational precepts has no bearing on the question of reward. Samuel ben Ḥofni, who undoubtedly knew Saadia's work, moved in the same universe of theological discourse. His Genesis Commentary, a fragment of which is extant, has a passage that connects the "science of the precepts" (*'ilm al-miṣvot*) with the "knowledge of the Creator and the attributes," which is "also the knowledge of the will of our Creator, who has placed us in the world in order that we may submit to this will and gain our happiness. . . ."[43]

In Saadia's treatment of free will the Mu'tazilite pattern is clearly discernible. According to al-Ash'arī's report,[44] all Mu'tazilites "deny that God imposes a duty (*yukallifu*) for the fulfillment of which man is lacking the power (*yaqdiru*)." In other words, the fact of a man's obligation (*taklīf*) implies his freedom or power (*qudra*) to discharge it. Saadia adopted this notion: "The All-Wise does not impose an obligation (*yukallifu*) on anyone unless it lies within his competence and he is able to fulfill it."[45] Again in keeping with the Mu'tazilites' concern to safeguard the concept of Divine justice (*'adl*),[46] Saadia argued the case of man's power and ability on the ground of belief in God's justice and kindness toward man.[47] Treatise four of the *Amānāt*, where the subject is discussed, bears the title, "Obedience and Disobedience, Compulsion and Justice." Were God to exercise compulsion (*jabr*) upon human acts, Saadia pointed out, there would be no sense in either law or punishment.[48] How strongly Saadia felt the need to emphasize the principle of Divine justice may be gauged from the fact that in his *Psalms Translation and Commentary* he consistently rendered passages that might seem to question the justice of God by taking out the sting, that is, by rendering the Hebrew *lamah* ("why") in the sense of the Arabic negative particle *lam*. Thus he translated *lamah 'azavtani* (Ps. 22:2) "Thou wilt not abandon me," and he rendered *lamah paraṣta gedereha* (Ps. 80:13) "Do not break down her fences." There are numerous instances of this kind of forced exegesis, which Saadia chose to apply in order to avoid the impression that the Psalmist occasionally questioned the justice of God. He distinctly declared that it was his "way to explain every question concerned with the petition for release negatively."[49] He adopted this rule because he considered it "absurd" to associate injustice with the Creator, whose motive in creating was to "benefit" his creatures.[50] It was from the very same theological considerations that in his *Psalms Translation and Commentary* Saadia took great care to interpret passages like *hadrikheni be-'ammitekha* (Ps. 25:5) and *me-YHWH miṣ'adey gever konanu* (Ps. 37:23) as implying no suggestion of Divine compulsion (*jabr*).[51] The words *temokh ashuray* (Ps. 17:5), he said in his commentary, were not "a petition for *jabr* but for an inclination toward obedience." It is unlikely that Saadia would have approved the type of Islamic prayer known as *istikhāra*, to which Professor Goitein has drawn attention.[52] Invoking God's guidance when faced with an important decision would probably have been regarded by him as something coming dangerously close to a petition for *jabr* or to abdication of responsibility.

Before discussing man's freedom of choice, Saadia explains more fully the power (*qudra*) or ability (*istiṭā'a*) to act.[53] He declares that "The ability to act must precede the act itself," for were the ability synchronous with the act, the relationship of cause and effect would become a matter of doubt. Differently expressed, the potency must be prior to the act, as Aristotle had asserted against the Megarians' view that a thing only has potency when it functions.[54] Saadia points out that unless the ability were prior to the act, the agent would have no opportunity either to act or to desist from acting, the latter being tantamount to acting in the opposite way since in the case of man—as distinct from God—refraining from doing a specific thing was an act producing the contrary: If a man does not love, he hates.[55] In stating his view about the priority of the ability, Saadia seems to have echoed Abū l-Hudhayl's theory of "phases" of acting but whereas Kalām discussions of this theme tended to confuse the power of acting with the power of willing,[56] Saadia drew a clear distinction between *istiṭā'a* and *ikhtiyār*, between the potency of acting and free choice. As for the potency of acting, he obviously had in mind the passages in Aristotle's *Metaphysics* IX.ii and IX.v, where rational potencies are said to be capable of producing either of two contraries. In speaking of the ability as being prior to the act and as offering an opportunity for either performing or not performing the act, and in defining this alternative in terms of opposites Saadia echoed Aristotle. As far as his assertion of free will is concerned, he probably equated Aristotle's "choice" with absolute free will[57] or *liberum arbitrium*.[58]

The power of acting, Aristotle says, requires a "deciding factor" if one of the two contraries is to be enacted. In the case of animals, children, and incontinent men, the deciding factor may be appetite or anger. The continent man, however, acts with choice, which involves a rational principle and thought.[59] In Saadia's words, man cannot be considered a responsible "agent" of an act unless he is freely choosing (*mukhtār*) to perform it and acts in the exercise of his free choice.[60] Saadia adds that a man is not punishable for a freely committed act if he was ignorant of what caused the act: E.g., one that "killeth any person through error" (Deut. 19:5) is not liable to suffer the death penalty because his only guilt lies in negligence to take precautions. Although he acted with deliberate intent (*muta'ammid*) and with free choice (*mukhtār*) in wielding the axe to cut wood, the ensuing homicide was not premeditated or, as Saadia put it, he was "ignorant" of the causal connection. Similarly, a person that profanes the Sabbath in ignorance of the fact that the day on which he does it is the Sabbath cannot be held accountable.[61] Saadia's discussion reflects Aristotle's passage in *Nicomachean Ethics* III.i, where it is explained that "Everything that is done by reason of ignorance is *not* voluntary," and that by ignorance is meant any unawareness of the circumstances of one's action. By using the term "ignorance" to cover all cases of involuntary crimes and by applying it to the instance of homicide through negligence, where it ill fits, Saadia betrays the Aristotelian background of his treatment of the theme.

The view that God does not interfere with the actions of men and exercises no compulsion upon them is a corollary of the doctrine of human potency and free will. Saadia offers two arguments in support of absolute freedom and in rejection of *jabr*. First, man is conscious of his power to speak or to be silent, to take hold of things or to leave them alone. He is not conscious of any power (*quwwa*) that would prevent him from acting or not acting.[62] Judah Ha-Levi said likewise that free choice is attested by our being aware of the power we have over speech and silence as long as we are under the dominion of reason and not subject to certain accidents.[63] Both Saadia and Ha-Levi may have quoted from some *Vorlage*, for a passage in al-Ghazālī's *Iḥyā' 'Ulūm al-Dīn*, speaking in similar terms,[64] says that man instinctively apprehends the difference between an action that is voluntary and mere reflexes that are involuntary, and al-Shahrastānī makes the same observation.[65] The second argument against *jabr* utilizes a point made in previous passages in refutation of dualism: One act cannot possibly have two authors.[66] The assumption of *jabr* amounts to attributing human acts to two agents, which is absurd.[67] Saadia opposes Ḍirār's formula, "one act, two agents," which expressed the view that every single human act comes from two agents, i.e., from God, who creates, and from man, who acquires it.[68] This theory attempted to reconcile God's omnipotence with human responsibility, and it was eventually adopted as orthodox doctrine by the Ash'ariyya.[69] Saadia would have none of it, and Maimonides referred to it only in order to reject it. He quoted the formula "There is no act of man but there may be an acquisition (*al-iktisāb*)" as a meaningless kind of statement.[70]

Saadia would not acknowledge any ambiguity concerning free will and predestination that one might find in the Scriptures and in the rabbinic sources. As for biblical passages, he took good care to eliminate any problems in his capacity as Bible translator and commentator. In his *Amānāt* he quoted a number of scriptural verses in support of the doctrine of absolute free will, starting with Deut. 30:19: "Therefore choose life." As for rabbinic dicta, he cited the popular saying of R. Ḥanina, "All is in the hands of Heaven except the fear of Heaven."[71] It may be noted that in one of the three talmudic contexts in which this saying occurs,[72] it is linked with the haggadic statement of R. Ḥanina bar Pappa, the Palestinian Amora of the third generation, concerning the human sperm brought before God by the angel in charge of conception, and about the Divine decree predetermining the fate of man in all respects save whether he is to be righteous or wicked, this depending on his free will. Martin Schreiner suggested[73] that this haggadic statement came to be adopted by Wāṣil ibn 'Aṭā, the first Mu'tazilite, who, according to al-Shahrastānī,[74] interpreted a certain tradition of a predestinarian character to mean that everything was preordained except man's good and evil deeds. The pre-Qur'anic tradition concerned represents a variant of R. Ḥanina bar Pappa's haggada: the things decreed at the time when the embryo has passed forty-two days in the womb are its sex, its sustenance, its life-span, and its state of misery or happiness. The texts in al-Bukhārī and al-Ash'arī list in addition its work (*'amal*), i.e., deeds of piety or impiety, which reflects the orthodox view of the predetermined character of man's actions.[75] While Saadia offers no comment on R. Ḥanina's saying quoted by him, the Karaite Salmōn ben Yerūḥīm does so in his *Commentary on Kohelet*: "What remains in man's power is obedience and disobedience. The decision between the one and the other is entrusted (*mufawwaḍ*) to man, for he is free in his choice (*mukhtār*). This is what the ancients taught: 'All is in the hands of Heaven except the fear of Heaven.'"[76]

In trying to characterize Saadia's type of piety as it emerges from his discussion of man's free will, we may say that it is one of confidence that reason has an answer to all problems; that God's omnipotence and human freedom do not collide; and that predestination and determinism need not be resorted to in order to account for the seeming perplexities of man's existence.

We meet a different type of thinker in Baḥya ibn Paquda. Like Saadia, he stresses the freedom of choice that is given to man in the sphere of action but, unlike Saadia, he is intensely aware of the all-pervading will of God. Speaking about the "mystery of motion" (*sirr al-ḥaraka*), he points out that by our contemplation of it we shall realize our dependence on God: all our movements will be seen to be "bound" (*mazmūm*) to the will (*irāda*) of the Creator and to his regimen (*tadbīr*) and desire (*mashī'a*) except for that which has been "entrusted" (*fuwwiḍa*) to us and left to our free choice (*ikhtiyār*) concerning obedience and disobedience.[77] In this particular context the question as to how man's utter dependence on God's will can be squared with human freedom is not posed as a problem. Baḥya had no intention, however, to ignore it, although in one passage (V.5) he might seem to shrug off the doubts about free will as a mere stratagem of the evil one, called by him *al-hawa* (passion), which appears as *yeṣer* in the Hebrew version.[78] The evil inclination, he says, will try to "plunge thee into a sea of doubts concerning the subject of compulsion and justice (*al-jabr wa-l-'adl*), and when noticing your negligence in regard to acts of obedience and your inclination toward disobedience, it will seek to demonstrate to your satisfaction, by recourse to Scripture and Tradition, that you do act under compulsion." Yet on other occasions when secular matters are at issue, the *yeṣer* will make an effort to convince you that success or failure in your enterprises do not depend on God but on your own devices. Baḥya counsels extreme vigilance and quotes R. Ḥanina's *dictum*—referred to as "a saying of the ancients"—thereby implying that in all matters outside the sphere of moral and religious action man has to be considered to be subject to compulsion (*jabr*).[79]

In another passage, however, Baḥya treats the problem not as a mere ruse of the evil one but as a most serious question indeed. The passage concerned is placed in the context of the celebrated dialog between soul and intellect.[80] The soul confesses to being perplexed by the contradictory utterances concerning this matter found in the Scriptures: Some of these affirm compulsion (*jabr*) and predestination (*qadar*), regimen (*ḥukm*) and Divine will (*irāda*), while others indicate man's free choice. More precisely: Numerous scriptural passages seem to attest that "man and all other living beings are instruments prepared by God for the furnishing of the world, moving as they do solely by his permission, power (*quwwa*) and ability (*qudra*), and coming to rest when He causes them to rest."[81] This doctrine, Baḥya says, is reaffirmed, without any dissenting opinion, in the writings of the ancients, i.e., in rabbinic literature. Yet the Scriptures presented also a different view: Man's own acts"[82] are "entrusted" (*mufawwad*)[83] to him, are due to his will (*irāda*) and free choice (*ikhtiyār*), and man incurs reward and punishment for his obedience and disobedience on this account. All that is said in our books, that is, in rabbinic literature, about the Law (*sharī'a*), good manners (*adab*), and the commandment (*waṣīya*) indicates the soundness of this doctrine. The soul, addressing the intellect, finds this contradiction difficult and the reconciliation of it very hard of accomplishment.[84]

In reply, the intellect mentions first an empirical observation: We find that our actions, at times, turn out to accord with the purposes for which they were intended, while at other times they do not, which shows that they are under the bond (*zamām*) and control (*thaqāfa*)[85] of the Creator. Thus, sometimes we are hampered in our speech, hearing, and seeing.[86] Experience therefore indicates, Baḥya means to say, that we are indeed both free and not free in our acts. Intellect then records three ways in which the scholars attempted to reconcile *jabr* and *'adl*. (1) All human actions follow from man's free choice, power (*qudra*), and capacity (*ṭāqa*), all of which God has "entrusted" to man. Consequently,

God is "free" (*barā'*) from responsibility for human acts,[87] and reward and punishment are just. This view, which "solves" the problem by simply denying *jabr*, is obviously meant to reflect the Mu'tazilite outlook. (2) Every movement that is innovated in the world happens by the permission (*idhn*), predestination (*qadar*) and regimen (*ḥukm*) of the Creator and thus is under his bond (*zamām*). As for the justice of reward and punishment, the answer is: "We are ignorant of the form and procedure of judgment; God is just and commits no injustice; our intellect is too weak to comprehend the nature (lit. being) of his wisdom." This theory, which blissfully ignores the problem of justice, is easily recognizable as Ash'arite. (3) Since subscribing to either view involves sin and error as a result of one's getting immersed (*al-khā'iḍ*) in one of two extremes,[88] both views are to be believed in the sense that we act on the assumption of the correctness of both. Through assuming that our actions are "entrusted" to us, which entails the justice of reward and punishment, we shall make every effort to do what benefits us in this world and the next. By assuming, at the same time, that all our acts and movements are subject to the predestination, permission, and bond of the Creator; that He has the last word in argument, and that man has no case against Him, we shall surely put our trust in Him.[89]

Theory (3) clearly represents Baḥya's own "solution." "This view," he says, "comes closest to a release (*khalāṣ*), compared to all other [views], for it is true and fair to admit ignorance in matters of this kind."[90] We fail to understand, he points out, the mysterious workings of the astrolabe, the weighing-machine and the millstone; how then can we hope to grasp the operations of Divine justice?[91] Baḥya thus combines the Mu'tazilite and Ash'arite positions, not by way of harmonization and synthesis, which would be impossible by the nature of things, but from what would seem to be a pragmatic viewpoint. Yet his formula is more than a mere working hypothesis. It binds together his faith in Divine justice with his religious experience of utter dependence on God. This sense of dependence is clearly expressed in his concept of trust in God (*tawakkul*). This concept, which plays a major role in Baḥya's religious thought,[92] ties in with his notion of the "mystery of motion" by which he indicated his consciousness of being under the "bond" of God, i.e., under the direct control of the Divine will. Baḥya admitted the operation of secondary causes. Unlike the Ṣūfīs, who went to extremes in disregarding them, he counseled prudence and shunned fatalism.[93] Yet he maintained that the functioning of secondary causes depended on the decree of God,[94] and that all our movements were controlled by God's all-pervading will.

The type of piety that Baḥya represents has a mystical tinge of both the Neoplatonic and Ṣūfī kind of flavor, and closely resembles the stance of Abraham Maimonides who, about a hundred and fifty years later, was also much impressed by Ṣūfī piety. Abraham Maimonides described "reliance upon proximate, external, ordinary causes" as an attitude of unbelief.[95] We have to believe, he said, that natural causes and the ordinary means are disposed (*maṣrūf*) in accordance with the particular will of God in regard to every individual person, time, and situation, whereby the causes operate or are deflected from their nature.[96] Trust in God (*tawakkul*) is tantamount to being conscious of the fact that no benefit will accrue to one's labors except if so determined by God.[97] Abraham Maimonides's emphasis on *tawakkul* may have been indebted to Baḥya's influence in addition to that of the Ṣūfīs.

We now turn to the last thinker on our list, Moses Maimonides, whose earliest reference to our subject is found in his *Mishna Commentary* on Berakhot 9:7. The reference was occasioned by what he considered to be the literal meaning of Ps. 119:126, the verse quoted in the Mishna. Maimonides understood the words *ʿet la-ʿasōt la-YHWH heferū toratekha* to mean: When the time for action by God [i.e., the preordained time for punishment] arrives, they [i.e., the sinners deserving of punishment because of guilt incurred in the past], will break thy law [and thus they will not be allowed to escape their just deserts]. In all likelihood, Maimonides was thinking of Divine actions such as the hardening of Pharaoh's heart, which he explained as a measure employed by God to prevent Pharaoh's last-minute repentance by which he would have averted his just punishment.[98] Maimonides's comment reads:[99]

> When the time of retribution (*iqtiṣāṣ*) and vengeance (*intiqām*) arrives, certain causes will bring about men's [continued] breaking of the law in order that this [retribution] may befall them according to their deserts

(*bi-istiḥqāq*). This subject is long and recondite, "deep, deep, who can find it out?" (Eccl. 7 : 24), for in touching it we deal with the question of predestination (*al-qaḍā'*) and of the decree (*al-qadar*).[100]

Maimonides declines to discuss this subject in the present context and promises to treat it fully in his comments on the tractate Avot. He does, however, make a few remarks right here. In a manner reminiscent of Baḥya, he refers to the fact that the Scriptures and the talmudic sages (*al-ḥakhamim*) make contradictory statements on the subject. Again like Baḥya, he utters a warning against "immersing oneself" in a particular theory,[101] for, as he put it, "everyone who tried to immerse himself in it, followers of our law or others, failed to be particularly successful in the end. In the phrase of our sages, peace be upon them, he dived into deep waters and brought up a mere potsherd" (B.Q. 91a). Taking his cue once more probably from Baḥya, Maimonides declares that "the basic principle (*al-qā'ida*) of the matter is that God approves [the deeds of] the good and punishes the wicked," for his justice is clearly attested in the Scriptures.[102] Yet "to comprehend the mode of justice employed by Him is not within the capacity (*ṭāqa*) of man."

The final part of Maimonides's disquisition expresses a disavowal of Kalām and a firm approval of the way in which the *falāsifa* deal with the problem:

If concerning the subject you find in the words of the Mutakallimūn some imaginative idea (*takhayyul*) or rhetorical phrase resembling a proof (*ḥujja*), it is no proof. Once you make a determined effort in speculation, the beauty (*ṭalāwa*) of the alleged proof vanishes and the contradictions return. We are then back to where we were before but only at the price of long-winded speech and the writing of books. On the other hand, the discourse on this matter by the philosophers (*kalām al-falāsifa*) . . . is something wonderful, most extraordinary and subtle, requiring many preliminary propositions and training in the sciences. An intelligent man will consider those statements and show the accord of what they say with His word, be He praised and exalted: "See, I have set before thee this day life and good, death and evil . . ." (Deut. 30 : 15), word by word. He will conclude from their words something that approximates to the principle I have indicated to you, or that is even more profound and subtle. We shall say more about this subject in [our comments on] the tractate Avot, and shall show you some of the harmony that prevails between the words of the competent philosophers and our sages (*al-ḥakhamim*) in all matters.[103]

In chapter eight of *Shemona Peraqim*, the introductory part of his *Mishna Commentary* on Avot, Maimonides amplifies the remarks made in his comments on Berakhot. He formulates the principle of free choice by declaring that "all actions of man are within his discretion (*maṣrūfa ilaihi*), there being no compulsion (*jabr*) or influence[104] from outside whatever that could sway him toward virtue or vice;[105] that "if he so wills, he acts, and if he so wills, he does not act, there being no compulsion (*jabr*) or *force* (*qahr*) exercised upon him."[106] The thrust of this passage is directed against the astrologers who claim that the constellation of the stars at a person's birth endows him with virtue or vice and that for this reason man acts under compulsion.[107] The terms "compulsion," "influence," "force" used here are obviously intended as synonyms denoting the external constraint under which man is said to labor, according to the "chimerical ideas" (*hadhayānāt*) of the astrologers. In the present context, *jabr* no longer signifies a direct Divine intervention. The Kalām doctrine asserting the constant activity of God's will comes up for rebuttal later.[108] Maimonides's concern at the moment is the safeguarding of human free choice against fatalism.[109] As he explains, the belief in astral compulsion is incompatible with the assumption of free choice (*ikhtiyār*) and it renders the commandments and prohibitions of the Law futile. It also implies that all training in the arts and sciences as well as all efforts to form one's character are to no purpose. Moreover, it invalidates the justice of reward and punishment. The entire system of Divine legislation is based on the notion of man's freedom of choice as expressed in such biblical verses as Deut. 20:15 and 30:19 ("choose life").[110]

Maimonides leaves no doubt that in his view the doctrine of free choice is held in common by "our Law" and "Greek philosophy," and has been verified by "true proofs."[111] By "Greek philosophy" he means Aristotle and his followers among the *falāsifa*, particularly al-Fārābī, whose *Fuṣūl al-Madanī* has been shown to be reflected in the *Shemona Peraqim*,[112] and whose other ethicopolitical works, which contain distinct references to the notion of free will, were certainly known to him.[113] He knew, above all, al-Fārābī's (lost) Commentary on the *Nicomachean Ethics*,[114] and there is no reason to suspect that the Arabic version of the *Ethics* itself was unknown to him.[115] The Aristotelian background of our passage is patent. In denying that man invariably acts under "external influence" and under "compulsion" as claimed by the astrologers, Maimonides echoes Aristotle's distinction between the voluntary, of which "the moving principle is in the agent himself," and the involuntary that may be due to compulsion, the compulsory being that "of which the moving principle is outside."[116] In stating that man is a free agent for "if he so wills, he acts, and if he so wills, he does not act," Maimonides almost literally repeats Aristotle's words, "Where it is in our power to act it is also in our power not to act, and vice versa."[117] That the assumption of free will underlies all legislation and dispensation of justice is likewise taken from Aristotle who in the same context expatiates on this subject.[118] Maimonides's view that "our Law" and Aristotle agree with respect to the attribution of free choice to man is fundamentally sound. As Eduard Zeller pointed out, "It is Aristotle's firm conviction that we ourselves are the authors of our actions, and that it is within our power to be good or bad."[119] There is, however, a slight difference in the way in which Aristotle and Maimonides assess the impact of acquired traits of character. According to Aristotle, a man who has become unjust will not cease to be so by wishing to be just; he is morally sick as it were, and he can no longer change his character.[120] Maimonides, on the other hand, believes in the possibility of curing the ills of the soul. He outlines a therapy that is based on the notion of innate propensities due to temperament. While every man is free in the exercise of his will, he is either aided or hampered by his inborn "disposition" (*isti'dād*) but never compelled by it to act in a certain way.[121]

Having adopted the Aristotelian doctrine of free choice in its broad outline, Maimonides feels on safe philosophical ground in discussing the theological issue of predestination (which plays no part in Aristotle). He deals at length with R. Ḥanina's above-mentioned saying on the subject, which he declares to have been frequently misunderstood. His interpretation is clearly a case of a philosopher's piety versus popular religion. As he points out, it is erroneous to consider purely voluntary actions such as marrying a particular woman or enriching oneself by theft as due to Divine compulsion (*jabr*) and to justify such belief by invoking R. Ḥanina's statement. The term "all" as used in the sentence "all is in the hands of Heaven except the fear of Heaven" includes only "natural things concerning which man has no free choice," e.g., being of tall or small stature, rainfall or drought, the salubriousness or harmfulness of the air in a certain climate, etc.[122] Obedience or disobedience, however, and likewise such matters as marrying and coming into the possession of wealth were not preordained. They depended neither on God's decree (*qadar*) nor on his will (*mashī'a*) but solely on the will (*irāda*) of man. As he put it elsewhere,[123] it was but "the fools among the Gentiles[124] [viz., the astrologers] and most of the uneducated among the Jews" who mistakenly believed that God "preordained" (*gozer*) whether a man was to become a righteous man (*ṣaddiq*) or a wicked one (*rasha'*).[125]

In the same context Maimonides makes a pointed reference to the Kalām doctrine of the Divine will. He sums it up as proclaiming that "the will of God is continually, time after time, [active] in everything."[126] This is a fair description of what constitutes a belief common to both Mu'tazilites and Ash'arites. Neither of them assumes the operation of an eternal will of God in human affairs. Some Mu'tazilites dispense with the notion of Divine "willing" in the strict sense of the term: "Willing" by God, they say, really means creating, and his "willing" men's acts means commanding, while his "eternal will" signifies eternal knowledge.[127] Those Mu'tazilites who accept the term "will" in its literal sense admit only successive acts of temporal volitions but no eternal will. The Ash'arites, on the other hand, take the notion of Divine will most seriously, yet they too conceive of it as being temporal and concerned with the renewal of existence from moment to moment.[128] The "eternal will" of God, they declare, refers only to the temporal renewal of things that are perpetually renewed, not to human actions.[129] Maimonides rejects the Kalām notion of continually operative discrete acts of Divine volition, be they related to either the natural or volitional sphere. Upholding as he does the Aristotelian concept of a perpetual natural order, he affirms the belief that "the will [of God operated] in the six days of creation" and that "all things occur continually according to their nature, as it is said, 'That which hath been is that which shall be, and that which hath been done is that which shall be done, and there is nothing new under the sun' (Eccl. 1:9).[130]

Maimonides thus excludes from the realm of natural happenings and, *a fortiori*, from that of voluntary human acts any re-creating or innovating operation of the will of God. He seems to limit the activity of the Divine will to the initial creative act which, as he explains, made provision for occasional deviations from the natural order by way of miracle.[131] This almost deistic stance enables him to declare invalid certain pious assertions found in popular sayings: E.g., the saying expressing the belief that all of man's movements such as his standing up and sitting down are due to the will of God—a belief attested also in scriptural and rabbinic texts—has to be interpreted in a nonliteral sense. It means that God originally created man with the natural capacity of standing and sitting according to free choice. It cannot possibly be understood to mean that ad hoc created acts of the Divine will are the direct cause of every single movement of man.[132] In similar vein, though with a different emphasis, Maimonides says in his *Guide of the Perplexed* (II, 48) that it is characteristic of the prophetic way of speech to ascribe directly to God what occurs through natural or voluntary causes or by chance, the three types of causality assumed by Aristotle.[133] In his insistence on the autonomous functioning of the natural order, Maimonides markedly differs from Baḥya, who had stressed God's direct control of man's movements, and from Abraham Maimonides, who will emphasize the subjection of natural causes to the guiding will of God.

There remains an ambiguity as to Maimonides's notion of God's eternal will. He repeatedly identified the will and wisdom of God in the *Guide*.[134] Yet he did not reduce God's will to his wisdom, as did the Mu'tazilites, who declared God's eternal willing to be nothing else but his eternal knowledge.[135] He obviously considered it necessary to establish the operation of the Divine will in creation. Why? To formulate the question more precisely: Assuming that Maimonides had to posit a Divine will so as to exclude the assumption of a necessary, noncontingent world, why did he have to reject necessity even in the sense of a necessity flowing from the will of God? A necessity of this kind was postulated by Averroes as sufficient to meet the objections against the *falāsifa* raised by al-Ghazālī. According to Averroes, will and necessity are compatible: God's will necessarily wills the best, a view that expresses the ultimate intent of Plotinus's concept of emanation and necessity,[136] and in Jewish philosophy was adopted by Albalag and Crescas.[137]

As Averroes put it, Divine causality is neither natural nor voluntaristic, if by "voluntaristic" we mean free choosing from two opposites in the sense of *liberum arbitrium*. The term "will" as applied to Divine causality bears a meaning totally different from that of the term "will" as applied to man.[138] Since in the *Guide* Maimonides too insists on the homonymity of the term "will" in its application to man and God, why could he not have taken the road traveled by Averroes and his followers?

As Maimonides himself explains,[139] he was motivated by theological considerations. The doctrine of the *falāsifa* nullifies the Tora, particularly with regard to the possibility of miracles. One might ask why he was so anxious to uphold the possibility of miracles, seeing that according to his theory miracles are built into the natural order and thus are part of nature. A clue to answering the question is provided by Maimonides's discussion of free will in chapter eight of *Shemona Peraqim*. Our previous analysis has shown him to disallow any interference of the Divine will in human choices. God's eternal will relates to creation only. It does not disrupt the operations of the human will. This view, however, is not without qualification. God suspends man's exercise of free will when the decree of Divine justice so demands. Maimonides discusses at length God's hardening of Pharaoh's heart as a case in point. He had promised in his *Mishna Commentary* on Berakhot to elucidate the problem of predestination in the comments on Avot, and he now redeems that promise. Divine justice, he says, had ordained that Pharaoh be punished for his sins. His heart was hardened in order to prevent him from using his free will in an act of repentance that would have saved him from his well-deserved punishment. Other instances of Divine interference with human freedom of will that are quoted by Maimonides are Jeroboam's sudden incapacity to move his hand (I Kings 13:4) and the Sodomites' blindness (Gen. 19:11).[140] Maimonides's great concern with this subject is indicated by the elaborate manner in which he discusses it. Strangely enough, God's justice is said by him to operate in a sort of negative way: God occasionally suspends normal human functions such as the exercise of free will in order to make punishment possible. A striking parallel to this theory is found in Maimonides's doctrine of prophecy: While the act of prophesying is the natural result of a combination of certain factors and does not require a special act of will or grace by God, the unnatural supension of the prophetic capacity is due to God's intervention.[141] Maimonides describes such intervention as a miracle, and he obviously links the Divine governance of the world, especially the meting out of justice, with the will of God. The Divine will, however, is not conceived by him as arbitrary or *liberum arbitrium* but as wedded to wisdom and thereby directed toward justice.

It can hardly be assumed that Maimonides considered the "miracles" referred to as performed by ad hoc interventions. He must have understood them to operate, like all other miracles, through natural agencies. Seen from this angle, predestination may be defined as Divine justice decreed by the eternal will of God and operative through a concatenation of natural and voluntary causes. The question arises in what sense voluntary causes can be predetermined by God's will if man is endowed with absolute free choice or *liberum arbitrium*? There can be no doubt that in the *Mishna Commentary* and kindred texts of a theological character Maimonides subscribes to the theory that, no matter how strong the impact of circumstances and motivations, man is able to overrule them by his free choice.[142] This doctrine of absolute freedom does not appear, however, in the *Guide*, as has been noted by Shlomo Pines.[143] It can be shown, in fact, that in the *Guide* Maimonides tacitly replaces the view expressed in his theological works by a deterministic theory that must be considered to represent his esoteric doctrine. Pines suggests that many passages in the third book of the *Guide* bear out this interpretation, but he confines himself to an analysis of two chapters that he obviously regards as crucial. The first of these is the seventeenth chapter in Part III, which contains the following statement:

It is a basic principle of the Law of our teacher Moses, peace be upon him, and of all his followers that man possesses absolute capacity to act (*istiṭā'a muṭlaqa*), i.e., that by his nature, choice, and will he does all that a man can do, without anything being created that would interfere in any way. Likewise, all species of animals move by their own will. For God has willed it so, by which I mean to say that it is through His eternal will that, eternally, all living beings move by their will, and that man possesses the capacity to do what he wills or chooses from among the things he is capable of doing. This is a principle which, thank God, has never been heard to be contested within our community.[144]

As Pines rightly points out, the "absolute capacity to act" that Maimonides vindicates to man need not mean absolute freedom of will in the sense of *liberum arbitrium*. The use of this term and of the term "choice" (*ikhtiyār*) and "will" (*irāda*) does not rule out a deterministic interpretation of human acts based on the consideration of the impact of external circumstances and internal motivations. For the sole concern of Maimonides's statement is the rejection of the Mu'tazilite doctrine (mentioned earlier in the same chapter) according to which "the ability of man to act of his own accord is not absolute."[145] In the view of the Mosaic Law, Maimonides declares, the Kalām notion of "created will" (or that of "acquisition") has no place. Nothing is said as to whether the Jewish doctrine regards free choice as entirely sovereign or as conditioned by internal motivations. From the fact that Maimonides "finds it necessary" to impute the same freedom from Divine interference also to animal movements, Pines feels justified to infer that the statement does imply a deterministic view of human acts. "For it is difficult to see," he argues, "on what grounds the volitions of animals should be exempted from the reign of causality even in doctrines in which man's will is given a privileged status."[146] This line of reasoning does not seem to be compelling. Maimonides meticulously discriminates between animals, which he describes as moving by virtue of their will, and man, of whom he says that he has the ability of both willing (namely on the irrational level) and choosing (viz., as a rational being). The terminological distinction between *ikhtiyār* and *irāda* reflects Aristotle's distinction between "choice" (*proairesis*), which belongs to rational man alone, and the merely "voluntary" (*hekousios*), which extends to children and animals.[147] There is therefore nothing extraordinary in the fact that Maimonides mentions the animals, since Aristotle also does it. Moreover, the status of animals is variously discussed in this chapter. Hence there is no need to read into the passage an intent on Maimonides's part to place humans and animals on the same level, namely, to declare them equally subject to the laws of causality. In our view no definite conclusion can be drawn from this chapter.

It is different with Pines's second argument, which is based on Maimonides's statement on human will in chapter forty-eight of

Part II of the *Guide*.[148] The chapter opens with the statement that everything produced in time has a proximate cause, which in turn has a cause, and so on and so forth until the series reaches the First Cause, which is God's will and free choice. Maimonides then makes the point (referred to in a previous section of this essay) that it is typical of the prophetic way of speech to ignore the intermediate causes and to ascribe all events produced in time directly to the agency of God. The classification of the proximate causes offered by Maimonides lists three types: (1) essential or natural causes; (2) voluntary causes; and (3) accidental and fortuitous causes or chance. He explains the second class as consisting of either the "free choice" of a man or the "will" of an animal.[149] As Pines observes, "we find again that Maimonides appears to put on a par man's free choice and the volitions of the other animals, the former and the latter being caused by God."[150] Pines has a stronger case in this instance, since here Maimonides attributes both animal movements and human acts to a series of causes going ultimately back to God. The way in which Maimonides illustrates the matter fully corroborates Pines's thesis: "For inasmuch as the Deity, as has been established, is the One that arouses that volition in the irrational animal, and that has necessitated that free choice in the rational animal, and that has made the natural things pursue their course . . . it necessarily follows from all this that it may be said of the necessary results of these causes that God commanded them. . . ."[151] Pines concludes from this passage "that in Maimonides' opinion volition and choice are no less subject to causation than natural phenomena and do not form in this respect a domain governed by different laws or by no laws at all."[152] Indeed, looking at this passage one cannot avoid considering Maimonides a strict determinist. For our passage establishes a complete analogy between the necessities attending natural and volitional causes. As far as the latter are concerned, the necessary arousal of a particular volition in an animal (or in man at the level of irrationality) is an exact parallel to the necessity by which rational man makes his free choice. Moreover, certain results proceed necessarily from these causes, and the concatenation forming a causal series goes back to God's will, which justifies the prophetic manner of speech attributing all events directly to the First Cause. From the biblical specimens of such usage quoted by Maimonides, it becomes abundantly clear that the entire range of volitional causes comes under the category of necessary events. As for human free choice, Nebuchadnezzar's tyranny; Shimei ben Gera's cursing of David; Joseph's deliverance from prison; the Persians' and Medes' victory over the Chaldeans; and the widow's kindness in feeding Elijah; all these acts could be attributed to God's command because they were caused by motivations that necessitated the events.

The deterministic character of Maimonides's notion of free choice is attested also by other passages of the *Guide.* Chapter six of Part II discusses the Divine *modus operandi* through intermediate causes termed angels, "everyone carrying out an order being called an angel."[153] In this context Maimonides states that "the movements of animals, even nonrational ones, are said in Scripture to have been accomplished through an angel, if the motion was produced in accordance with the intention of God, who put a force in the animal that moved it." All acts of God are performed through an angel, this term denoting all natural and psychic forces. Maimonides quotes R. Yoḥanan's saying with reference to the story of Judah and Tamar: "Judah wanted to pass by but the Holy One, blessed be He, caused the angel that is in charge of lust—viz., the force of sexual desire—to present himself to him."[154] Here Judah's action is attributed to the impact of a desire which, against his intention, necessitated his choice; the overpowering desire is called an angel, i.e., an act of God. In the same context Maimonides cites the statement in *Kohelet Rabba* (10:20), "When man sleeps, his soul speaks to the angel, and the angel to the cherub," which he understands to mean that the force of imagination is called an angel, and that the intellect is called a cherub.[155] The implication is clear: What a man does under the impact of either imagination or intellect is likewise the necessary result of his motivation, which is traceable to a series of causes going back to the Divine will and hence is called an angel. There is no *liberum arbitrium.*

The denial of absolute free choice must not be construed, however, as a denial of freedom. This emerges from Maimonides's discussion of the free choice of the spheres and the separate intelligencies in chapter seven of Part II. Maimonides attributes free choice also to the celestial spheres and the intelligencies that are active in the preparation of matter and transmission of forms respectively to the sublunar world. Their choice, however, is said to be different from ours not only because they govern a realm distinct from the one "entrusted" to us but chiefly because they "always do what is good," whereas we "sometimes do things that are deficient."[156] It should be noted that Maimonides sees no incompatibility between free choice and choosing of necessity what is good, i.e., choosing what a rational being is bound to choose. That only on the level of intellect real freedom can be found is a truth that Plotinus recognized as the ultimate meaning of Aristotle's concept of free choice.[157] Al-Fārābī and Avicenna adopted this insight. Al-Fārābī speaks of three kinds of will: viz., one caused by desire, one by imagination, and one by intellect. Only the last one is called by him "free choice" (*ikhtiyār*) and said to enable a man to achieve ultimate felicity, which is tantamount to freedom.[158] Avicenna teaches that the intelligent man who chooses the highest good thereby actualizes the necessary, innate love of his very being for God. This choice alone makes a man free, although, truly speaking, he has no other choice.[159] Maimonides stands solidly in this Aristotelian-Plotinian tradition.

Maimonides's type of piety as expressed in the *Guide* is marked by the contemplative mood of the Neoplatonic Aristotelian. His theological writings reflect the same basic attitude tempered by the traditional belief in man's absolute freedom of will. Yet even there he allows himself a fair measure of philosophical independence. In his insistence on the autonomous functioning of nature and of the human will, he provides a striking contrast to Baḥya, who stressed God's direct control of man's movements, and who made trust in God one of the main categories of the spiritual life. In Maimonides the theme of *biṭaḥon* (*tawakkul*) plays hardly any role.[160] It is all the more remarkable that the first of Maimonides's thirteen principles of the Jewish religion as formulated in the credal statement found in the Daily Prayer Book (*Siddur*) affirms the belief that "God alone performed, performs, and will perform all actions."[161] In his paper on "Popular Religion . . ." presented at this conference, Professor Goitein drew attention to this formulation and suggested that, strange though this may sound, it testifies to the impact of Muslim orthodox theology (al-Ash'ari and al-Māturīdī) on Jewish religious belief. The matter would, however, seem to require further investigation. The crucial sentence in the text of the first principle as stated by Maimonides in the Introduction to his *Commentary on Mishna Sanhedrin*, Pereq Ḥeleq, reads:[162] "He is the cause of the existence of all existents; in Him is the foundation (*qiwām*) of their existence; and from Him derives their continued existence (*al-baqā'*)."[163] There is no reference in this text to human action as being caused by God. The credal formula in the *Siddur* probably used the term *ma'asim* not in the sense of "actions" but in the sense of "events" or "things happening." Yet even on this assumption it is still strange to find that "all events," including, presumably, events resulting from voluntary acts, are said to be due solely to Divine agency. As we have shown, Maimonides's theological writings distinctly affirm man's absolute freedom of will. The only explanation of this startling text can be provided by the deterministic view that Maimonides expressed in the *Guide*, and more specifically in his statement (*Guide*, III, 17) that prophetic parlance ascribes directly to God what is in effect the result of a series of intermediate causes. The author of the credal text obviously took his cue from this chapter. He adopted the prophetic way of speech as it were, and boldly proclaimed that everything that happens is done by God alone. This statement does not imply, however, that God actually creates—or participates in—every human act as Kalām doctrine has it. God works through intermediate causes, and it is only by using the license of prophetic speech that we ignore those causes and piously affirm God's exclusive agency.

NOTES

1. Thus formulated in a letter to me. The paper referred to appeared in S. D. Goitein, ed., *Religion in a Religious Age*. Proceedings of Regional Conferences etc. (Cambridge, Mass., 1974), 3–17.

2. See David Kaufmann, "Muammar as-Sulami und der unbekannte Gaon in Ibn Esra's Jesod Mora," *MGWJ*, 33 (1884): 332; Harry A. Wolfson, "The Jewish Kalām," *JQR*, 75 (1967): 550–53.

3. The term *anshey ha-meḥqar* designates in many instances the adepts of Jewish Kalām but it is also used to denote the philosophers. An investigation of the uses of this term and kindred ones (*anshey ha-tushiya; ḥakhmey shiqqul ha-da'at; ḥakhmey ha-'iyyun*) would be desirable. For references to the occurrence and meaning of *anshey* (*ba'aley; ḥakhmey*) *ha-meḥqar*, see M. Steinschneider, *Die hebräischen Übersetzungen des Mittelalters* . . . (1893; 1956), 6, n. 43; 133, n. 190; 161, n. 399; 303; 380, n. 85; 862, n. 92; 896, n. 271; *Idem, Jewish Literature* . . . (1857; 1967), 296; 310f; Martin Schreiner, *Der Kalām in der jüdischen Literatur* (Berlin, 1895), 41.

4. See David Kaufmann, op. cit., 327–32.

5. See H. Brody (ed.), *Hebräische Bibliographie*, 3 (1898): 88–91.

6. See *REJ*, 46 (1903): 179–86.

7. Shraga Abramson, *R. Nissim Gaon Libelli Quinque* (Jerusalem, 1965). See G. Vajda's review in *REJ*, 125 (1966): 422ff.

8. Particularly pertinent to our present subject is Vajda's article "De l'universalité de la loi morale selon Yusūf al-Baṣīr," *REJ*, (1969): 133–201.

9. See Martin Schreiner, *Studien über Jeschu'a ben Jehuda* (Berlin, 1900), 23–25.

10. See Vajda's article referred to in note 8.

11. The following previous Kalām studies by Professor Wolfson, in addition to the article mentioned in n. 2, have a direct bearing on our subject: "Ibn Khaldūn on Attributes and Predestination," *Speculum*, 34 (1959): 585–597; "The Controversy over Causality within the Kalām," *Mélanges Alexandre Koyré* (1964), 602–18; "The Khāṭirāni in the Kalām and Ghazālī as Inner Motive Powers of Human Actions," *Studies in Mysticism and Religion presented to Gershom G. Scholem* (Jerusalem, 1967), 363–79.

12. *Guide of the Perplexed*, I, 71, p. 122.6–9 (page references are to the Arabic edition by I. Joel, Jerusalem, 1930/31). Maimonides's view has been strongly contested by Schreiner, *Der Kalām*, 45, and by Wolfson, "The Jewish Kalām," 547f.

13. See Martin Schreiner, "Zur Charakteristik R. Samuel b. Chofni's und R. Hai's," *MGWJ*, 35 (1886): 314–19; E. E. Hildesheimer, "Mystik und Agada im Urteile der Gaonen R. Scherira und R. Hai," *Festschrift für Jacob Rosenheim* (Frankfurt a.M, 1931), 259–73; Gershom Scholem, *Major Trends in Jewish Mysticism*, Third Revised Edition, 49; 360, n. 26; 361, n. 47; Idem, *Ursprung und Anfänge der Kabbala* (Berlin, 1962), 96 and passim.

14. Mayer Lambert (ed. and tr.), *Commentaire sur le Séfer Yesira ou Livre de la Création par le Gaon Saadya de Fayyoum* (Paris, 1891).

15. Georges Vajda, *Sa'adyā Commentateur du "Livre de la Création"* (Paris, 1960), 8, 12f.

16. On Stoic influence, see S. Horovitz, *Ueber den Einfluss der griechischen Philosophie auf die Entwicklung des Kalam* (Breslau, 1909), 42f; concerning the impact of Saadia's doctrine of the Divine will on Kabbala, see Scholem, *Ursprung*, 197; 292f.

17. Lambert, *Commentaire* . . . , 37 (tr. 59); S. Landauer (ed.), *Kitāb al-Amānāt wa'l-I'tiqādāt* (Leiden, 1880), 11. Cf. Vajda, *Sa'adyā Commentateur* . . . , 14; Alexander Altmann, *Saadya Gaon: The Book of Doctrines and Beliefs* (Oxford, 1946), 32, n. 1; 34, n. 2.

18. See Louis Gardet, *Dieu et la Destinée de l'Homme* (Paris, 1967), 277.

19. See Harry A. Wolfson, "The Double Faith Theory in Clement, Saadia, Averroes and St. Thomas, and its origin in Aristotle and the Stoics," *JQR*, 33 (1942/43): 239.

20. *Amānāt*, Treatises VII and VIII.

21. Louis Gardet, "Quelques réflexions sur la place du *'ilm al-kalām* dans les 'sciences religieuses' musulmanes," *Arabic and Islamic Studies in Honor of Hamilton A. R. Gibb* (Leiden, 1965), 257–69 (quoted in G. Vajda's paper "Note sur le 'kalām' dans la pensée religieuse juive du Moyen Age," *Revue de l'Histoire des Religions* 1973: 144).

22. Richard M. Frank, "The Philosophy of the Kalām and its Theological Background," paper presented at the Colloquium "On Early Islamic Thought in honor of Professor Harry A. Wolfson," Harvard University, April 1971.

23. On this term see Gardet, *Dieu et la destinée*, 417–20.

24. *Amānāt*, 14–15.

25. *Amānāt*, 207–8; the same term occurs also on p. 247. See Jacob Guttmann, *Die Religionsphilosophie des Saadia* (Göttingen, 1882), 214, 237; Schreiner, *Der Kalām*, 66–67.

26. See A. S. Halkin (tr.), *Al-Baghdādī, Moslem Schisms and Sects*, Part II (Tel-Aviv, 1935); quoted by G. Scholem, *Von der mystischen Gestalt der Gottheit* (Zürich, 1962), 194, 297, n. 6.

27. See L. Nemoy (ed.), *Al-Qirqisānī, Kitāb al-Anwār wal-Marāqib*, II (1940), 315ff; quoted by Salo W. Baron, *A Social and Religious History of the Jews*, Second Edition, VII (New York, 1958), 331; and referred to by Scholem, *Von der mystischen Gestalt*, 195.

28. See the account given in Gardet, *Dieu et la destinée*, 96f.

29. See S. Horovitz (ed.), *Der Mikrokosmos des Josef Ibn Ṣaddiḳ* (Breslau, 1903), 72–73. Other quotations from the *Kitāb al-Manṣūrī* on pp. 44, 47; cf. Schreiner, *Der Kalām*, 29.

30. *Amānāt*, 208–9.
31. *Amānāt*, 173; see Guttmann, *Die Religionsphilosophie des Saadia*, 183.
32. *Amānāt*, 141–2.
33. *Guide*, III, 17, p. 340.7–10.
34. See Gardet, *Dieu et la destinée*, 297–300.
35. *Amānāt*, 169–172.
36. Cf. Gardet, op. cit., 298–9.
37. See D. S. (D. H.) Baneth, *Hathalat Sefer Ha-Miṣvot le-Rav Se'adya*, in: *Rav Se'adya Ga'on*, ed. by J. L. Fishman (Jerusalem, 5703/1943), 373–4.
38. *Amānāt*, 113.
39. *Qiddushin*, 31a.
40. *Amānāt*, 155.
41. Maimonides contradicts this view; see *Guide*; III, 17, p. 339, ll. 20–26.
42. See Shraga Abramson (ed.), *R. Nissim Gaon*, 330–31.
43. See W. Bacher, "Le Commentaire de Samuel Ibn Hofni sur le Pentateuque," *REJ*, 15 (1887), 118–19.
44. See W. Montgomery Watt, *Free Will and Predestination in Early Islam* (London, 1948), 69.
45. *Amānāt*, 150–1.
46. See Watt, op. cit., 68; Gardet, *Dieu et la destinée*, 88, 97.
47. *Amānāt*, 150.
48. *Amānāt*, 152.
49. See Joseph Qafaḥ (ed. and tr.), *Tehilim 'im Tirgum U-Ferush Ha-Ga'on Rabbenu Se'adya Ben Yosef Fayyumī* (Jerusalem, 5726), Ps. 74:1, p. 177. The method indicated is employed also in Ps. 10:1, 42:10, 43:2, 44:24.
50. *Amānāt*, 73.
51. See also Saadia's comment on Ps. 51:16. For a similar view cf. *Zohar* I, 59a on Ps. 86:11.
52. In his paper on "Religion . . ." referred to in note 1.
53. On *istiṭā'a*, see Gardet, *Dieu et la destinée*, 65ff., 139; Schreiner, *Der Kalām*, 15; Watt, op. cit., 90, n. 37.
54. Aristotle, *Metaph.*, IX.iii, 1046b 29ff.
55. *Amānāt*, 151.
56. See Watt, op. cit., 71f.
57. For the concept of "absolute freedom of the will" see H. A. Wolfson, "Philosophical Implications of the Pelagian Controversy," *Proceedings of the American Philosophical Society*, 103, No. 4 (August, 1959): 554f.; reprinted in Idem, *Religious Philosophy: A Group of Essays* (Cambridge, Mass., 1961), 158ff. See also Idem, "Philo on Free Will," *The Harvard Theological Review*, 35, No. 2 (April, 1942): 131–169.
58. For the doctrine of *liberum arbitrium* in patristic literature, see M. J. Rouet de Journel S. J., *Enchiridion Patristicum* (Freiburg Breisgau, 1956), 772, Index, No. 334, where many references are given. According to Bradwardine, not a single patristic author denied the *liberum arbitrium*: see Heiko A. Oberman, *Archbishop Thomas Bradwardine. A Fourteenth Century Augustinian* (Utrecht, 1957), 224. Two major scholastic interpretations of *liberum arbitrium* are discussed in Johannes Auer, *Die menschliche Willensfreiheit im Lehrsystem des Thomas von Aquin und Johannes Duns Scotus* (Munich, 1938).
59. Aristotle, *Metaph.*, IX. v, 1048a 1–24; *Eth. Nic.*, III. ii, 1111b 4–19; see also *De anima*, III, x–xi, 443a 10–434a 21.
60. *Amānāt*, 151–2.
61. *Amānāt*, 152.
62. Ibid.
63. *Kuzari*, V. 20. The essential part of the sentence is missing in H. Hirschfeld's edition of the Arabic text: *Das Buch Al-Chazari* . . . (Leipzig, 1887), 340.11.
64. See Schreiner, *Der Kalām*, 15, note 3; cf. al-Ghazālī, *Iḥyā' 'Ulūm al-Dīn* (1956), I, 98.22–23 and the passage in al-Juwainī, *Luma' fī Qawā'id Ahl al-Sunna*, ch. 19 (Michel Allard, S. J., *Textes apologétiques de Juwainī*, Beyrouth, 1968, 164–5).

65. The passage is quoted by Guttmann, op. cit., 167, n. 5.
66. *Amānāt*, 49–51; 82.
67. *Amānāt*, 152.
68. See Watt, op. cit., 104ff.; 83, 98.
69. See Gardet, *Dieu et la destinée*, 62.
70. *Guide*, I, 51, p. 76.28–77.1.
71. Berakhot 33b; Megilla 25a; Nidda 16b.
72. Namely, Nidda 16b.
73. Schreiner, *Der Kalām*, 4.
74. *Milal, I*, 32.
75. See Martin Schreiner, "Zur Geschichte des Ash'aritenthums," *Actes du Huitième Congrès International des Orientalistes*, 1889 (Leiden, 1893), II, 94; Watt, op. cit., 18; 30, n. 7.
76. See Georges Vajda, *Deux Commentaires Karaites sur l'Ecclésiaste* (Leiden, 1971), 25.
77. *Ḥovot Ha-Levavot*, II.5, p. 117.1–6 (page references are to the Arabic edition by A. S. Yahuda, Leiden, 1912). For a list of passages concerning free choice, see Moses Sister, "Bachja-Studien I," in: *Fünfzigster Bericht der Lehranstalt für die Wissenschaft des Judentums* (Berlin, 1936), 45f.
78. The term *khāṭir*, used in Islamic Kalām and by al-Ghāzālī, seems to be absent in Baḥya.
79. *Ḥovot Ha-Levavot*, V. 5, p. 250.15–251.9.
80. *Ḥovot Ha-Levavot*, III.8.
81. III.8, p. 161.23–162.14.
82. Lit., "the acts that appear from man."
83. III.8, p. 162.17. The same term occurs also p. 163.2, 14; 164.2, and is used by Salmōn ben Yeruhīm; see above, p. 44. As Vajda, *Deux Commentaires . . .*, 25 has pointed out, the term is characteristic of Kalām. Cf. Watt, op. cit., 33.
84. III.8, p. 162.15–163.4.
85. Lit., "seizure."
86. Lit., "this is manifest to you . . . from the movement of the tongue and from hearing and seeing" (163.10–11).
87. Cf. the Kalām principle of "not fixing evil upon God," mentioned by Watt, op. cit., 53 and passim.
88. III.8, p. 163.23. For the use of the same term by Maimonides see above, p. 48.
89. III.8, p. 163.4–164.5.
90. III.8, p. 164.6–7.
91. III.8, p. 164.14–165.12.
92. See G. Vajda, *La Théologie ascétique de Baḥya Ibn Paquda* (Paris, 1947), 60–85.
93. See *Ḥovot Ha-Levavot*, IV.4.
94. III.3, p. 190.10.
95. See Samuel Rosenblatt, *The High Ways to Perfection of Abraham Maimonides*, vol. II (Baltimore, 1938), p. 106.19–20.
96. Rosenblatt, op. cit., p. 110.12–18; 112.6-10.
97. Rosenblatt, op. cit., p. 90.19–21.
98. See above, p. 53.
99. In Joseph Qafaḥ's edition of Maimonides's *Mishna Commentary*, vol. I, 91. Qafaḥ's own Hebrew translation of *al-qaḍā'* and *al-qadar* by *ha-sakhar ve-ha-'onesh* misses the point.
100. For the meaning of these two terms, see Gardet, *Dieu et la destinée*, 116–120.
101. Using the same word as Baḥya did: *bi-l- khauḍ; khāḍa*.
102. Quoting Deut. 32:4.
103. In Qafaḥ's edition, I, 91–92.
104. Arab. *dā'iya*; see Qafaḥ's edition, IV, 397. The reading in M. Wolff's edition of *Shemona Peraqim* (Leiden, 1903), p. 27.13 makes no sense.
105. This sentence (Wolff, 27; Qafaḥ, IV, 397) has an exact parallel in Maimonides's *Letter on Astrology*, ed. by Alexander Marx, *HUCA*, 3 (1926): 354.23f.

106. Wolff, 28; Qafaḥ, IV, 397.
107. Wolff, 27; Qafaḥ, IV, 396.
108. Wolff, 30; Qafaḥ, IV, 399. See above, p. 52.
109. The same concern was prominent in Latin scholasticism. According to Archbishop Bradwardine, all Doctors agree that there is no such thing as "the fate in the stars." Etienne Tempier, bishop of Paris, decided in 1277 to condemn teachings expressing a tendency to fatalism. See Heiko A. Oberman, op. cit., 67.
110. Wolff, 27–28; Qafaḥ, IV, 397.
111. Wolff, 27; Qafaḥ, IV, 397.
112. See Herbert Davidson, "Maimonides' *Shemonah Peraqim* and Alfarabi's *Fuṣūl al-Madanī*," *PAAJR*, 31 (1963): 33–50.
113. We may single out al-Fārābī's *Kitāb fī Mabādi al-Mawjudāt* (*Sefer Ha-Hatḥalot*, ed. by Ṣevi Filipowski in *Sefer Ha-Assif*, Leipzig, 1849) and *Kitāb al-Siyāsa al-Madanīya*. For a more complete list see Shlomo Pines's introduction to his English translation of *The Guide of the Perplexed* (Chicago, 1963), lxxxvi–xcii. In Pines's view these writings had "a very strong influence on Maimonides."
114. See *Guide*, III, 18, p. 344.17–19.
115. See, however, Davidson, op. cit., 41 against David Rosin's stated assumption, with which the present writer is inclined to agree. Maimonides's quotations from the *Nicomachean Ethics* do not seem to be culled from al-Fārābī's political writings but from the text of the *Eth. Nic.*, which could have been known to him through al-Fārābī's Commentary or independently. On the Arabic version of *Eth. Nic.*, see the bibliographical references in Lawrence V. Berman's article in *Oriens*, 20 (1967): 32–33.
116. *Eth. Nic.*, III.i, 1109b–1110a; 1111a.
117. *Eth. Nic.*, III.v, 1113b.
118. *Eth. Nic.*, III.v, 1113b 21ff.
119. See Eduard Zeller, *Die Philosophie der Griechen in ihrer geschichtlichen Entwicklung*, II.2 (Hildesheim, 1963), 588f.
120. *Eth. Nic.*, III.v, 1114a 3–23.
121. See *Shemona Peraqim*, chs. 3, 4, 8; *Mishne Tora*, Hilkhot De'ot, chs. 2, 3.
122. Wolff, 28–29; Qafaḥ, IV, 398.
123. *Mishne Tora*, Hilkhot Teshuva, 5:2.
124. In his article "The Jewish Kalām" (quoted above, note 2), Wolfson interprets Maimonides's phrase *ṭippeshey ummot ha-'olam* to mean "the ignorant ones among the Gentiles," taking the term *ṭippeshim* to be the equivalent of Arabic *jāhilūn* and its cognates. Since the Arabic terms mentioned are invariably rendered in Hebrew by terms other than *ṭippeshim*, as Wolfson acknowledges (p. 557, note 34), our rendition ("fools") would seem to be preferable. Maimonides obviously refers to the astrologers, whom he holds in low esteem, and whom he designates as *ha-ṭippeshim* in his *Letter on Astrology* (*HUCA*, 3, 1926, p. 350.12). In a hand-written addendum to the reprint of his article in my possession Professor Wolfson wrote: "Similarly in his letter on astrology is *ṭippeshim* used as the opposite of *ḥakhamim* in the sense of those who are ignorant of philosophy." There follows a reference to the passage in *HUCA*.
125. The same view is expressed by Abraham Maimonides; see Rosenblatt, *The High Ways*, II, 88.19–20.
126. Wolff, 30; Qafaḥ, IV, 399.
127. See Alfred Guillaume (ed. and tr.), *Al-Shahrasṯānī, Kitāb Nihāyatu 'l-Iqdām fi 'Ilmi 'l-Kalām* (Oxford, 1934), 238; English section, p. 84.
128. Guillaume, op. cit., 248–9 (86–87).
129. Guillaume, op. cit., 257 (89).
130. Wolff, 30; Qafaḥ, IV, 399.
131. Ibid.
132. Wolff, 29–30; Qafaḥ, IV, 399.
133. See *Eth. Nic.*, III.iii, 1112a 31.
134. *Guide*, II, 18, p. 210.19–21; III, 13, p. 329.14; III, 17, p. 342.20.
135. See note 127.
136. See J. M. Rist., *Plotinus: The Road to Reality* (Cambridge, 1967), 66–83.

137. See Yehuda Arye (Georges) Vajda (ed.), *Sefer Tiqqun Ha-De'ot Le-Yiṣhaq Albalag* (Jerusalem, 1973), 23–25; 77–79.

138. See Simon van den Bergh (tr.), *Averroes' Tahafut Al-Tahafut* (London, 1945), I, 22; 264f.

139. *Guide*, II, 25, p. 229.21–26.

140. Wolff, 32–36; Qafaḥ, IV, 401–4.

141. *Guide*, II, 32.

142. See David Rosin, "Die Ethik des Maimonides," in: *Jahresbericht des jüdisch-theologischen Seminars*... (Breslau, 1876), 65; Leo Strauss, "Notes on Maimonides' Book of Knowledge," in: *Studies in Mysticism and Religion Presented to Gershom G. Scholem* (Jerusalem, 1967), 281ff.

143. Shlomo Pines, "Studies in Abul-Barakāt al-Baghdādī's Poetics and Metaphysics," in: *Studies in Philosophy, Scripta Hierosolymitana*, vol. VI (1960): 195–8; quoted by Pines in the introduction to his English translation of the *Guide*, xcv, n. 63.

144. *Guide*, III, 17, p. 338.24–30.

145. *Guide*, III, 17, p. 337.26–27.

146. Pines, op. cit., 196–7.

147. *Eth. Nic.*, III.ii, 1111b 6–9.

148. Mistakenly given as chapter 47.

149. *Guide*, II, 48, p. 292.25–29.

150. Pines, op. cit., 197.

151. *Guide*, II, 48, p. 293.4–10.

152. Pines, op. cit., 198.

153. *Guide*, II, 6, p. 182.15.

154. *Guide*, II, 6, p. 182.15–18; 184.3–4, 10–13.

155. *Guide*, II, 6, p. 184.15–18.

156. *Guide*, II, 7, p. 185.20–23.

157. See Paul Henry, "Le Problème de la liberté chez Plotin," *Revue Néo-Scolastique*, 8 (Louvain, 2nd series, 1931): 50–79, 180–215, 318–39; J. M. Rist, op. cit., 130–8.

158. See *Sefer Ha-Hatḥalot*, ed. Filipowski, 34ff.; the same text is found in P. Brönnle (ed.), *Die Staatsleitung von Alfarabi* (Leiden, 1904) [a German version of *Kitāb al-Siyāsat al-Madanīya*], 53ff.

159. For an appraisal, see Louis Gardet, *La Pensée réligieuse d'Avicenne* (Paris, 1951), 173.

160. Rabbi Menahem Meier, who searched for references at my request, found two, namely, *Mishne Tora*, Zera'im, Hilkhot Mattenot 'Aniyyim, 10:19 and Qinyan, Hilkhot Zekhiya u-Mattana, 12:17.

161. *We-hu' levado 'asah ve-'oseh ve-ya'aseh le-khol ha-ma'asim*. I have not been able to establish when and by whom this text was written, and when it was adopted into the *Siddur.*

162. See the Arabic text in J. Holzer, *Mose Maimūni's Einleitung zu Chelek* (Berlin, 1901), 20f., and Qafaḥ, IV, 210.

163. *Hu' 'illat meṣi'ut ha-nimṣa'im kulam bo qiyyum meṣi'utam u-mimmennu qiyyumam* in Shelomo ben Yiṣhaq's version. The text in Judah al-Ḥarīzī's translation renders the final part of the sentence more accurately: *u-mimmennu yimshekhu koaḥ ha-qiyyum*; see Moshe Goshen-Gottstein, "*Shelosh-'esre ha-'iqqarim le-ha-Rambam be-tirgum al-Ḥarizi,*" *Tarbiṣ*, 26 (1956): 188–9.

4 Maimonides's "Four Perfections"

Maimonides presents his account of the "four perfections" in the final chapter of the *Guide*[1] as derived from both the ancient and latter-day philosophers who had made it clear that the perfections (*al-kamālāt*) to be found in man consisted of four species (*anwā'*). The "ancient" authority claimed by Maimonides can be no other than Aristotle, as Munk already pointed out.[2] In the *Nicomachean Ethics*, which was well known to Maimonides,[3] Aristotle says that "things good have been divided into three classes, external goods on the one hand, and goods of the soul and of the body on the other,"[4] and that the happiness of the soul lies primarily in the activity of contemplation and secondarily in the exercise of moral virtue.[5] By distinguishing between two degrees of the soul's happiness and by thus subdividing the "goods of the soul," Aristotle does in fact recognize a fourfold division of things good. He declares distinctly that in addition to the happiness that belongs to moral virtue and to the life of contemplation man must also have bodily health and a supply of other requirements. These two latter classes are also lumped together as "external goods" as distinct from the goods of the soul.[6] Maimonides was therefore on sure ground in describing the fourfold division as "ancient." The question is to which source or sources he referred when he spoke about this division as one found in "latter-day" philosophers. At first blush it might seem that what he had in mind was al-Fārābī's scheme of four kinds of happiness in the *Kitāb taḥṣīl al-sa'āda*,[7] which appears in Averroes's Commentary on Plato's *Republic* as a scheme of four kinds of human "perfections."[8] On closer inspection, however, it turns out that the four classes listed by al-Fārābī and Averroes differ from those mentioned by Maimonides. Al-Fārābī and Averroes speak about (1) theoretical virtues (*al-faḍā'il al-naẓariyya*); (2) cogitative virtues (*al-faḍā'il al-fikriyya*); (3) moral virtues (*al-faḍā'il al-ḫulqiyya*); and (4) the practical arts (*al-ṣinā'āt al-'amaliyya*). Maimonides, on the other hand, enumerates the following perfections: (1) those of possessions; (2) those of the bodily constitution and shape; (3) the perfection of moral virtues; and (4) that of rational virtues. It is obvious that Maimonides used a *Vorlage* other than the al-Fārābī text that Averroes appropriated. We suggest that he based himself on the elaborate discussion of the four kinds of perfection found in Ibn Bājja's *Risālat al-widā'* ("Letter of Farewell").[9] A detailed comparison of the Maimonides passage with the treatment of the theme by Ibn Bājja will furnish evidence to this effect.[10]

Like Aristotle, who speaks of three classes of goods while, in fact, he recognizes four, Ibn Bājja opens his discourse by stating that there are three kinds of perfection (§ 19, line 1), but actually enumerates four and distinctly refers to the last as "the fourth perfection" (§ 21, line 1). Whereas in the case of Aristotle the number four is arrived at by subdividing the goods of the soul, the same result follows in Ibn Bājja's case by differentiating between external possessions and bodily health, a procedure that has its precedent in Aristotle's subdivision of "external goods" into "instruments" of actions and the well-being of the body.[11] Maimonides simplifies matters by introducing the fourfold division from the outset. He also simplifies the terminology. Whereas Ibn Bājja uses the two synonymous terms *al-tamāmāt* and *al-kamālāt* to denote "the perfections," Maimonides employs only the latter term. The transition from Aristotle's concept of "things good" to the notion of "perfections," as found in Ibn Bājja, Maimonides, and Averroes, was facilitated by Aristotle's description of pleasure as "a good"[12] and by his statement that the degrees of pleasure corresponded to the activity that engendered the pleasure and perfected the person performing it. "It is therefore that pleasure, or those pleasures, by which the activity, or the activities, of the perfect and supremely happy man are perfected, that must be pronounced human in the fullest sense."[13] There exists, therefore, according to Aristotle, a scale of perfections corresponding to the types of activity, and "happiness" is said to attach to activity in accordance with virtue, and the highest degree of happiness is held to flow from the contemplative life.[14] The discussion of the degrees of perfection in both Ibn Bājja and Maimonides is clearly inspired by the ethos that informs book X of the *Nicomachean Ethics*. Al-Fārābī's and Averroes's discourses on the attainment of happiness reflect the same source.

1. The first of the perfections, Ibn Bājja tells us (§ 19), consists in the perfections of the artificial instruments (*al-ālāt al-ṣināʿiyya*) that serve useful ends. His use of the term "instruments" in a generic sense in this context reflects Aristotle's statement that happiness requires also external goods since "many noble actions require instruments for their performance, in the shape of friends or wealth or political power." The term "instruments" is used by Ibn Bājja also in its specific sense when in a subsequent passage (§ 22, line 1) the first class of perfections is "generally" designated as consisting in "possessions" (*al-amwāl*), of which, besides the "instruments," clothes (*al-thiyāb*) and costumes (*al-ziyy*) are mentioned as examples. Maimonides says similarly that the first class of perfections comprises property (*al-qunya*), i.e., that which belongs to a man in the way of possessions (*al-amwāl*), clothes (*al-thiyāb*), instruments (*al-ālāt*),"—all of which we have met in Ibn Bājja's account—as well as "slaves, land, and other things of this kind." Ibn Bājja (§ 19, lines 8–9) makes the point that, notwithstanding a man's intention to gain honor through his material acquisitions, their "relatedness" (*nisab*) to him neither confers excellence nor bestows greatness on the owner. Maimonides too contends that between this species of perfection and the individual there is no union but only "a certain relation" (*nisba mā*). According to Ibn Bājja (§ 19, lines 12–13), the honor held to attach to possessions of this kind does not obtain in reality. It seems to be real only at first sight but is actually worth nothing, although the soul does take pleasure in it. As stated in another passage (§ 22, lines 3–6), the joy felt about it is as unrealistic as the joy of a person asleep at being able to fly in his dream. Maimonides expressed the same idea briefly by saying that the efforts directed toward the acquisition of this perfection procured but "something purely imaginary" (*ḫayāl maḥḍ*) and that "most of the pleasure" was "purely imaginary." The upshot of Ibn Bājja's discussion is that the alleged perfection of man by means of possessions "expresses, in a primary and immediate sense, a deficiency in his essence," since having to be satisfied with this kind of perfection, which enters

from outside and is alien to man's essence, implies a lack of excellence in himself. Moreover, "when it is said that Zayd has these instruments and that he is therefore honored and respected, it is obvious that once he is divested of them, he will no longer enjoy respect" (§ 19; 22). The same line of thought is found in Maimonides: Possessions of this kind are not part of man's self; they are "outside his essence" (*ḫārijan ʻan dhātihi*), and once this relation (*nisba*) ceases, there is no difference between one who was a great king and one who is the most despicable of men, while in the things that had been related to him no change occurred. Maimonides adds that even assuming the permanency of these possessions throughout a man's life no perfection whatever accrues to his essence.

2. Ibn Bājja mentions next the "perfection and completeness of the bodily organs (*al-a̤ʻḍāʼ*), which is health" (§ 19, line 14; § 22, line 10), and Maimonides says likewise that the second species of perfection is the perfection of the bodily constitution (*binya*) and figure (*haiʼa*). According to Ibn Bājja (§ 22, line 11), "excellence of health alone" does not raise a man above the level of one who is "a slave by nature," for the mere possession of health establishes no difference between men and animals. Maimonides declares likewise that a bodily perfection belongs to man not qua man but qua animal. Ibn Bājja remarks (§ 22, lines 11–13) that in a certain respect man is worse off than the animal, since the latter is endowed with a faculty that directs its well-being whereas men are apt to be self-destructive if bereft of one who directs them. There is a parallel to this remark in *Guide* I, 72.[16] In our passage Maimonides varies the idea of man's inferiority, in a certain respect, compared with the animals. He puts a new complexion upon Ibn Bājja's remark by pointing out that even if the strength of a human individual reached its highest degree, it was still below the strength of a vigorous mule, let alone that of a lion or an elephant. Although he admits that bodily health has a greater connection with the essence of an individual than can be ascribed to material possessions, he clearly states that the soul draws no profit from this species of perfection. This categorical denial of any benefit that the soul might derive from bodily health is in strange contrast to Maimonides's statement in the "Eight Chapters" (ch. V) that the

study of medicine has a very great influence on the acquisition of the virtues and of the knowledge of God. It contradicts the strong awareness that he expressed of the interaction between body and soul.[17] It reflects, on the other hand, Ibn Bājja's radical view (§ 19, lines 16–17) that describing a person by the attribute of health implies neither praise nor reproach.[18] Maimonides seems to have understood this to mean that the possession of health is essentially irrelevant to the life of the soul, and he could obviously not resist following the rather heroic ethos of his *Vorlage*.

3. The third class of perfection listed by Ibn Bājja consists of the "virtues of the soul" (*al-faḍā'il al-nafsāniyya*) or, simply, the "virtues" (*al-faḍā'il*).[19] Correspondingly, Maimonides discusses the perfection of "the moral virtues" (*al-faḍā'il al-ḫulqiyya*) as the third species of perfections. Reflecting Aristotle's differentiation between means and ends and adopting his view that only the contemplative life represents the supreme good and final end,[20] Ibn Bājja says of the [moral] virtues that they too merely "serve," i.e., a higher purpose (§ 20, line 1); that they are "the preparation" or the stepping-stone (*al-tauṭi'a*) to the "ultimate purpose" (*al-ghāya al-quṣwā*).[21] In a similar vein Maimonides asserts that the perfection of the moral virtues too is but a "perfection" (*tauṭi'a*) for something else and "not an end in itself." Ibn Bājja, who considers the attainment of the highest perfection possible only in the ideal or perfect state (in the *madīna fāḍila*), limits the usefulness of the function of the "ethical virtues" (*al-faḍā'il al-shakliyya*) to the imperfect states. In such states, he declares, virtuous men will act like "the guardians" (*al-'urafā*) exercising authority over the people and perfecting the state since the ethical virtues improve sociability by which the state becomes perfect.[22] Maimonides neatly formulates this idea by saying that all moral virtues concern but the relations of men in society and that the moral perfection that an individual possesses has only the effect of making him "useful" (*li-manfa'a*) to people.[23] Hence moral perfection is but an "instrument" (*āla*) serving others. In drawing the conclusion from his view of the instrumental character of the ethical virtues, Ibn Bājja points out that unless their essential purpose (viz., the contemplative life in the ideal state) is achieved, their functions as "preparation" will "necessarily and in reality" prove to be "vain and idle"

(*bāṭilan wa-ʿabathan*); moreover, that once the ultimate purpose is reached, the preparation for it is rendered unnecessary (§ 20, lines 18–21). Again, Maimonides formulates Ibn Bājja's thought more precisely by pointing out its implication: "Should you, e.g., suppose [the existence of] an isolated human individual, who has no relation with anybody, you will find that all his moral virtues are in vain (*bāṭil*), unemployed and unneeded, and that they do not perfect the individual in anything. He only needs them and derives profit from them in regard to others." Ibn Bājja concedes that despite their instrumental character the moral virtues confer excellence upon those to whom they are attributed (§ 20, lines 2–3), and Maimonides likewise admits that moral perfection is to a greater degree a perfection in the "essence" or very self of the person than the perfection of health.

Ibn Bājja quotes (§ 20, lines 6–8) a statement by Abū Naṣr (al-Fārābī) that, he suggests, had, like similar ones, given rise to the thought that the [moral] virtues represented the ultimate purpose, while, on the contrary, the statement implied the opposite view: "Supposing a man knows all that is in the books of Aristotle but does not practice anything of what is [written] in them, whereas another man practices [the moral virtues] but has no scientific knowledge; the second will be more excellent than the first."[24] The statement quoted is a slightly abbreviated version of a passage that occurs in al-Fārābī's *Fuṣūl al-madanī* (§ 93), where it reads as follows:

> We posit two men, one of whom knows what is in all the books of Aristotle on natural science, logic, theology, political philosophy and mathematics, and all his actions or most of them are contrary to what is good at first sight in the opinion of all, and the actions of the other are all in accordance with what is good at first sight to all, even though he does not know the science which the first knows. Then this second man is nearer to being a philosopher than the first. . . .[25]

Maimonides, whose "Eight Chapters" have been shown to be greatly indebted to al-Fārābī's *Fuṣūl al-madanī*,[26] ignored Ibn Bājja's quotation of the passage in our particular context, where it obviously seemed to him too much of a digression. In his concise outline of the "four perfections" there was no place for a discussion of this kind. The al-Fārābī passage is reflected, however, in one of his early works, viz., the *Commentary on the Mishna*. In the Introduction to *Seder Zera'im*[27] Maimonides contrasts the philosopher or scientist who exercises no control over his passions with the moral man who is untrained in the sciences, and he says that the latter will be lacking in perfection yet will be more perfect than the former.[28]

4. The "fourth perfection" (*al-kamāl al-rābi'*), Ibn Bājja finally declares (§ 21, line 1), consists in the "cogitative virtues" (*al-faḍā'il al-fikriyya*).[29] Maimonides says: "The fourth species (*al-nau' al-rābi'*) is the true human perfection (*al-kamāl al-insānī al-ḥaqīqī*), i.e., the attainment of the rational virtues (*al-faḍā'il al-nutqiyya*), viz., the conception of the intelligibles (*taṣawwur ma'qūlāt*), which give us sound ideas on metaphysical subjects." As Ibn Bājja explains (§ 21, lines 1–3), this kind of perfection is not "relative" (*muḍāf*) [to something else outside itself] nor is [anything else] related to it, which we take to mean that the contemplative life is, unlike moral activity, entirely "self-sufficient," as Aristotle termed it.[30] The only relativity attaching to it, Ibn Bājja points out, is that of a potentiality to be actualized. Maimonides develops this idea further. He does so by following the trend of thought found in Aristotle's elaboration of the notion of the "self-sufficiency" (*autarkeia*) of the contemplative life. According to Aristotle, contemplation aims at no end beyond itself;[31] it is a divine activity, transcending the purely human level,[32] it represents the true self of each man;[33] not to engage in it is tantamount to not living one's own life but the life of some other than himself;[34] and while the moral virtues relate to our "composite" nature and yield a mere human happiness, the life of the intellect is "separate" [viz., from matter] and so is the happiness belonging to it.[35] Maimonides adopted the whole array of motives found in this passage and interpreted it in a sense that went far beyond Aristotle's own intentions. For Aristotle the moral virtues were not merely stepping-stones to the contemplative life. They too were "desirable in themselves" and were not merely "a means to something else." The happiness that derived from noble and virtuous deeds was, like the ultimate happiness, "self-sufficient," i.e., lacking nothing.[36] Maimonides tended to ignore the eudemonistic aspect of the virtuous

life and to focus attention exclusively on the happiness to be achieved by the intellectual virtues. In so doing he followed the precedent of Ibn Bājja, who in his *Tadbīr al-mutawaḥḥid* ("The Regimen of the Solitary"), advocated the pursuit of the contemplative life as unrelated to the well-being of the body and the moral concerns of the imperfect state.[37] Echoing Ibn Bājja's intellectually oriented individualism, he had said in an earlier chapter of the *Guide* (III, 51) that the intellectual love of God was best accomplished in solitude.[38] The stress he put on the intellectual virtues was also motivated by the consideration that it was the intellect that, in his view, established the bond between man and God that secured individual providence (III, 17; 51) and immortality. Aristotle too saw in the contemplative life the way to achieving immortality,[39] but he regarded the happiness attending the activity of intellect as an end in itself.[40]

Following in the footsteps of Ibn Bājja and, at the same time, reflecting his own reading of Aristotle, Maimonides offered three reasons for this contention that the intellectual virtues represented the "true human perfection" and the "ultimate purpose" of man's existence: The perfection was one that belonged to him alone; it conferred upon him immortality; and by virtue of it man was truly man. The first reason expresses in a nutshell the very essence of Ibn Bājja's individualism: "This ultimate perfection belongs to you alone; no one else sharing in it in any way." Maimonides reads this notion into a scriptural verse (Prov. 5:17): "They shall be only thine own. . . ." The contemplative life is man's most intimate and inalienable possession. In Aristotle's terms: It represents the true self of each man. The second reason is, likewise, derived from the Aristotelian concept of immortality: The life of the intellect is "separate" from the things that appertain to the body. In Maimonides's words: "You ought to be keen to achieve this thing, which will remain permanently with you." He bids man not to neglect his own soul by allowing the "bodily faculties" to gain dominion over it, thus failing to keep his own vineyard (Cant. 1:6) and surrendering his "splendor" unto others (Prov. 5:9). As for the third reason, it simply reflects the definition of man as a rational animal. It also expresses Aristotle's notion of the intellect as "the best part in us."[41] That the moral virtues by themselves do not constitute the nature of man qua man had been implied in Ibn Bājja's remark

(§ 28, lines 7–8) that man who possessed the moral virtues resembled the irrational animals which were endowed with noble qualities such as the lion's courage and the cock's generosity.

Maimonides concludes his discussion of the four perfections by an exegesis of Jeremiah 9:22–23, where he finds them stated in the same order, though reversed: "Thus saith the Lord: Let not the wise man [that is, 'him who possesses the moral virtues' and the 'perfection of moral habits'] glory in his wisdom, neither let the mighty man [i.e., him who has 'perfection of health'] glory in his might, let not the rich man [who has 'perfection of possession'] glory in his riches; but let him that glorieth glory in this, that he understandeth and knoweth Me [which is the true perfection and the 'ultimate purpose']. Maimonides points out, however, that the prophet requires, in addition to the apprehension (*idrāk*) of God, also the knowledge (*ma'rifa*) of his attributes (*ṣifāt*), and actions on the part of man that imitate God's loving-kindness, justice, and righteousness (Jer. 9:23). In elaborating this additional requirement and in laying particular stress on the practice of *imitatio Dei*, Maimonides might seem to depart from the whole tenor of his previous discussion and to raise, after all, the moral virtues to the rank of ultimate purpose.[42] Yet taking such a view is precluded by the mere fact that in the very context of his exegesis of the scriptural passage he declares that "all the actions prescribed by the Law, viz., the various species of worship and also the moral habits that are useful to all people in their dealings with one another" are not "to be compared with, nor equal to, this ultimate purpose," which is the "apprehension" of God. Maimonides obviously distinguishes between the moral virtues (the acquisition of which is aided by fulfilling the Divinely revealed Law, as he had pointed out before[43]) on the one hand and the imitation of the Divine attributes, which, unlike the moral virtues, is not the result of practical reasoning, but follows from theoretical, metaphysical considerations. *Imitatio Dei* is, therefore, but the practical consequence of the intellectual love of God and is part and parcel of the ultimate perfection. It should be noted that Maimonides treats it on a par not only with the knowledge of God and his attributes but also with the recognition of Divine providence as extending to the sublunar sphere in a manner befitting it, viz., corresponding to the degrees of intellectual perfection found among men. There is, therefore, no rift or inconsistency in Maimonides's discussion of the four perfections. Attention may be drawn to the fact that Abraham ibn Da'ūd's account of man's "perfections" also quotes the Jeremiah passage and also interprets the prophet's insistence on the imitation of God's loving-kindness, etc. as a putting into practice of God's attributes of action as known to the metaphysician. Ibn Da'ūd's *Vorlage* was clearly not the Ibn Bājja text used by Maimonides since he speaks of three perfections corresponding to the three psychic faculties, viz., the vegetative, animal, and rational soul.[44] It is, however, the same philosophical ethos that informs Ibn Da'ūd and Maimonides.

NOTES

1. *Le Guide des égarés*, ed. S. Munk, III, 133a–134a [459–563]; *Dalālat al-ḥa'irīn*, ed. I. Joel (Jerusalem, 1931), 467–469.

2. Munk, op. cit., III, 459, n. 5.

3. See *Guide*, II, 36; 40; III, 8; 49 (quoting *Eth. Nic.*, III, x, 11, 1118b, 2ff.: sense of touch); III, 49 (quoting VIII, i, 1155a, 3ff.: need for friendship). In *Guide*, III, 18 Maimonides cites al-Fārābī's (presumably lost) Commentary on *Eth. Nic.*

4. I, viii, 2, 1098b, 13–15.

5. X, vii, 1–viii, 8, 1177a, 13–1178b, 32.

6. See X, viii, 9, 1178b, 33–1179a, 1f.

7. Hyderabad, 1345 A.H., 2, 16 et passim.

8. See E. I. J. Rosenthal, *Averroes' Commentary on Plato's Republic* (Cambridge, 1956), 22 (I:10): *she-ha-shelemuyoth ha-'enushiyoth bi-khelal arba'ā mīnīm*. In his note (p. 256), Rosenthal refers to relevant passages in the *Ethica Nicomachea* and to al-Fārābī's *Kitāb taḥṣīl al-sa'āda*.

9. Edited by Miguel Asín Palacios with a Spanish translation, summary, and notes under the title, "La *Carta de Adiós* de Avempace," *Al-Andalus*, VIII:1–87 (Madrid-Granada, 1943). The three (four) perfections are discussed in sections 19–23; 28–30 (Arabic text: pp. 32–35; 37–39; Spanish translation: pp. 73–78; 82–85). It seems that Maimonides's dependence on Ibn Bājja was already noticed by Shemtobh ibn Falaqera and Joseph Kaspi. For both these commentators of the *Guide* quoted *ad locum* two passages in the name of Ibn Bājja, without, however, giving any further reference. See Falaqera, *Sefer Morē Ha-Morē*, ed. M. Bisliches (Pressburg, 1837), 137–138; Ibn Kaspi, *'Amudēy Kesef U-Maskiyot Kesef*, ed. S. Z. Werbluner (Frankfurt, a.M., 1848), 144–145. The first of the two passages is taken from Ibn Bājja's *Tadbīr al-mutawaḥḥid*, ed. M. Asín Palacios (Madrid-Granada, 1946), p. 61 (100f); the second is quoted from Ibn Bājja's *Risālat al-widā'*, in M. Asín's edition sections 28–30. Falaqera cites almost the entire text, omitting only the quotation from *al-Qur'ān*, III, 5 and of the *ḥadīth* on the creation of the intellect, whereas Ibn Kaspi offers but a short summary. My statement at the end of note 10 in the earlier version of this paper (see *Israel Oriental Studies II*, Tel Aviv University, 1972, p. 17) failed to take account of the second passage.

10. As I discovered after the completion of this paper, my theory of Maimonides's indebtedness to Ibn Bājja's *Risālat al-widā'* had been anticipated by Martin Schreiner as early as 1899. The Hebrew periodical *Mi-Mizraḥ U-Mi-Ma'arabh* (ed. R. Brainin), IV:37f. (Berlin, 1899) contains Schreiner's postscript ("Notes and Corrigenda") to his publication

in that periodical (II, Vienna, 1895, 96–106; IV, Berlin, 1899, 26–39) of Ḥayyim ibn Vivas's Hebrew version (*Iggereth Ha-Peṭirā*) of Ibn Bājja's *Risālat al-widā'*. In the course of his postscript Schreiner drew attention to the close similarity between the discussion of the human perfections in this particular treatise and in Maimonides's *Guide* III 54. He suggested that Maimonides's reference to "latter-day" philosophers had Ibn Bājja in mind. Schreiner did not go beyond this general observation and offered no detailed comparison. The Hebrew text corresponding to sections 19–23; 28–30 of the Arabic original is found in *Mi-Mizraḥ U-Mi-Ma'arabh* IV: 29–31; 32–33.

11. *Eth. Nic.* I, viii, 15–17, 1099a, 32–1099b, 8; cf. H. Rackham, *Aristotle* (XIX), *The Nicomachean Ethics* [The Loeb Classical Library], pp. 36f., note c.

12. *Eth. Nic.* X, ii, 3, 1172b, 26f.

13. *Eth. Nic.* X, v, 11, 1176a, 26–29.

14. *Eth. Nic.* X, vii, 1–7, 1177a, 12–1177b, 25.

15. *Eth. Nic.* I, viii, 15, 1099b, 1; for the use of the term "instruments" in a general sense see also *Eth. Nic.* I, vii, 3, 1097a, 28.

16. Munk, 102b–103a [369f.]; Joel, 131f.

17. See, e.g., [Theodor] Kroner (ed.), *Die Seelenhygiene des Maimonides, Auszug aus dem III. Kapitel des diätetischen Sendschreibens des Maimonides* (Frankfurt a.M., 1914).

18. Lit.: "The description of its possessor by it entails no nobility nor any perfection [namely, of the soul] on his part; nor does it entail any reproach of its possessor."

19. § 20, line 1; § 22, line 14. That Ibn Bājja speaks here of the moral virtues as distinct from the intellectual ones (see *Eth. Nic.* I, xiii, 20) is evident from the context.

20. *Eth. Nic.* I, vii, 1–5; X, vii–viii.

21. § 20, lines 8–10. The ultimate purpose is the culmination of the contemplative life in man's union with the Active Intellect, which represents the ultimate felicity. See my essay "Ibn Bājja on Man's Ultimate Felicity" in *Harry Austryn Wolfson Jubilee Volume*, English Section (Jerusalem, 1965), pp. 47–87, reprinted in my *Studies in Religious Philosophy and Mysticism* (Ithaca, N.Y., 1969), pp. 73–107.

22. § 20, lines 13–14; § 22, lines 14–21. See E. I. J. Rosenthal, *Political Thought in Medieval Islam* (Cambridge, 1958), 160f.; 287, n. 9.

23. For the same expression, see Ibn Bājja, § 20, line 14.

24. M. Asín Palacios (*Al-Andalus*, VIII, 33, n. 1) rightly prefers the reading of the MS Oxford.

25. D. M. Dunlop (ed.), *Al-Fārābī: Fuṣūl al-madanī, Aphorisms of the Statesman* (Cambridge 1961), Arabic text: p. 169; English translation: p. 76 (quoted here). M. Asín Palacios (p. 74, note 1) felt at a loss to place the passage.

26. See Herbert Davidson, "Maimonides' *Shemonah Peraqim* and Alfarabi's *Fuṣūl Al-Madanī*," *PAAJR*, XXXI: 33–50 (New York, 1963).

27. See *Pērūsh Ha-Mishnā le-Rabbi Moshē ben Maimon*, ed. S. Sassoon, I (Copenhagen, 1956), Plate 31.

28. See also E. Baneth (ed.), "Der Mischna-Traktat Abot mit Maimuni's arabischem Kommentar," *Dreiundzwanzigster Bericht über die Lehranstalt für die Wissenschaft des Judenthums* (Berlin, 1905), p. 23 on Abot 3 : 11: "This matter [viz., Rabbi Ḥanina ben Dosa's statement about the fear of sin having to precede wisdom] is agreed upon by the philosophers. . . ."

29. § 23, line 1. The term *al-faḍā'il al-fikriyya* is said to denote both the practical and theoretical virtues, but is used here preeminently in the latter sense.

30. *Eth. Nic.* X, vii, 4 1177a, 28ff.

31. *Eth. Nic.* X, vii, 7, 1177b, 20.

32. *Eth. Nic.* X, vii, 8.

33. *Eth. Nic.* X, vii, 9.

34. Ibid.

35. *Eth. Nic.* X, viii, 3, 1178a, 20–23.

36. *Eth. Nic.* X, vi, 2–3, 1176b, 3–9; I, xiii, 1. Cf. David Rosin, "Die Ethik des Maimonides," *Jahresbericht des jüdisch-theologischen Seminars* (Breslau, 1876), p. 101, n. 1.

37. See Miguel Asín Palacios (ed.), *El Regimen del Solitario por Avempace* (Madrid-Granada, 1946), Arabic text: p. 11f.; Spanish translation: p. 43; S. Munk, *Mélanges de philosophie juive et arabe* (Paris, 1927), 390; E. I. J. Rosenthal, *Political Thought in Medieval Islam*, 158–174.

38. Munk, III, 125a; Joel, 457; Shlomo Pines's Introduction to his translation of the *Guide of the Perplexed* (Chicago, 1963), p. cvii.

39. See the passage quoted in note 35 and *Eth. Nic.* X, vii, 8, 1177b, 30f.

40. See Isaak Heinemann, "Die Lehre von der Zweckbestimmung des Menschen im griechisch-römanischen Altertum und im jüdischen Mittelalter," *Bericht des jüdisch-theologischen Seminars* (Breslau, 1926), p. 67f.

41. *Eth. Nic.* X, vii, I, 1177a, 13.

42. Munk, III, 133b; Joel, 468.

43. Maimonides refers in this context to his discussion of *imitatio Dei* in *Guide* I, 54, where assimilation to the "thirteen attributes" of God is said to be "needed for the governance of cities." This political meaning of *imitatio Dei* in no way detracts from the supremacy of the theoretical life. It is the man of ultimate, that is, intellectual, perfection who is also fit to govern the city. For the political interpretation of *imitatio Dei*, see Lawrence V. Berman, "The Political Interpretation of the Maxim: The Purpose of Philosophy is the Imitation of God," *Studia Islamica* (ed. R. Brunschvig and J. Schacht) XV, 53–61 (Paris, 1961).

44. S. Weil (ed.), *Das Buch Emunah Ramah . . . von Abraham Ben David Halevi* (Frankfurt a.M., 1852), Hebrew text: p. 46; German translation: p. 59.

5 Maimonides and Thomas Aquinas: Natural or Divine Prophecy?

The question whether prophecy is a natural phenomenon or a divine gift goes back to classical antiquity. A natural explanation of divination in sleep was first attempted by Democritus, whose theory operates with the notion of "images" (*eidōla*) that affect the soul in dreams and foretell the future. Whence these images emanate does not seem to be too clear from the sources at our disposal.[1] Democritus is said to have described them as "great and gigantic . . . although not indestructible,"[2] and from this we may, perhaps, infer that he associated the images with the statues of gods to which the ancients ascribed an odd assortment of capacities.[3] The "images" may therefore signify certain emanations from those statues, especially since Aristotle distinctly speaks of Democritus's theory as one involving "images and emanations" that derive from certain objects.[4] The theory thus understood bears some resemblance to what Maimonides reports as the manner in which the Sabians explain prophecy: Statues in temples and holy trees give prophetic revelation to people.[5] Whatever the correct interpretation of Democritus's theory of dream visions, its intent was clearly scientific.[6] This first effort to see divination in naturalistic terms—Cicero criticized it as far too crude[7]—was to be superseded by Aristotle's more sophisticated theory in his small treatise *On Divination in Sleep*, which forms part of the so-called *Parva naturalia*.

Aristotle posed the question: What is the cause of veridical dreams?, and he inclined to assume that the veracity of at least some of them was due to mere "coincidence" (*symptōmata*).[8] Yet he pressed the search further. It seemed unlikely to him that divinatory dreams were "sent by God" (*theópempta*) since it was not "the best and wisest" who enjoyed such dreams but ordinary people and particularly those whose nature was garrulous and melancholic.[9] Being a scientist, he followed the clue and he reached the conclusion that there was a natural link between the easy response of such people to internal stimuli during sleep and their divinatory ability. He was able to develop this theory within the larger context of his theory of sleep as a state in which the senses were at rest and the bond (*desmós*) of rational thinking was also relaxed, thereby allowing for the free play of imagination. This syndrome —dormancy of senses and all controls on the one hand and uncontrolled activity of imagination on the other—was destined to become the archetypal pattern for practically all theories of divination and prophecy. The natural process thus described was said by Aristotle to be "demonic" for "nature was demonic, not divine,"[10] the term "demonic" signifying, as in Plato, something intermediate between the human and the divine.[11]

This scientific or naturalistic explanation of divination in sleep was a marked departure by Aristotle from the view he had expressed in his early work *On Philosophy*. "When the soul is by itself in sleep," he had said then, "it takes on its proper nature and prophesies and predicts the future. And it is in this state also when it is being separated from the body at the approach of death."[12] Echoes of this earlier view, which is characteristic of Aristotle's Platonic phase, are found also in his *Eudemian Ethics*, as Shlomo Pines has pointed out.[13] According to this Platonizing doctrine, the human soul is akin to the divine and for this reason may have intimations of things to come whenever untrammeled by the senses. Clearly, this view contains a theory that vindicates to the human soul a natural capacity for divination on account of its godlike nature, not because of physiological conditions.

The probably most instructive documentation of the classical and early Hellenistic discussion of the theme is found in Cicero's book *On Divination* which, as Isaac Heinemann has shown, draws in the main on Posidonius's work of the same title.[14] The Stoics took a position radically opposed to Aristotle's scientific approach in that they ascribed all divinatory phenomena to divine Providence. If there are gods who care about men, so the argument ran, there must be divination, a forewarning or cheering by prophetic dreams or in other ways.[15] There are two kinds of divination, natural and artificial, the natural type comprising veridical dreams and frenzy (*manía*, *furor*, *raptus*), the artificial signifying the interpretation of signs based on age-old empirical observation of sequences that correlates signs and events. The superiority of natural divination was recognized by Posidonius and Philo of Alexandria.[16] Stoicizing Peripatetics like Dicaearchus and Cratippus considered natural divination alone to be legitimate subjects of philosophic inquiry. Cratippus, in particular, took issue with Aristotle's suggestion that the veracity of dreams might be purely coincidental, a view that had been adopted also by Carneades.[17] Cratippus maintained the Stoic notion of veridical dreams as sent by a solicitous Providence and the Platonizing view of the divine nature of the human soul, which had also become part of the Stoic doctrine.[18] In his view, therefore, prophecy was natural in the sense that the soul possessed a natural capacity for divination.

As has been shown in an important study by Shlomo Pines,[19] the Arabic philosophers had no inkling of Aristotle's treatise *On Divination in Sleep* in its original and authentic form but knew it only in an Arabic version (now lost), which can be partly reconstructed from Averroes's *Epitome* of it[20] and from some quotations found in the *Risāla al-manāmiyya* (presumably by Avicenna)[21] and in Ibn Bājja's *Tadbīr al-mutawaḥḥid*.[22] According to this Arabic version, veridical dreams are bestowed by divine Providence, through the Active Intelligence, upon the human imagination, which thereby receives the knowledge of future events either in clear terms ("as they are going to be") or in a "hidden," i.e., figurized form.[23] As in Cratippus, we find in this theory the assumption of divine origin combined with a naturalistic approach, seeing that both the activity of the Active Intelligence and the mimetic function of the imagination are natural as distinct from the divine initiative. It is this theory of veridical dreams that underlies the doctrines of prophecy developed by al-Fārābī and Avicenna. It forms the starting point and structural nucleus of these more complex theories. Like veridical dreams, prophecy in its various higher forms is said to be due to an emanation from God mediated by the Active Intelligence, the difference being that in prophecy proper both imagination and intellect are involved. Averroes, who elaborated the doctrine of veridical dreams in his *Epitome* of the Arabic version of Aristotle's treatise, made the explicit point that essentially there was no difference between veridical dreams and prophecy or for that matter between the two and technical forms of divination (*kihāna*). The only difference was one of degree. For this reason it had been said that "dream was a certain part of prophecy." Averroes alluded here to a widely quoted and much varied *ḥadīth* according to which Muḥammad is said to have defined a dream as being the forty-sixth part of prophecy.[24] In his *Epitome* Averroes also pointed out that veridical dreams were confined to disclosures of future happenings and to information in the practical arts such as medicine, many cures having been revealed in dreams, but could not convey knowledge in the theoretical sciences. Revelations of the latter kind, particularly about things divine, were possible only in prophecy.[25]

Maimonides was not acquainted with Averroes's *Epitome*, as we happen to know from the letter written by him to his disciple Yosef ben Shime'on in 1190–91.[26] Yet his discussion of veridical dreams in *Guide* 2:36 is strikingly similar to Averroes's. Maimonides too makes the point that there is only a difference in degree between dreams and prophecy, and one of the rabbinic *dicta* (Berakhot 57b) quoted by him in support ("dream is the sixtieth part of prophecy") is probably the source from which the *ḥadīth* cited by Averroes ultimately derived. In other chapters (2:37, 38), he made it clear that prophets alone received intimations of a theoretical nature in addition to knowledge of future events, but whether or not the medical art stood to profit from dreams is not spelled out by him. Gersonides took it for granted that he denied such a possibility and that his psychological explanation of misguided prophetic claims in 2:38 was a veiled attack against Galen, who had attributed some of his cures to revelation in dreams.[27] We may safely assume that Maimonides's accord with Averroes was due to the fact that both of them used the Arabic version of the Aristotelian treatise, and that both followed in the al-Fārābī and Avicenna tradition that had grown out of it. It is this intellectual background that accounts in large measure for Maimonides's theory of prophecy.

Thomas Aquinas's philosophical background was in many respects different. He shared with Maimonides a knowledge, at least to some extent, of the Arabic philosophers, particularly of Avicenna.[28] He was not acquainted, however, with the Arabic version of Aristotle's *On Divination in Sleep*, even assuming that he knew the Latin version of Averroes's *Epitome* of the *Parva naturalia*, which was, in part, based on that version.[29] This is evident from the fact that both he and his teacher, Albertus Magnus, quote the authentic Aristotelian view that veridical dreams cannot be sent by God, seeing that they do not occur to the wisest and best.[30] Both Albert and he believed Aristotle to hold a purely naturalistic notion of veridical dreams, and this suited both of them very well. It enabled them to assign the phenomenon of prophecy as attested in pagan literature to purely natural agencies in contrast to biblical prophecy, which they attributed to the agency of God and designated as divine prophecy.[31] There were more differences in the intellectual heritage of Maimonides and St. Thomas. Maimonides's knowledge of the philosophical tradition concerning theories of prophecy was limited to the works of the Arabic and a few Jewish philosophers, whereas Thomas, like Albert, had at his disposal a large array of Latin sources as well.[32] Moreover, Thomas could draw on an extensive body of patristic writings, especially St. Augustine's Twelfth Book in *De Genesi ad litteram*, that dealt with prophecy.[33] Finally, both he and Albert were quite at home with Maimonides's treatment of the subject in the *Guide* and made ample use of it, as has been shown in a number of studies tracing his borrowings.[34]

It is remarkable that Thomas Aquinas could adopt a great many points from Maimonides's theory of prophecy, notwithstanding the radical difference in their fundamental outlook, which may be summed up in the antithesis between "natural" and "divine" prophecy that forms the subject of this paper. The ultimate reason for this difference must be sought in the dissimilarity of ontological assumptions that divide them. Maimonides subscribes to the Avicennian type of ontology,[35] which sees the total reality, including God, as a continuum in which the flow of emanations from God through the hierarchy of Intelligences reaches down to the Active Intelligence as the immediate fountainhead of the activity of forms in the sublunar world. This entire universe is a system of free-flowing grace as it were,[36] and does not require special acts of divine grace for special purposes. Here grace is abounding at all times, and its reception and efficacy depend solely on the receptivity or disposition of the recipient. "Envy is banished from the celestial choir," Plato had said,[37] and this statement is echoed in Avicenna's declaration, "Yonder there is no veiling (*iḥtijāb*) nor avarice (*bukhl*),"[38] a formulation that reappears somewhat abbreviated in Judah Halevi, Joseph ibn Ṣaddiq, and Abraham ibn

Da'ūd.[39] For Maimonides the flow of emanations that results in the bestowal of forms upon matter in the physical world is identical with the flow of emanations that constitutes the exercise of Providence and the gift of prophecy.[40] The interposition of mediating agencies like the Active Intelligence does not detract from the divine character of the various bestowals. At the same time, the natural endowments of matter and of the material intellect of man, if properly conditioned, render the bestowal of the divine overflow a natural process. Maimonides says distinctly (2:32) that "it is a natural thing for everyone who according to his natural disposition is fit for prophecy . . . to become a prophet." True, he makes the actualization of the prophetic potentiality dependent upon the Divine Will that may or may not miraculously prevent it, but the "Divine Will"—designated here as *mashi'a*, not *irāda*—has to be understood as the primordial Will of God that is identical with God's Wisdom.[41] Hence the gift of prophecy is not due to an ad hoc dispensation, but is grounded in the ultimate mystery of the Divine essence in which Will and Wisdom are intertwined. Maimonides's stipulation that links prophecy to the Divine Will is not meant to annul its natural character; it only corroborates it. For the natural happening is thereby legitimized, as it were, as divinely preordained and as of an order above mechanical and blind necessity. Maimonides's insistence upon the operation of Will in the flow of emanations comes close to the way in which some modern interpreters have understood Plotinus's notion of emanation as a blend of necessity and will.[42] It would therefore seem that even if Maimonides's stipulation meant to disguise his view—as some commentators assume it does[43]—his stress on the Divine Will does represent his true opinion and it allows, at the same time, for a naturalistic theory of prophecy.

Thomas Aquinas, on the other hand, breaks with the Avicennian ontological scheme that had dominated the Neoplatonic phase of Latin scholasticism, although he retains some of its Augustinian features.[44] The most radical step in this direction was the relocation of the Aristotelian active intellect from the semidivine and transcendent position that it had been assigned to in the Alexander of Aphrodisias tradition down to Averroes. Thomas interpreted the active intellect as a part of the human intellect.[45] He adhered to the concept of Intelligences correlated to the celestial bodies, but cancelled the emanationist theory and thereby did away with the notion of a divine continuum in which grace is a matter of free-flowing divine activity. In the Augustinian-Avicennian tradition the boundaries of grace and nature had been blurred. All cognition had been described as a seeing in the divine light. St. Thomas sharply differentiated between nature and grace. *Gratia perficit naturam*, which means that the two are not a single activity any more. Whereas in the al-Fārābī-Avicenna type of epistemology the highest stage of human knowledge amounts to an act of mystical union with the Active Intelligence, and prophecy is this very act, termed variously the "angelic intellect" or "holy intellect" or "holy spirit" or "divine power,"[46] Thomas frees the cognitive act from any link with the transcendent. Hence for him prophecy cannot be a mere perfect act of the natural order of intellection. It becomes a pure "gift of God" (*donum Dei* or *donum Spiritus sancti*).[47] It is no longer the result of natural dispositions as in Maimonides. Nor can it ever be a *habitus*, since it is a transient gift, like light in the air.[48] At best, it may be a *habilitas*, a certain readiness or state of being attuned after previous experiences of that gift.[49]

At the same time, Thomas admits the naturalness of veridical dreams and of pagan prophecy. He offers two definitions of natural prophecy. The first of these is based on Aristotle's notion of the "natural" as "that which has the principle of motion within itself," e.g., it being natural for fire to rise upward.[50] Those who hold the soul to be naturally gifted to foresee the future take the term "natural" in this sense of "natural power."[51] Yet this theory must be rejected, he says, for various reasons, chiefly because the human mind cannot naturally arrive at a cognition to which no way leads from self-evident principles of knowledge.[52] The second definition of natural prophecy starts from the concept of "natural" as a principle of dispositions or aptitudes insofar as these are the necessary preconditions for the attainment of certain perfections, e.g., the suitable disposition of the human body for the infusion of the rational soul.[53] Natural prophecy in this sense of the term would seem to be identical with the al-Fārābī-Avicenna-Maimonides sponsored view that makes prophecy dependent on natural dispositions for the reception of the divine overflow. St. Thomas adopts this kind of theory, without its emanationist implications, as an adequate explanation of veridical dreams and natural prophecy. He rules it out of court as far as true prophecy—the one "about which we talk"—is concerned.[54] He believes that in the case of veridical dreams the natural aptitude or disposition enables the dreamer to receive certain "impressions" from the celestial bodies in which the "preparations" of future events reside. The soul, by virtue of its subtlety, is able to previsualize those events from certain "similitudes" left in the imagination as a result of those impressions.[55] This theory goes back to Avicenna, who attributes to the celestial bodies an influence upon the imagination of suitably disposed people, without, however, attaching too much significance to dreams in this manner.[56] St. Thomas obviously assigns a far greater importance to the impact of the celestial bodies upon the human imagination. There is a great deal of evidence to show that in his view the celestial bodies are responsible for sublunar happenings that are not reducible to the elemental powers, including such occult phenomena as magnetism.[57] As far as natural prophecy is concerned, St. Thomas believes it to consist in the reception of certain information from the Intelligences which, unlike Maimonides, he does not equate with the angels.[58] He makes the point, however, that even information conveyed by the angels is still within the confines of natural prophecy.[59] This theory of natural prophecy clearly follows the Maimonidean pattern but relegates it to a lower level. Defined in the most concise formulation offered by Thomas, natural prophecy is one "ex virtute creata."[60] This includes both intelligences and angels.

It is obvious that divine prophecy, according to St. Thomas, can do without the dispositions that Maimonides laid down as conditional for the coming-into-being of prophecy.[61] If prophecy is but a gift of God, it will be unnecessary for the prophet to be endowed with a high degree of imagination and intellectual capacity, to have developed his mental powers through training, and to be possessed of moral perfection. All these preconditions were required by Maimonides under the assumption that only the most favorable preparation of "matter" rendered an individual fit for the reception of the divine emanation, i.e., for union with the Active Intelligence. More specifically, only at the stage of the acquired intellect could the divine influx assume such proportions as to set in motion the rational faculty as well as the imagination in adequate measure. On the one hand, Thomas adopts the phenomenology of the prophetic process described by Maimonides also for divine prophecy. He actually quotes Maimonides when referring to this process: "Prophecy begins in the intellect and is completed in the imagination,"[62] for "from the fullness of the intellectual light a redundancy arises that spills over into imagination there to form an imaginative vision."[63] Yet in discussing the question "Whether any natural disposition is required for prophecy,"[64] Thomas points out that as a divine gift prophecy cannot be due to any natural cause (*ex virtute alicuius causae creatae*). At times God confers this gift precisely upon the seemingly most unfit in order thereby to indicate the operation of divine power.[65] Hence prophecy cannot be something merited by certain perfections. It is all a matter of unmerited grace.[66]

In thus divorcing the gift of prophecy from all natural dispositions, Thomas Aquinas subscribes to the very view that Maimonides (2:32) had listed as the opinion of the ignorant multitude among pagans and Jews, i.e., the one that held prophecy to be independent of natural capacities and that considered it purely a matter of Divine Will. At the same time Thomas does not deny that dispositional qualities are indeed needed to make the divine gift of prophecy operational. He therefore assumes that God, who is the creator of both form and matter, supplies not only the *lumen propheticum* but also the necessary disposition in case it is lacking. Thus, in the absence of a sufficiently strong power of imagination God will ameliorate the complexion of the organ that is responsible for the imaginative faculty.[67] This is an interesting case of combining Maimonides's phenomenology of the prophetic act with the exigencies of a supernaturalistic view of prophecy. The naturalistic point of view remains intact, but it is integrated into a supernaturalistic framework. Divine grace creates the natural conditions for the effective reception of the charisma.

What is meant by this kind of divine intervention becomes clear from Thomas's discussion of the role of angels in prophecy, another *topos* that bears some resemblance to Maimonides's doctrine. Before entering into this area of discussion, let us first present Thomas's important and fundamental distinction between two aspects of the prophetic act that he calls *acceptio* (or *receptio*) and *iudicium*.[68] As Benoit Garceau has shown in his monograph on the subject,[69] these two terms signify, in this context at least, the imaginative vision on the one hand and its intellectual interpretation or meaning on the other. In a sense, *acceptio* and *iudicium* correspond to the terms *taṣawwur* and *taṣdīq*, concept and affirmation, which form the two main divisions in the logical systems of the Arabic philosophers,[70] and go back to Aristotle's distinction between the *What* and the *That* in the beginning of the *Posterior Analytics* (l. 1). Thomas Aquinas points out that the mere reception of an image in dream or vision does not make one a prophet. Pharaoh's dream vision did not amount to prophecy. Joseph, who received a *iudicium*, an intellectual understanding of Pharaoh's dream, did thereby show himself to be a prophet. *A fortiori*, one who has both the *receptio* of a species or similitude and the intellectual *iudicium* concerning it is a prophet. He is the most superior prophet whose very *receptio* consists of an intellectual vision (unalloyed by imaginative components) as well as a divinely imparted *iudicium*.[71] It is not difficult to recognize in this tripartite division the contours of Maimonides's three levels of prophecy, the lowest being purely imaginative (as in veridical dreams); the intermediate combining imaginative and intellectual cognition; and the highest involving the intellect alone (as in Moses's prophecy).[72]

Thomas Aquinas describes the *acceptio supernaturalis*, i.e., the divinely caused reception of some vision, as *nova formatio specierum*, i.e., as a new formation of images or similitudes, it being new either as signifying something not previously contained in the imagination, or as a novel combination of previously held images.[73] The formation of images he attributes to the activity of the angels in the sense that it is the angels' job to move the imagination. This assumption, he explains, follows from St. Augustine's and Dionysius's doctrine that all created corporeal nature is administered by created spiritual natures.[74] In light of this statement we may assume that the furnishing by God of the requisite quality of the imagination whenever necessary is to be understood as part of the angelic function. As for the *iudicium supernaturale*, he characterizes it as an "infused light" (*lumen infusum*) or as an "illumination of the mind" (*mentis illustratio*), a terminology somewhat reminiscent of the Maimonidean definition of prophecy as an "overflow (*faiḍ*) from God through the Active Intelligence upon intellect and imagination. Thomas Aquinas must, however, not be understood as reverting to an emanationist position. He certainly does not consider the infused light to flow from God by way of the Active Intelligence; yet there remain certain ambiguities. On the one hand, he describes the *lumen infusum* in terms of its function, which is the "strengthening" or "preparation" of the human mind for the reception of the *lumen propheticum*.[75] On the other hand, he defines it as a process by which the *lumen divinum*, something utterly simple and universal, is communicated to the human mind. The *lumen infusum* is the filtering as it were of the incomprehensible divine light by way of the angelic intellect. By passing through the angelic intellect the divine light is somehow "contracted" and "specified" and thereby accommodated to the prophetic intellect.[76] One is reminded of the kabbalistic doctrine of "contraction" (*ṣimṣum*), which serves a somewhat similar purpose.

It follows that in the doctrine of St. Thomas the supernatural act of prophetic illumination is not as direct and immediate as one might have assumed from its definition as *donum Dei*. It turns out to be an act mediated by angelic activity, not entirely unlike the view held by Maimonides. The revelation of prophecy, St. Thomas says, "descends from God to an angel, and from the angel to man."[77] Maimonides, too, describes all prophecy, with the exception of Moses's, as mediated by angels, but this parallel holds good only insofar as the role of the Intelligences as transmitters of the emanation is concerned. In all other respects the analogy breaks down. In Maimonides's doctrine the angels that are said to mediate prophecy are, as a rule, the imaginative faculty of each prophet, the term "cherub" being used to denote the intellect.[78] Thomas Aquinas does not accept Maimonides's designation of natural faculties or propensities as "angels."[79] Nor does he agree that the angels seen in prophetic dreams and visions are mere projections of the imagination. According to Maimonides, the "created forms" that the prophet visualizes are but forms "created" by the imagination,[80] and they include the forms of angels and men. In St. Thomas's view, the role of angels in prophecy is of a metaphysical, not merely psychological, order. Their role is confined, however, to a subsidiary function, while the initiative and the content of the prophetic gift remain the preserve of God. Were angels to communicate to men any knowledge they possess on their own, without divine revelation as its source, the prophecy thus constituted would come under the rubric of natural, not divine, prophecy.[81]

Maimonides emphatically differentiates between Moses's prophecy and that of all other prophets. He goes so far as to say that the term "prophet" as used with reference to Moses and to the others is "amphibolous" (*bi-tashkīk*).[82] We take the term "amphibolous" to be used here in the sense of "analogical."[83] This implies a relationship between exemplar and copy, and allows for both distance and proximity between Moses and the rest of the prophets. Moses is the "master of the prophets" and at the same time, he shares with them the general characteristics of all prophecy, i.e., the naturalness of the prophetic act within the metaphysical continuum of a universe in which divine grace abounds and is freely available to all according to degrees of receptivity. It has been suggested that, according to Maimonides, Moses's prophecy involved a direct bestowal of the prophetic gift by God, without mediation by secondary causes such as the Active Intelligence.[84] This view cannot be upheld. Even Moses, it would seem, received his prophecy through the Active Intelligence. That this is Maimonides's view can be substantiated from a close reading of the way in which he interprets the biblical passages describing the uniqueness of Moses's prophecy. God spoke to him "mouth to mouth" (Num. 12:8) is paraphrased: "The mighty divine overflow reached him" (2:24), i.e., he received an abundant measure of the divine emanation that passes through the Active Intelligence. "Whom the Lord knew face to face" (Deut. 34:10): "His apprehension was different from that of all who came after him" (2:35). "And the Lord spoke unto Moses face to face" (Exod. 33:11) is said to mean: "as a presence to another presence, without an intermediary"; for "the hearing of a speech without the intermediacy of an angel is described as 'face to face'" (1:37). In plain words: "The imaginative faculty did not enter into his prophecy, since the intellect overflowed toward him without the former's intermediation; for . . . he did not, like the other prophets, prophesy by means of parables" (2:37). It is the purely intellectual nature of Moses's prophecy that alone is held to justify the striking figures of speech used to characterize his supreme rank.

St. Thomas clearly reflects Maimonides's view when he describes Moses's purely intellectual vision as an infusion of the divine light without angelic help.[85] He makes the point, however, that even at this level of prophecy imagination is used, if only for the benefit of the multitude, while the prophet himself has no need for the figurization of the truth apprehended by him.[86] Al-Fārābī had expressed the same view when he said that the figurative language used by the Lawgiver-Prophet is invented "not in order to understand [for] himself the higher realities . . . but as symbols and images for others."[87] Maimonides could not have held otherwise since he was acutely aware of the need to interpret the figurative language of the Torah. His reference to Moses's faculty of imagination (2:36) makes sense from this point of view.[88] The essential difference between Maimonides and Thomas is here, as elsewhere, the difference between natural and divine prophecy. In Maimonides's view even Moses's prophecy was the natural result of a specific disposition which, though unique, was still natural. The highest possible degree of perfection that is natural to the human species, he says, must necessarily be realized in at least one particular individual (2:32). Moses was that individual. Hence, Moses is no exception to the general rule that prophecy is a natural phenomenon within a divinely controlled universe. Maimonides's portrayal of Moses's spirituality in *Guide* 3:51 makes it evident that he considered the attainment of his exceptional rank to have been the natural result of his dispositions and mode of life. We might say that his union with the Active Intelligence was held to have been consequent upon his decorporealization as it were, a stage reminiscent of Ibn Bājja's ultimate stage that arises from an existential break with matter.[89] We may also call it the achievement of merited grace. St. Thomas, on the other hand, sees Moses's prophecy as the ultimate degree of divine prophecy in the sense of unmerited grace.[90]

One final point. Avicenna had suggested that Providence, which took such care of the comforts of the human race as to provide men with eyelashes and concave soles, could not have left him without making provision for politically gifted men who would take care of law and order, thereby securing the survival of the species. For, as Aristotle had said,[91] man was "political by nature," i.e., in dire need of political organization.[92] In taking up this theme Maimonides pointed out that the striking social divisiveness due to differences in character between men required the authority of rulers and lawgivers in order to neutralize the "natural diversity" by the imposition of "conventional accord." In this way, "the law, although it is not nature, enters into what is natural" (2:40). In other words, convention is designed to help nature against nature. It is tacitly assumed that only the prophet, not the philosopher, is capable of effectively imposing a unifying law upon a nation or group of people. The prophet is thus seen as a necessity of nature, a view that inevitably implies that prophecy is a natural phenomenon. This is, at any rate, St. Thomas's reading of the Avicennian thesis according to which prophets are indispensable for the preservation of humanity. Thomas lists this viewpoint as one of the nineteen arguments adduced by him in favor of the naturalistic approach to prophecy.[93] He quotes as a scriptural prooftext Prov. 29:18: "Where there is no vision, the people cast off restraint," interpreting "vision" as the exercise of the prophetic office. He may have hit upon this particular verse by his own intuition, and it is interesting to note that Gersonides, in his *Commentary on Proverbs*, explains it in the very same way. Thomas rejects Avicenna's argument. The sociopolitical order, he says, will be taken care of with or without prophets. Nature will be responsible for the satisfaction of man's need. The prophet is not a necessity of nature. He is required to give direction toward life eternal, not to secure justice in the political order. The supernatural goal is attainable through the "justice of faith" of which prophecy is the principle.[94] Thomas has nothing further to say, in this context at least, on the political function of prophecy, a theme of tremendous significance to Maimonides, who sees in the Law of the Torah the perfect constitution of the ideal city.[95]

St. Thomas's silence on the political function of prophecy—to be more precise: his denial of such a function—set him apart from the entire school of thought, Islamic and Jewish, that ranged itself with the Platonic search for the "ideal city" on earth. In developing that tradition, the *falāsifa* and their Jewish partisans, including Maimonides, had good reason for stressing the role of imagination in prophecy. It was the political function of the prophet that necessitated the veiling of metaphysical notions by figurization. By radically ignoring the political aspect, St. Thomas deprived himself of the means of suggesting a cogent rationale for the significance of the imaginative element in prophecy. On the one hand, he fully subscribed to the interpretation of the prophetic act as one involving the imagination. On the other, he had little to offer in explanation of this theory beyond the general observation that truth was hard of access to the multitude.[96] Yet the problem could not easily be ignored. Albertus Magnus had quoted the Greek poet Simonides, who suggested that it was the envy of the gods that caused their revelations to be veiled in figurative language.[97] A decisive step toward a more appreciative evaluation was taken when the mimetic function of imagination in the service of the intellect was discovered, probably in Middle Platonism.[98] In the Arabic version of Aristotle's *On Divination in Sleep*[99] this new insight already plays some part, if only a minor one. Finally, al-Fārābī put it into the service of the political interpretation of prophecy, and Maimonides took it from there. Yet how sensitive an area this was may be gauged from the fact not hitherto observed, that when listing the required dispositions of prophecy in his popular writings, Maimonides mentioned only intellectual and moral perfection but omitted imagination. He obviously considered it imprudent to disclose this particular requirement to the very audience that was to benefit from the veiling of the truth. To what extent Maimonides adopted the political view of prophecy and in what manner he modified it to suit his own purposes is another matter. There is, however, enough evidence to show that the adoption of this viewpoint reinforced his naturalistic concept of prophecy, while the rejection of it in St. Thomas was part and parcel of his supernaturalistic doctrine.

NOTES

1. See Werner Jaeger, *The Theology of the Early Greek Philosophers* (Oxford, 1947), pp. 180–1, 249, n. 36; Saul Horowitz, *Die Psychologie bei den jüdischen Religionsphilosophen des Mittelalters von Saadia bis Maimuni* (Breslau, 1898; reprint ed., Westmead, 1970), p. 189, n. 133.
2. Sextus Empiricus *Adversus physicos* 1. 19.
3. For references, see Arthur Stanley Pease, ed., *M. Tulli Ciceronis de divinatione* (University of Illinois, 1920–23), 1:271–72.
4. Aristotle *De divinatione per somnum* 2. 464a11.
5. Maimonides, *The Guide of the Perplexed*, 3:45.
6. See Jaeger, *Theology*, p. 181. The notion of "images" is used by Democritus also in connection with the theory of poetic inspiration. See Pease, *De divinatione*, 1:237–38.
7. Cicero *De natura deorum* 1. 38–39; *De divinatione* 2. 67.137–39.
8. Aristotle *De divinatione per somnum* 1. 462b28, 463b1; 2. 464a5.
9. Aristotle *De divinatione* 1. 462b19–24, 463b13–18, 464a33. For Aristotle's dream

theory referred to in what follows in the text, see his *De somno et vigilia* 1. 454b8–11; *De somniis* 3. 460b.28–461a30, 461b27–462a32.

10. *De divinatione per somnum* 2. 463b13–15.

11. Sometimes Aristotle identifies the "demonic" with the "divine"; see Hermann Bonitz, *Index Aristotelicus*, 2d ed, p. 164, s.v. *daimonios*. For nature as below the divine, see the statement of Themistius quoted by H. A. Wolfson, "Hallevi and Maimonides on Design, Chance and Necessity," *Preceedings of the American Academy for Jewish Research* 11 (1941): 148–49, 153 (republished in H. A. Wolfson, *Studies in the History of Philosophy and Religion*, ed. Isadore Twersky and George H. Williams [Cambridge, Mass., 1977], 2:44–45, 49). For the development of the notion of the "demonic" in the Platonic tradition, see Frank Regen, *Apuleius philosophus Platonicus* (Berlin and New York, 1971).

12. Sextus Empiricus *Adversus mathematicos* 1. 20–21, quoted by Cicero *De divinatione* 1. 30, 63 from either Cratippus or Posidonius, as suggested by Isaac Heinemann, *Poseidonios' metaphysische Schriften* (Breslau, 1928), 2:354. Cf. Simon van den Bergh, trans., *Averroes' Tahafut Al-Tahafut* (London, 1954), 2:167.

13. Shlomo Pines, "The Arabic Recension of *Parva Naturalia* and the Philosophical Doctrine Concerning Veridical Dreams According to *al-Risāla al-Manāmiyya* and Other Sources," *Israel Oriental Studies* 4 (1974): 141–42.

14. See Heinemann, *Schriften*, p. 328 and passim.

15. Cicero *De divinatione* 1. 38. 82–83, 39. 84; 2. 49. 101. The argument is reported in the name of Chrysippus, who wrote a treatise on divination, and others. The reverse argument: "if there is divination, there must be gods" is found in Aristotle's *On Philosophy* (see Sextus *Adv. phys.* 1. 20) and in Posidonius (see Heinemann, *Schriften*, p. 346).

16. Cicero *De div.* 1. 50. 113; Philo *Vita Mosis* 1. 277 (see Heinemann, *Schriften*, p. 333).

17. Cicero *De div.* 1. 13. 23; on Carneades see Heinemann, *Schriften*, p. 341.

18. Cicero *De div.* 1. 32. 70, 2. 58. 119. Heinemann (*Schriften*, p. 354) leaves it undecided whether Cratippus adopted the Stoic view or whether Cicero formulated Cratippus's view in Stoic fashion. On Cratippus, see Pease, *De divinitatione*, 1: 59.

19. Referred to in n. 13.

20. See Harry Blumberg's edition of the Arabic text of Averroes's *Epitome of Parva Naturalia* (1972), his edition of the Hebrew translation of this text (1954); and E. L. Shields's edition (with H. Blumberg's assistance) of the Latin version (1949), all published by The Mediaeval Academy of America, Cambridge, Mass.

21. See Pines, "Arabic Recension," pp. 120–1.

22. See Miguel Asín Palacios, trans., *El régimen del solitario por Avempace* (Madrid and Granada, 1946), pp. 22–24 (54–55); quoted and partly translated by Pines, pp. 137–38.

23. See the texts quoted by Pines, pp. 114–21, 137–38; Averroes's *Epitome of Parva Naturalia*; Arabic 72. 7, 73. 4–7, 79. 7–12, 84. 7–9; Hebrew 47. 9–10, 48. 1–3, 51. 16–52. 3, 55. 3–5; Latin 101. 35–36, 102. 49–52, 109. 4–9, 116. 17–18.

24. Averroes's *Epitome*: Arabic 67. 4–11, 84. 11; Hebrew 44. 3–9, 55. 6–7; Latin 116. 23. On the *ḥadīth* and its many variations, see M. J. Kister, "The Interpretation of Dreams . . . ," *Israel Oriental Studies* 4 (1974): 71. To the list should be added: Franz Rosenthal, trans., *Ibn Khaldūn The Muqaddimah* (Bollingen Series 43, 1958), 1: 208–9.

25. Averroes's *Epitome*: Arabic 67. 8–10, 73. 4, 88. 9–91. 3; Hebrew 44. 6–9, 47. 16–48. 1, 57. 14–59. 9; Latin 102. 48–49, 120. 7–123. 41. The attribution of medical prognosis to dream revelation is a well-known *topos* in ancient philosophy. For references, see Pease, *De divinatione*, 2:572. Heinemann, *Schriften*, p. 332 quotes a reference concerning the discovery, in a dream, of the efficacy of *aristolachia* against snake poisoning.

26. See Solomon Munk, "Notice sur Joseph ben-Iehouda . . . . ," *Journal asiatique* 3d ser. 14 (1842): 22, 24–25, 31; D. H. Baneth, ed., *Moses Ben Maimon Epistulae* (Hebrew), vol. 1 (Jerusalem, 1946), p. 70. Baneth (p. 22) confirmed Munk's dating of the letter.

27. *Sefer milḥamot ha-shem* (Riva di Trento, 1560), 2: 4, fols. 17c–18b.

28. For bibliographical details (translations, etc.) and texts quoted by St. Thomas, see C. Vansteenkiste, "Autori Arabi e Giudei nell' opera di S. Tommaso," *Angelicum* 32 (1960).

29. The *Versio Vulgata* is variously attributed to Gerard of Cremona (d. 1187) and Michael Scot (d. c. 1235). See Shields's edition, p. xiii.

30. Albertus Magnus, *Opera Omnia*, vol. 9 (Paris, 1891), Lib. III, *De somno et vigilia*, Tract. 1, C. 2, p. 179; Thomas Aquinas, *Quaestiones disputatae* (*QD*), 1, *De veritate*, ed. Raimondo Spiazzi (Turin and Rome, 1953), 12. 5 (4), 246a; idem, *Summa theologiae*, 45, ed. R. Potter (Manchester, 1970), 2: 2 (*ST*), 172. 4 (4).

31. Cf. Albertus Magnus, *Opera*, 3. 1. 1, p. 178: "hoc quod dicit Aristoteles plus accedit veritati, quam aliquid quod ante vel post scripsit aliquis Philosophorum, cujus scripta ad nos devenerunt."

32. Of the range of literature available to Albertus Magnus, one catches a glimpse from the quotations found in his *De somno et vigilia*.

33. St. Augustine, *De Genesi ad litteram*, 12. 1–37, in J.P. Migne, *Patrologiae cursus completum, Series latina*, 34: 454–86.

34. See Jacob Guttmann, *Das Verhältnis des Thomas von Aquino zum Judenthum und zur jüdischen Litteratur* (Göttingen, 1891), pp. 73–79; Ernst Salomon Koplowitz, *Die Abhängigkeit Thomas von Aquins von R. Mose Ben Maimon* (Mir, 1935), pp. 89–93; and the excellent monograph by José Maria Casciaro, *El diálogo teológico de Santo Tomás con musulmanes y judíos, el tema de la profecía y la revelación* (Madrid, 1969). On some early polemics concerning the degree of Thomas's "dependence" on Maimonides, see the valuable essay by Joseph Mausbach, "Die Stellung des hl. Thomas von Aquin zu Maimonides in der Lehre von der Prophetie," *Theologische Quartalsschrift* 81 (1899): 553–79.

35. He does so with some reservations, as is evident from his remark in *Guide*, 1: 72 *in fine*. A searching analysis of the Avicennian ontology is found in Herbert Davidson's study, "Alfarabi and Avicenna on the Active Intellect," *Viator Medieval and Renaissance Studies* 3 (1972): 109–78.

36. I borrow this term from H.A. Wolfson's translation of Maimonides's definition of prophecy (2: 36) as "a free grace flowing from God through the medium of the Active Intellect to man's rational faculty first and then to his imaginative faculty." As Wolfson explains, the term *faiḍ*, which is usually translated as "emanation," actually denotes the "element of liberality and generosity in the act of emanation" and is correctly rendered by *largitas* in the old Latin translation (Paris, 1520). See Wolfson, "Hallevi and Maimonides on Prophecy," *JQR*, n.s. 33 (1943): 71 (republished in Wolfson, *Studies in the History of Philosophy and Religion*, 2 [1977]: 60–119; cf. p. 108).

37. *Phaedrus* 247A; see also *Timaeus* 29E; Aristotle *Metaphysics* 1. 2. 12 938a2: "It is impossible for the Deity to be jealous."

38. See Fazlur Rahman, ed., *Avicenna's De Anima* (London, 1959), p. 178; S. van Riet, ed., *Avicenna Latinus, Liber De Anima seu Sextus de Naturalibus* (Louvain and Leiden, 1968), p. 29: et non est illic occultatio aliqua nec avaritia.

39. Judah Halevi, *Kuzari*, 5: 10; Joseph ibn Ṣaddiq, *Microcosm*, ed. Saul Horovitz, p. 38; Abraham ibn Da'ūd, *'Emunah ramah*, ed. S. Weil, 74. 9–10; 36. 37–41: *ki 'ein sham kilut*.

40. Cf. *Guide*, 2: 12 (Munk 26a); 3: 18 (Munk, 37b).

41. See Avraham Nuriel, "Ha-raṣon ha-'elohi be-moreh nevukhim," in *Tarbiz* 39 (1970): 39–61.

42. See Paul Henry, "Le Problème de la liberté chez Plotin," in *Revue néo-scolastique*, 2d ser., 8 (1931); J. M. Rist, *Plotinus: The Road to Reality* (Cambridge, 1967); Klaus Kremer, "Das 'Warum' der Schöpfung: 'quia bonus' vel / et 'quia voluit'? Ein Beitrag zum Verhältnis von Neoplatonismus und Christentum an Hand des Prinzips 'bonum est diffusivum sui'," in Kurt Flasch, ed., *Parousia, Festgabe für Johannes Hirschberger* (Frankfurt, 1965), pp. 241–64.

43. See Joseph Kaspi, Moses Narboni, and Shemtov ben Joseph ad loc. (2: 32).

44. See Gallus M. Manser, *Das Wesen des Thomismus*, 3d ed. (Freiburg, Switzerland, 1949), pp. 140–52, 166–79; Etienne Gilson, "Les Sources gréco-arabes de l'augustinisme avicennisant," *Archives d'histoire doctrinale et littéraire du Moyen Age*, 1929–30, pp. 5–107.

45. Cf. Martin Grabmann, *Mittelalterliche Deutung und Umbildung der aristotelischen Lehre vom nous poietikos* (Munich, 1936), pp. 47ff.

46. Angelic intellect: Avicenna, *Tis' rasā'il* (Cairo, 1326 A.H.), 122. 12 (*al-'aql al-malakī*); holy intellect: Avicenna, *De anima* (ed. Rahman), 248. 18 (*'aql qudsī*); holy spirit: *Tis' rasā'il*, 64. 2; holy spirit: *De anima*, 249. 1 (*al-rūḥ al-qudsiyya*); divine power: *De anima*, 250. 4 (*quwwa qudsiyya*). The notion of "angelic intellect" is implied in al-Fārābī's statement that one who has achieved contact with the Active Intelligence was considered an "angel" (*malak*) by the ancients; see *Al-siyāsāt al-madiniyyaḥ* (Hyderabad, 1346 A.H.), p. 49. The Hebrew version (*Sefer ha-hatḥalot*, ed. Filipowski, p. 40, bottom line) reads *melekh* (king), and the reading *malik* (king) in the Arabic text is followed by Fazlur Rahman, *Prophecy in Islam* (London, 1958), p. 30 and Ralph Lerner and Muhsin Mahdi, eds., *Medieval Political Philosophy: A Sourcebook* (Chicago, 1963), p. 36. Paul Brönnle, ed., *Die Staatsleitung von Alfarabi, Deutsche Bearbeitung* (Leiden, 1904), p. 61 translates "Engel," and this reading corresponds to the statement in Averroes's *Epitome of Parva Naturalia*: "These men, if they exist, are men only in an equivocal sense, and they are more nearly angels than men" (Arabic 90. 2–3; Hebrew 58. 12; Latin 122. 23–24).

47. *QD*, 12. 4, p. 245a; 12. 5, p. 246a–b; 12. 8, p. 253a; *ST*, 2. 2. 172. 1, 172. 2 and passim.

48. *QD*, 12. 1, p. 236a; *ST*, 171. 2.

49. *QD*, 12. 1, p. 236b; *ST*, 171. 2 (2).

50. *QD*, 12. 3, p. 241a. See Aristotle *Physics* 2. 1 192b–193a1.

51. Thomas reports this view (which was discussed above, pp. 78–79) in the name of St. Augustine who refutes it. See *De Genesi ad litteram*, 12:13.

52. *QD*, 12. 3, p. 241a.

53. *QD*, 12. 3, p. 241a–b. Cf. Aristotle *De generatione animalium* 2. 3 736b28. Thomas Aquinas offers two different sets of definitions of the "natural" in *QD*, *De veritate*, 24. 10, p. 454a and 25. 6, p. 479a.

54. *QD*, 12. 3, p. 241b: "prophetia . . . de qua nunc loquitur; prophetia de qua loquimur."

55. *QD*, 12. 3 (*ad* 1 and 5), pp. 242b and 243a.

56. Avicenna, *De anima* (ed. Rahman), 180. 4–7; (ed. van Riet), 31. 29–33.

57. See Thomas Litt, *Les Corps célestes dans l'univers de Saint Thomas d'Aquin* (Paris, 1963), pp. 113ff., 117, 122–23, 129. Litt analyzes Thomas's treatise "De occultis operationibus naturae" and shows that in his view of the celestial bodies he followed Albertus Magnus. For Avicenna's doctrine, see S. van den Bergh, *Tahafut*, 2: 166–67.

58. *QD*, 12. 3 (*ad* 1), p. 242b; (*ad* 5), p. 243a; 12. 4, p. 245; 12. 8 (3), p. 253a; *ST*, 172. 1 (2).

59. *QD*, 12. 8 (*ad* 3), p. 253b.

60. *QD*, 12. 3, p. 241b; 12. 4, p. 245a; 12. 8, p. 253a.

61. *QD*, 12. 4–5; *ST*, 172. 3–4.

62. *QD*, 12. 12 (6), p. 261a.

63. *QD*, 12. 12 (2), p. 260b.

64. *QD*, 12. 4, p. 245a.

65. Ibid. (*ad* 6), p. 245b.

66. Ibid. (*ad* 4).

67. Ibid. (2), p. 244b.

68. *QD*, 12. 7, p. 251a–b (see also 12. 3 [*ad* 1], p. 242b); cf. *ST*, 174. 2–3.

69. Benoit Garceau, *Judicium, vocabulaire, sources, doctrine de Saint Thomas d'Aquin* (Montreal and Paris, 1968), pp. 38–39.

70. See H.A. Wolfson, "The Terms *Taṣawwur* and *Taṣdīq* in Arabic Philosophy and Their Greek, Latin and Hebrew Equivalents," *Moslem World* 33 (1943): 1–15 (republished in *Studies*, 1: 478–92; cf. 2: 564–65).

71. *QD*, 12. 7 and 12. 12; *ST*, 174. 2–3.

72. Thomas's view derives, in the first place, from Augustine's. See *De genesi*, 12.9 (*Prophetiam ad mentem pertinere*). As for the lowest level of prophecy, there is an echo of Maimonides's description of veridical dreams (2: 36) as *novelet nevu'ah*, a term quoted from *Genesis Rabba*, 17:5, 44:17. Thomas (*ST*, 173. 2) refers undoubedly to this term when he says that mere imaginative apparitions are "called by some *casus prophetiae*" (this being the correct reading in place of *extasis prophetiae*, which makes no sense). The refer-

ence becomes perfectly clear from a passage in Albertus Magnus, *De somno et vigilia*, 3. 1. 3. p. 181: "propter quod tradiderunt Philosophi, quod somnium aliquod futurum praenuntians est casus a prophetia factus. Casus enim vocatur immaturus fructus decidens, qui tamen figuram et saporem fructus etiam aliquo modo praetendit." Manuel Joel, *Verhältnis Albert des Grossen zu Moses Maimonides* (Breslau, 1863; 2d ed. 1876, here quoted, p. 25, first drew attention to the use in this passage (in the name of the 'philosophers') of Maimonides's quotation and interpretation of the midrashic phrase, *casus* being obviously the rendition of *novelet* (i.e., the fruit "falling" prematurely off the tree) in the Latin version by Augustinus Iustinianus, which was based on Judah al-Ḥarizi's Hebrew translation (see W. Kluxen, "Literargeschichtliches zum lateinischen Moses Maimonides," in *Recherches de théologie ancienne et médiévale* 21 (1954): 23–50). Joel did not verify his assumption,but the Paris 1520 edition of the old Latin version (reprint ed., Frankfurt, 1964), fol. 63b does indeed contain this term: "Dixit etiam in eadem ratione quod casus prophetiae somnium est." Johannes Buxtorf jun. (*Doctor Perplexorum*, [Basle, 1629), p. 293) renders the midrashic statement: "Deciduum Prophetiae est Somnium." Cf. Jacob Guttmann, *Die Scholastik des dreizehnten Jahrhunderts* (Breslau, 1902), pp. 113–14. The dependence of the Thomas Aquinas passage on Maimonides was definitively established by Joseph Mausbach (see n. 34), p. 563, n. 1 by suggesting the reading "*casus*" (following the note in the Bar-le-Duc edition). José M. Casciaro (see n. 34), pp. 165–66 adopts Mausbach's reading.

73. *QD*, 12. 8, p. 253a.

74. *QD*, 12. 8, p. 253a–b.

75. *QD*, 12. 8, p. 253a.

76. *QD*, 12. 8, p. 253a–b.

77. *QD*, 12. 13, p. 265b.

78. See *Guide*, 2: 45 *in fine*; 2:6 (Munk 17b–18a). The "separate intellects" that are said to appear to the prophets (ibid., Munk 16b) are figurized in corporeal form by the imagination (1: 49, 2: 41–42), which is the mediating agency par excellence in all prophecies, except Moses's.

79. See Jacob Guttmann, *Das Verhältnis . . .*, pp. 73–75.

80. *Guide*, 1:46 (Munk 52b). Zvi Diesendruck, "Maimonides' Lehre von der Prophetie," in *Jewish Studies in Memory of Israel Abrahams* (New York, 1927), pp. 124ff., interpreted this passage in the sense of prophecy being a divine creation. This view cannot be upheld.

81. See n. 39.

82. *Guide*, 2:35. On the various shades of meaning of this term, see H.A. Wolfson, "The Amphibolous Terms in Aristotle, Arabic Philosophy and Maimonides," *Harvard Theological Review* 31 (1938): 151–73; idem, "Maimonides and Gersonides on Divine Attributes as Ambiguous Terms," *Mordecai M. Kaplan Jubilee Volume* (New York, 1953), pp. 515–30 (republished in *Studies*, 1: 455–77, 2: 231–46).

83. For this meaning of the term, see Wolfson's two essays referred to in the preceding note.

84. H.A. Wolfson, "Hallevi and Maimonides on Prophecy" (see n. 36), p. 71.

85. *QD*, 12. 14, p. 266b.

86. *QD*, 12. 12 (*ad* 2), pp. 262b–263a.

87. See Rahman, *Prophecy in Islam*, pp. 76–77 (n. 37), quoting al-Fārābī, *Taḥṣīl al-sa'āda*, p. 44.

88. *Guide*, 2: 36 (Munk 80a). For a different interpretation, see Kaspi, ad loc.

89. See Alexander Altmann, "Ibn Bājja on Man's Ultimate Felicity," *Harry Austryn Wolfson Jubilee Volume* (Jerusalem, 1965), 1: 74 and passim (republished in Alexander Altmann, *Studies in Religious Philosophy and Mysticism* [Ithaca, N.Y. and London, 1969], p. 96 and passim.

90. *QD*, 12. 14; *ST*, 174. 4.

91. *Politics* 1. 1. 9 1253a2; 3. 4. 2. 1278b19; *Ethica Nichomachea* 1. 7. 6 1097b11; 9. 9. 3 1169b18. It can be shown that the manner in which the Arabic philosophers and Maimonides elaborate the statement presupposes some knowledge of its use in the *Politics*, not merely in the *Ethics*. This corroborates S. Pines's suggestion that some recension, paraphrase, or summary of Aristotle's *Politics* was known to the Arabs. See his article "Aristotle's *Politics* in Arabic Philosophy," *Israel Oriental Studies* 5 (1975): 157.

92. Avicenna, *Al-Shifā', Al-Ilāhiyyāt* (2), ed. Ibrahim Madkour (Cairo, 1960), 10: 2, pp. 441–42.

93. *QD*, 12. 3 (11), p. 240a; *ST*, 172. 1 (4).

94. Ibid. (*ad* 11), p. 243a–b (*ad* 4).

95. *Guide*, 2: 39–40, 3: 29–34.

96. *QD*, 12. 12 passim.

97. Albertus Magnus, *De somno et vigilia*, 3. 1. 2., p. 179: ut dicit Simonides, "Deus invidet hanc scientiam homini, et ideo velat eam sub metaphora et deceptione." On Simonides, see Pease, *De divinatione*, 1: 194.

98. See Richard Walzer, "Al-Fārābī's Theory of Prophecy and Divination," in *Journal of Hellenic Studies* 1 (1957): 144ff. (republished in Walzer, *Greek into Arabic* [Cambridge, Mass., 1962], pp. 211ff.

99. See above, p. 79.

6 *Ars Rhetorica* as Reflected in Some Jewish Figures of the Italian Renaissance

Jews living in Renaissance Italy had access to two different philosophical traditions: (1) the Arabic and Judeo-Arabic one, which was inherited from the Middle Ages, and (2) the Latin one, which was being enriched by the discoveries of fresh texts, Latin and Greek, and was being infused with a new spirit, that of humanism. The two traditions did not necessarily converge toward a unified pattern. Their respective attitudes toward the art of rhetoric is a case in point. The Latin sphere of philosophical culture had been able to draw, throughout the medieval period, upon a rich classical legacy that included the writings of Aristotle, Cicero, and Quintilian,[1] while Arabic philosophy had known only Aristotle.[2] The translations of Arabic texts into Latin produced from the twelfth century onward had reinforced the Aristotelian perspective of rhetoric in Latin culture but had hardly changed the overall picture. Rhetoric in the Latin West remained more or less under the dominance of the Ciceronian tradition, no matter how arid and formalistic in its application. The revival of a broader concept of classical rhetoric in the Renaissance was due, to a large extent, to the rediscovery of Quintilian's complete text and of Cicero's *De oratore* in 1416 and 1421 respectively. The Italian Jews of the Renaissance were therefore confronted with two somewhat divergent legacies and, as could have been expected, they were by no means unanimous in the choice of options presented to them. Elijah del Medigo, for example, seems to have decided to adhere to the medieval orientation,[3] while other prominent figures like Judah ben Yeḥiel Messer Leon, ʻAzarya dei Rossi, and Judah Moscato clearly reflect the impact of Renaissance thinking.

What was the role and place of rhetorical art in the Arabic and Judeo-Arabic tradition? Aristotle had defined rhetoric as "the faculty of discovering the possible means of persuasion in reference to any subject whatever" (*Rhetorica*, I.ii.1). Proofs common to all branches of rhetoric were said by him to be of two kinds, example and enthymeme, and to correspond to the use of induction and syllogism in the art of dialectical argumentation, rhetoric being as it were "an offshoot of dialectic" (I.ii.7–8; II.xx.1). As a parallel to the possible "topics" of the dialectical syllogism discussed in *Topica*, Aristotle deals with the specifically rhetorical topics (II. xxiii). The *Rhetorica* does not contrast the art of persuasion and dialectic with the science of demonstration. Aristotle's view concerning the relationship between these three types of argument is spelled out in his logical writings and it may be summed up as follows: The dialectic syllogism and the rhetorical enthymeme proceed from probable premises and arrive at conclusions that are merely probable, whereas strict demonstration or scientific proof is based on incontrovertibly true, i.e., self-evident, premises and reaches equally true conclusions (*Anal. Prior*, II.xxiii, xxvii; *Topica*, I.1). It was this suggestion of a descending scale of logical validity that was seized upon by the Arabic philosophers in determining the place of the *Rhetorica* (and *Poetica*) as the last treatises in the *Organon*, thus highlighting the art of rhetoric as inferior in logical terms to both scientific and dialectical proofs, the difference between dialectic and rhetoric consisting in the kind of probable premises from which they proceed: dialectical probable premises being generally accepted by well-informed people, whereas rhetorical probable premises were accepted by the common people.

This relegation of rhetoric to a logically inferior position, though in accord with Aristotle's stated opinion, tended to ignore the important function that the *Rhetorica* assigns to the art of persuasion in the context of political life and, more precisely, in relation to ethics (*Rhetorica*, I.ii.7). It also failed to attach due prominence to the three kinds of rhetoric (deliberative, forensic, and epideictic), by the careful delineation of which (I.iii.1–6 and passim) Aristotle illuminated the significant role rhetoric exercised in society. By fastening upon the *logical* status of the art, the Arabic philosophers succeeded in downplaying the orator in contrast to the philosopher, and by stressing the close proximity of orator and dialectician, if not their essential identity, they deliberately sought to equate theology and rhetoric. While Aristotle considered oratory the legitimate province of political reality and projected a thoroughly approved use of it in the three kinds of rhetorical activity spelled out in rich detail, the *falāsifa* narrowed down this field of applicability by focusing upon the theologians or preachers of religion as the representatives of a logically faulty rhetoric. To be sure, they did not deny the politically useful role of this particular form of rhetoric, but whereas for Aristotle politics and rhetoric were organically connected, these two elements were now linked in a somewhat artificial manner: For the sake of the common people's happiness—which is the goal of politics—the philosophical truth can be communicated only in the disguise of rhetoric, that is, by proceeding from premises accepted by the common people.

This reading of Aristotle in the light of changed religious and social conditions was initiated by Alfarabi, continued by Avicenna and perfected by Averroes. Alfarabi's *Kitāb al-Ḫaṭāba* ("Book of Rhetoric") was part of the lost *Muḫtaṣar al-Mantiq* ("Abridgment of Logic"), and it has been described by its editor (Jacques Langhade) as a work in which "le point de vue logique prédomine tout au long de l'oeuvre. C'est par des définitions logiques qu'Al-Fārābī commence, et c'est en logicien qu'il continue à envisager et à expliquer la Rhétorique" (p. 26). Alfarabi's lost commentary on the *Rhetorica* seems to have been on a grand scale, but the introduction to it (which is known from Hermann the German's *Didascalia in Rhetoricam Aristotelis ex Glosa Alpharabii*, a simple translation of the introduction and folio 1 of the text) is again heavily weighted on the side of logic. In the words of its editor (Mario Grignaschi), "L'idée maitresse d'Al-Fārābī" was "que la rhétorique et la poétique font partie de la logique" (p. 139). It is in complete agreement with this idea that Alfarabi's *Iḥṣā' al-'ulūm* ("Enumeration of Sciences") lists rhetoric and poetics as the last topics (nos. 7 and 8) under the rubric of logic (*'ilm al-manṭiq*). Avicenna followed this trend. The very first chapter of his rhetoric in *Al-Šifā'* (I.8) is related to Alfarabi's *Kitāb al-Ḫaṭāba*, as Grignaschi suggested (p. 132). As for Averroes, he wrote a *Middle Commentary (Talḫīṣ)* as well as a *Short Commentary* (*Jāmi'*) on Aristotle's *Rhetorica*, and, according to the incisive analysis of the former by its editor and translator (Charles E. Butterworth), he included rhetoric and poetics in the *Organon* in order to alert the reader to the inferior status of rhetorical and poetical arguments compared with demonstrative and even dialectical proofs. Averroes is said to have indicated the advisability of the use of rhetoric rather than dialectic by the theologians, which tallies with the stance he took in his *Faṣl al-Maqāl* ("The Decisive Treatise"): For every Muslim the Law has offered a specific way to truth according to his nature, through demonstrative, dialectical, or rhetorical methods. In Scripture, dialectical and rhetorical arguments are preferred because it is the purpose of Scripture to teach and guide the majority of men.[4]

Medieval Jewish philosophy adopted this assessment of rhetoric. Moses ibn Ezra's *Poetics* (*Kitāb al-muḥāḍara wal-mudhākara*) opens its chapter on "Rhetoric and Rhetoricians"[5] by defining the art, in the name of Aristotle, as "persuasive speech" but, significantly, adds the qualification "below firm opinion" and further explains that there are five logical arts in all: demonstrative, dialectical, poetical, rhetorical, and sophistical. Maimonides briefly discusses the difference between demonstrative, dialectical, rhetorical, sophistical, and poetical syllogisms in his *Maqāla fī sana'at al-mantiq* (*Millot ha-Higayon*), ch. VIII. He describes the difference between dialectical and rhetorical proofs as proceeding from generally accepted and traditionally received opinions respectively. Rhetoric is thereby closely associated with religious revealed doctrine. In the *Guide of the Perplexed* there is only a single reference to Aristotle's *Rhetorica* (III, 49), but it must be assumed that his famous interpretation of Rabbi Yishma'el's dictum, *dibbra Tora ki-leshon beney adam* expresses a distinctly rhetorical device. "The meaning of this is," says Maimonides (I,26), that everything that all men are capable of understanding and representing to themselves at first thought (*bi-awwal fikrihi*; *bi-teḥilat ha-maḥshava*) has been ascribed to Him." The term "at first thought" has a rhetorical connotation. Alfarabi used its equivalent when describing the condition under which the enthymeme (the rhetorical syllogism) becomes persuasive "for the immediate common view" (*fī bādī al-ra'y al-muštarak*; Langhade, p. 62; s. note), and Averroes in his *Short Commentary on the Rhetorica* did likewise when defining the enthymeme as a syllogism leading to a conclusion that "corresponds to the immediate view (Butterworth: 'unexamined opinion') previously existing among all or most people" (*bi-ḥasabi bādī al-ra'y* . . . ; Butterworth, pp. 63, 170). The "first" or "immediate" (unexamined) view of the multitude has to be addressed and persuaded by rhetoric, and this is why Maimonides's defense of anthropomorphic language in Scripture amounts to a vindication of rhetoric. Yet the fact remains that for him (and Averroes) scriptural language, however necessary, is *only* rhetoric. Strangely enough, he has little or no use for the artistic element of rhetoric. Aristotle's elaborate discussion of the various elements of style and arrangement evokes no response. He does not refer to this aspect of rhetoric when dealing with the "figurative expressions and rhetorical speeches" of the prophets in *Guide*, II, 29, where the hyperbolic language of eschatological passages might have invited some reference to the persuasiveness achieved by certain rhetorical devices. All he mentions in this respect is the fact that "every prophet has a kind of speech peculiar to him," as noted already in the Talmud (Sanh. 89a). Rhetoric somehow dwindles down to the comparative evaluation of its place in the hierarchy of logical syllogisms, and its low rank is determined by its function to persuade the multitude, a view that persisted throughout the medieval period and can still be discerned in Elijah del Medigo's *Beḥinat ha-Dath*.[6]

A radically new attitude to the art of rhetoric is manifested in Judah ben Yeḥiel Messer Leon's *Nofet Ṣufim*, which was written some time between 1454 and 1474 and appeared in print shortly afterwards (Mantua, 1476–80 ?) as one of the first Hebrew incunabula. Adolf Jellinek, who republished it (Vienna, 1863), correctly described it on the German title page as a "Rhetorik nach Aristoteles, Cicero und Quintilian, mit besonderer Beziehung auf die Heilige Schrift." In other words, it is a full-fledged treatise on rhetoric, not a manual designed for the benefit of pulpit oratory, as Moritz Steinschneider (*Hebr. Übers.*, 78) suggested. As such, it takes its place alongside some of the major works on the subject that were produced in the fifteenth and sixteenth centuries in response to the Ciceronianism that pervaded the age. Thus, prior to the *Nofet Ṣufim* the Greek émigré George of Trebizond known as Trapezuntius (1395–1486), having studied Cicero with Guarino Veronese, wrote his *Rhetoricorum libri quinque* in 1436 or 1437. To the following century belong Philipp Melanchthon's *Institu-*

tiones rhetoricae, Leonard Cox's *Rhetorike* (London, c. 1530) and, perhaps the closest analogue to Messer Leon's work, Thomas Wilson's *The Arte of Rhetorique* (London, 1585).

Messer Leon's openness to Ciceronian humanism is all the more noteworthy in light of the fact that he also continued the medieval tradition of studying, presenting, and commenting upon Aristotle. In 1453/54 he wrote a compendium of Aristotelian logic (*Mikhlal Yofi*), which, significantly, does not comprise the *Rhetorica* and *Poetica*, a departure from the medieval pattern that may be said to point to the more independent status of these two arts about to emerge. The rhetorical concern is evident already in this early work, for the introduction states the purpose of presenting "old and new subject matters in excellent order (*be-siddur nifla'*) and in the utmost degree of elegance and beauty attainable (*be-takhlit ma she-'efshar be-'erki min ha-hiddur ve-ha-yofi*)" so as to duly impress the reader and facilitate his understanding. He wrote, in addition, a commentary on Averroes's *Middle Commentary* to the first five books of the *Organon*, which Jacob Anatoli had translated into Hebrew in 1232. According to his son's report, he also commented on other Aristotelian works.

Messer Leon's *Nofet Ṣufim* may be characterized as a judiciously performed synthesis or amalgam of most of the classical texts on rhetoric, selecting from each one what seemed to be the clearest and most felicitous passages dealing with the manifold issues discussed. The following sources are used in the compilation:

1. Aristotle's *Rheṭorica* (*halaṣa*) as quoted and discussed in Averroes's *Middle Commentary* known to Leon in the Hebrew version by Ṭodros ben Meshullam (1337), the text edited by Jacob Goldenthal (Leipzig, 1842). Leon's use of this version is attested by the terminology he employed. E.g., the term *haspaqa* for "persuasion" was obviously taken from Ṭodros's Hebrew version, which renders Arab. *qanāʿa* and/or *iqnāʿ*. Likewise, *siman* (pp. 135, 137) in the sense of "enthymeme" is borrowed from Ṭodros's version, where it translates Arab. *ḍamīr*. Steinschneider already noted that Leon consulted Averroes's *Middle Commentary* rather than the original Aristotle. Yet it is possible that he knew also the Latin version of the *Rhetorica*.

2. The (pseudo-Aristotelian) *Rhetorica ad Alexandrum* (*ha-*

halaṣa asher 'asah le-Alexander), the genuineness of which was first doubted by Erasmus of Rotterdam, is but rarely quoted. It is referred to also as an "abridgment" of the *Rhetorica (qiṣṣuro sheshalaḥ le-Alexander*; s. p. 16).

3. Cicero's *De inventione*, known also as the *Rhetorica vetus*, is referred to by Leon as *Tullio ba-halaṣa ha-yeshana.*

4. (Pseudo-) Cicero's *Rhetorica ad Herrenium*, known also as the *Rhetorica nova*, is referred to by Leon as *Tullio ba-halaṣa ha-ḥadasha.* It was, again, Erasmus who questioned first the genuineness of the work.

5. Fabius Laurentius Victorinus's *Explanationes in Rhetoricam M. Tullii Ciceronis* is referred to by Leon as *Vittorio ha-mefaresh.* The author is a fourth-century rhetorician who is mentioned by St. Augustine (*Confessio* VII.ix), and the work quoted is a commentary on Cicero's *De inventione.*[7]

6. Quintilian's *Institutio oratoria*, the most elaborate and accomplished work in rhetorical literature, is referred to by Leon simply as *Quintiliano ba-pereq . . me-ha-ḥeleq ha- . . (min ha-ma'amar ha- . .).* It was the impact of the rediscovery of the complete text by Poggio Bracciolini in 1416 that helped to rekindle the enthusiasm for the rhetorical art as a potent element in education. Leon's fulsome quotations from this work in all its parts show the remarkable extent of his familiarity with it.[8]

A major work not quoted by Leon is Cicero's *De oratore*, the complete text of which had been rediscovered by Bishop Gerardo Landriani five years after the find of Quintilian's opus.[9] He probably did not come across this work in either its mutilated form (which had been used by Petrarch) or in its completeness. Otherwise he would have used it, since the image of the orator drawn therein would have suited his purposes.

What motivated Messer Leon to write the *Nofet Ṣufim*? It is obvious from the scholarship he invested in this work as well as from the lofty style he employed that he was fascinated by the new look at rhetoric that dominated the era and by the classical texts themselves that he had studied. He could not have failed to notice that the ancient authors (Aristotle, Cicero, Quintilian) were able to illustrate the rhetorical rules by an abundance of quotations from their own literature, and he must therefore have felt the urge to discover the rhetorical dimension also in the Hebrew Bible. It seems that it was the prospect of finding the rhetorical principles embodied in biblical speech that gave wings to his efforts. For this is how he summed up, at the opening of the fourth and last part of his work, what he had so far accomplished:

After the foregoing account of the subject-matters of this book and having entered into their domains by searching every section of the writings of the ancient and modern rhetoricians for precious material (*divrey ḥefeṣ*), it now remains for us to treat the various categories of rhetorical embellishment . . . and most of what we shall have to say thereon will be taken from Cicero's *Rhetorica (ad Herrenium)* and from part III of Aristotle's *Rhetorica.* Yet the illustrations (*ha-meshalim lahem*) I shall adduce from our own glorious sanctuary, from the words of the prophets and from the biblical narratives that "sit first in the kingdom" (Esther 1 : 14) of rhetorical perfection (*ha-'arevut ve-ha-ṣaḥut*) and which "cannot be gotten for gold neither shall the exchange thereof be vessels of fine gold" (Job 28 : 15, 17). (p. 147)

The assertion that biblical oratory occupied the highest rank in the "kingdom of rhetoric" has to be understood not merely as an expression of piety, but, more particularly, as an attempt to cope with the awareness so characteristic for the Renaissance that there was a common human element, a universal law as it were that ruled rhetoric, the art of communication, everywhere. The universalism that was all-pervasive in the syncretistic culture of the period made it psychologically imperative for a Jewish traditionalist like Messer Leon to stress the superiority of the Jewish heritage within the commonality of mankind. He was sophisticated enough to realise that the enthusiastic manner in which he applied, to the Hebrew Bible, the rules of rhetoric formulated by the ancient pagans presented some problems. To obviate any misunderstanding he made his position clear at the end of the introduction to *Nofet Ṣufim*: Addressing the reader, he emphatically warned him against assuming that it was the conformity of the prophets' speeches to the rhetorical rules of the Gentiles that constituted, in his view, their claim to greatness. One who were to interpret him in this fashion would be utterly wrong. He continued: "Yet if it occurred to you that I turned to those writings because they approximate to the words of the prophets and formed a close link with them, you would guess my intent correctly." Classical rhetoric is thus described not as a yardstick for biblical oratory but as an intriguing parallel that caught his fancy. The true facts of the case are not so clear-cut, however. Messer Leon was obviously first drawn to the classical works on the subject, found them highly illuminating, and then sought to discover their rules and devices in the biblical texts. In so doing he brought a hitherto untried method to bear on the comprehension of the Bible. Whereas Maimonides and those following him saw in biblical rhetoric a mere concession to the need of addressing the multitude in terms compatible with their mental capacity, rhetoric now took on the character of a noble art indispensable for effective communication on all levels of public life. It was, above all, the figure of the orator that now commanded a new respect.

The heightened importance attached to oratory and orator is clearly reflected in the *Nofet Ṣufim*. Quintilian (II.xv) had passed in review the various definitions of the art of rhetoric previously advanced. They had apparently all taken their cue from the role of the art in sophistry. Hence the tendency to equate rhetoric with persuasiveness, which was adopted also in Aristotle's definition. By contrast, Quintilian professed to have undertaken the task of molding the perfect orator who had to be a good man, and he therefore proposed the definition of rhetoric as "the science of speaking well" (*bene dicendi scientiam*). This definition was meant to imply that "no man could speak well unless he was good himself." The corollary of this definition was the view that the orator and his art were independent of results (II.xvii). Indeed, the speaker aimed at victory, but if he spoke well, he had lived up to the ideals of his art, even if he was defeated. Like Quintilian, Messer Leon (I.1) reviewed the possible definitions of rhetoric but, unlike Quintilian, he suggested that they all amounted to the same thing and could be squared with Aristotle's. He did not mention the famous definition that Cicero gave in *De optimo genere oratorum* (I.3–4): "The supreme orator, then, is the one whose speech instructs, delights, and moves the minds of his audience," a definition not referred to in Quintilian's discussion either. He quoted instead Cicero's statement in *De inventione* (I.v.6) that the function of eloquence was to persuade by speech. In the end he suggested that one might distinguish between the inner and outer purpose of oratory, the one being the inner quality of the speech ("speaking well"), the other the outer effect ("persuasion"). He saw the inner purpose alluded to in Isa. 50:4, "The Lord hath given me the tongue of them that are taught" (*leshon limmudim*), and the outer purpose indicated by Prov. 10:32, "The lips of the righteous know what is acceptable" (*siftey ṣaddiq yed'un raṣon*), persuasion being *hafaqat ha-raṣon be-ma'amar* (*persuadere dictione*). The orator is tacitly identified with the *ṣaddiq* (Quintilian's *vir bonus*), a view that is not just coincidental but will be pursued later.

Messer Leon is not unmindful of the havoc and misery that may be effected by eloquent speech and, like Cicero (*De inv.* I.i.1) and Quintilian (II.xvi.1–4), he dwells at some length upon the ruin wrought by the wicked whose "tongue walketh through the earth" (Ps. 73:9). This gloomy picture serves, however, only as a counterpoint to the brightness of the portrait he draws of the immense benefit that a nation derives from its great orators. In answer to the question "What is the orator?" (*mahu ha-meliṣ*), he now completely identifies himself with Quintilian's idealistic image, which he finds also supported by the commentators: It is impossible for the perfect orator (*ha-meliṣ ha-shalem*) not to be a "good and righteous man" (*adam tov ve-ṣaddiq*) (I.2, p. 9). How could he be a leader of men wielding full power of persuasion unless he was utterly sincere (*piv ve-libo shalem*)? Moreover, he had to master the three branches of sciences, viz., the natural, political, and linguistic fields of knowledge, into which Quintilian had divided philosophy. The last-mentioned science (comprising the *artes sermocinales*) included logic, rhetoric and grammar, while natural science embraced the divine science (metaphysics), as Victorinus had pointed out. To be sure, the orator was not supposed to discuss philosophical subjects in all their technical details and in great depth, for persuasion was achieved only if things were presented to the audience in a manner easily comprehensible to all. It is clear, however, that Messer Leon wished to depict the orator as a figure of considerable philosophic erudition, whose words were both eloquent and weighty.

The image of the orator drawn by Messer Leon corresponds to the humanist aspirations which, following Cicero's vision, sought to combine philosophy and rhetoric, a trend that had been initiated by Petrarch and was continued by men like Coluccio Salutati, Leonardo Bruni and, in a way, also by Lorenzo Valla, who would subordinate philosophy to rhetoric.[10] The *Nofet Ṣufim* was written prior to the revolution of the "New Logic" that was started by Rudolph Agricola (1444–1485) and was brought to fruition by Peter Ramus (1515–1572). The meaning of that revolt was the creation of a unified field of logic by breaking down the barriers between the *topoi* of dialectic and rhetoric established by Aristotle. It thereby signified the relegation of rhetoric to pure eloquence. It expressed, at its deepest level, a protest against the intrusion of person-to-person communication into the realm of intellectual life, and thus it marked the transition from dialog to the scientific age of reason.[11] Messer Leon belonged to the "dialogical" humanism of the Renaissance, and to him the nontechnical orator-philosopher represents the ideal figure because of the role he is destined to play in the nation.

This favorable evaluation is articulated in striking fashion by the equation of the orator with the *ṣaddiq*, brief mention of which has already been made. We have here an interpretation of the *ṣaddiq* figure poles apart from the understanding of that term in contemporary Kabbala. Leon quotes Prov. 10:20, "The tongue of the *ṣaddiq* is as choice silver," and he understands it as a characterization of the orator as a man "perfect in his character and philosophical notions" (*shalem ha-middot ve-ha-de'ot*). There were numerous biblical verses testifying to the same view of the orator, and he concludes the chapter (I.2) by describing the prophets of Israel as the most illustrious representatives of this type. All this, he points out, supported Quintilian's definition of oratory.

The following are a few selected examples of the way in which Messer Leon projected rhetorical rules upon biblical material. In Deut. 32:2, the opening of Moses's farewell song, he (I.4) discovers an affirmation, in poetic language, of the five operations in which, according to Cicero (*De inv.* I.vii.9; see also *Ad Herr.* I.ii.3) and Quintilian (III.iii.1ff.), the art of rhetoric consists: invention (*inventio*, *hamṣa'a*); arrangement (*dispositio*, *seder*); style (*elocutio*, *ṣaḥut*); memory (*memoria*, *zekhira*); and delivery (*pronunciatio*, *remiza*). Invention and style are said to be alluded to by the term *leqaḥ* (*liqḥi*), which denotes a "taking hold" of the subject-matter as well as the "winning" power achieved by beauty of language. Arrangement and memory are hinted at in the metaphors "dropping as the rain" and "distilling as the dew" respectively. The metaphors "as the small rain upon the tender grass" and "as the showers upon the herb" are interpreted as the persuasive power of the oration, which is attuned to all levels of the audience's understanding. They are also applied to the successful delivery, i.e., the appropriate manner of tone and gesticulation. Moses invoked the testimony of heaven and earth (32:1) for his intention of delivering a speech in which none of the five operations constituting a perfect oration shall be missing. The constrained and artificial manner of Messer Leon's exegesis illustrates his keen desire to find some biblical *locus probandi* for so prominent a rule as the one concerning the five elements of oratory.

Judah's oration before Joseph (Gen. 44:18–34) is seen by Messer Leon as structured according to the sixpartite division of forensic (*'iṣṣumi*) speech advocated by Cicero (*De inv.* I.xiv.19; *Ad Herr.* I.iii.7): introduction (*exordium*, *petiḥa*); statement of fact (*narratio*, *sippur*); partition (*partitio*, *ḥilluq*); confirmation (*confirmatio*, *qiyyum*); refutation (*reprehensio* or *confutatio*, *hatara*); and peroration (*conclusio*, *ḥatima*). Leon inaccurately attributed the same division also to Aristotle and Cicero, who prescribe, however, only four and five parts respectively (*Rhet.* III.xiii; *Inst. or.* III.ix). In I.7 (p. 24) he does refer, though, to Aristotle's statement (*Rhet.* III.xiii) that in speeches of an epideictic (*meqayyem*) or deliberative (*'aṣati*) kind—as distinct from forensic oratory—only two parts are required: the statement of subject and the proof. He also quotes Cicero's counsel against counterproductive introductions (*De inv.* I.xviii.26) and mentions Quintilian's similar caveat (IV.i.72–73), it being the purpose of the exordium to make the audience attentive (*attentum*, *maqshiv*); well-disposed (*benevolum*, *meḥabbev*); and ready to receive instruction (*docilem*, *mitlammed*) (I.5; *Ad Alex.* XXIX 1436a; *Inst. or.* IV.i.5). The conclusion Leon draws from these various points of view is the realisation of the need for a certain flexibility, which he finds confirmed by biblical testimony: "If you consider the Holy Scriptures, you will find that what Aristotle and Quintilian said is undoubtedly true." Only in rare cases, he points out, did biblical speeches contain all six parts. Abigail's oration (1 Sam. 25:24–31), he tries to show, was structured in the following way: statement of fact (24a); exordium (24b); confirmation (25a); refutation (25b); conclusion (26). The rest is amplification and rhetorical embellishment. Messer Leon regards this speech as a model of oration hardly matched by any other (p. 26).

Of particular significance is Messer Leon's attention to the style peculiar to biblical oratory. From the *Rhetorica ad Herrenium* (IV.viii.11) he probably took the distinction between three kinds of style called "types" (*figuras*, *ṣurot*): the grand (*gravem*, *nisa'*), the middle (*mediocrem*, *beynoni*) and the simple (*extenuatam*, *shafal*). He (I.14) characterizes the grand style as one employing special or figurative words of utmost elegance or as one of speeches that include amplification (*amplificatio*, *harḥava*)—see II.11; *Ad Herr.* II.xxix.48ff.—and pathetic form (*conquestio*, *raḥmanut*; see *Ad Herr.* III.xiii.24; *De inv.* I.lv.106) or a combination of rhetorical embellishments (*yippuyim halaṣiim*). He considers most of the speeches of Isaiah and some of the narrations of Ezekiel the very epitome of the grand style.

These specimens of Messer Leon's recourse to biblical rhetoric unmistakably show how profoundly he was impressed by the elaborate structure of the rhetorical art as manifested in the sources at his disposal, and how strongly he felt the need to project those rules upon the biblical material. An almost autobiographical note to this effect occurs in I.13 (pp. 47–48), where he pleads for the study of the secular sciences as help toward an increased awareness of the riches contained in the Holy Scriptures. The "science of rhetoric" (*ḥokhmat ha-halaṣa*), he says, is particularly useful in this regard.

For when I had studied the Tora in the habitual way, I had not been able to fathom that it embraced that science [of rhetoric] or part of it. Only after I had learned, searched and mastered it [rhetoric] in all its depth from the writings of the Gentiles, could I visualize, when returning to the Holy Scriptures, what they were like. Now the eyes of my understanding were opened and I saw that there was, in fact, a vast difference (*hevdel muflag*) between the pleasantness and elegance of their speeches (*'arevut amareha ve-ṣaḥiyuteha*) . . . and all that is found, in this (genre), among the rest of the nations, the difference resembling that between "the hyssop out of the wall" and "the cedar that is in Lebanon" (1 Kings 5:13).

Yet for all its emphasis on the uniqueness of the Bible, the aesthetic viewpoint, which Leon pushed to the foreground, contained the seed of secularism, for it saw the Scriptures as great "literature." This approach had been anticipated, under the influence of Aristotle's *Poetica*, in Moses ibn Ezra's *Kitāb al-muḥāḍara wal-mudhākara* and in Abu'l-Barakāt's *Kitāb al-mu'tabar* in the twelfth century,[12] but the Middle Ages had not been hospitable to the idea. It was different now in the intellectual climate of Renaissance thought. From Judah Messer Leon's *Nofet Ṣufim* the road leads to 'Azarya dei Rossi in the sixteenth century and thence to Robert Lowth and Moses Mendelssohn in the eighteenth.

While Messer Leon applied the classical rules of rhetorical art to the Hebrew Scriptures, 'Azarya dei Rossi took the novel step of referring to them, albeit in limited degree, when dealing with rabbinic Aggada. In so doing he consciously followed in Leon's footsteps. He quoted him twice in *Imrey Bina* and once in *Maṣref la-Kesef*. The first passage[13] draws attention to "the book *Nofet Ṣufim* of the great scholar R. Judah known as Messer Leon of Mantua," in particular to the statement at the end of I.13 (cited above), which he sums up in these words: "From the indications of the rhetorical embellishments to which the Gentile scholars alert us we come to recognize how superbly beautiful and pleasant are the Holy Scriptures." He then literally reproduces Messer Leon's concluding remark in which he deprecates the unwillingness of many rabbis to accept the truth from foreign sources. The second passage is more specific. It occurs in a context (I. B., 234–239) discussing the rabbinic use of hyperbole as a rhetorical device and makes corroborative reference to the acknowledgment of the same device by the Gentile rhetoricians as a praiseworthy one, "as you find it stated by their leading writers, Cicero (*Tullio*) in *Topica* IV [should read: X, 44–45] and Quintilian in *Institutio oratoria* (*be-halaṣato*) VIII.vi [67–76], from whom the Jewish rhetorician (*ha-meliṣ ha-yehudi*), author of the *Nofet Ṣufim*, borrowed in IV.43 (*Pereq Ha-Guzma'*)" (p. 236).

Interestingly enough, dei Rossi considers it necessary to refer to Gentile support for an oratorical form of expression which, as his talmudic references show, was fully recognized within the Jewish tradition. He was obviously motivated by the desire to legitimize the use of this kind of interpretation also concerning matters that *prima facie* are asserted as historical facts. For he uses it subsequently in an effort to show that R. Yoḥanan's statement (b. Yoma

19a) about the number (over 300) of high priests during the Second Temple period was not historical but hyperbolic (ibid.). Quintilian's phrase describing the hyperbole as "an elegant straining of the truth" must have appealed to him. He might have quoted other sources such as Aristotle, *Rhetorica* III.X.15–16 and the *Ad Herrenium* IV.xxxiii. The third passage is similar in intent to the second. It is found in *Maṣref la-Kesef* II.13 (p. 107, note) and relates to a rabbinic statement (Ned. 37b) about the Sinaitic origin of certain masoretic elements. Dei Rossi considers it a purely rhetorical assertion, "for in all languages do we find essential embellishments (*yippuyim 'aṣmiim*) and all the more so in this holy and primeval language, as has been shown by the scholarly author of *Nofet Ṣufim* who adduced Scriptural examples for every form of rhetorical embellishment found therein." It appears from these statements by dei Rossi that he valued rhetorical theory as an aid to historical scholarship.

In similar fashion oratorical technique is resorted to as the explanation of the talmudic-midrashic legend about the strange punishment God decreed upon Titus (b. Giṭṭin 56b; Pirqey R. Eliezer 49), which seemed unbelievable to dei Rossi as an historical account (I.B. 214–219). He quoted "the mellifluous speaker of theirs"—a reference to Cicero—and "our truly wise sages" (*ḥakhamenu ha-meḥukamim be-emmet*) who would purposely invent stories of this kind in order to impress people by their fancifulness and thereby drive home certain moral or intellectual verities (p. 217). Oratory as seen from this perspective comes close to poetry, and dei Rossi, in a mood of poetic inspiration, felicitously likens the *aggadot* of the rabbis to those groups of angels that are said to arise from the "fiery stream" (*nehar di-nur*), deliver their song, and, having fulfilled their purpose, return to that element not to be seen again. He takes great pains to collect the numerous rabbinic dicta in which the fluidity of *Aggada* is contrasted with the exactness of *Halakha* and the rule is laid down that in aggadic matters contentious debate is out of place (*eyn maqshin be-aggada'*) (I.B. 210–212). He has a whole section on poetic theory in which he quotes, among others, Moses ibn Ḥabib's *Darkhey No'am* (I.B. 477–484). In *Maṣref la-Kesef* he refers to Horace's *De arte poetica* (p. 121). He was clearly groping for a rabbinic rhetoric and poetic and he was well equipped to undertake such a task. Yet he remained content to use certain aspects of both in the service of historical research.

Judah Moscato (1530–c. 1593), contemporary of dei Rossi (b. 1513) and his friend and supporter, represented the Hebrew version of the Renaissance in the most accomplished manner. His erudition was steeped in classical, medieval, and Renaissance literature, and his superb Hebrew style exemplified, and not merely discoursed upon, the humanist concern for *ars rhetorica*. Yet there is no lack of direct references to oratorical theory in both his published works, the sermonic collection *Nefuṣot Yehuda*[14] and the commentary on Judah Hallevi's *Sefer Ha-Kuzari* called *Qol Yehuda*.[15] With dei Rossi, he shared, among other things, a sense of indebtedness to Messer Leon's pioneering work in Hebrew rhetoric. In Sermon V (fol. 19 d) he quoted, *in extenso*, the concluding passage of the introduction to *Nofet Ṣufim*[16] in which Leon had sought to define his priorities. Moscato obviously wished to identify himself with the sentiments expressed. He was not, however, an uncritical follower of Leon's outline of rhetoric. He used additional sources such as Cicero's *De partitione oratoria* (19d) and Rudolph Agricola's *De inventione dialectica* (20a), which had been published 1538 in Paris, and he reached, partly, different conclusions. He acknowledged five operations of rhetoric instead of six (*Qol Yehuda* on II.72, p. 161f.) and four parts of speech instead of six (*Nefuṣot* 19d–20a). He somewhat changed the terminology. The term *haspaqa* ("persuasion"), which was an imitation of Arab. *qinā'a*, he replaced by the more idiomatic Hebrew phrase *hafaqat raṣon* (20a), which Leon had used only occasionally. Instead of *sippur*, he used *haṣa'a* to denote the *narratio* (statement of fact; 19d); and in designating the rhetorical operations by their Italian terms, he referred to *elocutio* (style; *ṣahut*) as *enunciatione*.

The strong impression that classical rhetoric made upon Moscato's mind is strikingly attested by his attempt to rediscover some of its features in rabbinic sources. Like dei Rossi, he applied the urge for projections of this kind to rabbinic literature, seeing that Messer Leon had focused his attention on biblical material. There are two rather bizzare examples of this procedure. The first concerns the aggadic story told in b. Sanhedrin 44b: The angel (Rashi: Gabriel) appointed for the defense of Israel before the heavenly court protests, in exceedingly bold language, against the harsh words uttered by God to Ezekiel (16:3) about the patriarchs. The question is asked whether the angel did not overstep his authority in using such language before God. The answer given is to the effect that he was within his rights, for he bore three names spelling out his legitimate functions: *pisqon*, i.e., the one who lays down things before God; *iṭmon*, i.e., the one who suppresses the sins of Israel; and *sigron*, i.e., he who, having closed the case, does not reopen it. Moscato finds in these three names of the celestial forensic advocate of Israel a reference to three of the four parts of forensic oratory mentioned in Cicero's *De partitione*: statement of fact; proof and refutation; peroration. What is missing is the exordium, but Moscato is delighted to discover this missing part in the list of four names attributed to the angel (*Meṭaṭron*) in *Tiqquney Ha-Zohar* (no. 57): *pisqon, pitḥon, sigron, iṭmon. Pitḥon* stands, of course, for the exordium. The fact that this part is omitted in the talmudic passage is not disturbing to Moscato, for, as he points out, the introductory part is but a "preparation" to what follows and, besides, may be dispensed with in certain circumstances, as had been stated by Agricola in his *De inventione dialectica* (II.22). To be sure, the talmudic story could not be taken literally, but it was appropriate to depict, metaphorically, the proceedings in the celestial court in analogy to the rules obtaining in the terrestrial court (*Nefuṣot* 19b–20a).

The other example refers to a discussion in b. Sanhedrin 100a where the phrase *ve-'alehu li-terufa* ("and the leaf thereof for healing," Ezek. 47:12) is anagrammatically explained in various ways: 1. The leaf has the power *le-hatir peh shel ma'la*, i.e., to confer eloquence on the dumb; 2. *le-hatir peh shel maṭa*, i.e., to open the womb of the sterile; 3. *le-to'ar panim shel ba'ale lashon*, i.e., to enliven the facial expression of the speaker. Moscato sees in these three terms an allusion to the five operations of rhetorical art as prescribed by Cicero: the opening of the womb means three of these: *inventione*, *dispositione*, *memoria*, for they entail creative activity; the conferment of eloquence denotes the faculty of *enunciatione* (*elocutio*, delivery); and the improvement of facial expression points to *pronunciatione*, which includes gesticulation, a subject discussed at length, as Moscato recalls, in the eleventh book of Quintilian's *Institutio oratoria* (*Qol Yehuda* on II.72, pp.

161f.). We may say that it is precisely the far-fetched nature of these cases of eisegesis that illustrates the degree to which Moscato was preoccupied with classical rhetoric.

Indigenous rabbinic oratory comes into its own in Sermon XII, where Moscato elaborates on *Canticles Rabba* IV: 11, 1. The passage chosen by him offers five different views of the verse "Thy lips . . . drop honey—Honey and milk are under thy tongue . . . ," all of which do agree on the application of its praises to the public orator delivering words of Tora, and all of which declare that "If one discourses on the Tora in public and his words are not tasteful (*'arevim*) to his hearers . . . , it were better that he had not spoken." Here we have a genuinely rabbinic stress on the elements of persuasive rhetoric, and all Moscato does is to conceptualize the various poetic descriptions of pleasantness presented by the rabbis. They amount, in his view, (1) to the clarity ("sifting") of the material that forms the subject-matter of the oration; (2) to the quality of the disposition ("as honey from the comb"); (3) to the combination of (1) and (2) ("as honey with milk"); (4) to the element of beauty ("as a bride sitting in her chamber"); (5) to the moral quality of the orator ("as a bride to her husband"). The upshot of his discussion is a summary portrayal of what a public orator discoursing on the Tora should be like: "He must be of pleasant speech, presenting matters in proper order and in conformity to intellectual speculation, being also a man of excellent character." The last condition is best expressed by the rabbinic phrase "*na'eh doresh ve-na'eh meqayyem*" (36c–37b). This image, though authentically rabbinic, conforms, at the same time, to the concept of the ideal orator drawn by Quintilian and eagerly adopted by Messer Leon.

The perfect orator, according to humanist sentiment, is also the perfect man, and this larger perspective was not absent from Moscato's consciousness. In Sermon IX (22d) he permitted himself to quote a lengthy passage from another of his writings—he gave no hint as to its whereabouts—in which he described "the speech of perfect men." There was no "tasteless word" (*milla tefela*) on their lips, he said, and a certain "fragrance and beauty" (*reaḥ ṭov ve-yofi*) radiated from their faces, for beauty was but the fragrance of goodness (*reaḥ ha-ṭoviut*), as the Platonists (*ba'aley berit Aflaṭon*) would say.[17] Moscato linked eloquence of rhetoric also to the dignity of man, another celebrated *topos* of humanist thought, on which Gianozzo Manetti and Pico della Mirandola had written in the fifteenth century.[18] In *Qol Yehuda* (II.68, p. 157), he pointed out that the faculty of speech was the special prerogative of man and that its quality had to be considered the criterion of the rank of a nation. Hence, given the unique character of the Jewish people, its language had to be of the utmost perfection. Moscato shared the belief predominantly held by Jewish scholars (see dei Rossi, *Imrey Bina*, 453) that Hebrew was the primeval language, the *lingua Adamica*. In his *Qol Yehuda* (II.67, p. 153ff.), Moscato quoted Abraham ibn Ezra's *Safa berura* in support of his critique of *Genesis Rabba* 18.6, which led him to a new interpretation of this midrashic passage. In his view the burden of the proof that "the Tora was given in the holy tongue" had to be placed upon the fact that the etymologies of proper names offered in the Tora (e.g., Adam: adama; Qayin: qaniti) could not possibly be regarded as translations from another, earlier tongue because translations invariably left *nomina propria* in their original form. Dei Rossi, who recalled Isaac 'Arama's skepticism about the midrashic argument from the consonance of the nouns *'ish* ("man") and *'isha* ("woman") allegedly peculiar to Hebrew and who adopted Moscato's proof, relates yet another argument which, he says, Moscato had "taught" him: Hebrew is the primeval language, for God, who is perfect, can bestow only perfection. He, who bestowed circularity, the most perfect form (Aristotle, *De coelo* II.iv), upon matter when creating the heaven, could have endowed Adam with but the most perfect language. The argument entails two assumptions: (1) that Hebrew is the most perfect tongue, a view corroborated by dei Rossi from a variety of sources; and (2) that the language of the first man was not his own invention but a Divine gift. Moscato clearly affirms this view in *Qol Yehuda* when commenting on *Kuzari* II.72 (p. 162): The Hebrew language is not conventional (*muskemet mi-beney adam*) but a *creatio ex nihilo* (*me-'ayin timaṣe'*), as Hallevi's phrase *ha-noṣeret ha-beru'a* (Juda ibn Tibbon's rendition of *al-maḫlūqa al-muḫtara'a*) means to indicate. The revealed character of Hebrew had been stressed also in *Kuzari* IV.25 and in a passage from Profiat Duran's *Ma'aseh Efod* (ch. 3) quoted approvingly by Moscato earlier on (p. 155). From Gen. 2:20, Maimonides (*Guide*, II.30) had inferred that languages, including Hebrew, are conventional, and Naḥmanides (*Commentary on the Tora*: Ex. 30:13) had opposed this doctrine from a mystically inspired position. Moscato explicitly noted (p. 162) that Gen. 2:20 did not disprove the view held by Hallevi. As for all other languages, they were conventional.[19] Moscato's position on this issue is clear: The Hebrew language is both *lingua Adamica* and God-given.

What introduces a Renaissance flavor into the medieval texture of this position is Moscato's fondness of syncretistic etymologies. Since Hebrew was the original language of the human race, he found it quite natural that, as he believed, many Hebrew words survived in the other tongues. This belief helped to restore a sense of universal human kinship that the consciousness of Hebrew singularity might have been apt to undermine. Hence the search for words common to many languages, while assuming the primacy of Hebrew, tended, at the same time, to create a bridge between the cultures. It was the counterpart to the intellectual syncretism that permitted Christian Renaissance philosophers to defer, in all innocence, to the pagan deities, and that made it inoffensive in Moscato's eyes to follow the Platonists and Pico in calling the first hypostasis in the process of emanations by the name of the "Son of God" (*Nefuṣot* 23c; see Pico, *Discourse on Love* I.iii). It seems that Moscato's excursions into the nebulous region of etymology owed some stimulus to the treatise *Doṛ ha-Pelaga* written by his friend David Provençal, one of the three Provençal brothers whom dei Rossi described as the "upholders of Tora" (*tofsey ha-tora*) in Mantua (*Imrey Bina*, p. 146). In this well-intentioned work, more than two thousand Hebrew words had been collected that were said to be found also in Greek, Latin, Italian and/or other tongues. Examples recorded by dei Rossi (I.B., p. 456f.) include the following: *'ezer—uxor*; *pilegesh—paelex*, *pallakis*; *osef dalim—hospidale*; *qol yafe—Kalliope*; *bet 'eqed—academia*. A list of etymologies found in Moscato's writings has been compiled by Abba Apfelbaum in his valuable monograph on Moscato.[20] Among others, we meet here again *Kalliope*, the first of the nine Muses and protectress of music, as bearing a name derived from Hebrew *qol yafe (Nefuṣot* 1c). "Music" is said to be a word identical with Hebrew *mezeg* in the sense of a "well-proportioned" arrangement of voices (1b). "Simile" is identical with *mashal* (88c); etc. The most striking etymology concerns the name Moshe (Moses), which is said to be akin (*qarov*) to *Musa*, from which name the noun "music" is derived (3c). Moscato adds that, according to some writers, the word music comes from Egyptian *moys*, denoting water, for the art originated near the water (where reeds grow?). This, he says, agrees with Exod. 2:10 ("Moses . . . Because I drew him out of the water"). The same derivation occurs also in the famous encyclopaedia of the sciences written by the monk and imperial father confessor Gregorius Reisch and known as the *Margarita philosophica*,[21] where also Greek *Musa* is mentioned as a possible derivation. Moscato knew and made use of this work, which he described as "well-known among the Gentiles" (*sefer mefursam eṣlam*; 2d), and it is most likely that his etymology is indebted to it. The knowledge of the Egyptian word for water was probably obtained from Philo's *Moses* I.17: "Since he had been taken up from the water, the princess gave him a name derived from this, and called him Moses, for Möu is the Egyptian word for water."

These playful theories as well as the concern for establishing the precise character and origin of the Hebrew language are all part of the larger preoccupation with language as the vehicle of human communication and with the *ars rhetorica* as the ultimate consummation of man's faculty of speech. As we have seen, the three writers whom we have analyzed made a determined effort, each in his own way, to adapt the understanding of the Scriptures and of rabbinic literature to the spirit of Renaissance humanism.

NOTES

1. See Richard McKeon, "Rhetoric in the Middle Ages," in: *Speculum*, XVII (1942): 1–32; James J. Murphy, *Rhetoric in the Middle Ages* (Berkeley, Los Angeles, London, 1974).

2. See J. Langhade and M. Grignaschi, *Al-Fārābī, Deux ouvrages inédits sur la rhétorique* (Beyrouth, 1971); Charles E. Butterworth (ed. and tr.), *Averroës' Three Short Commentaries on Aristotle's "Topics," "Rhetoric," and "Poetics,"* (Albany, 1977).

3. See below and n. 6.

4. See George F. Hourani, *Averroes on the Harmony of Religion and Philosophy* (London, 1961), pp. 45, 49, 63. The logical orientation of the *falāsifa*'s approach to the *Rhetoric* (and *Poetics*) was well perceived by Hermann the German. In his Prologue to the "Rhetoric," he wrote: Quod autem hi duo libri logicales sint, nemo dubitat qui libros perspexerit arabum famosorum, Alfarabii videlicet et Avicennae et Avenrosdi et quorundam aliorum. See William F. Boggess, "Hermannus Alemanus's Rhetorical Translations," in: *Viator*, II (1971): 249–250. For a discussion of the Averroes Latinus on Poetics, see H. A.

Kelly, "Aristotle on Tragedy: The Influence of the 'Poetics' on the Latin Middle Ages," in: *Viator*, X (1979): 161–209.

5. See A. S. Halkin, *Moshe ben Ya'aqov ibn Ezra, Kitāb al-Muḥāḍara wal-Mudhākara Liber Discussionis et Commemorationis (Poetica Hebraica)* (Jerusalem, 1975), p. 13.

6. See Elijah del Medigo, *Sefer Beḥinat Ha-Dat*, ed. by Isaac Reggio (Vienna, 1833), p. 5.

7. For the text, see Charles Halm, *Rhetores latini minores* (Leipzig, 1863), pp. 155–304. Another commentator (on Cicero?) referred to by Leon (pp. 6, 9) as *ha-mefaresh Alano* could not be identified with certainty. Steinschneider (*Hebr. Übers.*, p. 79) suggested that Alano was the Italianized form of Aelianus. He obviously had in mind Claudius Aelianus (c. 170–235), the Roman author and teacher of rhetoric, but I have been unable to trace a reference to, let alone a manuscript or printed edition of, a commentary by him on Cicero. No reference to such a commentary occurs in Halm's *Rhetores latini minores*.

8. For the story of the recovery of the text, see James J. Murphy, loc. cit., pp. 357–363.

9. See ibid., 360f.

10. See Hannah Holborn Gray, "Renaissance Humanism: The Pursuit of Eloquence," in: *Journal of the History of Ideas*, 24 (1963); Jerrold E. Seigel, *Rhetoric and Philosophy in Renaissance Humanism* (Princeton, N.J., 1968); Eckhard Kessler, *Petrarca und die Geschichte* (Munich, 1978); Jan Lindhardt, *Rhetor. Poeta, Historicus* (Leiden, 1979); Edward E. Hale, Jr., "Ideas on Rhetoric in the Sixteenth Century," in: *Publications of the Modern Language Association of America*, XVII (1903): 424–444 deals only with sixteenth century England.

11. See Walter J. Ong, *Ramus, Method and the Decay of Dialogue* (Cambridge, Mass., 1959), p. 288f.

12. See Shlomo Pines, "Studies in Abu'l-Barakāt al-Baghdādī's Poetics and Metaphysics," in: *The Collected Works of Shlomo Pines, Vol. I: Studies in Abu'l-Barakāt al-Baghdādī Physics and Metaphysics* (Jerusalem-Leiden, 1979), pp. 259–334.

13. 'Azarya min Ha-Edomim, *Sefer Me'or 'Eynayim*, ed. by David Cassel (Vilna, 1866), *Imrey Binah*, p. 89.

14. Venice, 1589; quoted here from the Lemberg, 1850 edition.

15. Venice, 1594; quoted here from the Warsaw, 1880 edition.

16. See above, p. 104.

17. See Plotinus, *Enneads*, V.i.6; Pico della Mirandola's *Discourse on Love*, II.1: "Love is a species of desire; beauty of good"; Pico's *Discourse* is quoted in *Nefuṣot*, 23c.

18. See Paul Oskar Kristeller, *Humanism and Renaissance*, II (Munich, 1976), pp. 110, 120–123.

19. For the theories of language in medieval Islam, see Bernard G. Weiss's article on the subject in *ZDMG*, 124.1 (1974): 33–41.

20. Abba Apfelbaum, *Sefer Toledot Ha-Ga'on Rabbi Yehuda Moscato* (Drohobicz, 1900), p. 12.

21. The first edition probably appeared in 1496; the work is quoted here from the 1504 edition, V.i.2.

7 Moses Mendelssohn's Proofs for the Existence of God

Moses Mendelssohn (1729–1786) made a lifelong effort to refine and reformulate the two major proofs for the existence of God that had been presented by the Leibniz-Wolff-Baumgarten school. The proofs concerned are known as the ontological or a priori and the cosmological or a posteriori argument respectively. He vigorously strove to demonstrate their validity against mounting opposition. In the first half of the eighteenth century the ontological argument had been attacked by Samuel Werenfels, Andreas Rüdiger, Johann Lorenz Mosheim, and Christian August Crusius.[1] Kant criticized it first in his *Nova dilucidatio* (1755). He objected to both proofs in his book *The Only Possible Argument Demonstrating the Existence of God* (1763),[2] in which he set out to establish a novel proof of God as the ground of all reality.[3] In the *Critique of Pure Reason* (1781) and in his subsequent lectures on metaphysics and on rational theology,[4] he discarded all transcendental proofs as illusory.[5] Mendelssohn, on the other hand, offered careful formulations of the two arguments for the first time in his essay on evidence in metaphysical sciences, which won the Berlin Academy prize in 1763.[6] His effort elicited critical comments from Johann Daniel Schumann, Johann Bernhard Basedow, and Marcus Herz.[7] Mendelssohn refrained from replying until challenged to do so by the appearance, in 1776, of a Latin essay by Goeden, a Dutchman, which presented the various formulations of the ontological argument from Anselm to Mendelssohn and expressed lavish praise for the latter, yet criticized him. In answer to both Goeden and his earlier critics, Mendelssohn tried his hand again at refurbishing the ontological proof (1778). He wrote a short essay, which he circulated among his critics. The autographs of this unpublished text and of the replies received from Schumann, Basedow, and Herz are fortunately preserved.[8]

Mendelssohn's final effort in vindication of both arguments was made in 1785, shortly before his death, in what undoubtedly was his most accomplished philosophical work. He published *Morning Hours or Lectures on the Existence of God* with the more or less concealed purpose of forestalling any disturbing effects that Friedrich Heinrich Jacobi might produce by his expected disclosures of Lessing's alleged Spinozism. The long-smoldering feud between Mendelssohn and Jacobi, known as the *Pantheismus-Streit*, burst into the open through the simultaneous publication of *Morning Hours* by Mendelssohn and *The Doctrine of Spinoza in Letters to Mr. Moses Mendelssohn* by Jacobi.[9] *Morning Hours* contained an interpretation of Lessing's philosophical creed that sought to redeem it from the charge of atheism. Yet the bulk of the book was an elaborate defense of the two proofs for the existence of God, preceded by epistemological analyses of the meaning of truth, illusion, and error.

In his preface Mendelssohn candidly admitted that owing to the impact of his protracted illness—a nervous debility that had plagued him since early 1771—he had been unable to profit from the more recent works of such metaphysicians as Lambert, Tetens, Platner, and "the all-crushing Kant." The little he knew about them had come from reports by friends and from scholarly reviews.[10] His own philosophy, he said with Stoic resignation, was no longer the philosophy of the times. Yet he had felt the urge to transmit to posterity what he considered to be the truth.

As we shall see, Mendelssohn did make an effort to face up, in some measure, to Kant's criticism of the ontological argument. His presentation of the proofs ignored, however, the invalidation of dogmatic metaphysics that followed from the *Critique of Pure Reason*. From the hindsight of history the appearance in 1785, four years after the *Critique*, of Mendelssohn's *Morning Hours* looks like an outright anachronism. Yet this was not felt to be the case by Mendelssohn's contemporaries, including Kant and the early Kantians. The critical philosophy was then still far from being recognized for what it was. Only a handful of people comprehended it. Many thought it hardly worth the effort of close study, as may be gathered from private letters written at the time.[11] It should cause no surprise therefore that in the view of some readers Mendelssohn's *Morning Hours* had successfully defied Kant and managed to reinstate metaphysics. One of Kant's followers, Ludwig Heinrich Jacob, grew alarmed and alerted Kant to the situation. Rumor had it that Kant was about to write a refutation of Mendelssohn. What did happen was something less dramatic. Jacob published a painstaking critical analysis of Mendelssohn's proofs, and Kant added some observations of his own.[12] Neither Kant nor Jacob denied the merit of Mendelssohn's work. On the contrary, both acknowledged the superb manner in which Mendelssohn had presented the case of dogmatic metaphysics. In a letter to Christian Gottfried Schütz, another early follower of his, Kant described *Morning Hours* as "the final bequest of dogmatizing metaphysics" and as its "most perfect product." Philosophy, he said, stood to gain by it since it ideally called forth a critique of pure reason.[13] Kant's letter was published by Schütz as an epilog to his own review of *Morning Hours* in the literary organ of the Kantians, the Jena *Allgemeine Literatur-Zeitung*, of which Schütz was the editor.[14]

This positive evaluation of Mendelssohn's *Morning Hours* was still maintained in Carl Leonhard Reinhold's *Letters on the Kantian Philosophy*, which appeared in 1790 and did much to propagate Kant's *Critique.*[15] Reinhold made the point that if ill health had indeed prevented the late Mendelssohn from studying Kant's work in depth, this was by no means a lamentable fact; for had Mendelssohn studied Kant, *Morning Hours* would have remained unwritten and the world would have missed a book that "with rare lucidity develops the illusory metaphysical proofs from their fundamental presuppositions, shows them in their maximum strength, and seeks to augment them by new arguments." In Reinhold's view Mendelssohn had presented the case of dogmatic theism with a clarity, thoroughness, and precision that were sure to facilitate the successful accomplishment of a critique of pure reason.

What then were Mendelssohn's proofs? I shall present them in the order in which they appear in *Morning Hours*, where the cosmological proof precedes the ontological.[16] The cosmological argument is stated there in three different forms: as proof from creation; as proof from contingency; and as an entirely novel proof that we might call the argument from the limitations of subjective minds. Mendelssohn's discussion of the ontological proof is based largely on the pattern established in the prize-essay yet strikes out novel paths and confronts the critics.

The first form of the cosmological argument presented by Mendelssohn is the one known in the history of philosophy as the proof from creation.[17] It is based on two assumptions: the principle of causality, and the thesis that the world does not exist from eternity but has a beginning in time. If we grant the noneternity of the world, we have to admit its createdness and, by implication, the existence of God as its Creator. Since the principle of causality is not in doubt, everything hinges on our ability to prove the noneternity of the causal series, i.e., of the world as a process in time. Mendelssohn mentions the following proof: "An endless series cannot ever become real; for its endlessness consists in its never being completed, there existing always the possibility of adding to it. . . . In the same way beginninglessness is a mere thought that is incapable of realisation. . . . Both the endlessness and the beginningless require an eternity to be realised, and an eternity can never elapse." The corollary of this proof is the assumption of an absolute beginning, i.e., of a necessary being that exists without beginning and end. This necessary being is God, who is eternal. The chain of causes and effects, which has been shown to require a beginning, does not hang suspended in midair as it were but, in Mendelssohn's poetic phrase, is attached to the throne of the Almighty. It comes into existence by its connection with the necessary being.[18]

That the world has a beginning in time because it is impossible for an infinite series to have elapsed is also stated in the thesis of Kant's first antinomy.[19] Historically the proof goes back to John Philoponus (5th–6th cent. C.E.), from whom it passed into Islamic and Jewish Kalam.[20] It is found in Saadia's fourth proof for creation and in Baḥya ibn Paḳuda and Judah Hallevi among others.[21] Mendelssohn was undoubtedly familiar with it from his acquaintance with Hebrew philosophical literature. He knew the argument from creation also from more recent philosophical writings. It had been adopted by the Cambridge Platonists (Ralph Cudworth; Henry More) and by William Wollaston, whose widely-read book *The Religion of Nature Delineated* (1724) used the Homeric image of a chain suspended from an unknown height as an illustration of an infinite series. Hermann Samuel Reimarus, the most radical proponent of natural religion in Germany, had borrowed this simile from Wollaston, and it seems that Mendelssohn took it from Reimarus.[22]

Mendelssohn made it perfectly clear that the proof from creation was unsatisfactory. "Many a philosopher," he said, had found fault with it. He did not name its opponents but he probably thought of Maimonides, Wolff, and Gottfried Ploucquet.[23] He mentioned the objection that had been raised (by Ploucquet) to drawing an analogy from future to past time: Granted that an eternity can never elapse in the future, it may still be possible for an infinity *a parte ante* to have passed away without having had a start at the beginning. In Mendelssohn's apt formulation: The proof for a beginning of the world is begging the question. We ask whether a series that has no beginning can be real, and the answer takes it for granted that a beginningless series cannot elapse.[24] The objection he raised is applicable to Kant's proof for the thesis of his first antinomy. Essentially the same objection can be found in Norman Kemp Smith's *Commentary*:[25] "That we cannot comprehend how, from an infinitude that has no beginning, the present should ever have been reached, is no sufficient reason for denying what by the very nature of time we are compelled to accept as a correct description of the situation which is being analyzed."[26]

In Mendelssohn's view the proof from the impossibility of an infinite series was open to grave doubt. He made the trenchant remark that if the Divine mind could think the infinite series of causes of every contingent being,[27] one might as well assume the actual reality of the infinite even without a first cause.[28] He did not discuss the question whether the proof from creation, assuming its validity were granted, was capable of establishing a necessary being, not merely a first cause. When Kant argued for an absolutely necessary being, he did so in the fourth antinomy.[29] For establishing a first cause the argument from creation is not required, as Mendelssohn well understood. Aristotle, who assumed the world to be without beginning, proved the existence of a first cause or first mover by denying the legitimacy of an infinite regress.[30] Maimonides adopted Aristotle's proof. Similarly, the Leibnizians, including Mendelssohn, saw no incompatibility between the assumption of an eternal universe and the necessity of a first cause.[31]

Having discarded the proof from creation, Mendelssohn now presented the cosmological argument in the form known as the proof from the contingency of the world (*ex contingentia mundi*). This particular form of the argument goes back to Avicenna,[32] from whom it was adopted by Maimonides and Thomas Aquinas.[33] It is concerned with God as the necessary being, not merely as the first cause, and it proceeds as follows: From the fact that things which by their own nature are of merely possible existence do pass into being, i.e., become necessary by virtue of their causes, we may infer that there must be a being that is necessary not through any cause but by its very nature or essence. This being we define as one in which essence implies existence, and this being of necessary existence is God. This proof is clearly cosmological, for it starts out from the world. It infers necessary being from possible beings that are data of our experience, and it therefore differs from the ontological argument, which infers the existence of God from the very concept of his being. We may note that the ontological argument remained unknown in medieval Islamic and Jewish philosophy.[34] Hegel suggested that only in Christian philosophy the ontological argument could have arisen, for it was in the Christian world that subjectivity and objectivity became a problem. In Hegel's view the ontological argument was meant to overcome this opposition.[35] One has to be a thoroughbred Hegelian to accept the validity of this reasoning.

Mendelssohn offers the Avicennian argument in the specific form given to it by Leibniz. The Leibnizian proof differs from the Avicennian by its emphasis on the principle of sufficient reason, one of the hallmarks of Leibniz's philosophy. For Avicenna the possible is simply that which owes its existence to an external cause and ultimately depends on the necessary being. For Leibniz the possible is the contingent, i.e., the merely factual, which has temporal existence, in opposition to the ideational, which is eternal. The *vérités de fait* are distinct from the *vérités de raison*.[36] Eternal truths have their sufficient reason in their logical necessity. Temporal facts lack logical necessity. They are bereft, in themselves, of sufficient reason. Even an infinite series of causes and effects contains only temporal data without an ultimate sufficient reason. Hence we have to posit the required sufficient reason in a noncontingent, necessary being outside the entire series. This being we call God.[37]

Wolff, in his *Theologia Naturalis* and also in his more popular German Metaphysics,[38] had adopted this Leibnizian proof from contingency, and Mendelssohn had been following Wolff's exposition of it in his prize-essay.[39] In *Morning Hours*, Mendelssohn laid particular stress on a certain aspect of Leibniz's doctrine that Wolff does not seem to have utilized in his presentation of the proof. I am referring to Leibniz's view that contingent truths depend on the principle of fitness or choice of the best in contrast to eternal truths, which follow from God's understanding.[40]

In introducing this aspect Mendelssohn pointed out that everything real must have a sufficient reason by which the coming into being of the thing becomes intelligible. In the case of contingent beings we do not find this reason in the thing itself, for its thinkability or possibility fails to explain its existence. Nor do we find this reason in the proximate causes of the thing since these are in themselves contingent and incapable of giving a reason for their existence, their opposite being equally thinkable. The same is true of the remote causes, and we may ascend the ladder of being as high as we wish, we never come any closer to the sufficient reason. The question is merely deferred, not answered. Even an infinite chain of causes cannot contain the sufficient reason why a contingent being does, rather than does not, exist. Yet since contingent beings do exist, there must be a necessary being that contains the cause for their existence but has the cause of its own existence not outside itself but in its own inner possibility, i.e., in its own essence.[41]

So far no mention has been made of the principle of fitness or choice of the best. This principle will now be expounded by Mendelssohn. He interprets the proof from contingency in the light of the Leibnizian distinction between the Divine intellect as the locus of eternal truths on the one hand, and the Divine will or choice as the locus of contingent truths on the other.[42] He links this metaphysical distinction with his own epistemological theory of the difference between thinking, willing, and approving, a tripartite division of the faculties of the soul that had enabled him to understand the appreciation of art as something distinct from both thinking and willing, and which prefigured Kant's aesthetic concept of "disinterested pleasure."[43] In the context of *Morning Hours* the faculty of approval (*Billigungsvermögen*) is raised to metaphysical status by its linkage to the principle of Divine choice or will. The existence of contingent things, we have seen, does not follow from their inner possibility or thinkability. For if this were the case, they would be necessary beings and would exist eternally. Nor does it follow from an infinite series of contingent causes. It can be sought only in their dependence on an absolutely necessary cause that precludes their nonexistence. This preclusion of their nonexistence cannot be due to the intellect of the necessary being. For if dependence on the necessary being were such as to make nonexistence unthinkable, the contingent being would itself have to be necessary and immutable since that which necessarily follows from a necessary truth must itself be necessary and would have to exist not here and now but always. As an object of the intellect of the necessary being, it would be immutable and eternal like an eternal truth. Hence a contingent being cannot come into existence as an object of the necessary being's intellect but does so only as an object of its will, i.e., of its choice and approbation that considers it from eternity as the best and fittest for a certain time and for a certain place. It follows that the sufficient reason of contingent beings existing anywhere and at any place[44] lies in an act of Divine choice.[45]

In reviewing Mendelssohn's version of the proof from contingency, one is struck by the fact that somewhat paradoxically an act of will constitutes the sufficient reason and the ultimate necessity. This is good predestinarian doctrine but somehow falls short of the quest for a rational theology. In making Leibniz's view so thoroughly his own Mendelssohn departed from the classical line of medieval Jewish philosophy, which refused to separate intellect and will in God.[46] Another observation may be in place. The proof leads at best to a sufficient cause of the world but not to an absolutely necessary being, i.e., a being whose necessity is unrelated to the world and rests in itself. As Kant already noticed, the argument from contingency establishes only an independent being that might itself be contingent.[47] Mendelssohn seems to have had an inkling of this possible objection, for he asked:[48] "As for this necessary being itself, where does the reason for its own existence lie?" and his answer was a referral to the ontological argument. It would seem that he thereby indicated the need for the cosmological argument to fall back upon the ontological, a view that would coincide with Kant's.[49]

Yet Mendelssohn did make an attempt to render the cosmological argument self-sufficient. In a recapitulation of the proof in chapter XVI of *Morning Hours*, he drew a distinction between the independent and the necessary being of God. Both aspects, he said, followed from the premise that contingent beings exist. For contingency had two aspects. It meant (a) that the thinkability or possibility of the contingent did not entail existence; and (b) that contingent beings depended on things other than themselves. Hence their sufficient reason had to be a cause that was both independent and necessary: independent in the sense that its reality was thinkable without a cause; and necessary in the sense that its thinkability was sufficient to explain its existence. It was real because it was thinkable or possible, and its nonexistence was unthinkable. The novelty of this deduction lies in the fact that it tries to prove God's necessary being from the very concept of contingency as a cosmological datum. The nerve of the argument is the definition of the contingent as that whose existence is not implied in its thinkability. By starting out from this meaning of contingency, we are led to the concept of God as *causa sui* in the very sense in which the ontological argument understands it,[50] yet without actually employing the ontological proof. Here the cosmological argument appears to yield the existence of an absolutely necessary being. Yet on closer inspection one has to admit that the necessary being arrived at is still tied to the world of contingent beings and not necessary in an absolute sense. Kant's objection stands.

Before turning to the ontological proof as such, Mendelssohn undertook to offer the argument from contingency in yet another way, one, he said, which, to the best of his knowledge, had not been touched upon by any previous philosopher.[51] This proof argues the existence of an infinite intellect that thinks all things real and possible. The proof proceeds from the observation that a man's contingent existence contains far more than his powers of perception and awareness are able to grasp; and that both his potentialities and his real condition at any time—complex as they are—would be nonentities unless being thought by some intellect. Hence, there must be an intellect that has a complete and clear conception of all things possible and real. The crux of this argument is the assumption that the possible cannot be considered possible unless actually thought to be so; and that the real too, apart from also being possible and on this score alone requiring to be an object of thought, cannot be said to have objective reality unless recognized as such by some subjective mind. In other words, no thing is true unless it is the object of conceptual thinking. A truth that no one knows is no truth, has no evidence. Kant, who seems to have found this proof rather intriguing, wrote in his letter to Schütz:[52]

> In presenting the subjective conditions of the use of our reason the author [Mendelssohn] comes in the end to the conclusion that nothing is *thinkable* unless it is actually thought by some being, and that altogether no *object* actually exists without there being a *concept* of it. From this he infers that an infinite and active intellect must exist since predicates of things have meaning only in relation to their possibility or reality.

Kant lauded this "extremely sagacious pursuance of the chain of our concepts which extends them to include totality" in response to "an essential urge of human reason and its natural propensity." He, nevertheless, rejected the argument on the grounds that one had to differentiate between "the merely subjective conditions of the use of reason and the conditions indicating objective validity." What he probably meant was more fully expressed in Jacob's critique of Mendelssohn's proof:[53]

> If by "possible" we understand merely the subjectively possible it is manifest that all possibles must be thought since they consist in mere thoughts and thoughts cannot hover around outside thinking beings. If, however, by "possible" we understand the objectively possible, i.e., the laws according to which things hang together and achieve reality, or even the objects which may once achieve reality, there is no reason why these have to be thought.

The same, Jacob said, was true of the real. For the real had to be objectively possible, i.e., it had to conform to the laws of nature, but it was not necessary for it to be subjectively possible, i.e., to be represented in a thinking being. It seems to us that these objections failed to live up to the point made by Mendelssohn.

The novel proof suggested by Mendelssohn must not be confounded with a Leibnizian argument to which it bears a certain resemblance. In the *Monadology* Leibniz inferred from the existence of eternal truths the being of God as their "source" and "region."[54] This proof had been adopted by Johann Heinrich Lambert, and in 1766 Mendelssohn had criticized it in a review of the *New Organon* in which it had appeared.[55] As he put it, one could not so easily conclude from eternal truths to an eternal *suppositum intelligens* or Divine mind as the origin of these truths. The transition from the possibility of representations to the existence of a representing entity was an unwarranted step. The novel proof in *Morning Hours* was a deliberate departure from the Leibniz-Lambert argument. It started not from eternal but from contingent truths, and here the transition from possible and real things to the infinite mind that thinks them was not a mere postulate. It was based on the thesis that the thinkable must be actually thought by some mind if it is to be possible or real. This particular notion had its origin in a suggestion that had been put to Mendelssohn when his *Phaedon* appeared in 1767. In that work Mendelssohn had demonstrated the immateriality of the soul by pointing out that we had to presuppose the soul's activity in order to explain that an aggregate or any combination of parts into units presented itself to the mind. Isaak Iselin, Mendelssohn's Swiss friend, had suggested that the proof might also be used to show the immaterial nature and unity of God, and Mendelssohn had been "much pleased" with this "happy thought." "I consider it possible and also very useful to implement it," he had written in reply. The novel proof in *Morning Hours*, seventeen years later, offered the implementation of Iselin's suggestion: The infinite and perfect intellect that comprises the universe in all its aspects is conceived upon the analogy of the unifying power of the human soul.[56]

The refining process that Mendelssohn applied to the cosmological argument is very much in evidence also when we turn to his treatment of the ontological or a priori proof which, as we noted, occupied him to an even larger extent. He may be said to have been its last prominent defender until Hegel renewed it in the nineteenth century. In the prize-essay he presented this proof in the following way:[57] The most perfect being cannot be considered impossible since only the self-contradictory is impossible, and the most perfect being is by definition that which contains all "realities," i.e., affirmative determinations, and no negations or limitations. Nor can the most perfect being be held to be merely possible, for a being whose existence is merely possible is one that possesses existence not intrinsically but as a mere mode, while the most perfect being, by definition, excludes existence as a mere mode. For it is evident that intrinsic or essential existence is a greater perfection than existence as a mere mode, the latter implying contingency. The proposition "The most perfect being has contingent existence" is self-contradictory. Since therefore the most perfect being can be neither impossible nor merely possible, it must be real.

Mendelssohn tried to reach the same result also by simply spelling out the implications of the concept of existence according to Alexander Gottlieb Baumgarten's ontology which he, like Kant, prized above Wolff's.[58] The latter had defined existence as a "complement" of the essence or possibility (*complementum possibilitatis*), i.e., as something added to the internal possibility of the thing, whereas Baumgarten had seen in it the factuality of a thing's total determination in its essential as well as contingent predicates. According to Baumgarten all that exists is totally (*omnimode*) determined, and the reverse is equally true: Everything that is totally determined exists. In the case of the most perfect being only essential or inner determinations can apply. Hence it is sufficiently determined by dint of its essence, and it either exists or it is altogether indeterminate and impossible. Since it cannot be impossible, as has been shown, it necessarily exists.[59]

Both presentations of the a priori proof in the prize-essay have for their premise the concept of the most perfect being—not that of the necessary being—and both make it their business to show the possibility of the most perfect being as a prerequisite of the validity of the proof. In this latter respect they follow Leibniz who insisted, in criticism of Descartes, that before any inference could be drawn from the concept of the most perfect being, the possibility of such a being had to be demonstrated first.[60] In concentrating on the most perfect being Mendelssohn patterns his proof on the procedure adopted by Baumgarten, who was content to rely on the a priori argument for the most perfect being in the first place, deriving the existence of the necessary being only secondarily from the other. Wolff had chosen a different way in leaning upon the cosmological proof for the necessary being in formulating the ontological argument. Mendelssohn's allegiance to Baumgarten clearly emerges from his procedure as well as from his employment of Baumgarten's ontological concepts.[61]

Mendelssohn's reformulation of the ontological argument in the prize-essay encountered two major objections. It was criticized by Schumann[62] for what, to all intents and purposes, appeared to be an intrusion of the cosmological proof into the ontological mode of reasoning. Mendelssohn had argued that contingency had no place in the most perfect being because intrinsic existence was a greater perfection than existence as a mere mode. By contrasting dependent and independent existence, he had allegedly introduced the cosmological concept of sufficient reason and thereby vitiated the purity of the a priori proof. In fact, one might reply, Mendelssohn had stayed well within the confines of pure ontology. He had used the distinction between necessary and contingent being only in an ontological sense. He had not inferred the necessary being from the fact of contingent existence, which was the characteristic feature of the cosmological proof.[63]

The second and more common objection echoed the standard criticism that had been raised by the opponents of the ontological argument since its very inception, had become prominent through Thomas Aquinas's critique of it, and had been voiced again earlier in the eighteenth century. Now it was invoked again by Mendelssohn's critics (Schumann; Basedow; Herz; Goeden). In Schumann's formulation it ran as follows: From the mere idea no existence can be inferred unless one obliterates the distinction between thinking and being. Mendelssohn's argument proved only that the concept of existence was part of the concept of the most perfect being; that in thinking the most perfect being we necessarily thought of it as existing; but there was no warrant for the inference that this being really existed.[64] The short essay Mendelssohn wrote in answer to this criticism bore the defiant title: "The Existence of God Demonstrated a priori."[65]

The essay contains two distinct kinds of proof. The first kind (*Erste Art*) demonstrates the thesis "The necessary being exists in reality objectively," while the second (*Zwote Art*) sets out to do the same for the thesis "The most perfect being exists in reality." The presentation of the ontological argument in this twofold manner is highly significant. It clearly shows that Mendelssohn was well aware of the two forms that the ontological proof had assumed since Descartes and, more outspokenly, since Leibniz.[66] Yet the way he formulated the two proofs was entirely novel, as far as we can see. His first proof reads:

> Assuming the necessary being has no existence outside my mind, and further assuming that every truth must be thinkable, the proposition "The necessary being does not exist in reality" must be capable of being subjectively thought. Yet this proposition is unthinkable, for its subject flatly contradicts its predicate. Hence the proposition cannot be objectively true, and the necessary being must have real existence.

The second proof reads:

> The most perfect being is unthinkable without objective existence. For at least some of its determinations are infinite and of the highest degree, and as such cannot coexist with any deficiency. Lacking reality is a deficiency, and hence is incompatible with a being of the utmost perfection. Since, however, the most perfect being is a *thinkable* concept, the proposition "The most perfect being does not exist" cannot be objectively true. Its opposite must be true: The most perfect being exists.

The novelty of these proofs lies in the distinction between objective being and subjective thinking, and in the endeavor to show that what is objectively untrue cannot be subjectively thought and, vice versa, what is subjectively unthinkable cannot be objectively true. In a postscript Mendelssohn dwelt at length on the difference between two kinds of intramental existence: one that signified the mere presence of an idea in the mind, and one that was meant to represent some objective reality. The first could be termed a "mental image" (*Denkbild*)—Mendelssohn's translation of the Dutch term *Denkbeeld*—while the second was "subjective" in the sense that it reflected objectivity and was intimately related to objective reality. No inference as to objectivity could be drawn from a mere

Denkbild but a great deal was to be inferred from subjective existence. As I have shown in another place,[67] this line of thought arose out of Mendelssohn's correspondence with Doctor Allard Hulshoff, a Baptist minister in Amsterdam, who had coined the term *Denkbeeld* in an essay of his on the ontological proof.

Mendelssohn's short essay is remarkable in yet another respect. In an explanatory note to the second proof, Mendelssohn made an observation that indicates that he had tried to make the proof safe against Kant's denial of the qualitative character of existence. Kant had expressed this particular criticism of the ontological argument in his 1763 treatise on the only possible argument, and Mendelssohn could hardly ignore it. The same objection became famous through its restatement in the *Critique of Pure Reason*, in which Kant reiterated the striking simile of the hundred *thalers* that had appeared only a year earlier in Johann Bering's *Examination* of the two forms of the ontological proof.[68] In 1778, the year in which Mendelssohn wrote the short essay, he was faced only with Kant's 1763 treatise, which had rejected Wolff's definition of existence as a "complement" of possibility as well as Baumgarten's definition of it as the total determination of a thing. Existence, Kant had said, did not make the thing more complete or perfect. It indicated merely the positing of the thing.[69] In the short essay Mendelssohn wrote:[70] "By the way, I made no assumption to the effect that existence was either a reality or perfection. I take it, no one will deny that it is a positive determination (*determinatio positiva*) or, since words are irrelevant, that it can be transformed into a positing predicate (*predicatum ponens*)." Obviously, this was an attempt at invalidating Kant's objection to the ontological argument. By equating existence with a positive determination and reducing the latter to a positing predicate, Mendelssohn sought to dissolve the criticism into a mere verbal quibble (*Wortstreit*), a method of which he was extremely fond.[71] He was, at any rate, more inclined to concede Kant's point than was his friend Johann August Eberhard in Halle, Kant's foe in later years.[72] A letter written by Eberhard to Mendelssohn that very year (1778) confessed to a sense of grave doubt whether Kant's objection to Wolff and Baumgarten was valid and implored Mendelssohn to rescue him from his perplexity.[73]

When in *Morning Hours* Mendelssohn presented the ontological argument for the last time, his discussion of it reflected an even more acute awareness of Kant's objection to the proof. This is not surprising, for in the meantime the *Critique of Pure Reason* had appeared and despite Mendelssohn's disclaimer of any close acquaintance with the work, there is evidence to show that he took cognizance of it, albeit in a limited way.[74] The chapter dealing with the a priori proof—it is the last in the book—opens with the question:[75] Is it possible to prove the existence of the necessary being a priori, without resorting to any given reality, without any reference to the data of experience? In the prize-essay Mendelssohn's a priori proof had been concerned only with the most perfect being. In the short essay he had made an attempt to prove both the necessary and the most perfect being. Now he announced a proof a priori for the necessary being. He prepared the ground by characterizing the endeavor as one *sui generis* and without analogy: "Nowhere do we find a case of concluding from the concept to the thing, from ideal existence to real, objective existence, as we mean to do here with respect to the necessary being." The uniqueness of the case, he said, should not disturb us, for it was appropriate to the unique subject to which it applied.

Strangely enough, Mendelssohn did not pursue the proof for the existence of the necessary being in a direct manner. By way of historical reference he pointed out that Descartes, in his quest for this particular proof, had sought to facilitate his task by substituting the most perfect or infinite being for the necessary being. He had shown existence to be a perfect quality of things, and had concluded that the necessary being, qua the most perfect being, included existence, from which it followed that the necessary being actually existed.[76] Mendelssohn's Descartes exegesis is here somewhat doubtful,[77] and one wonders why he should have chosen to conflate the two forms of the ontological proof after he had clearly distinguished between them in the short essay. He obviously did no longer uphold the strict demarcation between the two aspects of the a priori argument. His subsequent account of the way Leibniz developed the proof again leads to the concept of the most perfect being, which is tacitly equated with that of the necessary being. The reason for his desire to shift the argument in this direction soon becomes clear. He was anxious to come to grips with

Kant's objection and, therefore, he had to present the proof in the form to which the objection had been directed, i.e., the Leibniz-Wolff-Baumgarten argument that existence was included in the predicates of the most perfect being. Once he had stated the argument in this form he presented the objection:[78]

By no means, some adversaries say; you . . . build upon a ground the solidity of which you have not sufficiently examined. Arbitrarily you form an abstract concept to which you attribute all positive qualities. We cannot deny you the freedom to do so, and we admit the concept. Yet hardly have you obtained this by surreptitious means when you reach out for existence and declare: To make the bundle complete we have to include in it also this quality and have to impart real existence to the concept. Is such a procedure not sycophantic?

The objection of the "adversaries" seems to reflect some of Kant's utterances on the subject as found in the *Critique of Pure Reason.*[79] Kant had said of the concept of an absolutely necessary being that it was "at first ventured upon blindly" (A 593).[80] This phrase appears to be echoed in Mendelssohn's sentence: "Arbitrarily you form an abstract concept." Kant had declared that he was "for the moment willing to allow" the claim according to which the noncontradictory character of a concept proved the possibility of its object (A 596). In Mendelssohn's paraphrase: "We cannot deny you the freedom to do so, and we admit the concept." Kant had described this concept as one into which the notion of existence had been introduced in disguise (A 597), a charge spelled out in the Mendelssohn passage: "To make the bundle complete" etc. The salient points made by Kant clearly reappear in this paragraph.

What was Mendelssohn's answer to these objections? The concepts referred to, i.e., those of the necessary and the most perfect being, were not "purely arbitrary," he contended. Their truth did not depend on our mere whim. They had to have ideal existence and had to be thinkable to be thought. Once the thinkability of these concepts was shown, we were compelled to think them as existing. That they were indeed thinkable or possible had been demonstrated by Leibniz,[81] and his own novel proof, he added, had likewise shown that a most perfect and infinite intellect was a possible concept.[82]

At this point Mendelssohn reiterated more fully the objection to the claim that the most perfect being was unthinkable without existence:[83]

> Precisely here, the adversaries exclaim, lies the surreption. You take existence to be a quality of the thing which is added to all its possible qualities so as to call them into being. According to your school definitions you consider existence a complement to essence. . . . [Yet] existence is no mere quality, no addition, no complement but the positing of all qualities and characteristics of the thing, without which all these remain mere abstract concepts.

The objection quoted is obviously a paraphrase of the passage in Kant's 1763 treatise to which the short essay had already briefly replied.[84] How did Mendelssohn answer this weighty objection here? "I can admit this," he declared.[85] Whether real existence was not a quality but the positing of all qualities or something else inexplicable yet well known to us, it was at any rate possible to think contingent beings without such positing. One could omit existence from the idea of the contingent without thereby canceling the idea. The idea still remained a concept, even though one without a corresponding real object. Not so in respect of the necessary being. From the idea of such a being its existence could not be separated without annihilating the idea itself. Everything depended on this important difference, and this difference rested by no means on an arbitrary definition. It followed from the very concept.

Mendelssohn reproduced, finally, the old standard objection:[86] Are you not inferring the thing from the mere idea of it? As he pungently expressed it: Must the necessary being exist because man cannot think otherwise? Who guarantees that what we must think as real is in fact real? By couching the objection in these terms Mendelssohn had provided an excellent cue for his answer:[87]

> Happy are we if so much is granted to us for the time being; if our opponents concede that man *must* think a Divine being as existing in reality. This [admission] would be a step of great importance. Everything would be gained thereby for the entire system of human insights, mental attitudes, and actions. For is a man capable of more than the pursuit of convictions and actions according to human powers?

Thus Mendelssohn was quite content to leave the debate at this point. The admission that man was inevitably led toward forming a concept of a necessary and most perfect being seemed to him a momentous step in the right direction and almost as beneficial to mankind as the acknowledgment of the validity of the proofs for the existence of God. There can be little doubt that in paying tribute to this admission he was not thinking of something merely hypothetical and desirable but had in mind Kant's notion of the "transcendental ideal" (A 576ff.).[88] Although Kant recognized the archetypal *ens realissimum* only as a "regulative idea," he left no doubt that on such grounds we not only *may* but *must* assume a wise and omnipotent Author of the world (A 725). Mendelssohn seems to have guessed, and rightly so, that there was solid common ground between him and Kant as far as ultimate beliefs were concerned. Kant's affirmation of God, freedom, and immortality as postulates of practical reason was akin to Mendelssohn's own philosophical creed, which embraced God, immortality, and providence.

If Kant discovered the validity of his beliefs from the aspect of the moral will, Mendelssohn saw his beliefs safeguarded by common sense, and Kant well understood that Mendelssohn's idea of common sense was firmly anchored in reason. He said so publicly after Mendelssohn's death in his essay "What Does It Mean: To Orient Oneself in Thinking?" in which he took a stand on behalf of Mendelssohn's rationality against Jacobi's enthusiasm.[89] What Mendelssohn's affirmation of common sense meant in terms of his religious beliefs cannot be discussed here.[90] It is clear, however, that the proofs for the existence of God that he so strenuously upheld were not the raison d'être of his faith. Both Mendelssohn and Kant were convinced of ultimate metaphysical truths on grounds other than purely theoretical.

NOTES

1. See Dieter Henrich, *Der ontologische Gottesbeweis*, 2nd ed. (Tübingen, 1967), pp. 90–115.

2. Immanuel Kant, *Der einzig mögliche Beweisgrund zu einer Demonstration des Daseins Gottes* (Königsberg, 1763), Dritte Abteilung, 1–5; *Immanuel Kants Werke*, ed. Ernst Cassirer, II (Berlin, 1922), pp. 164–172.

3. See Henrich, op. cit., pp. 140–154; 178–187.

4. See *Kant's gesammelte Schriften*, Academy edition, XXVIII: *Kant's Vorlesungen*, V, 1. 2/1-2 (Berlin, 1968; 1970; 1972).

5. Kant characterized both the ontological and the cosmological argument as "transcendental" in the sense of nonempirical: On closer inspection one finds that the a posteriori

proof does not presuppose more than a hypothetical existence of the world, and that it is as abstract as the a priori proof. See *Vorlesungen*, pp. 456, 1029f., 1149; *Kant's ges. Schriften*, XVIII, p. 209, Refl. 5530. The two proofs constitute transcendental or onto-theology. See *Vorlesungen*, pp. 451, 597ff., 1149, and passim. Kant discarded his own "only possible argument" of the 1763 treatise as lacking in apodictical certitude. See *Vorlesungen*, pp. 1034, 1260.

6. See Moses Mendelssohn, *Abhandlung über die Evidenz in Metaphysischen Wissenschaften . . .* (Berlin, 1764); *Moses Mendelssohn Gesammelte Schriften Jubiläumsausgabe* (henceforth: *JubA*), II (Berlin, 1931; reprint Stuttgart, 1972), pp. 297–311; Alexander Altmann, *Moses Mendelssohns Frühschriften zur Metaphysik* (Tübingen, 1969), pp. 299–302; 310–319.

7. See Alexander Altmann, *Moses Mendelssohn: A Biographical Study* (University, Alabama, 1973), p. 322ff.

8. See ibid., pp. 322–327. *JubA*, XII.2, pp. 117–19; 125–34.

9. See ibid., pp. 671–704, and Leo Strauss's Introduction to his annotated critical edition of *Morgenstunden* in *JubA*, III.2, pp. xii–xcv. *Morning Hours* (*Morgenstunden oder Vorlesungen über das Daseyn Gottes* [Berlin, 1785]) will be quoted here from Strauss's edition, *JubA*, III.2 (Stuttgart, 1974), pp. 1–175.

10. *JubA*, III.2, pp. 3–5. Cf. Altmann, *Mendelssohn*, pp. 629, 631.

11. Of special interest is Dr. Johann Albrecht Heinrich Reimarus's letter of October 2, 1785, addressed to Mendelssohn (autograph C II, No. 32 in "Depositum Robert von Mendelssohn," Staatsbibliothek Stiftung Preussischer Kulturbesitz, Berlin). *JubA*, XIII, p. 302.

12. See the correspondence between Ludwig Heinrich Jacob and Kant in *Kant's gesammelte Schriften*, Academy edition, X, 1 (1922), no. 264, pp. 435–438; no. 273, p. 450f.; no. 276, pp. 458–462; no. 281, p. 467f. Jacob published *Prüfung der Mendelssohnschen Morgenstunden oder aller spekulativen Beweise für das Daseyn Gottes in Vorlesungen. Nebst einer Abhandlung von Herrn Professor Kant* (Leipzig, 1786).

13. *Kant's gesammelte Schriften*, X, 1, no. 256, p. 428f.

14. *Allgemeine Literatur-Zeitung vom Jahre 1786*, I, no. 1, January 2, pp. 2–6; no. 7, January 9, pp. 49–56.

15. See Carl Leonhard Reinhold, *Briefe über die Kantische Philosophie* (Leipzig, 1790), pp. 141–145.

16. In the prize-essay, the ontological argument takes precedence.

17. See Harry A. Wolfson, "Notes on Proofs of the Existence of God in Jewish Philosophy," *Hebrew Union College Annual*, I (1924), p. 584ff.; idem, *The Philosophy of Spinoza* (New York, 1969), I, p. 192ff.

18. *JubA*, III.2, p. 92.

19. Norman Kemp Smith (tr.), *Immanuel Kant's Critique of Pure Reason* (London, 1953), p. 396f. (A 426, B 454).

20. See Harry A. Wolfson, "The Kalam Arguments from Creation in Saadia, Averroes, Maimonides and St. Thomas," *Saadia Anniversary Volume*, ed. American Academy for Jewish Research (New York, 1943), pp. 214–229; Herbert A. Davidson, "John Philoponus as a Source of Medieval Islamic and Jewish Proofs of Creation," *Journal of the American Oriental Society*, 89/2 (1969), pp. 357–391.

21. See Davidson, op. cit., p. 376f.

22. See Leo Strauss's note, *JubA*, III.2, p. 290f.; for Wollaston, see Alexander Altmann, *Studies in Religious Philosophy and Mysticism* (Ithaca, N.Y. & London, 1969), p. 229f.

23. See Strauss, op. cit., pp. 291–293, where passages from Samuel Clarke, Christian Wolff, and Gottfried Ploucquet are quoted.

24. *JubA*, III.2, p. 93.

25. Norman Kemp Smith, *A Commentary on Kant's 'Critique of Pure Reason'*, 2nd ed. (New York 1923; reprinted 1950), p. 484.

26. See also Smith, op. cit., p. 486, where Kant's own "better and abiding judgment" in the *Dissertation* of 1770 is quoted: "An intellect may exist, though not indeed a human intellect, which perceives a multiplicity distinctly in one intuition [*uno obtutu*] without the successive application of a measure." Smith interprets this to mean: "We must not

argue from the impossibility of mentally traversing the infinite to the impossibility of its existence."

27. An obvious reference to Leibniz's doctrine according to which contingent beings are reducible to an infinite series of causes and, finally, to God, whose mind alone encompasses the infinite. See *Monadology*, 35–38; *De Scientia Universali seu Calculo Philosophico* (Gerhardt, VII, p. 200). Cf. Altmann, *Mendelssohns Frühschriften*, pp. 40–50.

28. *JubA*, III.2, p. 94.

29. N. K. Smith (tr.), *Kant's Critique*, pp. 415–421 (A 452–460, B 480–488).

30. On the question how to reconcile the notion of the world's eternity with the rejection of an infinite regress of causes, see Davidson, op. cit., p. 381f.

31. See Altmann, *Mendelssohns Frühschriften*, p. 48; Strauss, *JubA*, III.2, p. 293.

32. See Wolfson, "Notes on Proofs," p. 586ff.; idem. *The Philosophy of Spinoza*, I, p. 193ff.

33. It figures as the third way of proof in both Maimonides and Thomas. See *Guide to the Perplexed*, II, 1; *Summa Theologica*, a.2.3.

34. Jacob Guttmann, *Die Religionsphilosophie des Abraham ibn Daud aus Toledo* (Göttingen, 1879), p. 121f. suggested that Ibn Da'ūd had anticipated the ontological argument. See, however, Wolfson, "Notes on Proofs," p. 583, where it is shown that Avicenna's proof, which underlies Ibn Da'ūd's, is cosmological, not ontological.

35. See Henrich, op. cit., p. 201f.

36. *Monadology*, 33; see Robert Latta (tr.), Leibniz *The Monadology and Other Philosophical Writings* (Oxford, 1898), p. 235f. and passim.

37. *Monadology*, 36–38.

38. Christian Wolff, *Theologia Naturalis* (Frankfurt & Leipzig, 1736), Pars. I, Cap. i, §24: "*Existit ens necessarium.* Anima humana existit, seu nos existimus. Quoniam nihil est sine ratione sufficiente, cur potius sit, quam non sit; ratio sufficiens detur necesse est, cur anima nostra existat, seu cur nos existamus. . . . consequenter ens necessarium existit." *Idem*, *Vernünfftige Gedancken von Gott, der Welt und der Seele des Menschen* (Halle, 1752), Cap. 6, §928.

39. See Altmann, *Mendelssohns Frühschriften*, pp. 316–318.

40. *Monadology*, 46, 53–55; *Essais de Théodicée*, I, B, §7.

41. *JubA*, III.2, p. 95f.

42. See n. 40.

43. See Altmann, *Mendelssohn*, p. 304f.

44. Mendelssohn's repeated reference to the contingent as being "somewhere" (*irgendwo*) and "at some time" (*irgendwann*) is no doubt borrowed from Christian August Crusius, *Entwurf der nothwendigen Vernunftwahrheiten wiefern sie den zufälligen entgegengesetzt werden* (Leipzig, 1745; reprint Hildesheim 1964), Cap. IV, §47–48, p. 76f. Kant distinctly mentions "Krusius Grundsatz vom Irgendwo und Irgendwann" in his "Lectures on Metaphysics"; see *Kant's gesammelte Schriften* (ed. Akademie der Wissenschaften), XXVIII, pp. 5, 188, 467 (cf. the Notes, ibid., p. 1373).

45. *JubA*, III.2, p. 96f.

46. See Alexander Altmann, "Free Will and Predestination in Saadia, Baḥya and Maimonides," *Religion in a Religious Age*, ed. by S. D. Goitein (Cambridge, Mass., 1974), pp. 38–41; above, pp. 50–54; Allan Lazaroff, *The Theology of Abraham Bibago, A Defense of the Divine Will, Knowledge and Providence in Fifteenth-Century Spanish-Jewish Philosophy* (Brandeis University Dissertation, 1973), Chap. III.

47. See Henrich, op. cit., p. 155.

48. *JubA*, III.2, p. 97.

49. See N. K. Smith (tr.), *Kant's Critique*, p. 509ff. (A 606–609, B 634–637); Kant, *Vorlesungen*, pp. 599f.;1006f.; 1149; 1260.

50. See Leibniz's formulation of the ontological argument in the "Memoirs de Trevoux" (Gerhardt, IV, p. 405f.).

51. *JubA*, III.2, pp. 141–147.

52. See n. 13.

53. Jacob, op. cit., p. 246f.

54. *Monadology*, 43–44.

55. Mendelssohn's review of J. H. Lambert's *Neues Organon*, I (Leipzig, 1764) was published in *Allgemeine deutsche Bibliothek*, III.1 (1766), pp. 1–23 (reproduced in *Moses Mendelssohn's gesammelte Schriften*, IV.2 (Leipzig, 1844), pp. 486–500; the criticism mentioned above is found on p. 500). See Strauss's important note, *JubA*, III.2, p. 306ff.

56. See Leo Strauss, *JubA*, III.2, p. 301; Altmann, *Mendelssohn*, p. 690.

57. *JubA*, II, p. 300f.; see Altmann, *Mendelssohns Frühschriften*, p. 310–315.

58. Kant based his lectures on rational theology on Baumgarten's *Metaphysica* (IV, §800–1000) and Eberhard's *Vorbereitung zur natürlichen Theologie* (Halle, 1781), of which he made a compendium (*Kant's Schriften*, Academy edition, XVIII, pp. 491–606); cf. *Vorlesungen*, p. 1515. For an account of the ontological concepts involved in the proof, see Altmann, *Mendelssohns Frühschriften*, pp. 310–313.

59. *JubA*, II, p. 301; see Altmann, ibid., p. 315f.

60. See the titleless short essay in "Memoires de Trevoux," (Gerhardt, IV, p. 405f.); *Meditationes de Cognitione, Veritate et Ideis* (Gerhardt, IV, p. 424); *Animadversiones in partem generalem Principiorum Cartesianorum* (Gerhardt, IV, p. 359); *De Synthesi et Analysi universali* etc. (Gerhardt, VII, p. 296); *Nouveaux Essais sur l'Entendment humain*, bk. IV, ch. xi, §8. Kant criticized Leibniz's supplementary proof as superfluous since it involved a *petitio principii*: it presupposed that a noncontradictory *omnitudo realitatis* was possible, but positive determinations might conceivably contradict each other (e.g., Divine love and punitive justice). See *Vorlesungen*, pp. 598, 783, 1024f.

61. See Altmann, *Mendelssohns Frühschriften*, pp. 313–316. For the difference between Wolff and Baumgarten, see Henrich, op. cit., pp. 55–68. Henrich's account of Mendelssohn's position (pp. 68–72) is rather summary.

62. In an anonymously published treatise, *Neue Bestätigung des Schlusses von der Möglichkeit des Allervollkommensten Wesens auf dessen Wirklichkeit. Nebst einigen Erinnerungen gegen des Hrn. Moses Mendelssohn neue Wendung dieses Beweises, in dessen Abhandlung über die Evidenz in den metaphysischen Wissenschaften* (Clausthal bey Wendeborn, 1771). A good account of this work is found in the elaborate review of it in *Allgemeine deutsche Bibliothek*, XXI.1 (1774), pp. 208–210. Johann David Schumann, director of the gymnasium in Hanover, is better known from his later role as Lessing's opponent in matters theological. He was the addressee of the latter's spirited reply, *Über den Beweis des Geistes und der Kraft* (Brunswick, 1777).

63. A similar point was made in the review of Schumann's treatise in *Allgemeine deutsche Bibliothek*.

64. See *Bibliothek*, p. 209.

65. Autograph B II, No. 11 in "Depositum Robert von Mendelssohn," Staatsbibliothek Stiftung Preussischer Kulturbesitz, Berlin. *JubA*, XII.2, pp. 117–19.

66. Henrich, op. cit., p. 71, asserts that Mendelssohn made a clear distinction between the two forms of the a priori argument only as late as in *Morgenstunden*. Henrich was obviously unacquainted with the short essay of 1778.

67. See Altmann, *Mendelssohn*, pp. 324–327.

68. This has been shown to be the case by Henrich, op. cit., p. 120.

69. *Kants Werke*, ed. Cassirer, II, pp. 76–81.

70. Loc. cit. (n. 65), fol. lv. *JubA*, XII.2, p. 118.

71. See Kant's criticism of this method as employed by Mendelssohn in "Einige Bemerkungen zu Ludwig Heinrich Jakobs Prüfung der Mendelssohnschen Morgenstunden," *Kants Werke*, ed. Cassirer, IV, p. 482f.

72. See Henry E. Allison, *The Kant-Eberhard Controversy* (Baltimore and London, 1973).

73. Eberhard's letter has been published by Jeremias Heinemann in *Sammlung theils noch ungedruckter . . . Aufsätze und Briefe . . .* (Leipzig, 1831), pp. 341–343. It is dated November 15, 1778. *JubA*, XII.2, pp. 139–41. Mendelssohn's reply is not extant.

74. See below, p. 135f.

75. *JubA*, III.2, p. 148f.

76. *JubA*, III.2, p. 149.

77. See Henrich, op. cit., p. 71; cf. pp. 10–22.
78. *JubA*, III.2, p. 150.
79. This was already noticed by Strauss, *JubA*, III.2, p. 309.
80. The translation of the Kantian phrases given here is taken from N. K. Smith (tr.), *Kant's Critique*, pp. 501–503.
81. See n. 60; Altmann, *Mendelssohns Frühschriften*, p. 314.
82. *JubA*, III.2, p. 151.
83. *JubA*, III.2, p. 151f.
84. See above, p. 133. Strauss, *JubA*, III.2, p. 309.
85. *JubA*, III.2, p. 152f.
86. *JubA*, III.2, p. 154.
87. *JubA*, III.2, pp. 154–157.
88. See also *Vorlesungen*, pp. 309f.; 451f.; 1013ff.; 1146ff.; 1260f.
89. Kant, "Was heißt: sich im Denken orientieren?", *Berlinische Monatsschrift* (1786), pp. 304–330; *Werke*, ed. Cassirer, IV, pp. 349–366. See Altmann, *Mendelssohn*, p. 751f.
90. See Strauss, *JubA*, III.2, pp. lxiv–lxxi.

8 Moses Mendelssohn on Miracles

Moses Mendelssohn was heir to both the medieval and modern Enlightenment discussions of miracles, and he seems to have encountered no serious difficulty in reconciling the two traditions. Maimonides on the one hand and Leibniz on the other served him as trusted guides along his path. Both recognized the possibility of miracles in a universe governed by natural causality. In the famous *Leibniz-Clarke Correspondence* (1715–16), both opponents were in agreement that miracles were possible; they only differed as to their nature and definition.[1] Mendelssohn could therefore feel on safe ground in ignoring the radicals within the modern Enlightenment (Hobbes, Spinoza, Reimarus, Hume; not to speak of the French *philosophes*) who held no brief for miracles.[2] Yet he could not remain altogether impervious to the general intellectual climate of the Enlightenment of which Paul Hazard has conveyed a good glimpse in the chapter "Miracles Denied" of his book *The European Mind: 1680–1715*.[3] In surveying Mendelssohn's scattered references to the subject, one does indeed become aware of a certain ambivalence and ambiguity on his part. At times he stresses the admissibility of miracles as Divine acts that infringe upon the natural order. On other occasions he almost downgrades the miracle as inferior to the operations of Divine providence enacted through natural causality. These alternations cannot be construed to follow a pattern of development, but are indicative of a dialectic pervading the entire span of his life.

Already in a notebook entry of March 16, 1753,[4] the earliest literary effort of Mendelssohn extant, he sounds the modernistic note:

> A wise man whom the arguments of true philosophy have convinced of the existence of a supreme Deity is much more impressed by a natural event, whose connection with the whole he can partially discern, than he is by a miracle. Inferior minds, however, are misled by the permanent connection of causes and effects into erroneously ignoring the hand of an intelligent free Being. They therefore cannot do without miracles.[5]

This is a clear echo of Spinoza's remark about the preference shown by vulgar people for miracles rather than natural causality.[6] Yet in the prize-essay "On Evidence in Metaphysical Sciences" (1763), Mendelssohn breaks a lance for miracles:

> Every natural event has a threefold cause: First, it can be understood from the Divine power that produces it from nothing, and without this cause it is altogether impossible. It has, secondly, its cause also in the system of Divine purposes, and this too is indispensable for its existence; for God would not will its production unless He approved of it. Finally, its existence can also be understood from the efficient causes in nature, and this cause can be dispensed with if necessary. For God can produce whatever conforms to his purposes by a miracle the existence of which cannot be explained through secondary causes.[7]

Mendelssohn points out that as a rule the system of efficient causes is in perfect harmony with the system of Divine purposes. A miracle, however, is something that "interrupts" (*unterbricht*) the course of nature.[8]

Mendelssohn's position is more fully explained in the section "Ueber die Wunder" in his "Gegenbetrachtungen über Bonnets Palingenesie" (1769),[9] in which his principal statement along traditional lines is offered. He starts out from a delineation of the problem that takes its cue from Bonnet:[10] "Are miracles preordained (*vorherverordnet*) by God and produced in time through laws of nature unknown to us, or do they involve a direct intervention of the All-Powerful (*eine unmittelbare Dazwischenkunft der Allmacht*), a suspension (*eine Aufhebung*) of the laws of nature?"[11] This alternative is more precisely defined by the remark that both these "systems" or theories reject the notion of a change in the Divine decree (*Rathschlusse*). In other words, both assume miracles to happen according to the eternal will of God and, in this sense, to be preordained. They differ only with regard to the manner in which miracles are effected. According to the theory proposed by Bonnet—we may call it the integrationist theory—God not merely preordained but also preestablished the miracles by "weaving" them, as Mendelssohn put it, into the "system of efficient causes." The adherents of what Mendelssohn designates as the more "common" hypothesis deny the assumption of any preestablishment of miracles and see in them events decreed, to be sure, by the eternal will of God yet enacted by certain infringements upon the normal series of causes and effects at appropriate points in time. We may call this the interventionist hypothesis, and Mendelssohn prefers it to the other while Bonnet favors the integrationist view.[12]

Before we proceed to analyze the arguments on both sides as aired by Mendelssohn, a word may be said concerning the historical antecedents of the two theories concerned. The doctrine of preordained miracles in its interventionist form goes back to Judah Hallevi's *Sefer Ha-Kuzari*, in which on the one hand miracles are said to be caused directly by God, without intermediate causes, and, on the other hand, they are nevertheless described as happening "within nature" in the sense that they are comprised by the eternal will of God that operated in the six days of creation. Their being somehow "within nature" is only another term for saying that they are preordained. Hallevi does not use any expression suggestive of the notion that miracles were "put" or integrated into the causal nexus. Hence, there is no contradiction between their preordainment and their direct causation in time.[13] John Buxtorf's (the son's) Latin version adds however by way of explanation: "ut, his vel illis temporibus, has vel illas miraculosas operationes *ederent*" (my emphasis),[14] and thereby suggests that by the Divine will nature has received the fitness to produce miracles as preordained. Accordingly, Hallevi would have to be regarded as the author of the doctrine of preestablished miracles. In fact, as we have seen, he subscribes to the interventionist view of preordained miracles.

The other view was first introduced by Maimonides, who speaks of miracles not only as preordained by the eternal will of God[15] but also as "put into the nature of things."[16] He emphasizes this point by denying that anything really "novel" happens when a miracle makes its preestablished appearance. The only novelty consists in the prophet's proclamation of its pending occurrence.[17] This theory has been criticized and even fiercely attacked as a misinterpretation of the rabbinic passages it seeks to explain.[18] It is, however, most likely that Maimonides himself withdrew from the opinion he had projected upon the rabbinic texts quoted by him. A careful reading of the way he presents it in the *Guide to the Perplexed* (II, 29) leaves little doubt that all he approves of is the "spirit" or attitude displayed in the texts, viz., the "avoidance" of even an implied denial of natural causality and the permanence of its order.[19] What he clearly does not wish to approve is the view of miracles as actually preestablished. Though he does not say so directly, the whole tenor of his discussion points in this direction.[20] Besides, and much more importantly, his entire metaphysics precludes such a simplistic notion as the one of "natural" miracles. The borderline between the natural and the miraculous remains to him intact.[21] Like Hallevi, he adopts the interventionist doctrine: Miracles are preordained but not preestablished.

Mendelssohn probably shared the view that neither Hallevi nor Maimonides can be regarded as protagonists of the integrationist theory. For he distinctly associated this view with the opinion held by "our rabbis" as interpreted by Maimonides. Having posed the two alternative "hypotheses," he ventures the surmise that "both are equally acceptable to all known religions." He adds: "Our rabbis, in particular, are not far removed from Mr. Bonnet's hypothesis. In fact, they explain the miracles of the Old Testament in a manner similar to the one in which Mr. Bonnet explains the miracles of the New Testament." In evidence he quotes the three passages in Maimonides in which the rabbinic view is presented.[22] He does not claim any direct or indirect dependence of Bonnet on this rabbinic view nor does he try to make plausible how Bonnet arrived at his theory. To Bonnet himself the integrationist doctrine seems to have appeared as a rather novel answer to an old problem.

> I know full well [he says] that one customarily regards a miracle as the effect of a direct act (*d'un Acte immédiat*) of the All-Powerful . . . because one does not consider it possible for a miracle to be contained (*renfermé*) within the realm (*la Sphère*) of the laws of nature. However, if it be in the nature of the Divine wisdom not to multiply acts unnecessarily; if the powerful Divine will (*la Volonté Efficace*) could by a single act produce or preordain all those modifications of the laws of nature which I call miracles, will it not be very probable, at the least, that it did so?[23]

It is the principle of economy (*la simplicité des voyes*) or least action that motivated Bonnet in his option for the integrationist theory. This principle had been stressed by Malebranche[24] and of late by Leibniz,[25] both having used it in the context of the problem of evil, yet with relevance also, on the part of Leibniz,[26] for the discussion of miracles. Mendelssohn quotes Bonnet's sentence about the wisdom of least action, and it is here that he detects a fundamental weakness of the integrationist theory. He writes:

> If I understand Mr. Bonnet correctly, he assumes the connection of causes and effects to have been introduced by God in order to absolve Him of the necessity of multiplying *actions*. To me this economy looks suspicious, for according to an old-established philosophical truth nature cannot be conserved by God without continuous actions. The entire system of intermediate causes does not suffice to conserve the creation for a single moment. Just as the creation out of nothing is a miracle, so is its conservation; for the latter is a continued creation. Except that in every moment of its conservation the entire universe is produced by God in a manner conforming to its preceding condition so that the conditions of the world will be as coherent as the parts of a supremely intelligible system. . . . As many moments as creation lasts, so many actions of the Infinite Being are unavoidable. Here no economizing through the system of intermediate causes is possible.[27]

Mendelssohn argues here from a position that he consistently held,[28] and that he inherited from Maimonides and Leibniz, both of whom emphasize the continuity of God's preservation of the universe.[29] In addition, he questions Bonnet's theory from yet another angle. The gist of his elaborate argumentation lies in the thought that certain miracles, e.g., the transformation of water into blood (Exod. 7:19–21), are of such a nature that they could not possibly have been integrated into the system of efficient natural causes without disrupting it as a whole. In other words, upon closer inspection the theory breaks down. Similarly Leibniz had argued that the transformation of water into wine at Kana could not have been "a miracle of first rank," i.e., one performed by God, but must have been enacted by superior beings (angels, substances) endowed with finer bodies, etc. and acting within a wider range of natural capacities than those possessed by men. For had this been a true miracle,

> God would have changed thereby the whole course of the universe by virtue of the connection of bodies; or else, He would have been obliged to suspend, again by way of miracle, this connection and to make the bodies—insofar as they are uninvolved in the miracle—act in complete disregard of the miracle. The miracle completed, He would have had to restore all things in the involved bodies to the condition in which they would have found themselves without the miracle; whereupon all would have reverted to its original course. The miracle would therefore have demanded more than it appeared to be.[30]

Mendelssohn's line of argument reflects Leibniz's but he applies it only to the integrationist position, which assumes miracles to happen according to a prearranged, irregular functioning of secondary causes. As an upholder of the interventionist theory he sees no need for secondary causes—regular or irregular—to bring about a miracle. For "why should it have been unbefitting the supreme Wisdom to produce directly (*unmittelbar*) this unique kind of event?"[31] He is obviously not troubled by Leibniz's point concerning the "connection of bodies," according to which even a temporary change wrought by direct intervention cannot remain without repercussions upon the whole. Leibniz himself speaks in the context referred to of creation, incarnation, and "some other acts of God" as miracles that "transcend all powers of creatures and are true miracles or even mysteries."[32] Similarly in another place: Though there are, perhaps, miracles that God performs through the intermediacy of angels and without any violation of the laws of nature, "it remains true nevertheless that the laws of nature are amenable to temporary suspension, whereas the eternal verities such as those of geometry are altogether indispensable."[33] The reason for this difference lies in Leibniz's distinction between geometrical and moral (i.e., elective) necessity, which in turn has to do with Leibniz's distinction between the Divine attributes of intellect and will. The laws of nature follow moral necessity and can therefore be set aside by God in certain cases.[34]

Mendelssohn could find in Leibniz also the notion of preordained miracles. In reply to the possible objection that in a world running to rule God could perform no miracles, Leibniz points out that the miracles that happen in the world "were also included and represented as possibles in this world considered in the state of pure possibility, and that God, who since effected them, decreed then to effect them, when He chose this world.[35] Having chosen the best world, God performed only the miracles that were unavoidable.[36] Differently put: "Since God can do nothing without reason, even when He acts miraculously, it follows that concerning individual events He has no volition that is not the consequence of a truth or a general volition."[37] This notion of preordainment excludes any particular original volitions on the part of God. Leibniz stresses, against Malebranche, the impossibility of an occasional cancellation of the general law to make room for an exception when order demands it. In his view God cancels one law only by substituting for it another, more applicable law. What order demands must conform to the rule of law.[38] In his "Metaphysical Discourse" of 1686, which remained unpublished until 1846 and was unknown to Mendelssohn,[39] Leibniz elaborated the concept of the superior order of general volition by which miracles come into being as preordained.

> Since nothing happens without conformity to order, one can say that miracles are just as much in order as are the natural operations which are called by that name because they conform to certain subordinate maxims designated by us as the nature of things. For one can say that this nature is but a custom of God (*n'est qu'une coustume de Dieu*) with which He can dispense on account of a stronger reason than the one that motivated Him to avail Himself of those maxims.[40]

"Miracles," he says in another place of the same Discourse, "always conform to the universal law of the general order, although they are above the subordinate maxims."[41] A "distinct comprehension" of the general order is beyond the capacity of any created mind. Hence miracles cannot be foreseen, while everything called natural is comprehensible because it depends on less general maxims.[42] It should be clear from these passages that Leibniz considers miracles as preordained not by way of being "put into nature," as the integrationist view suggests but, on the contrary, by being planned as part of a higher order in conformity to the general law and by being enacted at the appointed time in violation of the law of nature.[43] Most probably Mendelssohn understood Leibniz in the broad sense of these terms, and his criticism of Bonnet's theory was not unconnected with this understanding.

When in his *Morgenstunden oder Vorlesungen über das Daseyn Gottes* (1785), Mendelssohn resumes the theme of miracle, the "modernist" trend comes again to the fore. In chapter XV he reaches the point for the sake of which this esssentially polemical treatise had been written, viz., the presentation of Lessing's "purified pantheism" as allied to the "religion of reason."[44] No other author, Mendelssohn claims, had declared his belief in Divine providence with greater conviction than Lessing. "We need only recall those excellent scenes of his dramatic didactic poem [*Nathan the Wise*] in which he portrayed *ad oculos* the true doctrine of God's providence and governance as well as the harmfulness of the mentality that always looks for miracles in order to discover the finger of the Godhead."[45] Lessing's *Nathan*, Mendelssohn contends, was written as "a kind of *Anti-Candide*" in defense of Providence, a view that has a good deal to recommend itself.[46]

This characterization of Lessing, the highlight of the chapter and of the book as a whole, is initiated by a discussion of the nature of the miraculous, a procedure that is by no means arbitrary. For in *Nathan the Wise* the theme of miracle does indeed loom large. Recha, Nathan's stepdaughter, was rescued from a conflagration by the gallant Templar. She imagines the dazzling white-clad figure of her recollection as an angel sent by Heaven to save her miraculously. Nathan tries to disillusion her. "Why put an angel to the trouble?" when the entire concatenation of events leading to that episode is in itself a marvel, albeit one contrived by natural means? Daya, Recha's companion, sees no harm in the illusion of miracle: "Sure thus we feel ourselves nearer the great inscrutable First Cause of our deliverance," to which smug assurance Nathan retorts: "Pride—and nought but pride! The iron pot would fain be lifted up with tongs of silver from the kitchen fire, that it may deem itself a silver urn."[47]

It is with Recha in mind that earlier in his chapter Mendelssohn describes the "popular system" as one that sees the hand of God only "in extraordinary and astonishing cases or in miracles (*Wunderdingen*), i.e., in single events in which a definite purpose is strikingly evident and the concurrence (*Mitwürkung*) of a free Being acting with intent and deliberation cannot be denied."[48] He had expressed essentially the same thought in his notebook entry of 1753[49] but he offers here a novel definition of miracles[50] and Lessing's drama, for which he had unbounded admiration, adds a vivid color to it. Yet it is to Leibniz and Shaftesbury that he pays homage when contrasting the popular system with the one that he considers the most perfect in philosophy.

It is the highest triumph of human wisdom to recognize the complete harmony between the system of final causes (*Absichten*) and the system of efficient causes (*würkenden Ursachen*) and to see, with Shaftesbury and Leibniz, that the final causes of God and his concurrence extend to the minutest changes and to single events in the animate as well as the

> inanimate realms; . . . that every effect in nature agrees with the Divine purpose and, at the same time, flows from His power. Not to ignore God's governance and providence in the very minutest events, and not to ignore them precisely because these things happen in the ordinary course of nature; thus to revere God in natural events rather than in miracles; this, it seems to me, is the highest enoblement of human concepts, the most sublime manner of thinking about God, His governance and providence.[51]

In this panegyric to Leibniz's preestablished harmony, the role of miracles appears to be reduced to a superfluity. For if every single event in the natural order answers to a Divine purpose (the "general law") and follows from the Divine power, the raison d'être of miracles falls to the ground. The same conclusion obtrudes itself when one considers an earlier passage[52] in which Mendelssohn discusses the way philosophers before Shaftesbury and Leibniz viewed the problem of providence. They still adhered, he says there, to the old "philosophical prejudice" according to which God "acts solely by laws designed for the generality of things."[53] The particular was considered an object of Divine governance only insofar as it resulted from the general. As such it might conform to a Divine purpose or disagree with it; it had to be admitted by God simply because it was necessitated by the laws designed for the generality of things, or else it had to be put out of the way by a direct intervention, i.e., by a miracle.[54] Here miracle is described as a Divine act of redress from the ordinary course of nature, the assumption being that the particular as such is not an object of Divine providence. This had been the Aristotelian position with which Mendelssohn was familiar from Maimonides's presentation of it,[55] and it had also been the view of Malebranche, which Leibniz had rejected in the *Theodicy*.[56] The Leibnizian theory of Providence as presented here hardly envisages a situation calling for redress. In a world in which every particular is taken care of by Providence, the irregular can never happen. Leibniz does indeed affirm the operation of law in everything, including freaks and monsters.[57] We may display dots or lines on a surface as oddly as we like, the irregularity will nevertheless be amenable to order by some equation.[58] Contingent truths, i.e., truths of fact, though not demonstrable by a finite analysis, are *ex hypothesi* necessary and their integral reason is identifiable by an infinite analysis beyond the scope of the human mind.[59] When Leibniz speaks of the "general law" that transcends the maxims of the natural order comprehensible to the human intellect, he probably means the law that operates in the particular. By including the miracles—the particular *par excellence*—in the incomprehensible operations of the "general law," he confers upon them the status of necessary events. At the same time he robs them of their exceptional character. Mendelssohn does not draw all these consequences from Leibniz's doctrine. He is, after all, dealing here chiefly with Lessing. What emerges from his treatment of miracles in this context is a sense of the overriding importance of the natural as against the miraculous. His view has run full circle.

NOTES

1. Mendelssohn's early acquaintance with this *Correspondence* is attested in his letter of April 29, 1757, to Lessing. See *Moses Mendelssohn Gesammelte Werke Jubiläumsausgabe* (*JubA*), XI (Berlin, 1932; Stuttgart-Cannstatt, 1974), p. 117f.

2. Hobbes did nevertheless accommodate the belief in miracles within his "Christian Commonwealth" (see the references to *Leviathan* in *The English Works*, ed. Molesworth, XI, p. CXXV), and Hume's devastating essay "Of Miracles" ends surprisingly with a plea for faith in miracles (see *An Enquiry Concerning Human Understanding*, section X).

3. Paul Hazard, *The European Mind: 1680–1715* (Cleveland, Ohio, 1963), pp. 155–179.

4. See *JubA*, II (1931; reprint 1972), p. 3f.

5. Mendelssohn's *penchant* toward "revering God in natural events rather than in miracles" (see above, p. 150) bears all the marks of the Enlightenment. It must not be identified with Naḥmanides's mystical faith in the miracles concealed in natural causality. Scholem has rightly characterized Naḥmanides as "an occasionalist of the purest sort" (see Gershom Scholem, *Ursprung und Anfänge der Kabbala*, Berlin, 1962, p. 400f.).

6. See Spinoza, *Tractatus Theologico-Politicus*, ch. VI (§ 2, Bruder).

7. *JubA*, II, p. 307.

8. Ibid.; cf. Alexander Altmann, *Moses Mendelssohns Frühschriften zur Metaphysik* (Tübingen, 1969), pp. 321–3.

9. *JubA*, VII (1930; reprint 1974), pp. 77–9.

10. See below, n. 23.

11. *JubA*, VII, p. 78.

12. Ibid., p. 78; see below, n. 23.

13. See *Kuzari* (ed. Hirschfeld), III, 73, p. 222, lines 23–28; [p. 196]; our reading of Hallevi agrees basically with the interpretation offered in the late Professor Harry A. Wolfson's article, "Judah Halevi on Causality and Miracles," *Meyer Waxman Jubilee Volume* (Jerusalem-Tel Aviv, 1966), pp. 149–53.

14. *Liber Cosri* (Basle, 1660; reprint Westmead, 1971), p. 255.

15. See Maimonides, *Mishnah Commentary* (ed. Qafih), IV, p. 399f. ("Eight Chapters," ch. VIII; ed. Wolff, p. 30 [63ff.]); p. 456 (on Avot V, 5); *Guide of the Perplexed*, I, 66 (ed. Munk, I, p. 85a [295]).

16. *Mishnah Commentary* (ed. Qafih), IV, p. 456; *Guide*, II, 29 (ed. Munk, II, p. 64b [224]).

17. *Guide*, ibid.

18. For criticism, see Gersonides, *Milḥamot Ha-Shem*, VI.ii.10 (Berlin, 1922, p. 447f.; for the charge of misrepresentation, see Shemtob ben Joseph's *Commentary on the Guide*, II, 29, and particularly Isaac Abrabanel, *Naḥalat Avot*, V, 5 (ed. Zilberman, New York, 1953, pp. 323–31) and *Mif'alot Elohim* (Venice, 1592), X.1–6, pp. 72a–78a.

19. *Guide*, ed. Munk, p. 65a [225]. Maimonides expresses the same concern for this kind of "avoidance" (*harab*; *beriḥah*) in the *Treatise on Resurrection*, which was written after completion of the *Guide*. See *Maqālah fī teḥiyyat ha-metim*, ed. Joshua Finkel, *PAAJR*, IX (1938–39), p. 23.

20. This is also the way in which Shemtob ad locum understood the passage: *hinneh mitba'er ba-zeh shetey de'ot be-mofetim*. This line of interpretation is followed by Julius Guttmann, *Die Philosophie des Judentums* (Munich, 1933), pp. 192f.; 390, n. 451, who despite some reservation seems to have decided in its favor; Georges Vajda, *Introduction à la pensée juive du Moyen Age* (Paris, 1947), p. 139; and Joseph Heller, "Maimonides' Theory of Miracle," in: A. Altmann (ed.), *Between East and West: Essays Dedicated to the Memory of Bela Horovitz* (London, 1958), p. 115f., 125. For a different view, see Charles Touati, *La Pensée philosophique et théologique de Gersonide* (Paris, 1973), p. 475, n. 38. In our view, no clear inference as to their respective views can be drawn from the manner in which the translators rendered the text, notably the phrase *kalām gharība jiddan* (Munk, II, 64b, line 11). Though Ibn Tibbon translates it by *devarim zarim me'od*, a passage in his Letter concerning Providence (ed. Diesendruck, *HUCA*, XI, 1936, p. 358, lines 1–8) would seem to indicate that he identified Maimonides with the rabbinic doctrine.

21. Maimonides makes this point with particular force in the *Treatise on Resurrection*.

22. Mendelssohn refers to the Latin versions of the *Mishnah Commentary on Avot*, V; *Guide*, II, 29; and "Eight Chapters" (*Vorrede*, viz., to the *Commentary on Avot*). See *JubA*, VII, p. 77f.; and Rawidowicz's notes, p. 469f.

23. See Charles Bonnet, *La Palingénésie philosophique ou idées sur l'état passé et sur l'état futur des êtres vivans* (Geneva, 1769), II, p. 176. Mendelssohn had before him Johann Caspar Lavater's German version of this text: *Herrn Carl Bonnets philosophische Untersuchung der Beweise für das Christenthum* . . . (Zurich, 1769). In the Güstrow, 1773 edition of this work (which I was able to consult), the passage quoted above is found on p. 38f.

24. See Malebranche, *Traité de la nature et de la grâce* [Amsterdam, 1680], ed. Ginette Dreyfus (Paris, 1958), pp. 185–7; prefatory essay, p. 159.

25. See Leibniz, *Essais de Théodicée* [Amsterdam, 1710], II, § 208 (Gerhardt, VI, 241). Cf. Helmholtz, "Zur Geschichte des Prinzips der kleinsten Aktion," *Sitzungsberichte d. Berliner Akademie d. Wissenschaften*, 1887, 225ff.; Altmann, op. cit., 187ff.

26. *Essais de Théodicée*, II, § 248 (VI, 264).

27. *JubA*, VII, 78f.

28. See *JubA*, I, 23f.; III.2, 102, 222f.

29. Maimonides, *Guide*, I, 69; Leibniz, *Essais de Théodicée*, I, § 27; II, § 382 (VI, 118f., 342); *Causa Dei*, § 9 (VI, 440); H. G. Alexander (ed.), *The Leibniz-Clarke Correspondence* (Manchester-New York, 1956), Leibniz's Third Paper, § 16, p. 29.

30. *Essais de Théodicée*, II, § 249 (VI, 265).

31. *JubA*, VII, 79.

32. See n. 30.

33. *Essais de Théodicée*, Discours préliminaire, § 2–3 (VI, 50–1).

34. Ibid.

35. Ibid., I, § 53–5 (VI, 131f.).

36. Ibid., II, § 248 (VI, 264).

37. Ibid., II, § 206 (VI, 240).

38. Ibid., II, § 207 (VI, 240f.).

39. See C. I. Gerhardt (ed.), *Die philosophischen Schriften von G. W. Leibniz* (Berlin, 1880; reprint Hildesheim, 1960), IV, 410, note.

40. Leibniz, *Metaphysical Discourse*, VII (Gerhardt, IV, 432).

41. Leibniz, loc. cit., XVI (Gerhardt, IV, 441f.).

42. Ibid.

43. For a different view of Leibniz, see Harry A. Wolfson, *Religious Philosophy: A Group of Essays* (Cambridge, Mass., 1961; reprint New York, 1965), pp. 204–6.

44. See Alexander Altmann, *Moses Mendelssohn: A Biographical Study* (University, Alabama, 1973), pp. 686–98.

45. *JubA*, III.2, p. 129.

46. Georges Pons's paper, "Lessings Vorsehungs- und Fortschrittsglaube" (read at the International Lessing-Conference in Cincinnati, Ohio, on March 30, 1976) ably reinforces this view.

47. Lessing, *Nathan the Wise*, Act i, Scene i–ii (Translation by Patrick Maxwell).

48. *JubA*, III.2, p. 128.

49. See above, n. 4.

50. This definition was taken over from a note ("Ueber Wunder und wunderbar") written by Mendelssohn in preparation for *Morgenstunden*; s. *JubA*, VI.1.

51. *JubA*, III.2, p. 128f.

52. *JubA*, III.2, p. 128.

53. The reference is primarily to Malebranche and Bayle, as Leo Strauss, *JubA*, III.2, 305 has pointed out.

54. *JubA*, III.2, p. 128.

55. Maimonides, *Guide*, III, 17.

56. *Essais de Théodicée*, I, § 206 (VI, 240).

57. Ibid., III, § 241 (VI, 261).

58. Leibniz, *Metaphysical Discourse*, VI (Gerhardt, IV, 431).

59. Cf. Emile Bréhier, *The Seventeenth Century*, tr. Wade Baskin (Chicago and London, 1966), pp. 242–45.

9 The Philosophical Roots of Moses Mendelssohn's Plea for Emancipation

In the fall of 1781, when Christian Wilhelm Dohm's treatise "On the Civil Improvement of the Jews" appeared,[1] Moses Mendelssohn reimmersed himself in the study of natural law, a subject that had always attracted him, and certain aspects of which he had already touched upon in previous writings of his.[2] The reason that moved him to return to the subject is not far to seek. The issue of the civil admission of the Jews, which had been raised in Dohm's treatise, was entering a new stage after the promulgation of the Patent of Tolerance in Bohemia on October 19, 1781.[3] It was obviously desirable to foster a lively debate concerning the matter in Prussia, where the government showed no intention of following the precedent set by Joseph II. As Mendelssohn put it in a letter to his friend Friedrich Nicolai: "I think that at the present time one ought to keep the public constantly *en haleine* [in suspense] in regard to this matter, and that the pros and cons of this issue should continue to be a subject of debate."[4] He felt that as a philosopher he might interject into the discussion viewpoints of his own. Hence his resumed preoccupation with natural law. The first result of his efforts was a short fragment "On Perfect and Imperfect Duties," which was written in November 1781.[5] The ideas sketched therein became the nucleus of his theory of the relationship between church and state, a theory that was meant to undergird his plea for emancipation.[6]

Mendelssohn first presented his notions about church and state in the Preface to Marcus Herz's German version of Manasseh ben Israel's *Vindiciae Judaeorum*, published by him in the early spring of 1782 as a "Supplement" to Dohm's earlier treatise.[7] Mendelssohn modestly remarked that there was little he could add, Dohm having all but exhausted the philosophical and political aspects of the matter.[8] In actual fact, however, Mendelssohn added an entirely new dimension to Dohm's humanitarian plea by offering an outline of his theory of state and church that had a direct bearing on the civil admission of the Jews. Yet it did so only toward the end, and almost incidentally, in connection with his remonstration against the use of the ban by the rabbinate.[9] Even so, his remarks were widely noted and provoked diverse reactions, in response to which Mendelssohn wrote his treatise *Jerusalem or On Religious Power and Judaism* (1783).[10] It is here that we find his full-fledged treatment of state and religion, from which important consequences follow for the issue of civil equality. Although the plea for Jewish emancipation is not the overt theme of the book, no one reading it could fail to see the implications of Mendelssohn's political theory. It is the purpose of this paper to articulate what was deliberately left unsaid yet could not be missed upon the least reflection. In so doing we shall be tracing the philosophical roots of Mendelssohn's plea for the civil admission of the Jews.

The theory of the origin and functions of the state as presented in Part One of *Jerusalem* emerges from an elaborate discussion of the rights and duties incumbent upon man in the state of nature. Mendelssohn assumed that, even prior to the social contract, man has both rights and duties—a view he took over from the German natural law school (Samuel Pufendorf, Christian Wolff) and which he found stated also in Adam Ferguson's *Principles of Moral Philosophy* (1769). In 1772 Christian Garve had brought out an annotated German translation of this work,[11] and there is clear evidence that Mendelssohn availed himself of Garve's notes.[12] The distinction between perfect and imperfect rights and duties, which is the cornerstone of Mendelssohn's theory, goes back to Pufendorf: if a right or duty is of such a nature that it may be exacted by force, it is called a "perfect" right or duty. If it is merely in the nature of a claim that may be directed to another person's goodwill (e.g., asking for charity), it is termed an "imperfect" right, and the corresponding duty is an "imperfect" duty; that is, a mere duty of conscience, which is nonenforceable. Omitting to fulfill a perfect duty is tantamount to injustice, whereas noncompliance with a duty of conscience is merely unfair. Having clarified these elementary concepts, Mendelssohn continued: "Man cannot be happy without beneficence—whether it be passive, through receiving it, or active, through extending it. He cannot attain perfection except through mutual assistance." Man is therefore obliged to use for the benefit of his fellow men as much of his property as he can spare without detriment to his own well-being. Conversely, he may expect to be supported by others, should he find himself in need of help. In the state of nature it is left entirely to the individual's discretion to decide the amount, the timing, and the nature of his benefactions. There may be competing claims on his beneficence, and since a person's means are limited and not all claims can be satisfied, the benefactor must have the choice in the matter. "Hence, in the state of nature I—and I alone—am entitled to decide whether, to what extent, when, to whose benefit, and under what conditions I am obliged to practice benevolence." It follows that in the state of nature all *positive* duties are nonenforceable, imperfect duties; just as positive rights are imperfect rights. In the natural state only duties and rights of omission are perfect: I am perfectly (i.e., absolutely and unconditionally) obliged *not* to injure anyone, and I am just as perfectly empowered to prevent anyone from injuring me.[13]

The identical view (no doubt borrowed from Ferguson) had been expressed in 1773 by Samuel Johnson, as reported by James Boswell in his *Life of Johnson*: "Sir, you must consider that we have perfect and imperfect obligations. Perfect obligations, which are generally not to do something, are clear and positive, as 'thou shalt not kill.' But charity, for instance, is not definable by limits. It is a duty to give to the poor, but no man can say how much another should give to the poor."[14] Mendelssohn, however, added a rider: by concluding contracts, man left his natural state and entered into more or less defined social relationships. His own nature urged him to do this so as to change his undecided, unsettled rights and duties into something more settled and decided. Marriage contracts obviously reflected such a desire for stable relations. The social contract by which the state came into being was not essentially different from all other privately concluded agreements. Though the right to decide on the merits of competing claims and to dispense his goods rested with the individual, it seemed advisable to renounce the right of autonomous decision by means of a special contract; that is, by a legal agreement specifying what portions of his rights a person could be compelled to give up for the good of society. By virtue of the social contract a certain part of the person's duties of conscience therefore became compulsory duties; they were now enforceable by the state. Hence if a citizen was remiss in the fulfillment of his stipulated duties, the state had the authority and power to compel his action. The social contract conferring such authority and power had come into being either by tacit agreement or, in rare cases, by explicit compacts.

Underlying this derivation of state power from the transfer of personal privilege through the social contract, is a highly optimistic view of man in the state of nature. Mendelssohn distinctly rejected Hobbes's view that the social contract brought to an end man's natural state of anarchy, in which there was a war of all against all. If it were true, he argued, that natural man was under no moral obligation (as Hobbes had suggested), what could prevent him from breaking contracts at any time when he had the physical power to do so with impunity? He believed himself to have discovered evidence of an implied admission on Hobbes's part that natural man was, in fact, not devoid of morality.[15] In *Jerusalem*, Mendelssohn did not discuss Rousseau's theory, but we know from an earlier work of his that he interpreted Rousseau in a manner that brought the French philosopher somewhat into line with his own view. In the Epistle (*Sendschreiben*) to Lessing which he appended to his German translation (1756) of Rousseau's second *Discours*, he claimed that on closer inspection Rousseau credited even the savage with more than animal instincts. He pointed out that the feeling of pity ascribed by the *Discours* to presocial man, necessarily implied love, and that love, in turn, was based on the pleasure found in harmony and order; moreover, that Rousseau had also attributed to him *perfectibilité*, which could mean nothing less than a striving for perfection and hence an actual, not merely potential, propensity.[16] In reply to the Epistle, Lessing voiced doubts as to the correctness of Mendelssohn's reading of the *Discours*,[17] and it seems obvious from Martin Rang's incisive analysis of Rousseau's doctrine of man that Lessing was right. By *perfectibilité* Rousseau understood the almost infinite malleability of man, not any moral quality.[18] Yet such was Mendelssohn's faith in natural law that he could not conceive of man in any condition as bereft of reason and morality. For Rousseau, man became *man* only when he became a citizen; only the state and its laws make humane coexistence possible.[19] For Mendelssohn, on the other hand, the state only transforms imperfect into perfect duties; it cannot create compulsory obligations where no duties of conscience existed previously. Hence man must be assumed to have been man even prior to state law.[20] Mendelssohn would agree with Rousseau, however, that the state alone secures the equality of men.

This brings us to the heart of the matter that we wish to discuss: the way in which Mendelssohn views the nature and function of the state as inextricably bound up with civil equality. To put it succinctly: The social contract by which man relinquished the state of nature and surrendered the legislation of positive duties to the state must by its very nature be considered as limited in scope. It applies exclusively to such determination of positive duties as was within man's original power to surrender, but it has no validity in the sphere of inalienable rights and duties. In more concrete terms: Through the social contract the individual renounces his right to be the sole arbiter of the extent, manner, and timing of his benefactions; his contributions to the common weal are henceforth imposed upon him to a large extent by law, and the state has coercive power to secure them. Yet the individual can at no time have yielded to his fellow man in the state of nature, or to the state through the social contract, the right to determine his own thoughts and beliefs. No one can, for the sake of good fellowship or any earthly reason, go so far as to relinquish his innermost and private sentiments and convictions. Hence the state cannot have acquired the right of coercion where matters of personal conviction are concerned. The intimate domain of a person's faith must therefore remain inviolate, free from any kind of state interference.[21] A similar view had been expressed by Hobbes, Spinoza, and Locke. What was new in Mendelssohn's argumentation was the specific manner in which he established the principle from the very nature of the social contract. Yet this was not all. He went on to apply the principle in a highly ingenious manner: Granting the least privilege in civil matters to members of a certain church, or withholding certain freedoms from dissidents, he maintained, amounts to a kind of coercion. For every privilege is a bribe, and every denial of freedom is a punishment. A state that accords honor and dignity to one set of believers, and decrees or permits contempt and poverty for another, thereby coerces human beings to think and feel—or at least tempts them to think and feel—in a certain state-approved manner. For such coercion there is no valid legal foundation. Such an invasion of privacy is utterly beyond the competence of the state.[22]

With one masterful stroke Mendelssohn thus demolished all semblance of legitimacy attaching to civil discrimination against the Jew. The very definition of the state as the legal executor of the social contract was shown to invalidate any claim to preferential treatment granted to any church. The premium paid to any group in terms of civil rights was unmasked, as it were, as an unlawful act of coercion of conscience. Without uttering a plea, without a single word of direct appeal, Mendelssohn stated the case for the civil admission of the Jews. In his Preface to *Vindiciae Judaeorum*, he had noted that previous debates about tolerance had been concerned solely with dissident Christians, while Jews, Muslims, and believers in natural religion hardly entered into the picture at all. Lessing in his poem *Nathan the Wise* (1779), and Dohm in his treatise, had considered the "prerogatives of humanity as a whole," and an "admirable monarch" (Joseph II) had commenced to implement them.[23] In *Jerusalem*, Mendelssohn was more reserved. He praised Frederick the Great, his own monarch, for the "wise maxim" of tolerance, which he was the first ruler in the eighteenth century to apply, but he did not explicitly urge the king to do more than he had already done. Mendelssohn even condoned the prevailing discrimination and expected a change for the better only in the distant future. To quote his words: "True, with wise moderation he left the privileges of the public[24] religion intact, preserving thereby the *status quo*. Perhaps centuries of culture and preparation will still be required before men will understand that privileges accorded on grounds of religion are neither lawful nor really beneficial, and that it would be a true blessing if all civil discrimination based on religion were entirely abolished."[25] While leaving no doubt that he considered discrimination of this sort to be devoid of all legality, he was content to state his view without pleading the case of civil admission. It was an attitude worthy of a philosopher.

There was yet another philosophical approach that indirectly advanced the cause he had so much at heart. Its immediate concern was the separation of church and state. Locke had drawn a neat distinction between the "commonwealth" as "a society of men constituted only for the procuring, preserving and advancing of their own civil interests" and the church as "a voluntary society of men" devoted to "the public worshipping of God in such a manner as they judge acceptable to Him, and effectual to the salvation of their souls."[26] Mendelssohn advanced two objections to this strict division between the respective spheres of interest of church and state. First, if the state concerned itself exclusively with the temporal welfare of its citizens and left their eternal felicity entirely to the church, it was inevitable that the church, being in charge of men's ultimate vocation, would claim superiority over the state and assert its authority in cases of conflicting duties. Second, Mendelssohn considered it neither true nor in the best interests of man to distinguish so sharply between the temporal and the eternal. It seemed to him that Locke's radical separation of temporal and eternal welfare was bound to encourage men to neglect their duties as citizens on earth "in the hope of thereby becoming better citizens of heaven."[27] In a similar vein, Rousseau had voiced the fear that a truly good Christian might lose all interest in the mundane affairs of state, believing that only life eternal mattered.[28] Against such undue emphasis on the world-to-come, Mendelssohn quoted a well-known rabbinic saying (*Avot* 4:12), which he paraphrased as follows: "This life is a vestibule in which we have to conduct ourselves as we wish to appear in the innermost chamber."[29] This being the case, the bifurcation of society into state and religion should not mean a total separation. The state has no interest in religion insofar as strictly theological tenets are concerned, but the state is vitally interested in religion insofar as it teaches morality and social conduct. If the nation is to be governed ultimately by the inculcation of moral principles, rather than by fear of the coercive power of the state, the church must be considered an invaluable asset to the state.[30]

By emphasizing the moral function of religion, Mendelssohn found a way of integrating the church into the state's sphere of interest without permitting any state interference in the theologies and internal affairs of the various churches. By the same token he placed all religions on one and the same level vis-à-vis the state. Again, the principle of equality was asserted, and seeing that the Jew was being discriminated against on purely religious grounds, it followed with inexorable logic that the denial of civil equality to the Jew was unjustifiable. The state was entitled to apply one criterion only; namely, the degree of moral influence exercised by the various churches. It was by this yardstick, and it alone, that a religious community was to be judged from a political aspect.

How seriously Mendelssohn took this criterion may be gauged by the fact that he assigned to the state the duty as well as the right to supervise the churches in some broad fashion to prevent the spread of antisocial ideas. Locke had excluded atheists from the commonwealth on the assumption that "promises, covenants, and oaths, which are the bonds of human society, can have no hold upon an atheist."[31] The question of whether atheism and morality could exist together had been a major topic of debate for some time past. Pierre Bayle and John Toland, taking their cue from Plutarch, had argued that superstition and idolatry were far more injurious to morality than atheism, but Mendelssohn strongly contested this view.[32] In his *Jerusalem*, he referred again to this question, pointing out that one evil was as pernicious as the other, and suggesting that it was incumbent upon the state to ensure that doctrines that undermined the body politic would not take root. Yet he stressed the need to do so only "from a distance"—that is, in the most general way, without entering into philosophical or theological minutiae; in other words, without exercising coercive power and assuming the mantle of authority in the intellectual realm.[33]

I suggest that Mendelssohn's plea for noninterference by the state in matters of specific doctrine, religious or otherwise, serves again to underline his advocacy of the state's complete neutrality and impartiality vis-à-vis the churches. Dohm held exactly the same view. When the Austrian emperor expelled a deistic sect of Bohemian peasants and in the expulsion order invoked "the only saving faith," Dohm was outraged, both at the action itself and at the formula used, the latter being "wholly unworthy of the official style of an enlightened government."[34] Dohm's reaction shows that in his view the state was to conduct its business in a completely secular vein. The notion of a Christian state was utterly foreign to him. It was this secularized concept of the state that enabled Mendelssohn to base his hopes for the Jews' civil admission on the intrinsic character of the state-church relationship.

Mendelssohn's theory would have been a mere blueprint for

utopia had not the concept of the church itself undergone a radical metamorphosis in the more enlightened ecclesiastical circles that had adopted "collegianism."[35] This school of thought divested the church of its traditional character as a divinely founded mystical body, and considered it instead, by analogy with the state, as a free association of like-minded individuals, established by contract. The theory of the churches as mere "collegia" goes back to Hugo Grotius and Samuel Pufendorf. It was developed and designated "collegianism" by Christian M. Pfaff of Tübingen in his "Academic Addresses on Ecclesiastical Law" (1742). J. H. Boehmer's monumental *Jus Ecclesiasticum Protestanticum* reflected the fundamental outlook of collegianism in its repudiation of the ban as an instrument for the enforcement of church discipline.[36] A work of similar orientation was Israel Gottlieb Canz's *Disciplinae morales omnes*, from which Mendelssohn made excerpts in preparation for writing *Jerusalem*.[37] In one of his notes on those excerpts, Mendelssohn referred to an inconsistency in Canz's provisions for the treatment of dissidents: While they were not to be deprived of their civil rights, they had to forgo the ecclesiastical rights enjoyed by other members of the church.[38] We are not surprised to find that this position was regarded as unsatisfactory by Mendelssohn, who in his Preface to Manasseh's *Vindiciae Judaeorum* had made the point that ecclesiastical ostracism inevitably injured the social and civil status of a person.[39] His critique of Canz also anticipated the strong stand he made in *Jerusalem* on what he called the pretentious claim of the post-Reformation churches to undisputed authority and the right of coercion. In his view the churches still behaved as if they represented the Church (with a capital C), whereas in fact they were freely established religious associations —a fact conceded by collegianism, as we have noted. Whereas collegianism clung to the notion of the contractual origin of the churches, however, Mendelssohn strenuously denied this thesis. Only the state had come into being as a result of a social contract. In the case of religious associations the concept of contractual origin made no sense whatever. He considered this a point of tremendous significance, and he defined the difference as follows: The coercive power of the state is the corollary of the social contract. It derives from the surrender of the individuals' natural prerogative to decide in cases of competing claims, as has been explained above. In the case of religion or church the raison d'être for a social contract is lacking. The idea of a transference of the right to settle conflicting claims to one's benevolence simply has no place where religion is concerned. For religion is essentially a concern for one's relation to God. No conflict of duties toward God—the settling of which might have been passed on to the church—can be conceived. For which benefits could God receive from man? It follows that the church could never have acquired the right to use coercion. "Divine religion . . . does not prod men with an iron rod; it guides them with 'bands of love.' It draws no avenging sword, dispenses no worldly goods, arrogates to itself no right to earthly possessions, and usurps no external power over any person's mind. Its sole weapons are reason and persuasion; its strength is the divine power of truth."[40]

Mendelssohn concluded his Preface to *Vindiciae Judaeorum* with an appeal to the "most enlightened and most pious" among the rabbis and Jewish elders to renounce the weapon of *ḥerem*, and at the end of Part One of his *Jerusalem* he struck the same note again. Seen in the context of his concern for civil admission, this powerful advocacy of a totally noncoercive type of religion appears as the final effort on Mendelssohn's part to facilitate the integration of the Jews into the secular state. Coercive power in the form of *ḥerem* had indicated a measure of Jewish autonomy and was a relic of Jewish self-government in the Middle Ages. Unlike the excommunication practiced by the church, it was not entirely ecclesiastical, but had a certain political connotation. It was the vestige of a state within the state.[41] (Not that the exercise of this form of power had been left completely to the discretion of the rabbinate. We know, for example, that a royal resolution of May 5, 1781, deprived the chief rabbi of Altona of the right to pronounce the "great ban" against any member of the community.[42]) To Mendelssohn the use of *ḥerem* seemed incompatible with the desired integration of Jewry into the body politic. In the context of his theory of state and religion, it had lost all validity. The very desire to wield this instrument of power was to him evidence of an attitude that had to be overcome if the community was to qualify for civil admission.[43]

On the other hand, Mendelssohn saw no incompatibility between civil admission and the preservation of the Jews' separate identity as a nation. When Johann David Michaelis argued, against Dohm's plea, that so long as the Jews kept their laws they would be unable to coalesce with the citizenry, Mendelssohn published a spirited reply in Part Two of Dohm's treatise:[44] He did not deny that the Jews wished to preserve their separate national identity. In his view, however, a group's readiness to coalesce was no criterion of worthiness as far as civil rights were concerned. The only legitimate question was, Can the Jews be expected to discharge the duties incumbent upon citizens? He had no doubt that the answer to this question was in the affirmative. But the issue of *ḥerem* was of a different order.

A philosophical motif of a truly metaphysical nature, bearing on the plea for emancipation, appears in the last paragraph of *Jerusalem*. We may call it an argument for religious pluralism. It is embedded in an appeal to the Jewish community not to sacrifice Jewish identity on the altar of emancipation. It had become clear to Mendelssohn that the celebrated Patent of Tolerance as promulgated in Bohemia contained a clause that put a premium on conversion to Christianity.[45] He himself had been implored to lead his people toward a union with enlightened Christianity.[46] It seemed that the issue of civil rights was being linked to the lure of baptism or some more moderate form of religious unification. It was against this danger that Mendelssohn called upon his brethren to be on their guard. As he put it, there was no purpose in trying to effect a specious unity through some contrived theological formula of compromise. The endeavor to obliterate distinctiveness was tantamount to thwarting the purposes of Providence; for variety, not uniformity, was God's design. This metaphysical concept was not stated here for the first time or merely at random. It was part and parcel of Mendelssohn's philosophy. In 1777 the baron Karl Theodor von Dalberg had solicited Mendelssohn's opinion on the treatise "Reflections on the Universe," which Dalberg had published that year. According to Dalberg, the universal law governing the coexistence of things was to be found in their tendency to assimilate with each other. Mendelssohn had criticized this thesis. He had distinguished between sameness and unity. Sameness cancels the manifold, unity connects it. The degree of unity depends on the variety it combines. The more the manifold is connected, the greater the ensuing unity. The forces of nature seem to aim not so much at the obliteration of differences as at the connection of the manifold.[47] In *Jerusalem*, Mendelssohn applied this metaphysical principle to the socioreligious issue at stake. Religious pluralism, not uniformity, was the design of Providence. The civil admission of the Jews had to be dissociated from any demand for Jewish self-obliteration.

In his endeavor to secure the Jews' civil admission, Mendelssohn developed a theory of church and state that went beyond the principle of toleration advocated by Locke. What he propounded was a political doctrine conducive to equalitarianism. There is good reason to assume that Mendelssohn was emboldened to advance his strikingly progressive ideas because the principle of religious equality was just then being implemented in the wake of the American Revolution. That he closely followed the events across the Atlantic is obvious from a footnote at the end of *Jerusalem*: "Alas, now even the Congress in America rehashes the old slogan and speaks of a *dominant* religion."[48] This remark clearly shows that until this latest news reached him he had been greatly encouraged by the American example. He may have guessed that the setback was only a temporary affair. In the very year in which Mendelssohn wrote *Jerusalem* (1782), Thomas Jefferson wrote his *Notes on Virginia*, in which he expressed the view that a variety of religious opinions was in the best interests of progress and freedom; that the legitimate powers of government extended only to such acts as were injurious to others; and that nobody was injured by his neighbor's beliefs.[49]

Some similarity in outlook may be noted between Mendelssohn's political creed and the views expressed three years later by another admirer of the American Revolution, Richard Price, who was a fellow both of the Royal Society in England and of the Academy of Arts and Sciences in New England. Like Mendelssohn, he had criticized the moral-sense theory of Francis Hutcheson and, like Mendelssohn, he had shown considerable interest in the theory of probability.[50] In 1785 he published in London his *Observations on the Importance of the American Revolution*, in which he wrote as follows:

> In Liberty of Conscience I include much more than *Toleration*. . . . Not only all *Christians*, but all *men* of all religions ought to be considered by a State as equally entitled to its protection as far as they demean them-

selves honestly and peaceably. *Toleration* can take place only where there is a civil establishment of a particular mode of religion; that is, where a predominant sect enjoys *exclusive* advantages, and makes the encouragement of its own mode of faith and worship a part of the constitution of the State; but at the same time thinks fit to *suffer* the exercise of other modes of faith and worship. Thanks be to God, the new American States are at present strangers to such establishments. In this respect, as well as many others, they have shewn, in framing their constitution, a degree of wisdom and liberality which is above all praise.[51]

There is no evidence that Price's treatise came to Mendelssohn's notice. Yet Mendelssohn would have been highly pleased not only by the paragraph just quoted but also by another one bearing on an issue treated in Part One of *Jerusalem*, an issue that had involved Mendelssohn in some unpleasantness. He had attacked the imposition of oaths upon the appointment of ministers of religion, and he had dared to question the veracity of many of the oaths taken. In this context he had referred to the thirty-nine articles of faith to which the Anglican clergy, including the lord bishops of the realm, had to subscribe.[52] Johann David Michaelis had reprimanded him severely for what he considered a calumny, and Mendelssohn had to vindicate himself.[53] He would have been amused had he read what Price had to say on the very same subject:

The Church Establishment in *England* is one of the mildest and best sort. But even here what a snare has it been to integrity? And what a check to free enquiry? . . . What a burthen is it on the consciences of some of its best clergy, who, in consequence of being bound down to a system they do not approve, and having no support except that which they derive from conforming to it, find themselves under the hard necessity of either *prevaricating* or *starving*?—No one doubts but that the English clergy in general could with more truth declare that they *do not*, than that they *do* give their *unfeigned assent to all and every thing* contained in the thirty-nine Articles and the Book of Common-prayer; and yet, with a solemn declaration to this purpose, are they obliged to enter upon an office which above all offices requires those who exercise it to be examples of simplicity and sincerity.—Who can help execrating the cause of such an evil?[54]

It is astonishing to find how correctly Mendelssohn had diagnosed the situation created in England by the existence of an established church. The specific case he had presented was ostensibly concerned only with the separation of church and state. Yet the aim that was uppermost in his mind was the civil admission of the Jews.

In conclusion we may say: Mendelssohn's proposal to transcend all religious divisions as irrelevant in terms of human rights was a liberal solution. In arguing from certain premises of natural law, he clearly considered the state of nature not as a historical phase preceding the establishment of political society, but as a hypothesis abstracted from all the obligations voluntarily accepted by men for the best of society, a hypothesis that considered man in his very essence.[55] Whether Hobbes, Locke, and Rousseau regarded the state of nature as a merely hypothetical assumption or as a historical fact is a matter of debate among scholars. It seems that Mendelssohn looked upon the state of nature as a present reality insofar as the position of the Jews in civil society was concerned. In one of his notebooks he entered the following remark à propos Rousseau's Second *Discours*: "One whose rights are violated in an illicit fashion is being warred against: hence the Jews are continually being warred against."[56] The term "war" is reminiscent of Hobbes, as is the reference to the violation of rights. It was Hobbes who in the discussion of natural law shifted the emphasis from duties to rights, as Leo Strauss has shown:[57] In the natural state there are no absolute or unconditional duties; only the right of self-preservation is unconditional and absolute. Consequently, the prime function of civil society is the safeguarding of this natural right of each individual. Mendelssohn, though disagreeing with Hobbes in most respects, fully shared his emphasis on this inalienable right of the individual; and from this liberal doctrine followed the view that the Jew, who was constantly being warred against, must be emancipated.

NOTES

1. Christian Wilhelm Dohm, *Über die bürgerliche Verbesserung der Juden* (Berlin & Stettin, 1781). For the date of publication, see Alexander Altmann, *Moses Mendelssohn: A Biographical Study* (University, Alabama 1973) [hereafter referred to as *Mendelssohn*], p. 454.

2. See my essay "Moses Mendelssohn über Naturrecht und Naturzustand" in: Norbert Hinske, ed., *"Ich handle mit Vernunft"* (Hamburg, 1981).

3. See Jacob Katz's essay in *Zion*, vol. xxix (1964), pp. 127f., where the principal bibliographical references are given. The Austrian version of the Patent followed on January 2, 1782.

4. The letter that contains this statement was first published in Alexander Altmann, "Neuerschlossene Briefe Moses Mendelssohns an Friedrich Nicolai," *Lessing Yearbook V 1973* (Munich 1973), p. 42 (no. 49). The date is February 8, 1782.

5. Published first in *Moses Mendelssohn's gesammelte Schriften*, ed. by G. B. Mendelssohn (Leipzig 1843–1845) [hereafter referred to as *GS*], IV. 1, pp. 128–31.

6. The term "emancipation" is used here anachronistically, since it was not employed at the time. See Jacob Katz, "The Term 'Jewish Emancipation': Its Origin and Historical Impact," *Studies in Nineteenth-Century Jewish Intellectual History*, ed. by Alexander Altmann (Cambridge, Mass. 1964), pp. 1–25.

7. *Manasseh Ben Israel, Rettung der Juden. Aus dem Englischen übersetzt. Nebst einer Vorrede von Moses Mendelssohn. Als ein Anhang zu des Hrn. Kriegsraths Dohm Abhandlung: Über die bürgerliche Verbesserung der Juden* (Berlin & Stettin 1782); reproduced in *GS*, III, 177–254.

8. Ibid., p. 181.

9. Ibid., pp. 194–202.

10. *Jerusalem oder über religiöse Macht und Judentum* (Berlin 1883; *GS* III, 255–262). See below, pp. 170–89 and *Mendelssohn*, pp. 489–96, 502–13.

11. *Adam Fergusons Grundsätze der Moralphilosophie*. Übersetzt und mit einigen Anmerkungen versehen von Christian Garve (Leipzig 1772).

12. See *GS*, III, 279, note; *Mendelssohn*, pp. 523, 525.

13. *GS*, III, 269–81.

14. Quoted in *Mendelssohn*, p. 843, n. 74.

15. *GS*, III, 259–61. By acknowledging the sovereign's fear of Divine power (*Leviathan*, II, 30), Mendelssohn argued, Hobbes had shown the possible source of a "solemn right of nature."

16. See *Moses Mendelssohn gesammelte Schriften Jubiläumsausgabe* [*JubA*], II (Berlin 1931; reprint, Stuttgart 1972), 86–90.

17. See Lessing's letter of January 21, 1756; *JubA*, XI (Berlin 1932), 34.

18. See Martin Rang, *Rousseaus Lehre vom Menschen* (Göttingen 1959), pp. 129–40; Leo Strauss, *Natural Right and History* (Chicago 1953), p. 271.

19. Rang, op. cit., pp. 143–46.

20. *GS*, III, 196, 281.

21. Ibid., pp. 197, 285f.

22. Ibid., pp. 285–86.

23. Ibid., pp. 179–80.

24. Lit. "external" (*äusseren*), contrasting the interior worship of man with the external, public worship of the dominant church. The same sentiments are expressed in Christian Siegmund Krause's anonymously published work *Ueber kirchliche Gewalt. Nach Moses Mendelssohn* (Berlin 1786), in which Krause rejects the notion of an established religion as advocated by Emmerich de Vattel and G. L. Böhmer; see pp. 39, 44.

25. *GS*, III, pp. 300–02.

26. See *The Works of John Locke* (London 1823; reprint, Aalen 1963), VI, 5ff. ("A Letter concerning Toleration," First Letter); cf. *GS*, III, 261.

27. Ibid., pp. 262–63.

28. Jean-Jacques Rousseau, *Oeuvres complètes*, III, 465 (*Du Contrat social*, IV).

29. *GS*, III, 263.

30. Ibid., pp. 264–67.

31. Locke, op. cit., p. 47. See my essay "Gewissensfreiheit und Toleranz: Eine begriffsgeschichtliche Untersuchung" in: Cécile Lowenthal Hensel and Rudolf Elvers, ed., *Mendelssohn Studien* iv, (Berlin 1979), pp. 9–46, esp. pp. 43ff.

32. *JubA*, II, 21f.; see Fritz Bamberger's note, pp. 375f.

33. *GS*, III, 287.

34. See *Mendelssohn*, pp. 462f.

35. See ibid., pp. 518–19.

36. See *Iusti Henningii Boehmeri Ius Ecclesiasticum Protestanticum*, vol. V, 3d ed. (Halle, 1763), Book V, chap. 34, par. 55, pp. 962ff. See below, pp. 170–89.

37. See *Mendelssohn*, p. 519.

38. Ibid.

39. *GS*, III, 197–201.

40. Ibid., pp. 282, 294–98.

41. See below, p. 185.

42. See Heinz Mosche Graupe, *Die Statuten der drei Gemeinden Altona, Hamburg und Wandsbeck* (Hamburg 1973), I, 93, n. 118.

43. See *Mendelssohn*, p. 471.

44. See ibid., pp. 465f.

45. See ibid., p. 462.

46. See ibid., pp. 495f., 508ff.

47. *JubA*, XII.2, 90–92; *Mendelssohn*, pp. 313–15; 809, n. 5.

48. *GS*, III, 361, note.

49. See Anson Phelps Stokes, *Church and State in the United States* (New York 1950), I, 334f. It was due to James Madison's efforts that Patrick Henry's assessment bill imposing a federal tax "for the support of the Christian religion, or of some Christian church, denomination or communion of Christians, or of some form of Christian worship" did not become law. See ibid., I, 388f.

50. Richard Price, *Review of the Principal Questions and Difficulties in Morals* (1758; 3d ed. 1787), ed. by D. D. Raphael (Oxford 1948). Price's *Observations on Reversionary Payments* (1771), which laid the foundations of a scientific system of life insurance, was based on his work on a problem in the theory of probability; see *Encyclopaedia Britannica* (1964), vol. 18, pp. 467f.; and Thomas Bayes, *Facsimile of two papers* . . . I. An essay toward solving a problem in the doctrine of chances, with Richard Price's foreword and discussion . . . (Washington 1940). For Mendelssohn's critique of Hutcheson, see my *Moses Mendelssohns Frühschriften zur Metaphysik* (Tübingen 1969), pp. 170, 344–56; for his theory of probability, see ibid., pp. 209–51.

51. Richard Price, *Observations on the Importance of the American Revolution and the Means of making it a Benefit to the World* (London 1785), pp. 34–35.

52. *GS*, III, 291–92.

53. See *Mendelssohn*, pp. 529–31.

54. Price, op. cit., pp. 36–37.

55. See *JubA*, II, 92 and my article quoted in n. 2.

56. *JubA*, II, 8.

57. Op. cit., pp. 182f. For more detailed analyses of Mendelssohn's political views, see the following studies of mine: "Moses Mendelssohn's Quest for Liberty," in: *Humanität und Dialog. Lessing Yearbook XII* (1981); *Prinzipien politischer Theorie bei Mendelssohn und Kant.* Trierer Universitätsreden (Trier, 1981); and the essay quoted in n. 2.

10 Moses Mendelssohn on Excommunication: *The Ecclesiastical Law Background*

In my Mendelssohn biography[1] and in my edition of "Letters from Dohm to Mendelssohn,"[2] I have stated the facts concerning the amicable controversy between Mendelssohn and Dohm about the proposed granting of the *Bannrecht* to the Jewish "colony." Briefly, these facts are as follows. Dohm[3] had suggested that "like every other ecclesiastical society (*kirchliche Gesellschaft*), the Jewish one should possess, for a time or in perpetuity, the right of exclusion, and the sentence passed by the rabbis (*das Erkenntniß der Rabbinen*) should be aided by the magistrate." He had called this proposed right *Bannrecht*, a term that in the language of ecclesiastical law was ambiguous in that it related both to the mere exclusion from certain religious privileges ("minor ban") and to the denial of such privileges plus civil ostracism of varying degrees ("major ban"). What he had had in mind was the minor ban, as he pointed out in a letter (dated December 14, 1781) replying to Mendelssohn's privately communicated criticism.[4] In the same letter he expressed his desire to clarify the issue through an *addendum* in the forthcoming French edition of his treatise and he submitted the text he had prepared for Mendelssohn's approval. We must assume that Mendelssohn raised no objection at the time, for the French edition[5] as well as the revised edition of the German book[6] contain a caveat to the effect that the magistrate must never permit a rabbi to pronounce a ban that excludes a member of his community from social intercourse, degrades him in the eyes of his coreligionists, interferes with his business, or even exposes him to persecution by the mob. The imposition of fines was likewise declared to be inappropriate as a punishment of religious precepts. In accordance with the principle of keeping church membership and citizenship apart, rabbinic power was to be confined to the exclusion of transgressors from the synagogue and the privileges connected therewith.

How little Mendelssohn was satisfied with Dohm's distinction could be gauged already from Moses Wessely's pamphlet, *Anmerkungen zu der Schrift des Herrn Dohm, über die bürgerliche Verfassung [sic] der Juden* (Altona, 1782), which appeared under the initials of Johann Christoph Unzer, a respected citizen of Altona, and which bore the impress of Mendelssohn's thought on the subject, anticipating the point made later in the year in Mendelssohn's Preface to *Manasseh Ben Israel Rettung der Juden aus dem Englischen übersetzt.* Wessely took issue with the very solution suggested by Dohm. Is it true, he asked, that an ejected member of the church can retain his status as a very useful and respected citizen? Do not ban and excommunication invariably result in civil injury, and is this not in fact their avowed object? In a footnote Wessely referred to an instance of "abuse" of ecclesiastical power that had become a sort of cause célèbre: the imposition of a minor ban (*Unterbann*; *nidduy*) accompanied by the threat of the great anathema (*des großen Fluchbanns*, *ḥerem*) upon a certain Samuel Marcus jun. in Altona by the chief rabbi of that community. A tract by August Friedrich Cranz, *Ueber den Missbrauch der geistlichen Macht und der weltlichen Herrschaft in Glaubenssachen durch Beispiele aus dem jetzigen Jahrhundert ins Licht gesetzt* (Berlin, 1781), had exploited that incident. Because of his mistrust of the reliability of the author, Dohm had ignored this case when preparing the addendum for the French version of his treatise. After the publication of Wessely's pamphlet, Dohm no longer hesitated to refer to the Altona incident.[7] Mendelssohn himself made mention of it in his Preface to *Manasseh Ben Israel*, but he reserved judgment until the case was decided by the civil authorities before which it had been brought.[8] He obviously considered it germane to the issue of the *Bannrecht*, which figures so prominently in the Preface. The Altona chief rabbi, whose readiness to use the weapon of *ḥerem* he had had occasion to experience at close quarters not so long before,[9] had become to him something of a symbol in a way similar to the rôle Pastor Goeze had assumed in Lessing's life.[10]

In the Preface to *Manasseh Ben Israel* (dated March 19, 1782)

Mendelssohn openly voiced his opposition to Dohm's proposal and he reiterated the salient point, without reference to Dohm, a year later in his book *Jerusalem*.[11] His critique of Dohm is well known, but what seems to have escaped attention hitherto is the ultimate direction of his attack: the ecclesiastical law, or as he was fond of calling it "the so-called ecclesiastical law" (*das sogenannte Kirchenrecht*), "so-called" because he denied juridical status to the church as a body not entitled to coercive power.[12] He did indeed point out against Dohm that no excommunication was "without civil consequences" and that "the borderlines of this fine distinction between the civil and the ecclesiastic [forms of punishment] are hardly noticeable to the most sharp-sighted eye;"[13] and he summed up his objection in a most notable statement (repeated in *Jerusalem*):[14]

> To introduce church discipline (*Kirchenzucht*) and to preserve civil happiness intact seems to me to present a problem that still waits for its solution in politics. It amounts to the directive of the Supreme Judge to Satan: He [Job] is in your hands yet do spare his life. Break the barrel, as the commentators add, but do not let the wine escape.[15]

That Dohm's "solution" was unrealistic and impracticable was not, however, Mendelssohn's only point. He found fault with the very notion that all one had to guard against was the overspilling of the effects of the ban into the civil sphere, a concern that seemed to be at peace with the notion that a ban strictly limited to the ecclesiastical realm was perfectly legitimate. Dohm had felt quite comfortable in taking this position because he could shelter behind the ecclesiastical law. Mendelssohn had noticed this.. The *Bannrecht* to be entrusted to the Jewish colony, he quoted him as saying, "would never transcend religious society and it would have no effect whatever in the political sphere since the ejected member of the church could be a very useful and respected citizen, this differentiation representing a principle of the general ecclesiastical law not to be doubted any more in our times."[16] It is this position of the ecclesiastical law that Mendelssohn scrutinizes and finds wanting.

Mendelssohn admits "with heartfelt appreciation" (*herzlich gern*) that in granting the possibility of a person's being a very useful and respected citizen in spite of his expulsion from the church to which he belonged, the so-called ecclesiastical law had "at long last" given recognition to an "important principle." He was not satisfied, however, that shielding an excommunicate from civil injury was sufficient. He did not think that "this poor precautionary measure" had remedied the evil inherent in excommunication. Even assuming with Dohm that the danger of civil harm could be averted, the *Bannrecht* would still be a deplorable institution. Mendelssohn paints the picture of a man—a highly regarded citizen—who has the misfortune of being considered a dissident by his community and, in consequence, has suffered the fate of expulsion. His conscience forbids him to join another religious party, and thus he finds himself in the unhappy situation of being excluded from all religious assemblies and exercises. Though he owns a great fund of "inner religion," he may not be content to be a loner but still craves participation in the fellowship offered by "external religion." Yet he is, to all intents and purposes, a religious outcast.[17] (The image drawn could have been Mendelssohn's vision of Spinoza.[18]) Is it compatible with the purpose of the state, Mendelssohn asks, that it should tolerate any legal measures that cause unhappiness to any of its citizens?[19] If it be objected that every society has the right of exclusion—an argument he imputes to Dohm—his answer is: Indeed, every society has the right of exclusion, except for a church, seeing that exclusion is diametrically opposed to the very purpose of the church. A church is meant to facilitate a common edification. The devout mood that is supposed to prevail in it is irreconcilable with the expulsion of any of its members, be they dissidents of any kind—dissenters, heretics or schismatics (*Andersdenkenden, Irredenkenden, Abweichenden*). Troublemakers and disturbers of the peace are a different matter. They can be dealt with by the police.[20]

Mendelssohn sought to explain why a "dissenting" (*einsichtsvoller*) writer like Dohm should have argued for the granting of the *jus excommunicationis* to the Jewish colony. Dohm, he said, took things as they were, not as they ought to be. He regarded the dominant church as a "moral person"[21] endowed with certain privileges and, hence, in a position to invest other religions tolerated in the territory with the same privileges.

Now since the right to impose the ban and exclusion (*Bann- und Ausschließungsfreiheit*) is always the first right with which the dominant religion invests the tolerated one, Herr Dohm demands for the Jewish re-

> ligion the same right as is conceded to all other religious societies. He holds that as long as these still possessed the right of exclusion it would be inconsistent to suggest that the Jews be more constricted in this respect than all the rest.

Mendelssohn, on the other hand, preferred, as he put it, an outright inconsistency to the endowment of the Jewish colony with a privilege devoid of meaning, the religious right of coercion being a contradiction in terms.[22]

It is important to note that Mendelssohn understood Dohm to have derived any Jewish right to exercise the *Bannrecht* from the willingness of the dominant church, the legal holder of this right, to concede a share in it to the tolerated churches. In a similar way Mendelssohn had suggested in an earlier passage[23] that the right to reward or punish a person for opinions he held—a right actually claimed and exercised, however wrongly, by the State—might be bestowed upon a colony by the "maternal nation," another instance of tracing a right to its legitimate primary owner. Neither Dohm nor Mendelssohn offer any juridical or historical proof for this kind of derivation of rights nor do they indicate whether an explicit act of bestowal is required or whether tacit consent is sufficient. The important point is that both subscribed to this legal construction and that Mendelssohn's way of procedure was thereby determined. Since Dohm derived the legality of the proposed Jewish *Bannrecht* from the ecclesiastical law as its fountainhead, Mendelssohn's attack upon Dohm's proposal had to proceed along those lines. Hence Mendelssohn's denial of the *jus excommunicationis* takes the form of a repudiation of the ecclesiastical *Bannrecht*. While conceding that the latter had made undeniable progress in the direction of tolerance, he still found it to be remiss, and he opposed to it the still greater tolerance that he saw enshrined in the principles of natural law and in the implications of the social contract theory as he understood them. A considerable section of the Preface to *Manasseh Ben Israel* and of Part One of *Jerusalem* is devoted to a demonstration of the way in which the larger tolerance flows from those principles. Mendelssohn seeks to show that while the social contract established the coercive power of the state, its concept does not apply to the nature of the church; that no positive law could legalize a right of coercion (a "perfect right") that was not founded upon a moral claim (an "imperfect right") valid in natural law; and that, consequently, no legal grounds existed for the exercise of compulsory power by the church.[24]

The radical position that Mendelssohn took—a position that was widely rejected by ecclesiastics and laymen[25]—can be fully appreciated only if viewed in historical perspective. To this end we have to survey the debate on the *Bannrecht* as it proceeded among Protestant ecclesiastical lawyers in eighteenth-century Germany. This is all the more indicated in view of the fact that Mendelssohn knew a goodly number of "manuals of ecclesiastical law" (*Lehrbücher des Kirchenrechts*), as is apparent from several references to them in *Jerusalem*.[26] Unfortunately, he did not specify titles and the references in terms of content are too general to allow any identification. We are therefore left in the dark as to which of the numerous treatises in this field he perused or simply glanced at.[27] We may assume, however, that such major works of early eighteenth-century vintage as the following did not escape his attention: Justus Henning Boehmer's monumental *Ius Ecclesiasticum Protestanticum*, six vols. 1714–36 (5th ed. 1756–89);[28] Johann Georg Pertsch, *Vom Recht des Kirchenbannes, dessen Ursprung und Fortgang*, Halle, 1721 (2nd ed. Wolfenbüttel, 1738) and the same author's *Elementa Juris Canonici et Protestantium Ecclesiastici*, II (1731);[29] Johann Lorenz Fleischer, *Einleitung zum geistlichen Rechte*, Halle, 1724 (2nd ed. 1729);[30] and Christoph Matthäus Pfaff, *Academische Reden über das so wohl allgemeine als auch Teutsche Protestantische Kirchen-Recht*, Tübingen, 1742 (Reprint Frankfurt a. Main, 1963).[31] We know for sure that he read Israel Gottlieb Canz's voluminous *Disciplinae morales omnes*, Leipzig, 1739, at least in part.[32] This work, which was highly praised by Pfaff,[33] is a manual of ethics embroidered with jurisprudence and incorporates a great deal of ecclesiastical law. From these treatises and others that he may have known, Mendelssohn could glean not only their authors' respective positions on the *jus excommunicationis* but also much historical information concerning it. In reviewing this material we shall be traversing ground with which, in all probability, he himself was familiar.

As has been pointed out by Martin Heckel,[34] all Protestant jurists from the Reformation down to Benedikt Carpzov[35] insisted in principle on the unbroken continuity of canon law and Protestant Law and did so, surprisingly, even in such areas as excommunication. The Catholic division into *excommunicatio maior* (withdrawal of ecclesiastical rights and social ostracism) and *excommunicatio minor* (the mere denial of ecclesiastical rights) remained in use, although it contradicted the Lutheran concept of the church. One may add that the distinction between the major and the minor ban persisted down to the eighteenth century. In Pertsch's formulation, the major ban obtains "quando quis ab ecclesia & omni fidelium congregatione excluditur & eiicitur," while the minor ban is applied "ubi quis ab sacramentorum participatione removetur."[36] The anomaly noted by Heckel did, in fact, bother the eighteenth-century ecclesiastical lawyers, as we shall have occasion to observe. What is more, Johann Lorenz Fleischer thought that one might have expected to see the ban altogether "buried" as a result of the Reformation. Luther retained it, though, he explained, because of his belief that the institution as such was authorized by the New Testament and only needed to be purified of its papal elements. Hence, Luther taught, it was the duty of a pastor to deny the sacraments to unrepentant sinners. Calvin went further and established his Genevan Consistory as an ecclesiastical judiciary charged with the administration of "holy discipline" (*Kirchenzucht*), whereas Zwingli rejected the ban altogether.[37] Within Lutheran orthodoxy, one of the staunchest defenders of the canonical law of excommunication was Johann Fecht (1636–1716), who wrote a *Tractatus de excommunicatione ecclesiae* and *Kurtze Nachricht von dem Kirchenbann, dessen göttlicher Einsetzung und christlichen Billigkeit.*

Protestant advocacy of the ban is generally supported by the belief that its ultimate authority is found in the New Testament. The most favored *locus probandi*, it appears, is Matt. 16:19, from which verse the "power of the keys," i.e., to the kingdom of heaven (the *potestas clavium*), was derived and the view was developed that the excommunicate whose ban had not been dissolved on earth was bound also in heaven in perpetuity, a doctrine going back to Augustine and enthusiastically adopted by Fecht. Another prooftext was I Cor. 5:5: "To deliver such an one unto Satan for the destruction of the flesh, that the spirit may be saved. . . ." The understanding of this verse as a reference to the ban was said by Fleischer to date back to Ambrose and Jerome and to have been shared by such Catholic scholars as Cesare Baronius (1538–1607) and Louis Ellies Dupin (1657–1719) as well as by the Lutheran Johann Fecht.[38]

Opposition to the ban arose among ecclesiastical lawyers of the Erastian persuasion, who denied to the Church any semblance of state power.[39] It is significant that Thomas Erastus (1524–1583), the founder of this school of thought, developed his theory of state supremacy in matters both civil and ecclesiastical in a treatise the title of which poses the question: Does excommunication inasmuch as it bars people from the use of the sacraments rest upon a divine mandate or is it something excogitated by men?[40] His answer was that the ban had no foundation in either the Old or the New Testament, and that no one could be rightfully denied access to the sacraments. What had moved him to write this treatise was an attempt by extreme Calvinists like Caspar Olevianus to introduce the "holy discipline" in the Palatinate, where he, a native Swiss, was then residing.[41] No less characteristic is the title of a treatise by the Oxford Professor Ludovicus Molinaeus, a follower of Erastus: *Paraenesis ad aedificatores Imperii in Imperio*. In this "Exhortation to builders of a state within the state," i.e., to the advocates of ecclesiastical power, the interpretation of the *potestas clavium* as a divine ordainment of the ban is assailed as mistaken, for neither Christ nor the Apostles ever claimed judicial power.[42] Similarly, John Selden (1584–1654) in his *Tractatus de Synedriis Veterum Ebraeorum*, sought to show, on scholarly grounds, that the *potestas clavium* could not be understood as referring to the ban.[43] The very same point was made, with a similar abundance of learning, by Campegius Vitringa (c. 1659–1722) in his *De Synagoga Vetere.*[44] The Calvinist Samuel Basnage (1638–1721), on the other hand, while admitting that certain prooftexts were unreliable, still insisted that the ban was authorized by Scripture.[45] It appears that in all this discussion the ban spoken of was the minor ban as well as the major.

The German Territorialists (who may be said to represent a moderate form of Erastianism) unreservedly adopted the denial of New Testament authorization of the ban. They accepted as eagerly the alternative theory of its origin offered by Selden, Jean Morin (1591–1659), and Vitringa, all of whom had made a study of the ban as practiced in Judaism and had suggested that the primitive church instituted the ban under Jewish influence.[46] It appears, however, that they were not entirely unanimous in describing the exact nature of this influence. In one respect the Territorialists did agree: The ban applied by the primitive church did not affect the civil intercourse (*commercium civile*) of the excommunicate but merely barred him from the sharing of the sacraments (*ab omni sacrorum commercio*), as Tertullian had said.[47] In the light of this common assumption J. H. Boehmer stressed the difference between the Jewish and the Christian ban. Though admitting that there was some connection between the two and that the impact of the Jewish model gradually increased, he felt that the essentially religious nature of the Christian ban set it apart from the essentially sociopolitical character of the Jewish *nidduy* and *herem*.[48] While the latter was a form of punishment through social ostracism, the former was a self-protective measure of the struggling church, designed to keep itself pure and uncontaminated.[49]

J. L. Fleischer, on the other hand, considered both the Jewish and the Christian ban to have been necessitated by political circumstances and to have been sociopolitical in intent. It had been introduced by the Jews as a means of enforcing communal discipline at a time when their political sovereignty was in eclipse, probably after the Babylonian Exile or in Maccabean times.[50] Similarly, it had been initiated by the Christian community in the early centuries of its existence when it lacked protection from without. In this situation the need for internal discipline suggested the use of the ban, and expulsion from the sacraments, although in itself of a purely religious nature, served as a disciplinary measure because it meant the denial of the most cherished symbol of fellowship.[51] Boehmer was, in fact, not too far removed from this sociological appraisal of the early Christian ban, for in place of the *potestas clavium* as the raison d'être of the ban he put the *disciplina confederata*.[52]

The very recognition of the paramount importance the ban had in the primitive church implied a disapproval of its continued use after the Christianization of the Roman Empire in 313. Fleischer quite explicitly stated: "Da die Obrigkeit Christlich geworden ist, und sich der Kirche anzunehmen angefangen hat, hätte der Bann gantz und gar aufgehoben werden sollen. . . . Allein die Sache kehrte sich *just* um, und der Bann bekam noch ein viel grösseres

Ansehen."[53] Boehmer, from his slightly different perspective, condemned the steady expansion of the ban from the third century onward as a growing "accommodation" to the Jewish form of excommunication.[54] The historical accounts of the development of the *jus excommunicationis* presented in eighteenth-century Territorialist writings are heavily tinged with the Enlightenment sentiment that generally imputes the corruption of religion to the vices of the clergy. Boehmer, at the opening of his elaborate recital of the decline of the ban, speaks of the "ambition" of certain bishops and, in particular, of the "audacity" of Stephanus, Bishop of Rome, that set the ban on the road leading toward a totally new denegation of civil rights.[55] The Christian ban, he pointed out, increasingly degenerated into a measure of civil punishment, taking its cue from the Jewish ban and thereby exercising the right of the magistrate.[56] Fleischer is no less outspoken in his condemnation of the *Bannrecht* as it developed. Again in true Enlightenment fashion, he sees the "craftiness" (*Schlauheit*) of the clergy at work in the fact that "everything happened little by little."[57] He quotes Étienne Baluze's *Capitularia Regum Francorum* (1677) as the source of his contention that the clergy used the ban in many instances for trivial reasons in order to enrich itself.[58] It had been the avowed purpose of the ban to intimidate the laity and make it "dance to the clergy's tune," an accusation Fleischer quoted from the *Traité des benefices*, a work by Paolo Sarpi (1552–1623), a member of the Servite Order in Venice.[59]

Attention was also drawn to the anathematizing formulae that had come to be used in the pronouncements of the ban. Boehmer pointed out that they were copied from Jewish sources (*a moribus & institutis iudaicis*).[60] Fleischer castigated, without reference to Jewish origin, the "blasphemous" sort of *Bann-Formul* that had come into use. He found its earliest occurrence attested in an Epistle (79) of Synesius, Bishop of Ptolomais (c. 370–c. 414), and he quoted *in extenso* the ban formula contained in the *Decreta* of Burchard, Bishop of Worms (c. 965–1025) and St. Ivo, Bishop of Chartres (c. 1040–1116):[61]

Sie seyn verflucht in der Stadt, verflucht auf dem Felde, verflucht seyn ihre Scheuren, verflucht ihr Uberbleiben, verflucht die Frucht ihres Leibes, und die Frucht ihres Landes. Verflucht seyn sie, wenn sie eingehen, verflucht, wenn sie ausgehen, sie seyn in ihren Wohnungen verflucht, auf dem Felde flüchtig, es kommen alle die Flüche über sie, so GOtt durch Mosen über das Volck, so die Gesetze übertreten würde, zuschicken, gesagt hat. Sie seyn *Anathema, Maranatha*, d.i. Sie sollen untergehen in der andern Zukunfft des HErrn. Kein Christ soll sie grüssen, kein Aeltester soll sich unterstehen mit ihnen die Messe zu halten, oder ihnen die heilige Communion zu reichen. Sie sollen ein Esels-Begräbniß haben, und auf der Erden als ein Mist-Hauffen geachtet werden. Und wie diese Lichter, die wir aus unserer Hand werffen, heute ausgelöscht werden, so werde ihr Licht in alle Ewigkeit verlöschet, es sey denn, daß sie zur Erkänntniß kähmen, und der Kirche GOttes, welche sie beleidiget, durch Besserung und rechte Busse aussöhneten.

The citation of this text, which is almost entirely based on the *ḥerem* formula,[62] is paralleled by Boehmer's quotation from a more recent Protestant "ordination" that had been lauded by Johann Fecht:[63]

Derohalben ich, als dieser Christlichen Kirchen gemeiner Diener und Seelsorger, in dem Nahmen unsers HErrn JEsu Christi diesen unbußfertigen offenbahrlichen Sünder dem Teuffel irtzund übergebe zum Verderben des Fleisches, auf daß sein Geist selig werde am Tage des HErrn, wenn er sich wiederum bekehren wird. Verkündige ihm hiemit GOttes schrecklichen Zorn und Ungnade, und, daß er von der Gemeinschafft aller Heiligen im Himmel und auf Erden ausgeschlossen und abgeschnitten, und von allen Teufeln in der Hölle verflucht, und ewiglich verdammt sey so lange er in dieser Unbußfertigkeit verharret. Versage ihm auch damit alle Kirchen-Rechte, und aller heiligen Sacramenten Gemeinschafft, ausgenommen die Anhörung der Predigt. Bitte auch und vermahne alle Christen, daß sie mit diesem Menschen fernerhin nichts zu schaffen haben, und sich seiner Gemeinschafft gantz entschlagen, nicht mit ihm essen, oder trincken, ihn nicht zu Gevatter bitten, zu keiner Hochzeit oder anderer ehrlicher Gesellschafft laden, auch auf der Strasse oder sonst nicht grüssen; damit er beschämet oder gedemühtiget werde, und seine Sünde desto eher bekenne, und sich zu GOtt bekehre, und damit der Christlichen Kirchen, die er mit seinem Ungehorsam zum höchsten beleidiget und geärgert hat, versühne.

This text, a specimen of contemporary *Praxis Protestantium*, as Boehmer describes it, has a characteristically Christian ring. The ban pronounced in both formulae is obviously the *excommunicatio maior* since it imposes a twofold punishment: exclusion from the sacraments and social ostracism. Boehmer said of the text quoted by him that it included the infliction of disgrace and the prohibition of civil fellowship, measures that had been approved by Fecht since he believed this kind of penalty to be an essential part of excommunication. Boehmer himself condemned this view as manifestly false.[64] As a Territorialist he deprecated the intrusion of the ban into the civil sphere unless it was imposed by the magistrate. It appears that he had no objection to the minor ban although he, along with other Territorialist lawyers, regarded it as a regrettable innovation dating from the thirteenth century. In his and their view it had been introduced by Pope Innocent III in connection with the regular aural confession ordained by the Fourth Lateran Council, giving the priest the right to debar people from the sacraments if he considered them unworthy. According to this theory the minor ban was not to be confounded with the excommunication practiced in the early Church as a self-protective, nonpunitive, though disciplinary measure.[65] Boehmer was content to leave the minor ban uncontested because it entailed no serious civil effects such as injury to one's civil status (liberty, citizenship, family) and to one's "condition" by virtue of reputation, social intercourse and public offices held. All the minor ban might cause was a certain ill repute among the clergy and its followers, something that Boehmer obviously did not consider alarming. He assailed the major ban because of the social ostracism it enjoined. The curtailment of civil status, which he would not tolerate, thus included every form of social restriction.[66] A seventeenth century Territorialist like Johann Brunnemann (1608–1672) had been less scrupulous. He did admit the legality of the *excommunicatio maior*, "although it repels the excommunicate from social intercourse (*a conversatione cum aliis*)," because it was understood that his "civil rights" (*civilia iura*) were not affected.[67] Other eighteenth-century Territorialist lawyers like Pertsch and Fleischer tended to advocate the abolition of the ban altogether. Pertsch outspokenly declared that the entire reason for excommunication no longer fitted his times and that, at all events, it should be subjected to the judgment of the magistrate in case it was still practiced.[68] Fleischer was less explicit but the tenor of his discussion points in the same direction. He took it for granted that no ban was valid without confirmation by the magistrate. In admitting that much, he argued, Territorialist lawyers had tacitly granted that the ban belonged to the category of civil punishments. This being the case, why not do away with the ban altogether and leave it to the state to deal with all punishable offences?[69] Should the prince favor the retention of the ban in his territory, he ought to reserve the right of intervention and he would be well advised were he to interdict a number of features associated with the ban, such as the use of anathemas or "other superstitious formulae," the denial of a Christian burial, the application of the ban to dissenters, etc.[70] His summing-up reads:[71]

Es thut aber eine Obrigkeit am allerbesten, wenn sie den Bann gantz und gar abschaffet. Denn da ich bißhero gezeiget habe, daß es eine weltliche Straffe sey, und denen Geistlichen gar keine *Jurisdiction* zukomme, so ist es der *Republic* viel zuträglicher, wann die Verbrechen von denen ordentlichen Gerichten bestraffet werden. Und obgleich nicht alle Laster in denen bürgerlichen Gesetzen mit Straffen belegt seyn, so ist dieses auch nicht von nöthen, indem die Pflichten eines Fürsten nur dahin gehen, daß er den äusserlichen Frieden unter seinen Unterthanen erhalte, und die Friedens-Stöhrer bestraffe.[72]

The trend of Fleischer's arguments suggests that the ban he wished to see abolished was the major ban. Yet it seems that he took a dim view of the minor ban as well. In his account of the history of excommunication, he lumped major and minor ban together in the same vein of denigration.[73] "One began to divide the ban into the major and the minor. The latter's aim was the improvement of the sinner—so one tried to make people believe—his cleansing from sin and liberation from eternal punishment." It may safely be assumed, therefore, that Fleischer shared Pertsch's view that the ban had become an anachronism and that this verdict applied also to the minor ban although one could not argue against it in strictly juridical terms. What is common, then, to all Territorialist lawyers of the eighteenth century is the repudiation of the major ban because of its infraction of civil rights while with respect to the minor ban opinions were divided, ranging as they did from open disavowal to tacit approval.

We meet with a decidedly different position when we turn to the ecclesiastical lawyers of the Collegialist school, which considered the church a voluntary association (*collegium*)[74] distinct in its purpose from that of the state and not subject to the *jus majestatis* in matters of religion, that is, to the *jus circa sacra*, as was claimed by the Territorialists.[75] The patron saint of this school was Samuel Pufendorf (1632–1694) whose *De habitu religionis Christianae ad vitam civilem* (Bremen, 1685) had become the authoritative textbook of the Collegialists much in the way in which Christian Thomasius's (1655–1728) *Das Recht evangelischer Fürsten in theologischen Streitigkeiten* (Halle, 1696) enjoyed high authority among the Territorialists. Not that there was a strict division between their respective doctrines. Pufendorf was anything but consistent, and one marvels at the freedom with which he allowed himself to stray from his principles in the direction almost of Erastianism.[76] In *De habitu* (§ 27) he does make the point, however, that the church has the right to excommunicate unrepentant sinners and to prohibit social contact with them, it being understood that the ban has no consequences in the civil realm. The very same view was expressed by John Locke in his *A Letter Concerning Toleration* (written in the winter 1685/86 when Pufendorf's *De habitu* had just appeared).[77] Locke insisted that a religious society, though "destitute of all compulsive power" and in possession of no other means of enforcing internal discipline but "exhortations, admonitions and advice,"[78] must, nevertheless, be entitled to "cast out" offenders whose stubbornness and obstinacy give no ground to hope for their reformation. He added the proviso "that the sentence of excommunication, and the execution thereof, carry with it no rough usage, of work or action, whereby the ejected person may any ways be damnified in body or estate." For "Excommunication neither does nor can deprive the excommunicated person of any of those civil goods that he formerly possessed."[79]

The leading figure among the ecclesiastical lawyers of the Collegialist school in Germany was Christoph Matthäus Pfaff. In his *Academische Reden*[80] he declared it to be "perfectly natural" that free societies should deny certain rights to members or even exclude members who flout the established rules or cause unrest and annoyance. He designated the denial of certain rights *excommunicatio minor*, and he called expulsion from the society *excomminicatio major*. These highly charged ecclesiastical terms were thus given by him a general connotation applicable to procedures taken by any kind of society. As applied to the church, they signified the denial of the sacraments and ejection from the church respectively. Pfaff held that the early church practiced both the *excommunicatio minor* and the *excommunicatio major*, and with a stupendous array of sources he sought to refute the view held by

Territorialists like Boehmer, Pertsch, and others according to which the minor ban was not introduced before the thirteenth century.[81] In his view the "First Church" applied the minor ban by excluding sinners (*lapsi*) from the sacraments and also made use of the major ban by expelling them from the church. From this it would follow that both forms of the ban are legitimate. He pointed out, however, that nowadays the major ban had assumed the character of a civil punishment, the execution of which required the assistance of the secular arm, and it had, therefore, fallen into desuetude. He probably meant to imply that from a Collegialist point of view the major ban had lost its legality for two closely connected reasons: 1) It had been endowed with features that hurt the excommunicate's civil status; 2) it could no longer be enforced by the church itself (the *ministerium ecclesiasticum*), which would have to call in the power of the magistrate, something a Collegianist was not prepared to countenance. He added yet another reason for rescinding the major ban. Expulsion from the church prevented the excommunicate from listening to sermons and thereby defeated the very object of the penalty, the reformation of the sinner. Pfaff stressed this point as one applying to the major ban only. He would not extend the same consideration to the minor ban (as Pertsch had imputed to him). The fact that admission to the sacraments could "prepare men for penitence" should not be regarded as sufficient reason for the abolition of the minor ban.[82] In sum, Pfaff deprecated expulsion from the church but was all in favor of the denial of the sacraments to sinners. We may say in conclusion that Collegialists were unanimous in upholding the minor ban as a desirable institution but they were equally agreed that its complexion had changed from a mystically sanctioned right (*potestas clavium*) to a "natural" right inherent in any kind of voluntary society. Indeed, the character of the church itself had been redefined as that of a human society (*collegium*).

This then, to return to Mendelssohn, was the ecclesiastical law background against which he and Dohm argued the advisability or otherwise of granting the prospective Jewish colony the right of excommunication. In the light of the sources we have scanned, both Dohm's and Mendelssohn's positions can now be defined more precisely. Dohm's advocacy of the right of exclusion (*Ausschließungsrecht*) was obviously based on the Collegialist view, which claimed for every society such a right in principle and saw no difference in this respect between the church and other associations. Mendelssohn's retort: Every society, except a church—sounds like a rebuttal of Pfaff's basic position. Dohm's suggestion that the secular arm might be employed in the execution of a rabbinically imposed ban has a Territorialist ring. Mendelssohn, who rejected the *jus circa sacra* as state interference in religious matters,[83] could not entertain such a proposal. Dohm was, of course, perfectly correct in stating that according to a universally acknowledged principle of ecclesiastical law the ban must never harm the civil status of the excommunicate. As we have seen, Territorialists and Collegialists were in complete agreement on this point. The dissent of orthodox Lutherans like Fecht could be safely ignored. Dohm's statement, in the name of the ecclesiastical consensus that one ejected from the church might still remain a very useful and respected citizen, was probably his own formulation elaborated from the jurists' insistence that the civil status, reputation, public offices, etc. of the excommunicate must remain intact. Mendelssohn was not satisfied with this principle. It did not go beyond repudiating the major ban, but offered no argument against the minor ban nor against expulsion from the church once safeguards were offered that no civil harm would ensue. Locke had expressly affirmed this right and Pfaff had revoked it only because civil rights were involved, not on principle. Pfaff had voiced, however, a genuinely religious consideration that militated against the right of expulsion, namely, the concern for the religious welfare of the ejected member of the church. Strangely enough, he had stopped short of applying it in respect of the minor ban. Mendelssohn may have detected here, nevertheless, the beginnings of a new approach. As for the Territorialists, their disavowal of the major ban had been motivated by fear lest the *Bannrecht* establish a *status in stato* and by the growing tendency to separate church and state. Mendelssohn was in complete agreement with both the apprehension and the general trend toward the secularization of the state. What he missed was a new conception of the church as a purely spiritual entity, a conception that would nullify, at one stroke, every kind of ban, major as well as minor. He must have found it irritating that Locke, for all his magnificent portrayal of the noncoercive nature of the church, still approved the ban. He must have felt it all the more imperative to strike out new paths. To achieve this goal was one of the major purposes he set himself when writing the Preface to *Manasseh Ben Israel* and Part One of *Jerusalem*.

NOTES

1. Alexander Altmann, *Moses Mendelssohn: A Biographical Study* (University, Alabama, 1973), pp. 455–57.

2. *Salo Wittmayer Baron Jubilee Volume* (Jerusalem, 1975), I:43–45, 51–55.

3. Christian Wilhelm Dohm, *Über die bürgerliche Verbesserung der Juden* (Berlin & Stettin, 1781), p. 124.

4. *Baron Jubilee Volume*, I:51 (Letter No. 6).

5. Christian Wilhelm Dohm, *De la réforme politique des Juifs* (Dessau, 1782), pp. 165f.

6. Christian Wilhelm Dohm, *Über die bürgerliche Verbesserung der Juden*, Erster Theil (Berlin & Stettin, 1783), pp. 133f.

7. Ibid., p. 134.

8. See *Moses Mendelssohn's gesammelte Schriften*, ed. G. B. Mendelssohn (*GS*), III (Leipzig, 1843): 201.

9. See Altmann, *Mendelssohn*, pp. 383–88, 392f.

10. Ibid., pp. 561–64, 567–69, 571.

11. See *GS*, III:197–201; 296–98.

12. Ibid., 200, 265, 302.

13. Ibid., 200.

14. Ibid., 201, 297.

15. Quoting Job 2:6; Bava Batra 16a.

16. *GS*, III:199f.

17. Ibid., 200.

18. See *Moses Mendelssohn Gesammelte Schriften Jubiläumsausgabe* (*JubA*) I:14f.; III.2:188; XII.1:203 ("meines Mitbruders Spinoza").

19. According to Mendelssohn's political philosophy, the purpose of the state includes the promotion of the happiness of its citizens. See *GS*, III:264, 197; IV.1:136–45.

20. *GS*, III:198.

21. The conception of "moral personality" had been introduced by Pufendorf and other seventeenth-century lawyers in order to invest a group (*societas*, including the state) with the character of personality for legal (i.e., contractual) purposes. See J. W. Gough, *The Social Contract*, 2nd ed. (Oxford, 1957), pp. 47, 122f.

22. *GS*, III:198f.

23. Ibid., 197.

24. Ibid., 194–96; 281–84; 305f.

25. E.g., by Johann Friedrich Zöllner, *Über Moses Mendelssohn's Jerusalem* (Berlin, 1784) and August Wilhelm Rehberg, "Fernere Untersuchungen über allgemeine Toleranz und Freiheit in Glaubenssachen," *Berlinische Monatsschrift*, 13 (1789):327f.

26. See *GS*, III:258, 265, 285, 302.

27. A good introduction to the literature concerned can be found in Otto Mejer, *Lehrbuch des deutschen Kirchenrechts*, 3rd ed. (Göttingen, 1869).

28. The section dealing with the ban is found in Lib. V, Titulus XXXIX (*De Sententia Excommunicationis*), pp. 904–982. J. H. Boehmer (1674–1749), a disciple of Johann Samuel Stryk and Christian Thomasius, was professor in Halle. He represented a moderate, enlightened form of Territorialism.

29. J. G. Pertsch (1694–1754) was canon lawyer and church historian in Halle.

30. This work treats the theme of "Excommunication oder Kirchen-Bann" in the Second Book, Section (*Hauptstück*) XXXVII ("Von denen geistlichen Strafen"), § 10ff., pp. 790ff. Fleischer (1689–1749) too was a pupil of Thomasius and taught in Halle, later in Frankfort a.O. He describes his *Einleitung* on the title page as based on the law of nature, the principles of Holy Scripture, canon law, the *instrumentum pacis* (i.e., the provisions of the Peace of Westphalia, 1648) and the Church Orders of Protestant States.

31. Chapter 16 (pp. 265–271) is entitled "Von der Kirchen-*Disciplin* und *in specie* dem Kirchen-Bann etc." Pfaff (1686–1760) was chancellor of the universities of Tübingen and Giessen.

32. He made some excerpts relating to the issue of excommunication, which are preserved in an autograph of his first sketch of *Jerusalem* (see Altmann, *Mendelssohn*, pp. 515f.), from Canz's work.

33. *Academische Reden*, pp. 30, 395.

34. Martin Heckel, *Staat und Kirche nach den Lehren der evangelischen Juristen Deutschlands in der ersten Hälfte des siebzehnten Jahrhunderts* (Munich, 1968), p. 43.

35. Benedict Carpzov's *Jurisprudentia ecclesiastica seu consistorialis* (Leipzig, 1649) was "epoch-making" (O. Mejer) in that it combined the tradition of canon law with the practical needs of the Protestant territorial churches. B. Carpzov (1595–1666) was professor in Leipzig.

36. Pertsch, *Elementa*, II (1731), Lib. IV, Tit. XI, § 360.

37. Fleischer, *Einleitung*, pp. 823f.

38. See the extensive account given by Fleischer, *Einleitung*, pp. 793–801 and the quotation from Fecht in Boehmer, *Jus Ecclesiasticum*, V, xxxix, § xxii.

39. On Erastianism, its representatives, and historical context, see Joseph Lecler, *Toleration and the Reformation* (tr. by T. L. Westow), (New York and London, 1960), Index, p. 537, *s.v.*

40. Thomas Erastus, *Explicatio gravissimae questionis, utrum excommunicatio quatenus religionem intelligentes et amplexantes a sacramentorum usu propter admissum facinus arcet, mandato nitatur divino an excogitata sit ab hominibus* (Pesclavii, 1589). For a discussion of Erastus's doctrine, see Johannes Heckel, "Cura religionis Ius in sacra Ius circa sacra," *Festschrift Ulrich Stutz*, Kirchenrechtliche Abhandlungen, Vol. 117/118 (Stuttgart, 1938): 290–94.

41. See the dramatic account in Fleischer, *Einleitung*, pp. 824–27.

42. Ibid., pp. 827–28. The title of Chapter XII ("De excommunicatione") of *Paraenesis* declares: Excommunicatio melius concordat cum placitis pontificiorum quam cum moribus & praxi reformatorum (p. 259). On the history of the term "imperium in imperio" or "status in statu," see Jacob Katz, "A State Within a State," *The Israel Academy of Sciences and Humanities Proceedings*, Vol. IV, No. 3 (Jerusalem, 1969): 30–38.

43. See Fleischer, *Einleitung*, pp. 793f. John Selden's *De Synedriis & Praefecturis Veterum Ebraeorum Libri Tres* (Amsterdam, 1679; Frankfort, 1696) discourses in Chapter VIII (pp. 109–137) "De Excommunicationibus . . . Usu, Jure, Effectu . . . in Christianismo Primitivo per Apostulorum tempora."

44. Fleischer, loc. cit.; the reference is to Vitringa's *De Synagoga Vetere Libri Tres* (Franeker, 1696), Lib. 3, Pars I, Cap. IX.

45. Samuel Basnage, *Annales politico-ecclesiastici . . . Tomus Secundus* (Rotterdam, 1706); Fleischer, *Einleitung*, pp. 794f., 929 quotes Dissertatio I, § IV ("Tradere Satanae de immissio ab eo tormentis est intelligendum") and § VII ("Anathema non est exclusio a sacramentis").

46. Selden, De Synedriis, Lib. I, Cap. VII–VIII (quoted by Boehmer, *Ius Eccl.*, V, xxxix, § iv; Fleischer, *Einleitung*, pp. 790–93, 829); Morin (Morinus), *De administatione sacramentorum penitentium*, Lib. IV, Cap. 23ff. (quoted by Boehmer, ibid.); Vitringa, *De Synagoga Vetere*, Lib. 3, Pars I, Cap. IX–X (quoted by Boehmer, loc. cit., § vii; Fleischer, loc. cit., p. 794). Hugo Grotius, the leading figure in Dutch Territorialism, also traced the Christian ban to Jewish patterns, as Fleischer (p. 793) reports. A résumé of Selden's elaborate description of the Jewish ban is found in Fleischer's account (pp. 790–93). It draws not only on *De Synedriis* but also on passages in Selden's earlier treatise *De Iure Naturali & Gentium, Iuxta Disciplinam Ebraeorum Libri Septem* (London, 1640; last edition: Leipzig & Frankfort, 1695).

Selden's Hebrew sources (omitted by Fleischer) include the Palestinian and the Babylonian Talmud, Halakhot Gedolot, Moses b. Jacob of Coucy's *SeMaG*, Maimonides's *Mishneh Torah*, Jacob b. Asher's *Tur Yoreh De'ah*, Josef Karo's *Shulḥan 'Arukh*, etc. See *De Iure*, Cap. VIII (pp. 511–17): Causae, Ritus, ac Effectus Excommunicationis apud

Ebraeos . . . ; *De Synedriis*, Lib. I, Cap. VII (pp. 56–109): . . . praemittitur de ejusdam, apud Ebraeos veteres, Effectibus, Formulis, Speciebus seu Gradibus, Jure, Usû, ac Absolutione, Synopsis historica, nec solum è Talmudicis sed et partim à Karaeis desumta. In Cap. VII (pp. 506–8) of *De Iure* the full text of the ***nusaḥ ḥerem*** as given in *Sefer Kolbo* is quoted (Latin translation pp. 508–10). Basnages, ***Annales***, II, Dissertatio II (De Excommunicatione Judaica), pp. 478ff. quotes Selden *de Synedriis* and *de Iure Nat.*

47. Boehmer, *Jus Eccl.*, V, xxxix, § ix.

48. Ibid., §§ vi–vii.

49. Ibid., §§ vi, ix.

50. Fleischer, *Einleitung*, p. 790, quoting Selden, *De Synedriis*, Lib. I, Cap. VII, pp. 77ff. See also Vitringa, *De Synagoga Vetere*, Lib. 3, Pars I, p. 746f.: Origo illius arcessanda ab Exilio Babylonico; and Molinaeus, *Paraenesis*, Cap. XII (cf. n. 52 in fine). It may be assumed that Selden's theory was adopted also by Hobbes, who wrote in the Latin text of *Leviathan* (*Opera Omnia*, Amsterdam, 1668), Cap. 42, p. 238: Pars haec potestatis Ecclesiasticae Excommunicatio dicitur . . . & ritus erat etiam Iudaeis usitatus: sed ut videtur, post captivitatem Babylonicam . . . The same view appears in Pertsch, *Vom Recht des Kirchenbannes*, § 4ff. and Canz, *Disciplinae* (1752 edition), § 2681: Apud iudaeos cepisse excommunicationem initia, sub captivitate Babylonica, teste Seldeno, eam ob caussam, ut senioribus servaretur sua auctoritas. Canz obviously shared Selden's sociopolitical interpretation.

51. Fleischer, *Einleitung*, p. 800.

52. Boehmer, *Ius Eccl.*, V, xxxix, § iv. Cf. Selden, *De Synhedriis*, Lib. I, Cap. VIII, p. 109: De Christianorum tunc confoederata inter se disciplina, tempore Persecutiorum. Molinaeus, *Paraenesis*, Cap. XI, p. 259 described the Jewish ban as introduced by Ezra and Nehemiah "quo tempore coepit disciplina confoederata."

53. Fleischer, *Einleitung*, p. 800.

54. Boehmer, *Ius Eccl.*, V, xxxix, § xviii: quod mox ad disciplinam Iudaicam accomodata . . . quo ipso civiles accepit effectus, & in poenam civilem . . . degeneravit.

55. Ibid., § xviii.

56. Ibid.: & hoc modo iure magistratus ecclesiastici exerceri coeperit . . . quodam imperio sacro.

57. Fleischer, *Einleitung*, p. 800.

58. Ibid., pp. 801f.

59. Ibid., p. 803.

60. Boehmer, *Ius Eccl.*, V, xxxix, § xxix.

61. Fleischer, *Einleitung*, pp. 800f.

62. Cf. J. Wiesner, *Der Bann in seiner geschichtlichen Entwicklung auf dem Boden des Judenthumes* (Leipzig, 1864), pp. 40, 82. The possibility of a reverse influence of canon law upon medieval Jewry has been suggested by Salo W. Baron, *The Jewish Community*, Vol. II (Philadelphia, 1945): 229.

63. Boehmer, *Ius Eccl.*, V, xxxix, § lv.

64. Ibid.: Vides, in hac formula & notam quandam infamiae inuri, & communionem ciuilem prohiberi, quod ad palatum Fechtii est, qui excommunicationi hoc essentialiter inesse credit, quod oppido falsum est, quamuis legislator ciuilis tales effectus eidem tribuere queat.

65. Boehmer, *Ius Eccl.*, V, xxxviii (De Poenitentiis et Remissionibus), § xxxiii; V, xxxix, § lvii.

66. Boehmer, *Ius Eccl.*, V, xxxix, § v: De majori hic unice loquor; minori enim civiles non tribuunt effectus, nisi quod canonica infamia laborare dicatur excommunicatus, seu a sacramentorum usu exclusus, quae in hoc consistit, quod male audiat apud clersos, quorum iudicia facile sequuuntur plerique laicorum.

67. Brunnemann, *De Jure ecclesiastico*, Lib. II, Cap. XIX, § xi.

68. Pertsch, *Elementa*, II, Lib. IV, Tit. XI, § 368: totam excommunicationis rationem ad nostra tempora non quadrare: saltem ubi obtinet, arbitrio magistratus ad normam reliquarum poenarum subiacere.

69. Fleischer, *Einleitung*, pp. 832f.

70. Ibid., 834f.

71. Ibid., p. 835.

72. Cf. Christian Thomasius, *Das Recht evangelischer Fürsten in theologischen Streitigkeiten* (Halle, 1696), 4. Satz: Daß die Pflicht eines Fürsten als Fürsten nicht sey, seine Unterthanen recht tugendhafft zu machen. 5. Satz: Vielweniger ist er verbunden für die Seligkeit seiner Unterthanen zu sorgen (quoted by Martin Heckel, *Staat und Kirche*, p. 163).

73. Fleischer, *Einleitung*, p. 802.

74. This view of the church was shared by Territorialists like J. H. Boehmer. Representatives of Collegianism such as Pfaff, G. L. Boehmer, and Wiese in Germany and Gisbert Voetius in seventeenth-century Holland merely drew the conclusions from the distinctiveness of the church as a *collegium*. Cf. Martin Heckel, *Staat und Kirche*, p. 246.

75. On the Territorialist conception of the *jus circa sacra*, see Johannes Heckel's essay in the *Ulrich Stutz Festschrift*, pp. 283–98; Martin Heckel, *Staat und Kirche*, pp. 122ff. and passim (see Index, p. 263 *s.v.* Territorialsystem), especially the summary on pp. 241–48.

76. The conflicting sets of categories in Pufendorf's doctrine have been well analyzed by Leonard Krieger, *The Politics of Discretion: Pufendorf and the Acceptance of Natural Law* (Chicago & London, 1965), pp. 227–44. See also Horst Denzer, *Moralphilosophie und Naturrecht bei Samuel Pufendorf* (Munich, 1972), pp. 210–16. As for Thomasius, see Hildegard Doerr, *Thomasius Stellung zum Landesherrlichen Kirchenregiment* (Dissertation Bonn, 1917). Werner Schneiders's *Naturrecht und Liebesethik* (Hildesheim & New York, 1971) offers a sustained account of Thomasius's natural law doctrine in its historical context but does not go into his teachings on church and state. For a profile of the man, see Ernst Bloch, *Christian Thomasius Ein deutscher Gelehrter ohne Misere* (Berlin, 1953).

77. Quoted here from *The Works of John Locke*. A New Edition, Corrected, Vol. VI (London, 1823).

78. This passage seems to be echoed in Mendelssohn's words about the only power religion possesses: "durch Gründe zu gewinnen, zu überzeugen, und durch Überzeugung glückselig zu machen" (*GS*, III: 195; 284).

79. Locke, *Works*, VI: 16f.

80. C. 16, §2.

81. Ibid., §3.

82. Ibid., §2.

83. *GS*, III: 285–87; 306.

11 The New Style of Preaching in Nineteenth-Century German Jewry

The nineteenth century saw the rise and development of a new type of Jewish preaching, replacing the traditional *Derashah*. The changes involved in this innovation concerned not only the outward form and structure of the sermon but also its substance. The very concept of the purpose of preaching as well as the theology behind it underwent a radical transformation. Obviously, the impact of contemporary trends in the Christian pulpit and in the philosophical thinking of the period accounts for a great deal in this connection. The remarkable degree of symbiosis that characterized the integration of the Jews into the realm of German culture was manifested in the phenomenon of the modern Jewish sermon as it was in so many other fields.

The present study endeavors to trace the evolution of the new style of preaching in the context of the history of ideas in nineteenth-century theology and philosophy. In doing so, it resumes a line of investigation already pursued by the author's earlier study entitled "Zur Frühgeschichte der jüdischen Predigt in Deutschland: Leopold Zunz als Prediger" (*Publications of the Leo Baeck Institute, Year Book VI*, London, 1961, pp. 3–59). While the previous inquiry was devoted primarily to Zunz as one of the pioneers of the modern Jewish sermon, the present paper operates within a wider perimeter. It takes in the entire range of the century, without, however, laying claim to comprehensiveness. In a sense, its scope is narrower than that of the earlier study in that it is concerned with formative influences rather than with homiletical content. An analysis of the theology of the sermon is still a desideratum. Here nothing more is attempted than a preliminary orientation offering some signposts for a more detailed work.

CHRISTIAN MODELS OF PREACHING

The modern Jewish sermon arose at a time when the Protestant pulpit in Germany had reached its zenith in the art of rule-bound (*schulgerecht*) preaching. At no other period before or after was there a similar abundance of treatises on homiletics offering guidance in the preparation, composition, and delivery of a sermon.[1] The sermon had to conform to definite rules. It had to be *schulgerecht*. Homiletics was treated as a science. The classical work in the field, Johann Lorentz von Mosheim's *Anweisung erbaulich zu predigen* ("Directive for Edificatory Preaching")[2] laid down (1) general rules of ecclesiastical oratory (*geistliche Beredsamkeit*), (2) rules concerning the parts composing a sermon, and (3) the method of writing a sermon. Mosheim gave the collection of his own sermons the title *Heilige Reden* ("Holy Speeches")[3] in order to emphasize the character of the sermon as a piece of oratory in the service of religion. The stress laid by him and his followers on the rhetorical element in the sermon owes a great deal to the influence of the English and French schools of preachers.[4] By the time the modern Jewish sermon appeared on the scene (1808), Mosheim's manner of preaching had already become antiquated,[5] but the influence of his *Anweisung* still persisted.[6] His insistence on the essentially oratorical nature of the sermon commanded a large following. It also gave rise to strong misgivings. The old discussion as to whether oratory (*Beredsamkeit*) was legitimate in the pulpit still went on in the nineteenth century.[7] Some preachers decried the use of classical models of rhetoric (Cicero, Quintilian) as sheer paganism and deceitful mockery (*Gleissnerei*).[8] How perilous the rhetorical element could be to the evaluation of preaching may be gauged from Kant's remark that oratory—as distinct from mere eloquence and style—"is not to be commended either to courts of justice or to the pulpits" since it is "the art of persuading, i.e., of deceiving by beautiful semblance."[9]

Most works on homiletics do, however, consider preaching as an art belonging to the genre of rhetorics. Heinrich August Schott, who was professor of theology at Jena, disagreed with Kant and vindicated oratorical eloquence as a legitimate means of moving the feelings as well as of creating convictions. He defined ecclesiastical oratory as "the art . . . of producing . . . the particular direction of the mind toward the Eternal which is called Christian edification."[10] In still more radical fashion, an earlier theoretician of the sermon, Johann Friedrich Teller, had declared that "the preacher is meant to be an ecclesiastical orator [*geistlicher Redner*]" and that "he must differ from the general class of orator in nothing but his subject matter."[11] Other writers on homiletics pointed out the desirability of keeping oratory within the bounds of simplicity.[12] Perhaps the most eloquent plea in this direction came from Johann Friedrich Wilhelm Thym in his eminently readable *Briefe die Simplizität des Predigers betreffend* ("Letters Concerning the Simplicity of the Preacher").[13]

The sermon had evolved into a type of pulpit oratory decidedly different from the genre of the homily. It was not to be an exegetical discourse on scriptural verses loosely strung together but was to be a disquisition on some definite theme based on a text and presented according to a well-defined pattern of component parts. It was to be "synthetic" as distinct from the "analytical" homily. It had to avoid the scholastic aspect of the older dogmatic sermon, and the preacher was advised to shun subject matters and terms of too technical a nature. Its purpose was to "edify" the congregation, and it was to achieve this aim by observing the rules laid down in the manuals of homiletics. The customary parts of the sermon were the exordium, the prayer, the exposition, and the blessing. The sermon, at least the opening prayer, had to have "unction" (*Salbung*) so as to find the way to the heart in an exalted mood.[14] It is this type of sermon that the Jewish preachers in the early nineteenth century felt they had to imitate.

There is a wealth of evidence testifying to the fact that at its initial stage, if not later, Jewish preachers took the Protestant edificatory sermon for their model. They had hardly any choice in the matter, seeing that the traditional *Derashah* had become repugnant to current taste and no homiletical manuals comparable to the Christian ones were available.[15] It is, therefore, understandable that the early Jewish preachers—all of whom were virtuosos of religion, not accredited rabbis—turned to Christian models. Joseph Wolf (1762–1826), who had been bred in the spiritual climate of Mendelssohnian *Haskalah*, and who was teacher and community secretary at Dessau, took Georg Joachim Zollikofer's sermons for his guide.[16] Zollikofer (1730–1788) had cultivated the moralizing sermon[17] and, although he represented an older school of preaching, was still considered as one of the most important German pulpit orators.[18] Wolf's sermons deliberately avoided the complicated artfulness of the *Derashah*. His manner of preaching has been justifiably described as "lucid, simple, easily understandable," criteria that reflect the prevalent homiletical rules.[19] Gotthold Salomon (1784–1862), who achieved fame as a preacher at the Hamburg temple and was highly prolific in his sermonic output,[20] had spent his formative years in close association with Wolf at Dessau. A local minister, Pastor Demarées, introduced him to the sermons of Zollikofer, Johann Friedrich Wilhelm Jerusalem, Franz Volkmar Reinhard, and others, including some French preachers, and occasionally criticized his pulpit performances, pointing out offences against the homiletical rules.[21] His early homiletical library, he himself tells us, contained the sermons of Zollikofer, Reinhard, Marezoll, Löffler, and Claus Harms's *Winterpostille*.[22] This is an interesting collection, testifying to a rather catholic taste. Whereas Zollikofer and his disciple Marezoll[23] represent the moralizing sermon of the strictly rationalist school, Reinhard was the dominant figure on the right wing of *Aufklärung* theology, the so-called supernaturalist school. Although his influence was already waning, he could still be held up, as late as 1811, as a model preacher *par excellence*.[24] Claus Harms, on the other hand, was a revivalist preacher of great original power who believed in the "Spirit" rather than in homiletical rules, and found little to choose between the naturalist and supernaturalist schools of theology.[25]

Salomon's sermons invited comparison with Harms's because of their obvious warmth of feeling,[26] but the comparison is misleading. His manner of preaching is sentimental rather than inspirational. Salomon was also likened to the famous Johann Heinrich Bernhard Dräseke, from 1814 until 1832 pastor in Bremen, later bishop of Magdeburg.[27] A Christian reviewer of one of Salomon's earlier collections of sermons[28] in fact suggested that he had taken for his model "a well-known and renowned teacher of the Christian Church," an allusion that Salomon felt safe in considering a reference to Dräseke. His rejection of this particular allegation is of some interest. He felt flattered, he declared, by the insinuation;

to have chosen such an excellent model would reflect honor on any preacher, Jewish or Christian; in point of fact, however, Dräseke's sermons were unknown to him when he was writing the sermons in question.[29] He had, moreover, been careful not to appropriate or copy the manner and method of any single Christian preacher, notwithstanding the fact that many of the masterworks of Christian pulpit oratory had not remained wholly unknown to him. The manner in which he at times expounded the Scriptures he had learned from none other than the rabbis; strangely enough, he asserts, Dräseke's hermeneutics in many of his sermons bore the most striking resemblance to rabbinic exegesis, as he had had occasion to demonstrate to a Christian scholar who had since died.[30] It is interesting to observe how Salomon seeks to play down his indebtedness to Christian models. He is obviously motivated by a sense of Jewish pride. The compliment paid to him by another Christian author calling him "the Israelite Dräseke" he refuses to accept, since he "deserved neither the bee's honey nor its sting."[31] Yet the fact remains that Salomon felt no hesitation in using and occasionally even in borrowing from Christian models. A case in point is his devotional treatise *Selima's Stunden der Weihe*,[32] which emulates C. W. Spieker's *Emiliens Stunden der Andacht und des Nachdenkens.*[33] Both are addressed to educated young women, and Salomon's book appeared in the year (1816) in which the second edition of Spieker's came out. Salomon personally knew Spieker well. The latter was a Christian preacher in Dessau and took a friendly interest in Salomon.[34] The remarkable aspect about Salomon's book lies, however, not so much in the fact that it took Spieker's treatise for its model but that it contains a whole chapter on the vocation of man (*Bestimmung des Menschen*), which on closer scrutiny reveals itself as a mere paraphrase of Johann Joachim Spalding's famous essay under the same title.[35]

Other preachers were less reluctant to acknowledge their debt to Christian models. Isak Noa Mannheimer (1793–1865), the most vigorous and most endearing of the early preachers and undoubtedly the outstanding figure in the nineteenth-century Jewish pulpit,[36] is the least rule-bound and formalistic among his contemporaries. He is also in the forefront of those pressing for a closer link with the Jewish tradition in homiletics.[37] Yet he admits "that we as pupils and disciples, as novices in the art of preaching which we have been practicing only a little while, can learn a great deal from the masters of the art, and we have gratefully to accept every guidance and instruction offered to us in their schools."[38] Rule-bound (*schulgerechte*) homiletics, he declares, does have a useful purpose. It helps the preacher to express his thoughts in a manner that is comprehensible (*fasslich*), well ordered (*geregelt*), and pleasing (*gefällig*).[39] These criteria echo the leading concepts of current homiletics. On the other hand, Mannheimer exercises a sovereign freedom from the tyranny of rigid rules. What matters is not the smoothness of the outer form but the power of the preacher's innermost convictions. Only the "living spirit" will compel the respect of a receptive, though skeptical, congregation.[40] If Mannheimer refused the lead of Reinhard's homiletics according to rule, he was certainly imbued with the inspirational pattern of Claus Harms's preaching. Although Mannheimer does not mention Harms's name, there is evidence that Mannheimer, born and bred in Copenhagen, was well aware of the great preacher's activities in neighboring Lunden and Kiel in the province of Holstein.[41] The evidence lies not only in the constant use Mannheimer made of the concept of the "Spirit" in the sense in which it is employed by Harms. It may also be found in at least one definite literary borrowing. Mannheimer's simile of the sick man who instead of applying the medicine prescribed for him is content to carry the prescription with him and to read it morning and evening[42] is taken from Harms. In 1817, Harms had expressed the malaise of modern preaching in the words: "The character of their sermon is this: They make [the people] take the prescription instead of the medicine."[43] Mannheimer elaborated the simile in his own way, and used it more than once in his sermons.[44]

While Mannheimer's manner of preaching is decisively formed by the influence of Claus Harms, his friend Leopold Zunz experienced in Berlin at close quarters the impact of Schleiermacher's sermons. Although the letters from Zunz's early years in Berlin make no mention of the great Christian preacher, we have clear evidence from one of the sermons preached in 1821 that Schleiermacher served him as a model.[45] Zunz's activity as a preacher at the New Synagogue in Berlin, though only of short duration (1820–1822), was remarkably productive. Of the sixty-one sermons he delivered, eighteen appeared in print and thirty-nine are extant in his own hand. A close analysis of the entire material has shown the extent to which both Christian homiletical models and current philosophical trends are reflected in these sermons. Apart from Schleiermacher, Reinhard and Dräseke seem to have guided the young preacher.[46] We have no reason to assume that Zunz was in personal contact with Schleiermacher. We know, however, that at a slightly earlier period the young preachers at Jacobson's temple in Berlin (Isaac Levin Auerbach, Karl Siegfried Günsberg, Eduard Kley) had the benefit of such contact. A notice in the *Schlesisches Schriftsteller-Lexikon* reports:

> It was interesting to see how the most popular Christian preachers of the time, viz. Haunstein, [Georg Karl Benjamin] Ritschl, Schleiermacher, and others occasionally visited the German Synagogue on Sabbaths and listened attentively to the young preachers who had ventured into a new field not previously cultivated by their coreligionists; [it was interesting] to the young men themselves to receive, after the services, manifold hints and directives from those great preachers.[47]

The reliability of this priceless notice is borne out by a report in Julius Fürst's *Der Orient* describing the career of K. S. Günsberg. It mentions *inter alia* the "enthusiasm" with which in his younger days, jointly with Kley, he preached at the Berlin temple, "encouraged and esteemed by a Schleiermacher, a Ritschl, and other famous Christian orators."[48]

The novel spectacle of Jewish preachers imitating the style of the Protestant pulpit drew mixed reactions from non-Jewish observers in Germany. We have already recorded the instance of one of the reviews of Salomon's sermons. The "sting" wrapped up in the compliment did not pass unnoticed, as Salomon's retort indicates. There were a number of similar incidents. A review of Salomon Plessner's sermons states that they "follow closely the Christian pattern in both form and content (e.g., immortality, love of neighbor)" and that "one meets here once again a Christian preacher in Israelite garb, the like of whom there are several nowadays."[49] Plessner admits that the form of his sermons takes for its model the rule-bound (*schulgerechten*) Reinhard. He rejects, however, the suggestion that their content is likewise borrowed from Christianity. The Old Testament and rabbinic literature were sufficiently rich in content, including teachings on immortality and love of neighbor, to absolve a knowledgeable Jewish theologian of the necessity of borrowing.[50] In drawing a line between form and content, Plessner thought he had settled the issue. He was certainly right in his own case. His sermons are saturated with rabbinic and even Kabbalistic material. A scholar of note and imbued with traditional piety, Plessner is a somewhat unique figure among the Jewish preachers of the time. He is also a highly controversial figure, praised by some as "the Schleiermacher of the Jews" and severely criticized by others.[51] Far from following the rule-bound form of sermon, he rather inclines to the traditional *Derashah*.[52] The Christian reviewer could not have hit on a more un-Christian specimen of Jewish preaching. Applied to others, the charge was not entirely without foundation in regard to both form and content. In the case of the moralizing Jewish preachers there was little to distinguish them from their Christian models, except the absence of references to the New Testament. Whether their essential ethos was Christian or merely "enlightened" in the sense of *Aufklärung* theology is a moot point. The Jews certainly felt that the tenets of *Aufklärung* represented a common, neutral ground between the faiths rather than a sublimation of Christianity.[53] Many Christians, on the other hand, gave the Jews at best credit for being receptive to the enlightened ideas of their environment.[54] Others even resented Jewish receptivity. The progress of enlightenment and *Bildung* (education) among the Jews in Germany was felt to be incongruous with loyalty to Judaism. Thus, a reviewer of J. L. Saalschütz's devotional treatise *Mahnungen an Gott und Ewigkeit* (1840) takes umbrage at the term "spirit of eternal redemption" (*Geist ewiger Erlösung*) used by the author. The reviewer, Professor Ludwig August Kähler, feels that this term is "foreign" to Jewish sources and betrays the influence of "Christian *Bildung*" in contemporary Jewish thought and way of speech. The "sunrays" of *Bildung* had melted the "frozen soil of positive Judaism." Why, then, refuse to join Christianity and take root in the "warm soil of the spirit" that had given them a new interpretation of what the Jewish prophets had "merely hinted at in dark symbols"? Why should Jews deceive themselves by trying to revivify their religion?[55]

Saalschütz's reply merits to be quoted at some length because it expresses the prevalent Jewish attitude of the period. His first point is that *Bildung*, though specifically colored in every nation, is essentially universal and humanistic. The Jews living in Germany, being "children of the country," have a right to share in the specific forms of German culture that are not denied even to strangers. He, then, takes up the main challenge. "Perhaps, the culture [*Bildung*] of the modern world is Christian to such a degree that in absorbing it we automatically absorb Christian elements, thus becoming, in part, Christians in our way of thinking."[56] He denies this assumption. First, he points out, we have to differentiate between scientific and religious culture. Scientific *Bildung* is by no means Christian. "Even philosophy, which bears an intimate relation to religion, cannot start out, in its a priori method, from revealed teachings. Hence it cannot allow positive Christianity to dominate and guide the course of its investigations. It can only in the end meet religion in so far as the truth it has discovered independently appears to be identical with religion."[57] Obviously, Saalschütz alludes here to German Idealist philosophy, particularly Hegel's. His reading of it as merely "in the end" concurring with Christianity is, however, hardly correct.[58] He is on safer ground when he speaks of the moral aspect of religion. While crediting Christianity with the spread and deepening of morality in the world, he does not want to see the role of Judaism belittled. If it is a question of who is indebted to whom; Modern Judaism cannot owe more to modern Christianity than the Christian religion in its infancy owed to Judaism. The Old Testament is the basis of the New.[59] Moreover, and this is his final and crucial point, Christianity as a moral power is essentially one with Jewish teaching. He qualifies this statement by describing Jewish teaching as still full of vitality wherever taught according to the "truly Divine and pure spirit" that dwells in it. In other words, he confines the postulated identity of Christian moral teaching with Judaism to an enlightened version of Judaism such as is preached from modern Jewish pulpits. To Christian ears, he says, the preaching by Jews of a purified morality, of the solace of religion, and of a holy trust in God (*geläuterte Moral*, *Tröstungen*, *heilige Zuversicht*) sounds like a Christian message. "But we are conscious of the fact that thereby we say nothing foreign to our own religious sources or in conflict with the spirit . . . of our holy Scriptures, which is the spirit of eternal redemption as revealed in them too (albeit in a Jewish dogmatic sense)."[60] Hence, Saalschütz concludes, our morality as following from the principles of monotheism is "wholly and totally" Christian as much as Christian morality is "wholly and totally" identical with ours.[61]

It can hardly be assumed that this reply satisfied Saalschütz's critic. As Abraham Geiger remarked a few years later (1845), when answering Bruno Bauer's strictures upon Judaism, Christian resentment was directed particularly to Reform Judaism, which sought to preserve the Jews within the bounds of their faith by means of an enlightened approach. The employment of *Bildung* in the service of a revival of Judaism as understood by the Reform movement was for this very reason anathema to certain Christians. They would have preferred a clear-cut alternative between a rigid traditional Judaism and—baptism.[62] Seen in this light, the copying of Christian models of preaching in the nineteenth-century Jewish pulpit was bound to arouse the mixed feelings that we have noted. An awareness of this fact may help us toward a readier appreciation of the efforts made by the early preachers to express the message of Judaism in a manner commensurate with the tastes and ideas of their age. Starting from scratch, as it were, they soon mastered the art of which the Christian sermon furnished the model. In 1815, David Fränkel in an article in *Sulamith* surveyed the brief span of development from 1808 onward. In the course of his highly interesting account he takes occasion to counsel patience with the standard of Jewish sermons. One could not expect too much at the beginning, seeing that Jews had had no opportunity nor encouragement to train as pulpit orators. One could not, therefore, entertain the hope of finding preachers of the rank of a Demosthenes, Aeschines, Cicero, Spalding, Zollikofer, or a Reinhard, who aroused such general admiration and delight. It might, however, be expected that popular and famed preachers would arise among the Jews. The experiments of the last few years had proved that such hope was well founded.[63] Over two decades later (in 1839), Isaak Markus Jost could express admiration of the progress that Jewish pulpit oratory (*Kanzelberedsamkeit*) had made in the three decades since its inception. In his view, it had, generally speaking, ascended to the high level of the period, and Jewish preachers could, in some instances, be considered the equals of the best orators of the time. He wishes, however, to apply his praise only to nonrabbinic preachers, since the rabbis, with a few exceptions, were still suffering from a woeful neglect of homiletical training.[64]

TOWARD A JEWISH HOMILETICS

The moralizing type of sermon known as *Erbauungspredigt* ("edificatory sermon") held sway in the Jewish pulpit until the late thirties of the nineteenth century. It had not completely ousted the traditional *Derashah*, particularly in the eastern parts of Germany,[65] but was generally held to be incomparably superior to it. A modernized form of *Derashah* was cultivated by men like Hakam Isaac Bernays in Hamburg and Rabbi Solomon Judah Rapoport in Prague. A correspondent in Geiger's *Zeitschrift*[66] describes Bernays's manner of preaching as conducive to neither instruction nor edification. His sermons were as useless as, perhaps even less useful than, the earlier disputations and controversies displayed in the rabbinic *Derashah*. Passages chosen from Scripture, Talmud, and Midrash were "subjected to exegesis, etymological analysis, criticism and anatomical dissection of all kind without the audience understanding the least of it. Poor people! . . . How I pity them." Yet Heinrich Heine had a different estimate: "I have heard Bernays preach. He is a charlatan. None of the Jews understands him . . . but he is, nevertheless, an ingenious [*geistreicher*] man and he has more spirit within him than Dr. Kley, Salomon, Auerbach I and II."[67] Rapoport's scholarly mind found displeasure in the traditional halakic-haggadic type of *Derashah*, which he was obliged to deliver twice a year in accordance with time-honored custom.[68] He seems, however, to have developed also a modern type of *Derashah*, which greatly appealed to the more progressive section of the Prague community. A glowing report from the year 1844 on his manner of preaching speaks of his way of combining the ancient (*das Antike*) with the modern; of his unfolding of the past and showing how the present is reflected in it. "He vivifies and stimulates by the plenitude of his thought, astonishes by unexpected [*frappante*] interpretations, satisfies by brilliant explanations, and not only appeals to the heart but also gives food to the intellect." He is not a "popular orator" as the term is usually understood, for he presupposes in his listeners a "certain degree of education and scholarly receptivity." Yet the correspondent prefers him to the more glib popular preachers. "If one hears complaints that some famous preachers of our time lack profundity—substituting for it a superficial longwindedness [*seichte Breite*]—it would seem that it is precisely Rapoport's profundity . . . which repels the vulgar majority."[69]

The contrast between the richness of the more traditional type of preaching and the poverty of the modern one was bound to lead to some reappraisal of the situation. The enthusiasm with which the edificatory sermon had been received began to cool off. Its moralizing tone, plain rationality, and sentimentalism no longer satisfied. There is some irony in the fact that the charge of tediousness which had been leveled against the *Derashah* was now applied to the sermon.[70] It was increasingly felt that Jewish preaching should free itself from Christian tutelage and evolve a more genuinely Jewish approach. The clamor for a Jewish homiletics found expression in newspaper articles, critical reviews of sermons, prefaces to collections of sermons, and magazines. The prevailing sentiment was for a return, in some limited way, to a more exegetical type of sermon and a more liberal use of midrashic material. The first strong plea for greater freedom from Christian models came from Mannheimer, in the preface to a volume of sermons published in 1835. Notwithstanding his sense of obligation to the Christian "masters of the art," he does not want to forget "that in God's sanctuary we stand on our own native ground"; that "we have received a treasure from our Fathers which God has called upon us to preserve. . . It would be treason . . . if we wanted to erase with a single stroke of the pen the whole past of our nation or a few millennia in between, as would seem to be the manner of not a few." Referring specifically to the sermon, he says: "It is always better to feed on one's own resources than to live from alms, and it is better to cultivate one's own soil than to glean sparingly [*ein dürftige Nachlese halten*] on foreign ground." He does not want to regard the rule-bound sermon of the Protestant type as "the one and only form" and as possessing a salvational monopoly. "On the contrary, it would seem to me as if the acquisition of a form not particularly our own only served to cover up a poverty of spirit, without, however, concealing, let alone preventing it; for form cannot create ideas; it fetters rather than liberates the spirit."[71] Mannheimer's sermons fully live up to the principles he professed. They struck his contemporaries as extremely powerful and moving, precisely because of the Jewish spirit that animated them. Rapoport wrote to Samuel David Luzzatto in 1832: "I read one of his [Mannheimer's] sermons [*derashot*] for the seventh day of Pesach and found it truly precious."[72] The young Abraham Geiger writes in the same year to S. Frensdorf: "Mannheimer of Vienna was here [in Frankfurt], and I believe [myself] . . . to be right in considering him a very good Jewish preacher. He excerpts the Talmud and the Midrashim for use in his sermons."[73] It is significant that Mannheimer's concern with rabbinic material is specially mentioned. Such practice was obviously considered a novelty in a modern preacher. Mannheimer, in fact, appended to his sermons a table of source references that gives tangible evidence of his perusal of rabbinic material.

An attempt in the direction of a new theory of Jewish homiletics was made by Ludwig Philippson in an essay on the vocation of the Jewish preacher (1835).[74] In reviewing the situation he declared:

> There is one party which demands from the Israelite preacher only pure moralizing: the extremists of this party want the Israelite sermon to resemble altogether the sermon of other religions; indeed, an imitation and copying of the forms of speech [*Rede-Formeln*] of those [religions] is welcomed. Another party wants the Israelite sermon to be but a *Derashah* in a new garb; the more it approximates to the latter in form, content, and subject matter, the more worthy of approval it appears to be. As experience has taught me, the great majority [of people] takes the right road . . . by demanding an intermediate position.[75]

The theological considerations that prompted Philippson's attitude need not detain us here.[76] In the present context, his reappraisal of the form of the sermon is to be noted. In order to link up with tradition and achieve a more "organic" character, Jewish theology has to cultivate a type of sermon different from the Christian. It must not restrict itself to a "free exposition of a Biblical text" but has to utilize "our theological literature" in its wider range. Thereby it will reflect the "older [*bisherige*] popular wisdom" and come closer to actual life. The exposition must take on a historical color. Hence the analytical method is to be preferred to the synthetic. The difficulties of tracing teachings of a general character in historic events are not to be ignored. They call for greater acumen (*Scharfsinn*) in the production of a sermon. Seeing, however, that acumen is a characteristic trait of the Jewish nation, the appetite for it has to be satisfied.[77] Philippson amplified his homiletical theory in letters and essays published in collected form posthumously by Meyer Kayserling.[78] In the preface to *Siloah*, a two-volume work containing a collection of his own sermons,[79] he vigorously pleads for the right of the modern sermon to "lean upon her elder sister," namely, the *Derashah*, and to use "appropriate parts" from the mass of material offered by the Talmudim, Midrashim, and the liturgy. It could either preach on a theme based on a text or engage in an exegetical treatment of a Biblical or rabbinic passage.[80]

It cannot be said that Philippson's middle-of-the-road theory shows great depths of perception. It has the undoubted merit of having raised the problem of a Jewish homiletics, but it is rather superficial and not original even in its advocacy of a partial return to the analytical (exegetical) type of sermon. The same tendency prevailed also in the Christian pulpit of the time, and Philippson's use of the terms "synthetic" and "analytical" clearly indicates that he echoed the slogans of the discussion that went on in contemporary Christian circles. Some preachers regarded the analytical form or homily as deficient because it lacked "inner unity" (Schleiermacher) and was "filling but not satisfying" (Harms). Some approved of both types of preaching (Marheineke), while still others preferred the "freer" form of the homily to the synthetic sermon (Tholuck). The debate is reviewed in Christian Palmer's *Evangelische Homiletik* (1842). Palmer himself suggests that both methods have equal right, and that a good homily has much in common with a good sermon. For neither will a good homily lack inner coherence nor will a sermon of the synthetic type be anything but an exposition of the text.[81] Philippson's essay of 1835 obviously reflects the discussion that Palmer was to review some years later. It discerns the prevalent trend toward greater latitude in the method of preaching and applies it to good advantage for a revision of the Jewish sermon.

The same is true of an attempt made by a certain J. A. Fränkel in an essay published in 1840.[82] The author felt that the time had come for "establishing certain rules of homiletics from a Jewish point of view." While secular rhetoric of the classical models and the Christian oratory of a Reinhard,[83] Teller, Schleiermacher, or Theremin could be consulted with profit, the "fundament" of a Jewish homiletics had to be in harmony with Jewish principles. He, therefore, proposed to investigate the historical development of the Jewish sermon so as to derive the rules of Jewish homiletics a posteriori from the best sermons. Unfortunately, this laudable effort was undertaken with insufficient means,[84] and the result is extremely meager. Yet certain observations made by the author are noteworthy. He rejects the old type of *Derashah* still practiced by the Polish *darshanim* as repugnant to the taste of modern *Bildung* (education). He remarks, however, that it had been more effective than the best sermons of the most recent preachers. The question, then, was how to devise modern rules of homiletics that could be expected to take the place of the *Derashah*. Should the sermon be analytical or synthetic? In other words, should it take the form of the homily, or expound a set theme, or do both? Fränkel wishes to leave the decision to the free choice of the preacher who would have to consider the text, the theme, the occasion, etc. His sympathies, however, he admits, lie with the homily,[85] while, rather inconsistently, he pleads in the end for the synthetic sermon.[86] Like Philippson, he also makes a plea for the use of Talmud and Midrash, albeit restricted to "moral sentences."[87]

With infinitely greater authority Zacharias Frankel[88] called for a reorientation in Jewish preaching. Remarkably enough, he too echoes the Christian discussion of the topic sermon versus homily, and makes explicit reference to it. Writing as he did in 1845, he might have read Palmer's *Homiletik* of 1842, which Manuel Joel was to use from 1858 onward in his lectures on homiletics at the Breslau Seminary.[89]

> For every listener [Frankel says] especially the Jewish one, there lies an extraordinary charm in an ingenious [*geistreichen*] development and exposition of the text. . . . The sermon will thereby perhaps approach the homily but we see in this no disadvantage: even many excellent Christian pulpit orators desire a return to the homily, since the sermon, although a product of art, offers many a time too little that is essential [*wesentlich*] and of enduring value; it dwells on a single concept and flattens it out by rhetoric until it becomes tedious. For the Jew, whose vivacious mind loves the unexpected [*das Frappante*][90] and who is accustomed from former times to ingenious interpretations, the sermon is bound to be some-

what unsatisfactory. Hence our rabbis and orators should give more consideration to the characteristic element of Jewish homiletics and should not take the Christian sermon alone for their model.[91]

All these remonstrations did not have the effect of considerably altering the character of the Jewish sermon. True, preaching became less stilted and less subservient to rigid rules, but it did not revert to the homily or to a kind of modern Midrash. It did not evolve a specifically Jewish type of homiletics. Nor did it follow the example of the traditional *Derashah* by making a rabbinic haggadah or midrash the object of exegesis. A glance at the long list of published sermons compiled by Siegmund Maybaum toward the end of the century[92] clearly indicates that the form of the sermon remained more or less static: Most of the sermons deal with some general theme based on a biblical text. Maybaum only reflects the prevalent trend when he declares the exegesis of talmudic or midrashic passages on their own as impermissible in a sermon, and disagrees with Philippson's view to the contrary.[93] The deeper reason for this attitude lies in the fact that the concept of edification (*Erbauung*) as the purpose of preaching was never seriously challenged throughout the century, as will be shown further below.[94] The only change brought about by the groping for a more Jewish tone in the sermon was the use, in varying degree, made of talmudic and midrashic material in a subsidiary capacity. Maybaum himself gives unstinted approval to the judicious employment of such material in this limited sense.[95] As we have seen, Mannheimer had been the first to act in this manner. He was followed by Michael Sachs and later, on a more lavish scale, by Adolf Jellinek.

Sachs, who was preacher in Prague from 1836 until his appointment in Berlin in 1844, came under the influence of Solomon Judah Rapoport, who held a high opinion of him.[96] The atmosphere of learning in the Prague community of that time and, in particular, the impact of Rapoport's personality enabled him to develop an inner affinity with the authentic Jewish tradition.[97] As early as 1839 he conceived a plan to "describe the character of midrashic literature in its entire range." Zunz's *Die gottesdienstlichen Vorträge der Juden*, which had appeared in 1832, did not seem to him to do justice to the inner life pulsating in the Midrash. It was but an outline that needed filling in.[98] His friend Moritz Veit had urged him in 1837[99] to devote his attention to the Midrash. "If I were to become a Jewish preacher, I would engage in no other literature, for it [sc. Midrash] seems to me an inexhaustible store for the popular speaker."[100] He himself had just discovered, under the tutorship of Salomon Plessner,[101] the "true life" animating midrashic literature. Sachs's first literary effort in the midrashic field was an essay published in 1843[102] that was, however, rather poor and called forth Veit's undisguised criticism.[103] All the greater was the success of Sachs's *Die religiöse Poesie der Juden in Spanien* (Berlin, 1845). The introductory chapter contains an enthusiastic account of the character of the Midrash and the Talmud.[104] As a work of scholarship it is obviously unconcerned with the practical application of the insights won to the requirements of homiletics. Yet the fact that as result of his studies Sachs now "lived" in the world of the Midrash[105] was bound to express itself in his preaching. In contrast to Abraham Geiger, who saw in rabbinic exegesis a regrettable aberration,[106] Sachs was able to appreciate the sense of piety manifested in the midrashic way of interpreting Scripture as an ever-present guide to life.[107] The Midrash, as distinct from normative halakah, had been the veritable domain of popular teaching and had served the purpose of "edification"(*Erbauung*) and "elevation" (*Erhebung*).[108]

Sachs's posthumously published sermons,[109] though based on biblical texts throughout, indeed make ample use of rabbinic material. Talmudic and midrashic texts are skillfully interwoven with the exposition and help to introduce a traditional flavor. Passages of a decidedly mystical nature are interpreted in a rational sense and thus integrated into the prevalent tenor of the sermon. A few examples will illustrate the point. The statement (*Genesis Rabba* 47:6), "The patriarchs are the *merkabah*," means: The patriarchs founded the kingdom of a higher life in the world; they are the carriers of the highest thoughts: that is, the knowledge of God (I, 241). —Rabbi Akiba's warning: "When you come to the place of the pure marble plates, do not say 'Water! Water!'" (*Ḥagigah* 14b)—a reference to the dangers facing the mystic in his ascent[110]—is interpreted as a warning not to consider the fundamental pillars of the faith as subject to the flux of change (I, 349–350). —The haggadic motif (*Baba Bathra* 16b) of the pearl worn by Abraham hanging from his neck and, when he was about to die, fixed upon the sphere of the sun is said to refer to his wisdom (see Prov. 1:9), his most noble conviction openly confessed; when he died, his example had not been in vain; it did not become invisible and powerless. He had taught others to look up to heaven to draw courage and joy from those mysterious realms above (I, 202–203).

Sachs's concern with the Midrash and Haggadah is not merely the historian's interest in documents of the past. It evinces his desire to revive the true "spirit" of Judaism, which he sees throttled by a misconceived enlightenment. In the Midrash and Haggadah he sees an expression of a living spirit interpreting the present in the light of the past and integrating the past into the present. Imbued with this view of the "organic" character of the Jewish tradition, he is not content to use the old texts, biblical and rabbinic, merely as convenient proof texts to support some current opinion but senses in them the authentic power of the Jewish spirit.[111] Whether his own reading of midrashic and haggadic texts is correct may in many cases be doubted. The specimens just quoted negate such an assumption. Yet what matters to Sachs is the freedom of the Jewish spirit in every age to project itself into the past and to mould the past in the image of the present. To him, the "spirit" is "the vehicle for the free, creative interpretation of traditional religion by those who are neither stagnant nor blind and misled by a falsely understood enlightenment."[112] Unlike Mannheimer, whose concept of the "Spirit" reflects a revivalist theology, Sachs is obviously influenced by Hegel's notion of the "Spirit of God in His Community."[113] His letters to Veit (1839) mention his preoccupation with Hegel and quote the Hegelian phrase *Geist des Herrn in seiner Gemeinde* as being no less Jewish than Christian.[114] In one of his sermons Sachs speaks of "the Spirit of God offered to us as a free expression of the innermost life, as the free, living movement within the circle of God's Teaching."[115] His attitude to rabbinic literature and the use he makes of it in the sermon are thus geared to a definite philosophy, however vaguely conceived. They certainly do not represent a naïve return to the older sermonic practice.

The position is somewhat different in the case of Adolf Jellinek, the celebrated preacher of Vienna who succeeded Mannheimer.[116] A prolific scholar in the fields of the Midrash and Kabbalah, he excelled in the art of weaving an abundance of quotations from biblical and rabbinic sources into the texture of his sermons. His associative memory and the skillfulness of his interpretations, wedded to his oratorical brilliance, single him out as the most fascinating preacher of the period. In him Jewish homiletics as advocated by Zacharias Frankel certainly came into its own. Many of his sermons are mosaics of citations from the most variegated fields of Jewish literature without even indications of the sources except in footnotes to the printed editions. In a sense, they continue the process of free midrashic production by giving novel and unexpected turns of meaning to the texts quoted. In terms of their strong Jewish flavor they are poles apart from the sermons of the early nineteenth century and its later survivals.[117]

EDIFICATION AS THE PURPOSE OF THE SERMON

Throughout the nineteenth century Jewish preachers subscribed to the concept of edification (*Erbauung*) as the main purpose of the sermon. With it were linked such subsidiary notions as instruction (*Belehrung*), solace (*Trost*), enthusiasm (*Begeisterung*), and, above all, elevation (*Erhebung*), the latter being often used as almost synonymous with edification. Under Hegelian influence the term *Erhebung* acquired a specific connotation that tended to supersede the validity of elevation as the true end of preaching. Some prominent Jewish preachers (Sachs, Holdheim, Geiger, Joel) reflect this tendency without, however, discarding the concept of edification. At the end of the century, Maybaum sums up the purpose of the sermon as the "sentiment of edification," in which preacher and congregation jointly experience a sense of happy "connection" (*Zusammenhang*) with God.[118]

The term "edification" is a New Testament coinage and a key notion in Christian homiletics. Its acceptance by the Jewish preachers was facilitated by the fact that eighteenth-century *Aufklärung* theology had gradually emptied this concept of its specifically Christian connotation and invested it with a meaning that involved no conflict. The eighteenth-century development of this concept is therefore of paramount interest for an understanding of the significance it came to have for the Jewish preachers in search of a formula adequate to their purposes.

The New Testament passages concerned speak of edification (*oikodome*) as the "building" of a "holy temple": those who are "fellow-citizens with the saints" are "builded together" in God "for an habitation of God through the Spirit" (Eph. 2:19–22). One may "edify" another by preaching the kingdom of God (Rom. 14:19) and by seeking his good (Rom. 15:2). Through him that prophesies "the Church may receive edifying" (I Cor. 14:5). "Edification" becomes a technical term in the Pietist movement, initiated by Philip Jacob Spener (1635–1705). Mutual edification (*aedificatio mutua*) was introduced in 1670 at Spener's devotional meetings (*collegia pietatis*), which were considered more salutary than listening to sermons.[119] The stress on edification led, however, to a new conception of the sermon. In his *Pia Desideria* (1675) Spener advocated a reform of preaching in the direction of edification in order to counteract the excessive rationalism that had become rampant in the pulpit. The edificatory sermon in its extreme form was developed by Nicolaus Ludwig Count von Zinzendorf (1700–1760), founder of the "Herrenhuter Brüdergemeinde." His mystical-sensuous language and the eruptive, enthusiastic nature of his utterances testify to a sense of charismatic experience.[120] His emphasis on feeling influenced Schleiermacher, and his inspirational theory of preaching was echoed by Claus Harms.[121] To the Jewish preachers in the nineteenth century Pietism in its excessive form was utter anathema.[122]

The pietistic trend in preaching was strongly contested by the theology of *Aufklärung*. Mosheim took issue with the Spener school and created a type of edificatory sermon different from Spener's. In his *Anweisung erbaulich zu predigen* (1763), he defined the purpose of preaching as two-fold: (1) to confirm and enlarge the congregation's understanding (*Erkenntnis*) of religion, and (2) to awaken and encourage it toward a zeal and increase in the blissful state of soul called *Gottseligkeit* (happiness in God). The ultimate goal is *Gottseligkeit*. This term does not denote a mere state of pious emotion, nor is it "faith" in the Lutheran sense, but it indicates "holiness" as the state of grace.[123] Edification leading to *Gottseligkeit* concerns both the intellect and the will. "The will is edified when a good resolution is either entered into or, having existed before, is strengthened and confirmed."[124] In order to edify the will the preacher has to arouse the emotions by a vivid portrayal of the subject matter.[125] The arousal of emotions is clearly not an end in itself but merely a way of moving the will. Mosheim distinguishes between the arousal or "awakening" of those still in a state of corrupted nature and those already partaking of grace. The former will as a result of edification enter the state of grace. They will be edified in the sense of the New Testament meaning of the term: "putting on the new man." The latter will be encouraged to grow in *Gottseligkeit*, edification in this case meaning "to build a house on a groundwork already laid."[126] The edificatory sermon as understood by Mosheim has a thoroughly Christian character. It is meant to create the Christian state of grace and to confirm it in the converted. It does, however, not imply the operation of supranatural grace upon the emotions. It is the preacher's art and it alone that moves the will. The pietistic doctrine is clearly discarded.[127] Moreover, Mosheim's homiletical theory already tends in the direction of the moralizing sermon. It describes the edification of intellect and will in terms of their "improvement." "He who preaches wants to improve or edify . . . the intellect and will of his listeners."[128] This term foreshadows the moralistic interpretation of the term "edification" which became prominent in the latter part of the eighteenth century.

Mosheim's doctrine broke the pietistic monopoly of the concept of edification by adopting this term for a definition of the Christian sermon as such. His theory was taken up by Christian Friedrich Engelmann in his *Versuch einer Theorie über die Erbauung* (Breslau and Leipzig, 1771). From now on every treatise and manual on homiletics in Protestant literature in Germany will define preaching in terms of its edificatory purpose, and these publications will differ only in the interpretation of this term. Of the numerous tracts published in the period from 1771 down to Palmer's *Evangelische Homiletik* (1842),[129] we shall mention only a few as specimens of prevailing trends of development.

Like Mosheim, Johann Friedrich Teller tends toward the moralizing sermon. His *Theorie der christlichen Beredsamkeit* (Leipzig, 1774) sees the dual purpose of the sermon in the "improvement" of the intellect and the will. The sermon "wants to make the whole man wiser and more virtuous." It will achieve this goal by "moving" the listener, provided the effect is a lasting one. "In short," the sermon is to "edify" the congregation, which means to "pull down the old edifice and establish a new one in its place"; in other words, "to make man into a temple of God in which God's Spirit dwells." This, however, can be done only "with the help of God's cooperation," which is "indispensable" to the preacher. "Except the Lord *build* the house, they labor in vain that build it" (Psalm 127:1).[130] It is interesting to see how both Mosheim and Teller wish to preserve the Christian character of edification by invoking the New Testament imagery, supported in Teller's case by an ingenious exegesis of Ps. 127:1. Moral "improvement" is given a spiritual quality. It becomes the state of grace. While Mosheim, strangely enough, attributes the salvational effect to the preacher's art, Teller emphasizes the need for Divine cooperation. There is a Calvinist ring in his reference to making "the whole man" better and to the need of "pulling down" the old edifice. These theological references cannot, however, conceal the growing trend toward pure rationalism. They no longer express a predominantly theological orientation nor are they testimonies to a full-blooded religious experience. They bear a rather shadowy character and could be construed to signify mere metaphors of man's moral improvement. The Jewish preachers obviously regarded them in this light when, in the nineteenth century, they adopted the current notion of edification. They believed they could safely ignore its theological implications, such as the Christian doctrine of the Fall and of grace.

The moralistic interpretation of edification received a decisive stimulus from Johann Joachim Spalding, the eminent representative of the Berlin theology of *Aufklärung*. In attacking the Pietist notion of edification, his *Gedanken über den Werth der Gefühle in dem Christenthum*[131] made the point that the moral conscience and its sentiments (*Empfindungen*) are the sole evidence of the manifestation of God's Spirit in man.[132] The emotions (*Regungen*) of love, terror, shame, desire, doubt, trust, and joy, which are involved in the religious experience of conversion, are the work of the uniform Divine Power operating upon the conscience. It is the moral faculty of the soul that is awakened and vivified by the influence of the Divine Spirit. The diversity of feelings is due to the differences of individual temperament and to the play of the imagination.[133] Spalding denies the value of feelings unrelated to the moral edification of man. This view has an important bearing on the evaluation of preaching. In one of his sermons[134] Spalding explains that edification is to be measured by the fruits it produces. Edification means our moral improvement, by which alone we become pleasing in the eyes of God and achieve a state of mind (*Gemüthsverfassung*) characterized by peace of soul, contentedness, and hope.[135] A sermon that creates an enduring moral disposition may be called edificatory (*erbaulich*).[136] Spalding's view of the sermon is expressed on similar lines in his *Über die Nutzbarkeit des Predigtamtes und ihre Beförderung* (1772). His writings were still popular in the early part of the nineteenth century. Moses Mendelssohn's preoccupation with Spalding's *Bestimmung des Menschen* in response to Thomas Abbt's request[137] helped to enhance the Christian theologian's prestige among the Jews.[138] His doctrine of the purpose and character of preaching must, therefore, be reckoned among the formative influences upon the Jewish sermon.

In 1785 there appeared Immanuel Kant's *Grundlegung zur Metaphysik der Sitten*, to be followed in 1788 by his *Kritik der praktischen Vernunft* and in 1793 by his *Die Religion innerhalb der Grenzen der blossen Vernunft*. The impact of Kant's moral and religious philosophy on homiletics can be traced immediately in Johann Wilhelm Schmid's *Anleitung zum populären Kanzelvortrag*,[139] which defines edification as "the promotion of moral improvement in the spirit of the religion of Jesus." The preacher must "guide the listeners toward correct moral principles" that imply respect (*Achtung*) for the moral law and the preponderance of the moral viewpoint over the inclinations (*Neigungen*).[140] From the fairly large body of Kant-inspired works on homiletics,[141] we may also mention Johann Friedrich Wilhelm Thym's *Historisch-kritisches Lehrbuch der Homiletik* (Halle, 1880). It considers morality as "the chief purpose of all preaching." To teach religion is to "present the laws of practical reason as divine precepts." Hence "improvement is and remains the principal part of true edification."[142] There is, however, still another aspect to edification. The edificatory sermon not only perfects morality but also "awakens devotional feelings" (*Andachtsgefühle*).[143] This introduces a pietistic element into the definition of the purpose of preaching. The emotional element is, however, not an end in itself, as is the case in Pietism. It is subordinated to the moral purpose as a means toward it.[144] Herein, too, Thym follows the lead given by Kant. For Kant, devotion (*Andacht*) and the emotion (*Rührung*) accompanying it have meaning as leading toward moral improvement or edification. They help to attune the mind to the adoption of moral principles. Hence edification is the result of devotion, not identical with it. Kant derides the Pietists, who "believe themselves tremendously edified [*erbaut*] . . . while absolutely nothing has been built [*gebauet*], yea, where no hand has been put to the work." Edification as moral improvement becomes actual only if man, on the basis of firm principles squaring with well-understood concepts, "builds up a new man as a temple of God." This "building" can progress but slowly. It will not rise by itself, like the walls of Thebes, to the music of sighs and yearning wishes.[145] Thym adopted this view of edification as the combined result of *Andacht* and moral effort. *Erbauung* and *Andacht* henceforth appear frequently together as the purposes of preaching, although, strictly speaking, they are not coordinated but related to each other as means and end. By admitting devotional feeling as an integral, though subordinate, part of the purpose of the sermon, Thym, like Kant before him, paid a tribute to Pietism. He must have felt that the promotion of morality alone did not suffice as a raison d'être of preaching. Something more specifically religious was called for as an additional, albeit subsidiary, purpose. Devotional feeling seemed to supply the want. Yet on close inspection this undefined feeling turns out to be somewhat vague and barren. Being denied the full-blooded life of the Pietist religious experience and being made wholly subservient to moral ends without anchorage in theological doctrine, it is bereft of any substance of its own. It is this kind of pure feeling that becomes the locus of mere "sighs and yearning wishes," which Kant diagnosed in the Pietists but which soon turned out to be even more pronounced in the romantics, as Hegel pointed out.

In his *Phänomenologie des Geistes* (1807), Hegel characterized romantic religion as "bad subjectivity" or "unhappy consciousness," in which the mind (*Geist*) is unfree and as yet unrealized. In this state man is dominated by a sense of feeling that has itself as the object of this feeling. Sublime words like "eternal," "holy," "infinite" exercise an elevating power over him precisely because they are devoid of conceptual content. Whereas the Middle Ages and the scholasticism of seventeenth-century Enlightenment still possessed a "Heaven with an ample wealth of ideas and images," the eighteenth-century theology of *Aufklärung* had shrunk to mere shades and shells of concepts. In this impoverished state the mind, like a wanderer in the desert yearning for a mere drink of water, seemed to long for but a feeling of the Divine in order to revive itself. He who seeks to escape the vanity of the Finite is left with only a yearning for a vacuous Beyond, and thus religion is driven back upon mere feeling. "Religion builds in the heart of the individual its temple and altars, and sighing and prayers seek the God whose contemplation it denies itself." Knowledge and faith are replaced by edification. Viewed in this light, edification appears as purely subjective, unsubstantial, and inferior to knowledge and faith.[146] By the same token, the common type of devotion (*Andacht*) is rejected by Hegel. In it, "one rises above finitude and forgets it; but by forgetting it one has not really canceled it."[147] The devotion of the "unhappy consciousness" is mere *An-dacht*, that is, a mere approach to thinking, as it were (*es geht sozusagen nur an das Denken hin*); it remains "a musical thinking which fails to achieve conceptuality."[148] By way of contrast, the truly devout (*der Andächtige*) "immerses himself with his heart, his devotion, his will in his object so that at this highest point of devotion he has canceled the separation that prevails at the stage of consciousness."[149]

Hegel himself did not evolve a theory of preaching, but his philosophy of religion furnished the elements from which such a theory could be constructed. Of relevance in this respect are his notion of "elevation" (*Erhebung*) and of the *Kultus* as the means whereby the finite spirit becomes conscious of its oneness with the absolute Spirit. Hegel defines religion as "the knowledge of the divine Spirit of itself by the mediation of the finite spirit."[150] This involves two aspects: the activity of the divine Spirit as knowing itself in the finite spirit, and the activity of the finite spirit as knowing itself essentially one with the absolute Spirit. In the *Kultus* the finite spirit becomes conscious of its essence: that is, of its oneness with the absolute Spirit. The relation of God, the absolute Spirit, to the finite spirit is God's revelation to man. Correspondingly, the relation of the finite spirit to God is realized in the *Kultus*, in which man's elevation to God takes place. Religion comprises both aspects: It is God's moving toward man and man's moving toward God. In elevating itself to God, the spirit exercises its freedom. Man recognizes in everything accidental and finite something infinite and necessary. As he finds no satisfaction in the accidental nature of things, he elevates himself from the finite to the Absolute. In the *Kultus* Hegel sees therefore a conversion of the spirit, a return to the Absolute. In it the alienation that the consciousness experiences as soon as it awakens is being healed. Man relinquishes his isolation and finds his true self in the general. He liberates himself from the vanity of the finite and elevates himself to himself in truth.[151] This elevation demands a price: that is, the sacrificial abandonment of the finite, the annihilation of mere individuality. Yet in the *Kultus* such sacrifice becomes an object of supreme enjoyment. For in it man experiences the reconciliation of his finite spirit with the Absolute.[152]

In his *Grundlegung der Homiletik* (1811) Philipp Konrad Marheineke, the outstanding theologian of the Hegel school, elaborated his master's views from a homiletical viewpoint. "All priestly life and activity is borne upon the idea of sacrifice . . . sacrifice is the soul of priesthood. . . . For to sacrifice is but to consecrate what is transient and mere appearance to the eternal and primordial." Through the act of sacrifice, reconciliation is effected.[153] Edification is interpreted as the reconciliation between God and man in the sense in which Hegel had understood this term. This reconciliation, which, again following Hegel, is seen to be expressed in Christ as the God-man, forms "the one and only ever-recurrent and inexhaustible theme of the Christian sermon"; it is the ground "upon which a temple of God is to be built in every sermon." The preacher's task is neither teaching (for he is not concerned with ignorance) nor producing the sentiment of *Rührung* (being moved), but edification in the sense of reconciliation.[154]

The Christological element comes back also with full force in Schleiermacher's sermons and theory of homiletics. Notwithstanding his intimate concern with philosophy and the philosophical interpretation of religion, his sermons are imbued with a thoroughly Christian piety. They are intended solely for the "joint edification" (*gemeinsame Erbauung*) of Christians qua Christians. As Alexander Schweizer's penetrating account of Schleiermacher as a preacher has it, "He wanted to address his community as brethren so as to develop their Christian consciousness, not to found it; he wanted to show it to them, to purify and strengthen, not to impart it to them as something new."[155] The morality that he preached was not philosophical but Christian morality. Preaching, therefore, was to him not an exercise in moral improvement but was meant to communicate the preacher's own personal sense of piety. Schleiermacher defined the sermon as a "testifying to one's own experience so as to arouse in others a desire to have the same kind of experience."[156] As for edification, it is "the awakening and vivification of the pious consciousness," and it is based upon the communication of the pious self-consciousness reflecting upon itself (*Mitteilung des zum Gedanken gewordenen frommen Selbstbewusstseins*).[157] Finally, in Claus Harms's view of the sermon the *Aufklärung* approach is radically discarded. Reason is not the organ of religion. Only what comes from the heart goes to the heart. The Christian preacher must be oriented toward the Christian salvational order (*Heilsordnung*). His experience of inspiration and of love determines the sermon. Before he can edify others, he has to be edified himself.[158]

In all definitions of *Erbauung* the concept of edification is based on the New Testament meaning of the term. This semantic approach is responsible for the stress on the final achievement of the sermon: that is, the "building up" of the new man as a lasting effect. The emphasis on the true end and purpose of the sermon does not, however, obliterate the more colloquial meaning of the word *Erbauung* as "enjoyment" of a sublime kind. Nor is this particular meaning ignored or lost sight of. On closer inspection it will be found to be either implied or articulated in some way. It is assumed as a potent factor in the "mutual edification" cultivated by the Pietists. The *collegia pietatis* develop edification to a fine art of spiritual enjoyment of an individualistic character, and the Pietist sermon follows suit. The edificatory quality (*Erbaulichkeit*) assumes a highly subjective note. The German verb *erbauen* is from now on used with a reflexive pronoun: *sich erbauen*.[159] This expression clearly indicates a sense of enjoyment. Mosheim's term *Gottseligkeit* likewise signifies more than the objective achievement of the state of grace. It implies also the subjective element of *Seligkeit* (bliss, happiness). The theologians of *Aufklärung* seem to leave little scope for edification in the sense of enjoyment when they define this term in purely moralistic fashion. Yet they obviously regard moral edification as yielding a noble kind of spiritual satisfaction and uplift of soul. Even Kant, for all his rigorous emphasis on duty as opposed to the inclinations, speaks of the "moral enthusiasm" (*sittliche Begeisterung*) that the sermon is meant to arouse, and describes devotion (*Andacht*) as the "subjective aspect" of the effect of the moral idea.[160] The romantics' indulgence in "bad subjectivity" certainly produced a type of edification amounting to self-enjoyment. As for Hegel, the element of enjoyment is seen as a characteristic feature of the cultus: In the sacrifice of mere subjectivity that is the essence of the *Kultus* the people achieve the highest degree of self-enjoyment. As we have seen, Marheineke made this view fruitful for an understanding of what edification through the sermon means. We may add that he describes the "power of the Word" uttered by the preacher as "instructive, regenerative, and imparting a sense of blissfulness [*beseligend*]."[161]

This aspect of enjoyableness as the psychological secret of *Erbauung* was given its due emphasis in Palmer's *Evangelische Homiletik*. In his view, an analysis of edification has to proceed from the semantic value of the word as used in current speech, not from its original meaning in the New Testament. Consequently, the purpose of the sermon will be found to lie not merely in the ultimate fruits (regeneration, improvement) it is to produce but also in the present enjoyment it offers. "Not just the factual transformation, renewal and promotion of the spiritual life but the very enjoyment of the food which the word of God offers us in the sermon is edification." Even those whom the sermon will fail to "awaken" to a new life may still be "edified" by it.[162] This is an important observation. It explains the peculiar attraction that the sermon may have even for those who will not be converted by it. The fascination it holds is described as due to the fact that there is an element of sheer enjoyment in a good sermon. In a deeper sense, the enjoyment consists in the exhilarating effect of hearing the truth of the Scriptures expressed through the living personality of the preacher.[163] Palmer's homiletical theory broke new ground in the understanding of the nature of edification by articulating what had been vaguely felt before. In a sense, he de-Christianized the definition of *Erbauung* by reverting to the colloquial meaning of the term as "enjoyment" rather than "building up" the new man.

The Jewish preachers in the early nineteenth century were well aware of the various shades of meaning attaching to the term "edification." This is attested to by the far from uniform manner in which they speak about the concept of *Erbauung*. We hear echoes of Mosheim's discussion of the subject in David Fränkel's review of Jewish preaching in 1815, when he refers to the sermon as "highly salutary and necessary for the awakening [*Erweckung*] and vivification [*Belebung*] of religious virtues and for the promotion of morality."[164] The term *Gottseligkeit*, which, according to Mosheim, denotes the ultimate purpose of the edificatory sermon, occurs not infrequently in Jewish speech. Here it is understood as identical with either moral virtue or piety. Kley preached on "*Gottseligkeit* and virtue"[165] and treated as synonyms the "exhortation toward the good, encouragement toward virtue, and spur toward a way of life that is *gottselig*."[166] Mannheimer, on the other hand, preached *Gottseligkeit* in the sense of piety.[167] It may be noted that Moses Mendelssohn had already used the term in connection with the concept of edification.[168] Moral "improvement," which from Mosheim onward figured so prominently in the discussion of our topic, was likewise a recurrent theme in Jewish accounts of the purpose of the sermon. As late as 1841, G. Philippson could still sum up the aim of the sermon as "the improvement of the individual through edification."[169] It was the setting up of this goal that produced the moralizing type of sermon. In the Jewish social and political context "improvement" was, however, considered as a concern not merely of the individual. In the struggle for emancipation it came to signify the effort toward raising the moral level of the Jewish people as a prelude to "civil improvement" (*bürgerliche Verbesserung*). Dohm's famous treatise had blamed the oppression to which the Jews had been subjected as responsible for their moral degeneracy.[170] Mendelssohn had rejected the charge of moral inferiority,[171] but in the ensuing struggle for civil equality the Jews were eager to raise their moral, social, and cultural standards. "Improvement" or "ennoblement" (*Veredelung*) thus became a prominent topic in the pulpit. Zunz's sermons in particular stress the wider political aspect of this theme.[172] Moralizing preaching, though taking its cue from the *Aufklärung* sermon, is here fulfilling a specific function. The extent to which "improvement" came to denote a sociopolitical goal may be gauged from the fact that sermons sometimes stressed the need for occupational changes and pleaded with parents to give their children a training in agriculture and the handicrafts.[173] From the time of Mendelssohn onward this kind of change was constantly being advocated as a means toward creating healthier moral and social conditions. A reviewer in Fürst's *Annalen* praised a sermon published by Leopold Schott, rabbi of Randegg, because it urged the members of the congregation to effect such changes: "edification" was one thing, but it was not of lasting and practical value. It was necessary to implant the "true seed of improvement."[174] It is interesting to perceive the definition of edification as "improvement" in this critical remark.

In addition to improvement, devotion (*Andacht*) was considered to be an essential purpose of the sermon. As in Christian homiletics, the interpretation of the value and character of *Andacht* varied. For Zunz this term denoted the very *arcanum arcanorum* of religion. It was not merely, as it had been for Kant, a state of mind attuned to the acceptance of moral principles but an end in itself. It bears all the features of romanticism that Hegel had analyzed.[175] The same is true of Kley's concept of devotion. In a sermon preached in 1821 he defined *Andacht* as the "nostalgia and yearning of the heart for its home [in heaven]."[176] In another sermon (on "How to Achieve True Devotion") he explained *Andacht* as the mind's recalling ([*dar*]*an* [*ge*]*dacht*) of God, as attention directed toward God. It is "the highest feeling in the human breast," a remembering of our "home" (*Heimat*) in heaven, nay, our ability to feel being in heaven. This feeling is said to be denoted by the Hebrew term *kawwanah* and to constitute the worship of God *par excellence*.[177] Kley's semantic interpretation of *An-dacht* is reminiscent of Hegel's but, unlike his, it seeks to establish romantic devotion as the highest form of religion. In yet another context he described *Andacht* as the oil feeding the flame of prayer and as imparting a sense of consecration (*Weihe*). It is this sense of consecration that, in his view, constitutes the character of the religious life as distinct from "mere morality."[178] In a sermon preached at a synagogue consecration service in 1823, Kley connected the theme of *Andacht* with that of *Erbauung* and, like Teller before him, declared God to be the edifier in accordance with Ps. 127:1.

When devotion prevails among the worshippers, they cannot leave the temple except enriched in holiness, piety, faith and in the fear of God. Where devotion prevails God builds up anew in the heart what the world, alas, so often tears down: The higher life is raised up, the spirit is elevated, the heart is healed and restored; man feels edified [*erbaut*]. Here God himself builds the house; for he builds the true temple, the temple of your hearts. In this way, this house [that is, the newly built synagogue] achieves its purpose; otherwise, you have labored in vain who built it. You will have "built," but you will not be "edified."[179]

This passage comes extremely close to the Christian understanding of edification. It uses the New Testament image of edification as the building of a temple for the Spirit of God, and follows Teller's precedent in linking the theme with Ps. 127:1. The idea of God as the builder or edifier occurs also in the title of the homiletical journal *Erbauungen oder Gottes Werk und Wort*, edited by Kley jointly with Günsberg (Berlin, 1814–15).

Mannheimer's view of *Erbauung* and *Andacht* flowed from his inspirational concept of preaching, which, we have noted, was indebted to Claus Harms. True edification and devotion—the two were treated by him as practically synonymous—are possible only when the preacher's word is uttered and listened to as the word of God. The heart of man is likened to a "temple of devotion," and a "sacred fire" is seen to be lit upon its altar only by the glow of the Divine word. Where there is no ardor in the preacher nor a corresponding warmth in the congregation, *Andacht* becomes a mere *Glockenspiel* and empty pastime.[180] In a sermon describing "Hannah at prayer," Mannheimer sees the necessary precondition of all edification and true devotion in the heart's yearning for God as Hannah and the Psalmist (84:3) experienced it. The futility of preaching was in many cases due to the absence of a felt desire (*Bedürfniss*) to enter into communion (*Seelenverkehr*) with God and to regard the word of God as the "bread of life." Mannheimer castigated those who, rather than listening to the preacher as God's messenger, preferred to see in him merely a good orator. In such a frame of mind an attitude of devotion will not arise, and prayer will be bereft of soul.[181] How deeply Mannheimer was concerned with *Erbauung* and *Andacht* as the essential elements of religion may be seen from many of the opening prayers of his sermons. They often seek to create the very atmosphere and tone of devotion by praying for it. Their sincerity and beauty of language can be presumed to have produced the desired effect. A few examples will suffice to convey an impression of their quality:

> God who art enthroned in the heavens and powerfully rulest on earth; who hast ordered the times and ordained days and hours for Thy name's glory that we may announce Thy praise and hearken to Thy Divine word and receive Thy blessing on consecrated ground in an hour of grace—hallow Thou this hour in which we appear before Thee for the sake of the worship of Thy name, the illumination and edification of our spirit, the ennoblement and strengthening of our hearts, and the union of our souls in faith and love. Grant that it be a solemn, sacred hour, and that our work and deed be pleasing in Thine eyes. Grant that it be an hour of rest to the weary, and an hour of return to their Heavenly Father of those who have departed from Thy ways, O Lord; a joyful hour of grateful recognition to the fortunate ones; and a serene hour of heavenly comfort, spiritual strengthening and Divine consecration to the unfortunate and bereaved. . . .[182]

> Once more I have entered this place which in anticipatory feeling of hours of holiness and bliss to come we have consecrated to devotion [*Andacht*] and happiness in God [*Gottseligkeit*] . . . in order to place before you and commend to your hearts the word of faith and love in this hour of grace and solemn peace of soul when all voices of men have ceased around us and God's voice is sounding within us in clearness and purity. . . . May God in His mercy sanctify and bless His word in both you and me that it may issue forth and enter into you for salvation and for a blessing; granting me inner satisfaction and quietude, and helping you toward true illumination and edification for goodness; toward impelling and awakening of hearts and souls asleep . . . to be received in love and truth as it is offered you in love and truth. . . .[183]

The concern for *Erbauung* and *Andacht*, which Mannheimer expressed with such nobility and depth of feeling, was shared by all preachers. It epitomized the revolution in religious thinking that had occurred as a result of the breakdown of the ghetto and the cultural reorientation of German Jewry. The edificatory sermon was part and parcel of a new type of divine service that cultivated *Andacht* and had to this end taken over certain features (organ music, communal singing of hymns in German) from the Protestant service. At its lowest level, *Andacht* was identified with decorum and dignity (*Würde*). The loud and often uncontrolled manner of praying that had for a long time provoked sarcastic comment by non-Jews was felt to be undignified and incompatible with true devotion. The sermonic literature of the period contains many pleas for *Würde* and *Andacht* in the house of God. The style of the new sermon itself was designed for a setting in which devotion prevailed, and was meant to enhance devotion. The radical rejection of the traditional *Derashah* in the early period stemmed from the realization that this type of preaching now failed to "edify."[184] This was true not merely because the *Derashah* presupposed a degree of familiarity with Hebrew sources, biblical, talmudic, and midrashic, which no longer existed, but also because the type of piety it reflected had largely become defunct. The concentration of religion in specific hours of devotion as evidenced in the new cult of the "hour"[185] was in striking contrast to the halakic ordering of the Jew's total existence. The change from the *Derashah* to the *Predigt* (sermon) was therefore indicative of a deep-going transformation of Jewish outlook. It is interesting to note that discerning minds like Mannheimer and Sachs were well aware of the loss of substance that had been incurred. In one of his sermons Mannheimer nostalgically remarked that there was more religiosity in the loud crying of former times than in the concertlike performances of the decorous service. Real dignity and devotion were present then and were absent now.[186] Sachs expressed himself in similar terms.[187] The edifactory sermon, too, we have noted before, ran into serious criticism. Heine spoke bitingly of the "emotional moral sermons with the orthographical hymns [framing them]."[188] Above all, Hegel's critique of *Erbauung* began to make its impact felt and challenged the validity of the romantic type of edification as the avowed object of the sermon. It was Abraham Geiger who represented the new trend in its most vigorous form.

An analysis of Geiger's writings shows two stages in the development of his views on the sermon. At the first stage, he still regarded preaching as an exercise in the romantic type of edification. His essay on "the lack of sincere belief [*Glaubensinnigkeit*] in contemporary Jewry," written in 1835, reflects a mood wholly consonant with that of the early preachers. It castigates the rigidly orthodox on account of their opposition to "every innovation designed for the purpose of elevation [*Erhebung*] and edification [*Erbauung*]," such as the modern sermon, the introduction of instrumental music, singing and praying in the "mother tongue," all of which is "moving" (*ergreifend*) and "touches a chord in the heart."[189] His pamphlet on the Hamburg temple controversy, published in 1842, shows an entirely fresh approach. Now the type of reform represented by the Hamburg temple is criticized for its failure to produce more than aesthetic improvements in the service and more than a purely edificatory kind of sermon. It was important enough to restore to the service its lost edifying character, but the *Kultus* made sense only if it was part of a total religious organism that by its spirituality and life could generate true edification.[190] Reform must be guided not by mere aesthetic criteria but by principles.[191] Hence the need for a Jewish theology based on scholarship (*Wissenschaft*). The Hamburg temple had not initiated a movement in this direction. The literary activity that had emanated from it was confined to the editing of sermons. Unfortunately, those sermons had no scholarly and theological background. They lacked "firm principles" to guide them, and they therefore uncritically adopted from the *maggidim* of olden times and from modern preachers of all shades of opinion whatever appeared to suit their taste.[192] If the Jewish preachers had wanted to be more than mere "*maggidim* in a new dress," they might have endeavored to advance Jewish theology by scholarly pursuits and thereby to compensate for the loss of rabbinic activity that had been incurred by the deplorable divorce between the offices of rabbi and preacher in modern times.[193]

Geiger developed his views more fully in an article on "the task at the present time" published in 1844.[194] He admitted that the sermon was the only element in the service that attracted people to the synagogue. It was the spiritual and life-giving part of it. Yet "salvation" could not be expected from it unless it drew its strength from a definite and outspoken theology. "For, what is the sermon? It is the popular expression of a conviction come by and elaborated in a scholarly way. It is the exposition, in an ordered and substantiated manner, of some religious proposition which has its roots, in however impure and confused a form, also in the religious consciousness of the people." If the sermon shies away from the task of "making intelligible" (*verständlich machen*) what is dimly present in the religious consciousness and is acknowledged by scholarship, it will miss its purpose. In other words—if we understand Geiger correctly—the sermon that fails to tackle boldly the main religious issues of tradition in the light of modern historical scholarship stands condemned. It will not do if it "confines itself to general moral and religious questions" or if it "approaches the inner core of positive [*confessionell*] religious life" in but a vague and undecided manner. In either case it will leave unfulfilled the task of "making religion a vivifying force in all domains of life." It follows that the sermon by itself cannot be considered the "one and only ferment"; it presupposes a "veritable life of the spirit" (*wahrhaftes Geistesleben*) on which to draw.[195]

Geiger's new theory of the sermon bears all the marks of Hegelian influence. Its key notion is that of the "Spirit" (*Geist*). It signifies, in typical Hegelian fashion, both the Spirit of God and man's spirit as evolving in time. The "forms" of religion are said to manifest the Spirit and also to become redundant in time.[196] Yet there is one single life of the Spirit amid all change of direction and form. It binds together all individual members of a nation and all mankind.[197] This "eternal life of the Spirit" must be discerned "even in those times which we consider to be the dark ages."[198] The sermon seeks to connect the individual with the life of the Spirit that binds the generations together. It also wants him to "feel in himself the eternal, one Spirit which time cannot vanquish" and which is the "divine portion" in man.[199] How deeply Geiger's notion of the Spirit was indebted to Hegel may be seen from his more technical account in Hegelian terms of "the Idea, its entry into the phenomenal world, and its development," which occurs in Geiger's reply to Bruno Bauer.[200] It is, then, the impact of Hegel that caused him to reject the edificatory sermon as inadequate to the life of the Spirit.

Geiger's emphasis on the need for a Jewish theology as the necessary prerequisite of the sermon, again, voiced a fundamental Hegelian concern. Hegel had taught that while the absolute religion (which for him was identical with Christianity) possessed the truth in the form of faith or representation (*Vorstellung*), philosophy possessed the same truth in the form of thinking.[201] He had repeatedly warned against reducing religion to mere feeling. Doing so was courting the dissolution of religion. For "community is in [accepting] a doctrine, whereas each individual has his own feeling. . ."[202] Marheineke had extended the task of conceptualizing religious representations, beliefs, symbols to theology as a "science" (*Wissenschaft*).[203] Geiger's conception of theology as *Wissenschaft* was likewise Hegelian in spirit and akin to Marheineke's, except that its outlook was historical rather than metaphysical. The scholarly pursuits that he urged in his pamphlet of 1842 were intended to be on the lines of historical investigation. This is borne out by one of the letters of that year (addressed to Jakob Auerbach), which referred to the pamphlet he had just written on the Hamburg temple controversy, and enthusiastically described his research and lecturing in Jewish history.[204] The scholarship on which he wanted to see theology based was clearly historical learning. Interestingly enough, he assigned to the sermon the task of conceptualizing ("making intelligible") the representations ("impure and confused" notions) of popular religion. The sermon was thus to assume a function that, in Hegel's view, philosophy and, according to Marheineke, theology were to discharge. In Geiger's view, philosophy was hardly to be trusted to do justice to religion, and theology was historically oriented. His estimate of the philosophy of religion is expressed in his public letter to M. Mass (1858), who had characterized the "philosophical standpoint of contemporary Judaism" as "unsatisfactory." Geiger rejected the very notion of "philosophical standpoint of religion." "Religion," he declared, "teaches dispositions of mind [*Gesinnungen*], convictions, history, actions[205] without presenting them in an ordered system; philosophy . . . seeks to transform them into concepts." The history of philosophy, however, showed that the conceptualizing of religion by philosophy actually dissolved religion. This had been the case in medieval Aristotelianism, Renaissance Platonism, Kantianism ("which had no room for Christianity"), and Hegel's philosophy ("which sublimated Christian dogma and dissolved it in concepts without reality"). "We find," he concluded, "enough guidance in our religious standpoint toward true and authentic philosophy."[206] We infer from the trend of his discussion here and in the other places mentioned that the "true and authentic philosophy" of Judaism was to be presented in the sermon, which in turn was to be based on a theology founded on historical scholarship. It can hardly be asserted that Geiger's view was compatible with Hegel's. Yet it does reflect the spirit of Hegelianism in a broader sense, as we have pointed out before. Geiger himself admitted this. When the Protestant theologian H. J. Holtzmann[207] described Geiger as echoing ideas of Hegel (and Schleiermacher), he confessed that he "had attentively listened to the words of these masters" and that "without becoming a captive of theirs had adopted with pleasure from them" such "correct thoughts" as he "could find" in them. The manner, however, in which he had combined the "heterogeneous tendencies" they represented might be considered evidence of his essential independence of mind.[208]

Whether Geiger succeeded in welding into a unity the "heterogeneous tendencies" of the two "masters" is another matter. It would seem that he did not. While he was a Hegelian in his notion of the "life of the spirit," in his plea for conceptualism and in the short shrift he made of *Erbauung*, he still inclined to share Schleiermacher's view of religion as the life of "feeling." There are passages in his writings that read like restatements of Schleiermacher's romantic view of religion. Thus he said:

> The true essence of religion is precisely the innermost life of feeling [*das innerste Gemüthsleben*], which in its mobility [*Bewegtheit*], in its upward striving is of the highest value. . . . The unattainably high that rules above us and the consciousness of our smallness and puniness, the beauty and loving guidance that meets us everywhere, and the yearning that draws our heart towards it . . . those moments cause by their friendly touch the religious stirrings of the heart.[209]

True, this passage was written in 1835, when Geiger was still advocating the romantic view of edification. Yet he reaffirmed the same definition of religion in 1843 in opposition to the Young Hegelians: "I openly confess that I do not subscribe to pantheism; that I acknowledge that which exceeds mere immanence; that I recognize something ungraspable above us; that I concede the right of feeling which in its highest form is the *feeling of dependence* [Schleiermacher's definition!]. . . ."[210] It is this recognition of feeling as the "true essence" of religion that caused Geiger to retain a degree of romantic *Andacht* as an element in his sermons. This he wedded to the notion of *Erhebung* (elevation) and *Versöhnung* (reconciliation), both of which had acquired a specifically Hegelian ring. We quote a passage from the opening prayer of one of his sermons (preached in 1838) in order to illustrate our point:

> Let my word be a means of *elevation* toward Thee, who art holy and pure, to the end that the *spirit* strive upward toward Thee and humbly bow before Thee; let my word be a word of peace and *reconciliation* in order that in closeness of heart men unite in love for common deeds of charity . . . To this end I make supplication to Thee in quiet *devotion* [*in stiller Andacht*].[211]

Hegel's emphasis on the conceptual content of religion remained a potent influence in Jewish preaching in spite of the considerable force exercised by Schleiermacher's doctrine of feeling. The growing demand for a more specifically Jewish type of sermon stemmed, in part, from the impact of Hegel's speculative interpretation of Christianity as the "absolute religion," which was felt as a serious challenge.[212] The sermon will no longer be satisfactory with mere edification as its purpose. It will have to interpret the "idea" of Judaism; to lift into clear consciousness the "spirit" (*Geist*) that revealed itself in the history of the Jewish community. The function of the Jewish people in world history becomes a focus of interest. The horizon of the sermon expands far beyond the moralizing and emotional concerns of the earlier phase. The term "spirit" acquires a specifically Hegelian connotation. The phrase "Spirit to spirit," by which Hegel had described revealed religion,[213] is echoed by the Jewish preachers. It appears in Mannheimer, who, although his concept of the *Spirit* is essentially of a revivalist nature,[214] could not resist the impact of the Hegelian notion: "The spirit in him [sc. in man] is the eternally stirring living Spirit of the Lord. Keep it in order that the Spirit may address the spirit. . ."[215] Philippson contrasts, like Hegel, the nature god with the revealed God "who has given us, his children, of his Spirit which he can now address. . ."[216] The very character of the sermon is epitomized as "Spirit addressing spirit" in an inscription on the pulpit of the synagogue in Trier (consecrated in 1859), which read: "Where Spirit addresses spirit let the Word of God be thy soul's light."[217] This is an eloquent testimony to the popularity that the Hegelian phrase had attained in Jewish circles. It succinctly expressed, at the same time, the prevalent tendency to interpret Judaism as "*the* religion of the Spirit" (*die Religion des*

Geistes). Preachers like Salomon Formstecher, Samuel Hirsch, and David Einhorn elaborated the concept of the religion of the Spirit in speculative terms[218] and reflected it in more popular form in their sermons.[219]

Notwithstanding the Hegelian direction of Jewish preaching, edification continued to play an important role in homiletical thinking. The coexistence of the two tendencies is vividly illustrated in the manner in which Sachs formulated his program for a preacher, in the inaugural sermon he delivered in Berlin (1844): his aim was "to give expression to religious *thought*; to satisfy the felt desire for religion; to meet the holy divinations [*Ahnungen*] of the human breast, man's *yearning* for his God with the rich treasure of the Word of God."[220] This program represents a rather mixed bag, with its stress on religious thinking, yearning, psychological need, and the Word of God. Idealist pathos, romantic feeling, and revivalism are joined in a strange personal union. No wonder that Sachs's sermons and lectures evoked varied reactions. Moritz Lazarus was able to appreciate the many strands of their texture: every speech of Sachs's could be expected to

> illumine our spirit [*Geist*] and elevate our feeling [*Gemüt*]; he may . . . at once translate us to the ideal heights of *thought* by using for his text the words of the most exalted prophetic spirits and expounding the treasure of the noblest religious *sentiments* [*Empfindungen*]. . . . In every law he will reveal to us the *spirit* of the law. Thus we are elevated to the contemplation of the manner in which even the transient contains an abiding element . . . which we *are to know* [*erkennen sollen*].[221]

Simpler souls found his way of speaking "beautiful and florid" yet diffuse, "the central point evanescing,"[222] or even repellent by the impression of pretentiousness.[223] Sachs set himself the goal of making the sermon again a vehicle of "public instruction" so as to re-establish the "great and eternal basic thought [*Grundgedanke*] of Israel's teaching in its vital meaning."[224] The ideational content of his sermons is, however, lacking in clarity and precision. Geiger was not entirely wrong in describing Sachs as a romantic who, unlike Schleiermacher, had evaded the real issues of revelation and tradition.[225]

An attempt to separate the purposes of edification and instruction was made by Samuel Holdheim, Sachs's radical antagonist in Berlin. To prayer he assigned the function of *Erbauung*, whereas the sermon was to offer instruction. In a sense, prayer, he said, taught through edification, while the sermon edified through teaching. "To the edified . . . mind [*Gemüthe*] of man dawns an inner, purer light of the spirit which makes him see in greater clarity the otherwise confused contours of life. Teaching, on the other hand, will result in the adoption of better principles, and its inevitable fruit will be 'reconciliation' [*die Versöhnung*]."[226] The first of these two final ends of preaching harks back to Kant and the moralists; the second adopts without any hint of an explanation Hegel's and Marheineke's key notion, giving it a Jewish coloring by quoting the midrashic statement: "At the hour when the scholar [*ha-zaken*] sits and expounds [*Torah*], the Holy One, blessed be He, forgives all his sins."[227] In Holdheim's view, the sermon is not an indispensable part of the service, as prayer and edification are. An ideal congregation of scholars and preachers would not require it. Yet as a rule, the service will be fulfilling its purpose only with the help of the sermon. For the individual who in prayer has become one with the congregation will find his individuality restored through the sermon. By addressing him and making him see life in its true perspective the sermon will "illumine and ennoble" him. It will arouse more than a "transient edification" (*eine flüchtige Erbauung*), a "momentary soft and sentimental disposition and motion" (*Stimmung und Rührung*). It will give rise to "serious instruction" and will "strengthen principles." The preacher's office consists in teaching, and the Jewish preacher, in particular, has to teach Judaism as a historical religion, as "the product of the life of the spirit [*Geistesleben*] over the millennia." He has to interpret the historical tradition and by using its materials and its spirit he has to shape and order contemporary Jewish life.[228]

While Sachs and, in some measure, Geiger reflected both romantic and Hegelian elements, Holdheim sought to blend a historical approach with ideas borrowed from the older homiletics of *Aufklärung* theology. His notion of "illumination" (sc. of the intellect) and "ennoblement" (sc. of the will) reintroduced the well-worn definition of *Erbauung*, which goes back to Mosheim, without, however, admitting *Erbauung* as the purpose of the sermon. It may be assumed that Holdheim's reason for using the formula without the name lay in his realization that the name had meanwhile come to indicate a romantic concept that he was unwilling to accept. His whole character was indeed as unromantic and dry as could be. As for the moral aspect of the purpose of preaching, it can hardly be said to fit in with the function of "teaching," with which he sought to join it. The two simply do not go together. What he meant by the teaching purpose of the sermon becomes clear from his statement that the loss of Hebrew and traditional knowledge in modern Jewry necessitated a revival of Jewish loyalty through the sermon, as the only means still left for this end.[229] In one of his sermons (on "Hear, O Israel"), he declared that Judaism was not merely the sum total of certain religious ideas, but the history of these ideas in the sense of their impact on the development of the human race. To profess Judaism, therefore, meant more than knowing and acknowledging a set of fundamental ideas. It meant also the feeling for the historical significance of Judaism. This feeling engendered love and enthusiasm for the past and a sense of dignity in the present. Although the idea of monotheism was no longer a Jewish prerogative, since it was universally shared, the way Jews subscribed to it was different by virtue of historical memories and associations. Once these vanished from the Jewish consciousness, the *Shema*[c] *Yisrael* became an empty formula.[230] The function of the sermon was, then, essentially concerned with the invigoration of historical awareness of Judaism as a "form of culture [*Bildungsform*] of the human spirit."[231] Holdheim's program of radical reform was the logical corollary of this viewpoint, and vice versa. Its naked historicism can be described only as a travesty of the Hegelian spirit.

We are on different ground in Manuel Joel's homilectics. A scholar and preacher of high rank, he lectured on homiletics at the Breslau Seminary from 1858 until 1864,[232] taking Palmer's work for his model.[233] There is, however, a marked difference between his view of the sermon and Palmer's. For the latter the sermon was not to be subsumed under the genre of rhetoric. It "must be understood solely by itself and presented according to its specific concept; it is merely its external and less essential aspect in which it concurs with rhetoric."[234] For Joel the form of the sermon was identical with that of secular oratory as defined by the classical rules (Cicero, Quintilian), and it was "modified" only by the subject matter and certain conventions.[235] Hence his manner of preaching was intended to be "clerical" (*geistlich*) not so much in its form as in its content. He deliberately shunned the "exquisite tone of the pulpit" and wished to speak of things divine humanly.[236] While poetry addressed the feeling part (*Gemüth*), and prose spoke to the intellect, oratory sought to move the will. In order to influence the will it had to consider the nature of the listener. The motivation it wished to provide might in some cases depend on the ability to move the emotions, in others on reasoning and convincing. Nothing, however, convinced more than conviction on the part of the speaker himself.[237] The strength of Joel's own sermons lay in the power of his convictions and the crystal-clear manner in which they were expressed. With Hegel, he insisted on the elevation of religious teaching to the level of conscious knowledge (*bewusster Erkenntnis*).[238] The "edifying and elevating" aspect of the religious festivals consisted in our "elevation" to the eternal "idea" that they expressed.[239] Judaism was concerned with the "life of the spirit" as distinct from nature.[240] The experience of the "sublime" (*das Erhabene*) in nature was one thing; the "sublimity" (*Erhabenheit*) presented to the spirit in the act of revelation was another. "Before the sublimity of this [*Sinaitic*] historical revelation, the revelation of nature must keep silent" (interpreting the midrash about the hush that fell on all creatures at the moment of the Divine Revelation at Sinai).[241] The Festival of Revelation was not concerned with a historical remembrance only: it "challenges the most spiritual element within us"; it expects us to "relive the heartbeat of those that were affected by the event"; to "reexperience revelation in all its overwhelming power." In our "elevation" and "enthusiasm" the historical event becomes presentness, and we experience the "Holy."[242] Joel thus interpreted the edification and elevation that the sermon wants to create as an inner experience and not as a mere act of intellect or feeling. Hegel's "spirit" to which the "Spirit" reveals itself is seen in terms of a happening, as the total impact of the Spirit upon thinking, feeling, and willing.[243]

With Schleiermacher, Joel designated the religious experience also simply as "feeling." "In thinking God, we are separated from him; in feeling, we are united with him."[244] This immediate revelation, for which Hegel had only contempt, was for him the true revelation, a "thinking of the heart."[245] Joel particularly emphasized the experiential character of the religious act. The state of feeling or *Stimmung* in which and through which man becomes aware of himself as "spiritual" (*geistig*) in the innermost core of his being, as a citizen of a higher world, is called *Andacht*. In it man experiences himself in his elevated, higher nature, as a "child of heaven." The immediate, unreflected character of this "experience" is superior to any rational argument.[246] Obviously, Joel departs here significantly from Hegelian premises, in the direction of Schleiermacher. The supreme religious act is *Andacht*, not in Hegel's sense of one's "immersion in the object" but in Schleiermacher's sense of feeling. One of Joel's sermons ends with a prayer that echoes the famous sentence from Schleiermacher's *Speeches*, ". . . the religious feelings are to accompany every deed of man like a holy music; let him do everything with religion, not because of religion."[247] Joel's prayer ends: "Let religion accompany us throughout life like a holy melody in order that no unconsecrated sound may from the ear penetrate into our heart; that we may be able to say with the consecrated singer, 'Thy statutes have been a song unto me.'"[248]

In Joel's homiletics and preaching the nineteenth-century Jewish sermon reached its zenith so far as disciplined thinking and a true sense of purpose are concerned. After him a marked decline sets in. Jellinek's brilliant sermons lacked a firm philosophical orientation. *Erbauung* is conceived primarily in aesthetic terms. "The pre-eminence [*Vorzug*] of modern Judaism is revealed in its striving for beauty."[249] Jellinek was greatly concerned with the aspect of decorum in the service. "It is one of our most sacred duties to win honor for Judaism [*das Judentum zu Ehren zu bringen*] . . . by the forms of worship; to free it from the contempt that has weighed upon it long enough."[250] He praised the choral chant as characteristic of biblical worship,[251] and rejoiced in its restoration in many contemporary synagogues.[252] No doubt, his advocacy of beauty in the manner of worship was motivated not merely by a desire to improve the "image" of Judaism in the eyes of the world. Devotion and edification, too, demanded it. Yet there is a strong element of Jewish defense and apologetic in his sermons. They are concerned, above all, with the "honor" of Judaism. "How long are they [sc. the non-Jews] still to be misled concerning the character [*das Wesen*] of Judaism, to be permitted to believe that it is not a religion of the Spirit [*eine Religion des Geistes*], of the heart, of the loving deed, of holiness, justice, freedom, charity, and truth but [a religion] of petty externalities, unessential minutiae, antiquated customs?"[253]

Finally, Maybaum's homiletics sees in *Erbauung* the true purpose of the sermon. His theory tried to combine elements of the various definitions we have encountered in our survey. With Mosheim and his successors, he wanted the preacher to "awaken a better knowledge [*Erkenntnis*] in the listener and influence his will." With Schleiermacher and the romantics, he stressed the "feeling of edification" and the "edification of feeling" (*Erbauung des Gemütes*). With the Hegelians, he demanded the conceptualizing of religious truth resulting in the "blissful consciousness" of an edification that unites preacher and congregation and establishes their "connection" (*Zusammenhang*) with God. Lastly, with Palmer, he saw in the momentary edification produced by the sermon a value of its own, irrespective of whether a lasting effect was achieved. To be sure, he was confident that some salutary after effect was to be expected; that the Word of God uttered by the preacher would "not return void except it accomplish" its purpose (Isa. 55:11). Yet the preacher's work was, in a sense, done if it created an hour of "edificatory feeling" (*erbauliche Stimmung*.)[254] Such was Maybaum's faith in the religious significance of *Erbauung* that he could describe it as a substitute, in a way, for traditional observance.

> The more difficult and hopeless the struggle on behalf of the hallowing of the Sabbath becomes in the face of overwhelming conditions, the more one is forced . . . to realize the duty to use the sermon for influencing feeling [*auf die Gemüter zu wirken*] and, where one does not contrive to save the full Sabbath, at least to regain a few hours of the Sabbath for edification.[255]

In this sentence the whole chasm between the old *Derashah* and the modern sermon stands revealed. Edification became an end in itself in the measure in which religion came to be located in a state of soul variously described as *Andacht*, *Erhebung*, and the like. *Erbauung* as the purpose of the sermon thus epitomizes the transmutation of Judaism that happened in the nineteenth century: "Piety" was no longer conceived of in terms of obedience to the divine law as the precondition for the soul's closeness to God; it now stood on its own, drawing its nourishment from the autonomy of moral Reason, the subjectivity of feeling, and the objectivity of the Idea to which the spirit was able to elevate itself. It was this kind of piety that the sermon sought to cultivate and to reconcile with biblical and rabbinic theology. An analysis of the modifications that the leading theological concepts of Judaism underwent in the process lies beyond the compass of the present essay.

NOTES

1. "Maybe there was no period in which more was written on homiletics and in which more collections of sermons appeared than in the heyday of rationalism . . ." (Christian Palmer, *Evangelische Homiletik* [Stuttgart, 1842], p. 38). As early as in 1787 Johann Wilhelm Schmid speaks of "the great number of homiletical works" to which his *Anleitung zum populären Kanzelvortrag* was adding yet another specimen. See the preface to the first edition, reproduced in the second edition (Jena, 1795), p. vii.

For bibliographical data on homiletical manuals, see Philipp Heinrich Schuler, *Geschichte der Veränderungen des Geschmacks im Predigen . . .*, part III (Halle, 1794), pp. 106–108; August Hermann Niemeyer, *Grundriss der unmittelbaren Vorbereitungswissenschaften zur Führung des christlichen Predigtamtes . . .* (Halle, 1803), p. 119 et passim, Christoph Friedrich Ammon, *Geschichte der Homiletik* (Göttingen, 1804); and Georg Benedict Winer, *Handbuch der theologischen Literatur*, 3rd ed. I (Leipzig, 1838), II (1840).

2. Johann Lorentz von Mosheim, *Anweisung erbaulich zu predigen*, ed. by Christ[ian] Ernst von Windheim (Erlangen, 1763; II, 1771). See the account in Schuler, *Geschichte*, part II (Halle, 1793), pp. 162–163.

3. Johann Lorentz von Mosheim, *Sämmtliche Heilige Reden über wichtige Wahrheiten der Lehre Jesu Christi* (Hamburg, 1765).

4. Schuler, *Geschichte*, part II, pp. 112, 208–209, mentions in particular John Tillotson, archbishop of Canterbury (1630–94), and Jacques Saurin, preacher at the Hague (1677–1730).

5. See a remark to this effect in Heinrich Gottlieb Tzschirner's extremely interesting *Briefe veranlasst durch Reinhards Geständnisse seine Predigten und seine Bildung zum Prediger betreffend* (Leipzig, 1811), pp. 69–70.

6. See Johann Friedrich Wilhelm Thym, *Briefe die Simplizität des Predigers betreffend* (Halle, 1798), p. 80; idem, *Historisch-kritisches Lehrbuch der Homiletik* (Halle, 1800), p. 79.

7. Schleiermacher's sermons avoid all excess of rhetoric. See Alexander Schweizer, *Schleiermachers Wirksamkeit als Prediger* (Halle, 1834), pp. 79–83. On the illegitimacy of rhetoric in the pulpit, see Palmer, *Evangelische Homelitik*, pp. 13–17. The authentic "language of the sermon" is discussed by Claus Harms, *Ausgewählte Schriften und Predigtem*, ed. Peter Meinhold (Flensburg, 1955), II, 396f. Cf. Dietrich Rössler, "Zwischen Rationalismus und Erweckung, Zur Predigtlehre bei Claus Harms," *Zeitschrift für Kirchengeschichte*, fourth series, X, 73:71 (1962).

8. See Schuler, *Geschichte*, part II, pp. 201ff.

9. Immanuel Kant, *Kritik der Urtheilskraft* (Berlin, 1793) in *Werke* (1922–23), ed. Ernst Cassirer, V, 403, 396–397.

10. Heinrich August Schott, *Die Theorie der Beredsamkeit mit besonderer Anwendung auf die geistliche Beredsamkeit . . .*, I (Leipzig, 1815; 2nd ed., 1828 [quoted here]), 383. Schott cites in support Herder's essay, "Können wir deutsche Cicerone haben? und: sollen wir sie in den Kanzeln haben?" (p. 384).

11. Johann Friedrich Teller, *Theorie der christlichen Beredsamkeit* (Leipzig, 1774), p. 30.

12. Thus Schuler criticizes the "seraphic tone"—a "false glitter of oratory"—found among preachers bereft of natural eloquence and cultivated under English and French influence: such oratory "tickled the ear" but "left the heart empty." See *Geschichte*, III, 9–10.

13. See n. 6. Thym praises the "noble" (*edle*) simplicity of the sermons of Spalding, Teller, Zollikofer, and Löffler as distinct from mere "popular" simplicity. See pp. 26, 108. His ideas about simplicity are reiterated in his *Historisch-kritisches Lehrbuch*, pp. 129ff.

14. See Thym, *Briefe*, p. 54; Tzschirner, *Briefe*, p. 29: "Je lebendiger der religiöse Sinn und je reger das Andachtsgefühl ist, desto mehr wird der Kanzelredner mit Salbung zu reden vermögen." The term *Salbung* retains its positive quality during the first part of the nineteenth century. Its derogatory character in modern usage—e.g., describing a speech as *salbungsvoll*—is somewhat foreshadowed in Palmer's distinction between true *Salbung*, which is the hallmark of a sermon "filled with the divine Spirit," and the "high-pitched rhetoric and rule-bound declamation," which "should not be called *Salbung*" (see his *Evangelische Homiletik*, pp. 55–56). The term is of New Testament origin (I John 2:20, 27). Cf. Palmer, p. 6.

15. Joseph ben Shemtob's *'Eyn ha-Ḳore'*, a treatise on homiletics written shortly after 1455 (MSS Paris and Oxford), is still unpublished. Judah Messer Leon's work on rhetoric (*Nofet Ṣufim*), composed between 1454 and 1474, was printed in Mantua between 1476 and 1480 and republished by Adolf Jellinek (Vienna, 1863). The rare Mantua incunabulum could hardly have served the purpose of a Jewish manual for preaching in the early nineteenth century. A short treatise on rhetoric by Moses Hayyim Luzzatto was published from a manuscript in *Kerem Hemed* 6:1 (1841). A reviewer in *Israelitische Annalen*, ed. Isaak Markus Jost (1841), p. 295, expressed regret that this work had remained unknown until then; otherwise, it might have prevented the "Babylonian towers and senseless *Alfanzereien* [i.e., pilpulistic extravagances]" of the earlier preachers. It is, however, doubtful whether any of these works would have been of much use to nineteenth-century preachers.

16. See Ph[oebus] Philippson, *Biographische Skizzen*, books I and II (Leipzig, 1864), p. 186.

17. See C[arl] G[eorg] H[einrich] Lentz, *Geschichte der christlichen Homiletik*, part II (Brunswick, 1839), pp. 327–330.

18. See Tzschirner, *Briefe*, p. 69.

19. See Philippson, *Biographische Skizzen*, books I and II, pp. 186–187.

20. A list of his sermons is found in Philippson's *Biographische Skizzen*, book III (Leipzig, 1866), pp. 83–112, and in M[eyer] Kayserling, *Bibliothek jüdischer Kanzelredner*, I (1870), 156–173. A collection of speeches devoted to freemasonry (*Stimmen aus Osten*) appeared in Hamburg (1845). For a full bibliography of his writings see Philippson, *Biographische Skizzen*, book III, pp. 254–260.

21. See Philippson, *Biographische Skizzen*, book III, pp. 35, 81.

22. See preface to Salomon's *Festpredigten für alle Feiertage des Herrn* (Hamburg, 1829), quoted by Philippson, *Biographische Skizzen*, book III, pp. 116–117. Claus Harms's *Winterpostille, oder Predigten an den Sonn- und Fasttagen von Advent bis Ostern* (Kiel, 1812; 1817; 1820).

23. See Lentz, *Geschichte*, 329.

24. See Tzschirner's *Briefe*, with their impressive account of Reinhard's towering virtues as a preacher.

25. Although Claus Harms described himself as a "supernaturalist" (see Rössler, "Zwischen Rationalismus und Erweckung," p. 62), he belonged to a group of preachers in the early nineteenth century who sought a return to the "Christian sermon" beyond both naturalism and supernaturalism. See Palmer, *Evangelische Homiletik*, p. 40, n. 1, and pp. 36–41. For Schleiermacher's stand beyond the parties see Schweizer, *Schleiermachers Wirksamkeit als Prediger*, pp. 20ff., and Palmer, pp. 41–43.

26. See Philippson, *Biographische Skizzen*, book III, p. 82.

27. For a characterization of Dräseke, see Lentz, *Geschichte*, II, 257–259.

28. *Das Familienleben. Drei Predigten . . .* (Hamburg, 1821), reviewed in *Ergänzungs-*

blätter zur Allgemeinen Hallischen Literatur-Zeitung, no. 142 (December, 1821) (quoted in Philippson, *Biographische Skizzen*, book III, pp. 116–117).

29. At this point Salomon listed the items of his homiletical library (*Pastoral-Bibliothek*), mentioned above. See p. 193 and n. 22.

30. Professor Johann Samuel Ersch, joint editor of the *Hallische Literatur-Zeitung*. See preface to *Festpredigten*, quoted by Philippson, *Biographische Skizzen*, book III, pp. 116–118.

31. Philippson, *Biographische Skizzen*, book III, p. 118.

32. Gotthold Salomon, *Selima's Stunden der Weihe, eine moralisch-religiöse Schrift für die Gebildeten unter dem weiblichen Geschlecht* (Leipzig, 1816).

33. C. W. Spieker, *Emiliens Stunden der Andacht und des Nachdenkens. Für die erwachsenen Töchter der gebildeten Stände*, 2nd ed. (Reutlingen, 1816).

34. See Philippson, *Biographische Skizzen*, book III, p. 35.

35. The chapter on the vocation of man appeared first in *Sulamith*, vol. IV, part 2, pp. 8–31 (1815). Salomon indicates Spalding as the author of a passage literally quoted (p. 18), but thereby all the more obscures the fact that the entire discussion merely paraphrases Spalding. He may have assumed the readers' familiarity with the well-known treatise. It was first published in 1748; the 13th edition had appeared in 1794. See *Spaldings Bestimmung des Menschen*, ed. with an introduction by Horst Stephan (Giessen, 1908). Fichte confessed that Spalding's treatise had "injected the first seed of higher speculation into [his] soul." See Eduard Spranger's *Geleitwort* to Johann Gottlieb Fichte, *Die Bestimmung des Menschen* (Hamburg, 1954), p. 160.

36. For a biographical account see M. Rosenmann, *Isak Noa Mannheimer, Sein Leben und Wirken* (Vienna-Berlin, 1922). Many tributes to Mannheimer appeared in *Mannheimer-Album*, ed. Majer Kohn Bisstriz (Vienna, 1864).

37. See p. 201.

38. See I. N. Mannheimer, *Gottesdienstliche Vorträge über die Wochenabschnitte des Jahres*, I (Vienna, 1835), vii.

39. Ibid.

40. Ibid., x–xi.

41. Mannheimer was a young man of twenty-one when Harms preached his famous political sermon in 1814 in Lunden. It was the year of the emancipation of the Jews in Denmark. Two years later (1816), Mannheimer was appointed as "catechist" (teacher of religion) in the Copenhagen Jewish community. On Harms's pastoral activities, see Rössler, "Zwischen Rationalismus und Erweckung," pp. 62–73, particularly p. 68.

42. See Mannheimer, *Gottesdienstliche Vorträge gehalten im israelitischen Bethause . . .* (Vienna, 1834), p. 43.

43. See Harms, *Ausgewählte Schriften*, I, 217 (quoted by Rössler, "Zwischen Rationalismus und Erweckung," p. 73).

44. See Mannheimer, *Gottesdienstliche Vorträge* (1834), p. 43: ". . . und wie es Jenem ging, von dem ich Euch einmal erzählt habe."

45. See my article, "Zur Frühgeschichte der jüdischen Predigt in Deutschland . . ." (referred to above, page 190), p. 12.

46. Ibid., pp. 11–12.

47. Ibid., p. 11.

48. See *Der Orient*, no. 29, p. 222 (1840).

49. *Repertorium* (ed. Karl Gotthelf Gersdorf), 9:6, 521 (quoted by Plessner, see following note).

50. See Salomon Plessner, *Religiöse Vorträge, zunächst für Israeliten*, 2nd ed., I (Berlin, 1840), vii–viii.

51. Plessner is praised to the skies as *der Schleiermacher der Juden* and as in some respects even superior to Schleiermacher in *Allgemeine Zeitung des Judenthums*, 2:338 (1838). The bibliographer Joseph Zedner is "enchanted" (*entzückt*) by his sermons and describes him as "the first truly Jewish orator" he had heard. See Moritz Veit's letter to Michael Sachs (December 16, 1837) in *Michael Sachs und Moritz Veit Briefwechsel*, ed.

Ludwig Geiger (Frankfurt am Main, 1897), p. 9. See, however, Ludwig Philippson's severe criticism in *Allgemeine Zeitung des Judenthums*, 3:387 (1839). For Geiger's view of Plessner, see my article "Zur Frühgeschichte . . . ," p. 10, n. 40.

52. See the editor's remark in *Die Rhetorik und Homiletik von Dr. Ludwig Philippson*, ed. Meyer Kayserling (Leipzig, 1890), p. 51, note.

53. See Jacob Katz, *Tradition and Crisis* (New York, 1961), pp. 245–259; idem, *Exclusiveness and Tolerance* (Oxford, 1961), pp. 156–168.

54. A characteristic instance of this attitude is provided by the Göttingen physicist and astronomer Georg Christoph Lichtenberg, author of the satirical "apologia" *Timorus* (Göttingen, 1773), which ridiculed Lavater's missionary zeal. In a letter to J. D. Ramberg, secretary of war at Hannover, he ascribed Moses Mendelssohn's merits solely to the cultural influence of Berlin: "*Berlin* ist es und nicht Judaea oder Jerusalem, was ihm einigen Vorzug gab. Es müsste ja mit dem Teufel zugehen, wenn ein Geschöpf, das wenigstens Menschengestalt hat, nicht hie und da für Wahrheit empfänglich sein sollte. Mendelssohn in Berlin war empfänglich dafür, und das gereicht ihm zur Ehre, Aber ich wünsche nicht, dass er ein Zürcher sein sollte." (Quoted by Leo Weisz, "Georg Christoph Lichtenberg und Johann Caspar Lavater, I. Die Judentaufen," *Neue Zürcher Zeitung*, Literatur und Kunst, I April 1962, Blatt 5, no. 1279 [34].)

55. Kähler's review appeared in *Preussiche Provinzialblätter* (ed. O. W. L. Richter), January-February 1841. Saalschütz replied in the June issue of the same journal. An abstract of his reply was published in Jost's *Annalen*, nos. 35 and 36, pp. 274–277, 283–284 (1841). The gist of Kähler's review is given on pp. 273–274. Our account in the text is based on the abstract in *Annalen*. For a Jewish review of Saalschütz's book see *Literaturblatt des Orients*, no. 10, pp. 137–139 (1841). It suggests that it drew its inspiration from (Spieker's?) *Stunden der Andacht*.

56. Cf. Franz Rosenzweig's remarks in one of his early letters (November 6, 1909): "We are Christians in every respect; we live in a Christian state, attend Christian schools, read Christian books, in short, our whole 'culture' [*Kultur*] is fundamentally Christian" (*Franz Rosenzweig/Briefe*, ed. Edith Rosenzweig [Berlin, 1935], p. 45).

57. *Annalen* (1841), pp. 274–277.

58. See Karl Löwith, *Von Hegel zu Nietzsche*, 4th ed. (Stuttgart, 1958), p. 39: "Die christliche Lehre vom Leiden und von der Erlösung war ihm [sc. Hegel] massgebend auch für die Spekulation." Goethe rejected Hegel's connection of Reason and the Cross. See Löwith, pp. 28–31. The Christian elements in German Idealism have been stressed in recent years by Alois Dempf, Kurt Leese, H. Fuhrmans, and others.

59. *Annalen* (1841), p. 277.

60. *Annalen* (1841), p. 283.

61. *Annalen* (1841), pp. 283–284. The moral aspect of monotheism is the subject of an article ("Der Monotheismus in sittlicher Beziehung") which Saalschütz published in Geiger's *Wissenschaftliche Zeitschrift für jüdische Theologie*, 5:44ff., 152ff., 391ff. (1844).

62. See Abraham Geiger, "Bruno Bauer und die Juden," *Wissenschaftliche Zeitschrift für jüdische Theologie*, 5:329 (1844).

63. See David Fränkel, "Einige Worte über religiöse Reden und Predigten unter den Israeliten," *Sulamith* IV, II, part I, pp. 241–254, particularly pp. 250–251.

64. *Annalen* (1839), p. 319.

65. See my article, "Zur Frühgeschichte . . . ," p. 13, n. 55.

66. *Wissenschaftliche Zeitschrift für jüdische Theologie*, 2:590–591 (1836).

67. See *Heinrich Heine Briefe*, ed. Friedrich Hirth (Mainz, 1948), no. 62, pp. 71–72.

68. See his plaintive letter to Samuel David Luzzatto (dated Nisan 11, 5603/1843) in *S. L. Rappoport's hebräische Briefe*, ed. Eisig Gräber, part I (Przemysl, 1885), 132–133.

69. See "Bericht über Synagoge und Schule in Böhmen," *Zeitschrift für die religiösen Interessen des Judenthums* (ed. Z. Frankel), I:313 (1844). Rapoport's personality is described in glowing terms by another correspondent in *Der Orient*, no. 52, pp. 804–805 (1840).

70. E.g., the reviewer of Joseph Kahn's sermon *Das Pesach- als Aussöhnungsfest*

(Saarbrücken, 1841), in *Annalen* (1841), p. 304, welcomed sermons of this kind, which "compensate for the boredom offered us in this field more than anywhere else."

71. See Mannheimer, *Gottesdienstliche Vorträge*, I (1835), vii–ix.

72. Letter dated Tebet 5, 5592/1832, in *S. L. Rappoport's hebräische Briefe*, part II (1885), p. 228.

73. *Abraham Geiger's Nachgelassene Schriften*, ed. Ludwig Geiger, V (Berlin, 1878), 60. Mannheimer is reported to have followed in the footsteps of earlier *darshanim* such as Isaac 'Arama (*ca.* 1420–1494) and Isaiah Hurwitz (*ca.* 1555–*ca.* 1625). See Adolf Jellinek, *Rede bei der Gedächtnisfeier für den verewigten Prediger Herrn Isak Noa Mannheimer* (Vienna, 1865), p. 12: "Zwei Männer hatten, wie er mir einst mitteilte, auf seine Entwicklung als Prediger mächtig eingewirkt: Rabbi Jesaja Hurwitz . . . und Rabbi Isaac Arama . . . und in der Tat hatte er mit dem ersteren gemein die Gottinnigkeit, den werktätigen Glauben und die salbungsvolle Darstellung, und mit dem letzteren den weiten Blick, das Zusammenfassen des Mannigfaltigen und die Kunst der Auslegung der Hagada . . ." On closer scrutiny one may discern 'Arama's influence in the more philosophical sermons of Mannheimer: e.g., the one on Providence (*Gottesdienstliche Vorträge*, 1835, pp. 117–138). No trace can be detected, however, of Hurwitz's Kabbalistic trend of thought. Mannheimer's own testimony, as reported by Jellinek, may refer to a sense of inspiration rather than to anything specifically homiletical.

74. "Einiges über die Bestimmung des jüdischen Predigers," published in his *Israelitisches Predigt- und Schul-Magazin*, vol. 2 (1835); 2nd ed. (comprising vols. 1, 2, 3), Leipzig, 1854, pp. 364–370.

75. Ibid., p. 367.

76. They are related to the challenge presented by attacks upon Judaism by both the right and left wings of the Hegelian school. Philippson refers to these attacks in his article on "Homiletik" in *Allgemeine Zeitung des Judenthums*, Literarisches und homiletisches Beiblatt, vol. 1, no. 7, p. 26 (1838).

77. "Einiges über die Bestimmung . . . ," pp. 369–370. In the preface to the second edition of his *Magazin* (1854), p. ix, Philippson regretfully notes that the sermon of the most recent period had too frequently reverted to the "old sophistry" (*alte Spitzfindigkeit*), and that it suffered from a neglect of form. In the Christian pulpit, opposition to the rule-bound sermon had promoted almost a cult of the angular, negligent, incorrect way of speech. See Palmer, *Evangelische Homiletik*, pp. 442–443.

78. In a volume entitled *Die Rhetorik und Homiletik von Dr. Ludwig Philippson* (Leipzig, 1890). In his preface, Kayserling pointed out that Philippson—"one of the most celebrated preachers of our time"—was the first and only one to have established a theory of Jewish homiletics. The same year witnessed, however, the publication of Siegmund Maybaum's *Jüdische Homiletik* (Berlin, 1890).

79. Ludwig Philippson, *Siloah, Eine Auswahl von Predigten zur Erbauung* . . . , part I (Leipzig, 1843); part II (Leipzig, 1845); part I, 2nd ed. (Leipzig, 1859).

80. *Siloah*, part I, 2nd ed., ix.

81. See Palmer, *Evangelische Homiletik*, pp. 443–451.

82. "Zur Geschichte der Homiletik," *Literaturblatt des Orients*, 1840, nos. 35, 36, 37, 39. The author, otherwise unknown, is described as "cand. phil. aus Koerlin."

83. The text has "Reinhold," which is obviously a mistake.

84. No cognizance is taken of Zunz's *Gottesdienstliche Vorträge* (1832).

85. "Wenn wir . . . die Predigten gewissermassen nach Art der Derashot abgefasst wünschen . . ." (p. 558, n. 1).

86. See Fränkel, "Zur Geschichte der Homiletik," pp. 590–591.

87. Ibid., p. 590.

88. In a review of Elias Grünbaum's *Gottesdienstliche Vorträge* (Karlsruhe, 1844), published in Frankel's *Zeitschrift für die religiösen Interessen des Judenthums*, 2:63–66 (1845).

89. See p. 230.

90. The report on Rapoport's manner of preaching published in Frankel's *Zeitschrift* in 1844 had used the same expression. See p. 200.

91. See Frankel's *Zeitschrift*, 2:66 (1845). A somewhat critical review of a collection of sermons modeled on the *Derashah* appeared in Frankel's *Zeitschrift*, 3:142–145 (1846).
92. Siegmund Maybaum, *Jüdische Homiletik nebst einer Auswahl von Texten und Themen* (Berlin, 1890), pp. 191–385.
93. Ibid., pp. 45–48.
94. See the third section of this paper.
95. Maybaum, *Jüdische Homiletik*, pp. 47–48.
96. See *Rapoport's hebräische Briefe*, part I, p. 128.
97. This has been rightly stressed by Simon Bernfeld, *Michael Sachs, Me'ora'ot Ḥayyav u-fe'ulato ha-sifrutit* (Berlin, 1900), p. 15.
98. See *Michael Sachs und Moritz Veit Briefwechsel*, p. 25.
99. Ibid., pp. 8–10.
100. Ibid., p. 9.
101. Ibid., pp. 8–9.
102. "Zur Charakteristik des Judenthums, seiner Lehre und seiner Lehrer," *Kalender und Jahrbuch für Israeliten auf das Jahr 5604* (ed. Isidor Busch), 2:175–186 (Vienna, 1843).
103. See *Briefwechsel*, pp. 66–67.
104. Sachs had read this chapter in the manuscript to Rapoport and had won his warm approval. See *Briefwechsel*, p. 73.
105. See *Briefwechsel*, p. 25.
106. See Sachs's refutation of Geiger's view in *Die religiöse Poesie*, pp. 160–163.
107. See *Die religiöse Poesie*, pp. 148ff.
108. Ibid., p. 159.
109. *Predigten von Michael Sachs*, ed. David Rosin, vol. I (Berlin, 1867); vol II (Berlin, 1869).
110. See Gershom G. Scholem, *Major Trends in Jewish Mysticism* (New York, 1946), pp. 52–53; idem, *Jewish Gnosticism, Merkabah Mysticism and Talmudic Tradition* (New York, 1960), pp. 14–16.
111. See the highly enthusiastic letter to Veit (March 17, 1840) in *Briefwechsel*, pp. 33–37.
112. See *Predigten*, I, 245.
113. See *Hegel's Vorlesungen über die Philosophie der Religion*, vol. II (Berlin, 1832); 2nd ed. (Berlin, 1840), p. 191.
114. See *Briefwechsel*, pp. 16, 19, 23.
115. See *Predigten*, I, 170.
116. See Moses Rosenmann, *Dr. Adolf Jellinek: Sein Leben und Schaffen* (Vienna, 1931).
117. Jellinek's strong sense of Jewish nationalism blended with the ideal of *Humanität* is attested to both in his sermons and his *Der jüdische Stamm: Ethnographische Studien* (Vienna, 1869). In a sense, he preached a pre-Zionist humanistic Zionism (see, e. g., his sermons on "Zion," published in *Predigten*, part 2 [Vienna, 1863], pp. 155ff., 167ff.). For other tendencies in his sermons see below, page 232.
118. See his *Jüdische Homiletik*, p. 26.
119. On the "many quarrels and controversies" raised by the Pietists' plea for replacing the sermon by catechisms, biblical exegesis, and devotional hours (*Erbauungsstunden*) see Mosheim, *Anweisung*, p. 30.
120. See the account in Schuler, *Geschichte*, part III (1794), p. 12.
121. Cf. Harms's lecture entitled "Mit Zungen!! liebe Brüder, mit Zungen reden!" which describes the sermon as a work of inspiration, as *influxus spiritus sancti* (*Ausgewählte Schriften*, II, 395). His treatise "Dass es mit der Vernunftreligion nichts ist" (1819) attacked the view that regarded the sermon as a means of conveying knowledge (*Ausgewählte Schriften*, I, 301–370). Harms's inspirational theory of the sermon is foreshadowed in Novalis, "Aufzeichnungen zu einer Abhandlung über die Predigt," *Briefe und Werke* (Berlin, 1943), vol. III, *Die Fragmente*, pp. 281–284): "Predigten enthalten Betrachtungen Gottes—und Experimente Gottes. Jede Predigt ist eine Inspirationswirkung—eine Predigt

kann nur, muss genialisch sein [936].—Predigten müssen Assoziationen göttlicher Inspirationen, himmlische Anschauungen sein [937].—Der Prediger muss zuerst Enthusiasmus zu erregen suchen, denn dies ist das Element der Religion. Jedes Wort muss klar, heiss und herzlich sein . . . [943].—Der heilige Geist ist mehr als die Bibel. Er soll unser Lehrer des Christentums sein—und nicht toter, irdischer, zweideutiger Buchstabe [944]."

122. Michael Sachs (*Briefwechsel*, p. 48) speaks of "Pietisten und augenverdrehende Lügner." Pietism was rejected chiefly as a reactionary force in politics. Philipp Ehrenberg, writing to Leopold Zunz (1835), expects nothing good from the Puritans in England and the pietists in Prussia. See *Leopold and Adelheid Zunz, An Account in Letters 1815–1885*, ed. Nahum N. Glatzer (London, 1958), p. 87. Heinrich Graetz (*Geschichte der Juden*, XI, 181) speaks with contempt of *Herrenhuterei.*

123. See Mosheim, *Anweisung*, p. 12. *Gottseligkeit* and *Heiligkeit* (p. 13) are almost synonymous terms. In his sermon "Dass die Gottseligen klüger seyn als die Sünder" (*Sämmtliche Heilige Reden* . . . II, no. XIII, pp. 613–662), Mosheim says: "Ein Gottseliger ist ein Mensch, der sich durch die Gnade Gottes innerlich bekehren lassen, der durch diese Kraft der Gnaden sein Fleisch gekreuzigt hat samt den Lüsten und Begierden" (p. 620).

124. *Anweisung*, pp. 13, 178ff.

125. Ibid., pp. 184ff.

126. Ibid., pp. 13–14.

127. See Mosheim's references (p. 30) to the *Collegia pietatis.*

128. *Anweisung*, p.16.

129. See above, n. 1.

130. See the work quoted, pp. 44–49.

131. Leipzig, 1761; fifth edition, 1787; English translation by Arthur B. Evans under the title *Thoughts on the Value of Feelings in Religion* (London, 1827).

132. See preface to the second edition (1764), p. xvi.

133. Ibid., pp. xix–xx.

134. On the theme "Von dem, was erbaulich ist" in *Neue Predigten*, II (Berlin, 1784), 87–122.

135. Ibid., pp. 92–93.

136. Ibid., p. 105.

137. See *Moses Mendelssohn's gesammelte Schriften*, ed. G. B. Mendelssohn, V (Leipzig, 1844), 279–408.

138. Evidence of Spalding's popularity among Jews may be seen in Gotthold Salomon's paraphrase (see above, p. 194).

139. Part I (Jena, 1787); 2nd ed. (1795).

140. See 2nd ed., part I, pp. 2, 4–5.

141. In 1796 (1798) there had already appeared C. W. Flügge's *Versuch einer historisch-kritischen Darstellung des bisherigen Einflusses der Kantischen Philosophie auf alle Zweige der Wissenschaft und praktischen Theologie* (Hannover, 2 parts). A volume of *Predigten nach Kantischen Grundsätzen* was published in Königsberg (1794).

142. See the work quoted, pp. 90–91.

143. Ibid., p. 92.

144. "*Improvement* is and remains the principal part of true edification. . ." (ibid., pp. 92–93.).

145. Immanuel Kant, *Die Religion innerhalb der Grenzen der blossen Vernunft*, 2nd enlarged ed. (Königsberg, 1794), in *Werke*, ed. Cassirer, VI, 349–350.

146. See Georg Wilhelm Friedrich Hegel, *Phänomenologie des Geistes*, ed. Johann Hoffmeister, in *Sämtliche Werke*, V (Hamburg, 1952), 13–14; *Dokumente zu Hegel's Entwicklung*, ed. Johann Hoffmeister (Stuttgart, 1936), p. 364; cf. the account in Otto Pöggeler's *Hegels Kritik der Romantik* (Bonn, 1956), pp. 43, 103–106 and passim. See also my article, "Zur Frühgeschichte . . . ," pp. 35–37.

147. See *Hegel's Vorlesungen über die Philosophie der Religion*, vol. I (Berlin, 1832); 2nd ed. (Berlin, 1840), p. 122.

148. See Hegel, *Phänomenologie des Geistes*, p. 163.

149. See *Hegel's Vorlesungen über die Philosophie der Religion*, II, 195.

150. See *Hegel's Vorlesungen über die Philosophie der Religion*, I, 216.

151. The above account is indebted to the discussion of Hegel's doctrine in Johann Werner, *Hegels Offenbarungsbegriff* (Leipzig, 1887), pp. 43–48.

152. See Hegel, *Phänomenologie des Geistes*, pp. 498–502.

153. See Philipp [Konrad] Marheineke, *Grundlegung der Homiletik in einigen Vorlesungen über den wahren Charakter eines protestantischen Geistlichen* (Hamburg, 1811), pp. 12–13.

154. Ibid., pp. 58, 81–87.

155. See Alexander Schweizer, *Schleiermachers Wirksamkeit als Prediger*, p. 13.

156. See Schleiermacher, *The Christian Faith*, trans. H. R. Mackintosh and J. S. Stewart (Edinburgh, 1928), p. 69.

157. Quoted by Schweizer, *Schleiermachers Wirksamkeit als Prediger*, p. 61, from Schleiermacher's *Darstellung des theologischen Studiums*, §§ 279–280.

158. See the account in Rössler, "Zwischen Rationalismus und Erweckung," pp. 64, 66, 70.

159. Cf. the article "Erbauung," *Religion in Geschichte und Gegenwart*, 3rd ed., pp. 538ff.

160. See Kant, *Die Religion innerhalb* . . . , pp. 348 (note), 349.

161. Quoted by Palmer, *Evangelische Homiletik*, p. 673, from Marheineke's *Entwurf der protestantischen Theologie*, §§ 341–345.

162. See Palmer, *Evangelische Homiletik*, pp. 673–676.

163. Ibid., pp. 25–27, 688–720.

164. *Sulamith*, IV, part II: 241.

165. "Gottseligkeit und Tugend, sie haben ewige Jugend," in *Blätter der Erinnerung* (Hamburg, 1844) quoted by Kayserling, *Bibliothek*, I, 57.

166. See Kayserling, *Bibliothek*, I, 88.

167. Ibid., I, 305, 308.

168. Interestingly enough, Mendelssohn gave both terms a somewhat pietistic flavor. See his *Jerusalem oder über religiöse Macht und Judentum* (Berlin, 1783), section 1, pp. 94–95: "In der That, die wesentlichste Absicht religiöser Gesellschaften ist *gemeinschaftliche Erbauung*. Man will durch die Zauberkraft der Sympathie die Wahrheit aus dem Geist in das Herz übertragen, die zuweilen todte Vernunfterkenntniss durch Theilnehmung zu hohen Emfindnissen beleben. Wenn das Herz allzusehr an sinnlichen Lüsten klebt. . . . so werde es hier vom *Schauer der Gottseligkeit* ergriffen, und lerne *Freuden höherer Art* kennen, die auch hienieden schon den sinnlichen Freuden die Wage halten" (emphasis supplied). See also p. 92; section 2, p. 27.

169. *Literaturblatt des Orients*, 1841, no. 6, p. 77.

170. See Christian Wilhelm Dohm, *Über die bürgerliche Verbesserung der Juden*, part I (Berlin, 1781); part II (Stettin, 1783). "Die Geschichte zeigt, wie die Juden nur deshalb als Menschen und Bürger verderbt gewesen, weil man ihnen die Rechte beider versagt hat" (I, 3–4). Cf. also pp. 92–97.

171. In the preface to Manasseh Ben Israel, *Rettung der Juden, Moses Mendelssohn's gesammelte Schriften*, III, 182–183.

172. See my article "Zur Frühgeschichte . . . ," pp. 29–35.

173. See, e.g., L. Adler, *Vorträge zur Förderung der Humanität* (Kassel, 1860), pp. 71ff.

174. See *Annalen* (1840), p. 20.

175. See my article, "Zur Frühgeschichte . . . ," pp. 41–42.

176. See Kayserling, *Bibliothek*, I, 104.

177. See Eduard Kley, *Predigt-Skizzen: Beiträge zu einer künftigen Homiletik*, II (Leipzig, 1856), 85–86.

178. Ibid., p. 343 ("Die Weihestunden des höheren Lebens").

179. See Kayserling, *Bibliothek*, I, 79.

180. See Mannheimer, *Gottesdienstliche Vorträge, gehalten im israelitischen Bethause in Wien*, part II (Breslau, 1885), 20–37, particularly p. 31.

181. See Kayserling, *Bibliothek*, I, 294–303.

182. See Mannheimer, *Gottesdienstliche Vorträge* (1834), p. 3.

183. Ibid., p. 57 (opening prayer of a Yom Kippur sermon).

184. See Philippson, *Biographische Skizzen*, III, 78: "How could one be edified by the tedious *Derashah* of a Polish or Ashkenazi rabbi?"; David Fränkel, "Einige Worte über religiöse Reden und Predigten unter den Israeliten," *Sulamith*, IV, II, 3, p. 247: "It is altogether to be taken for granted that the former manner of preaching . . . is nowadays thoroughly useless, nay . . . damaging to the holy cause of religion. Those members of the community—their number is legion—who . . . are in no way edified by the content and delivery of some sermons . . . appear rarely or not at all in the synagogue." The same sentiments are expressed in Zunz's *Die gottesdienstlichen Vorträge der Juden, historisch entwickelt* (1832); 2nd ed. (Frankfurt, 1892), pp. 460–463, 464, 474–475.

185. Cf. the recurrent mention of the solemnity of the "hour" in the two opening prayers quoted from Mannheimer's sermons. The whole sermonic and devotional literature of the period abounds in references to "*Stunden* der Andacht" and "Weihe*stunden*."

186. See Mannheimer, *Gottesdienstliche Vorträge*, part I (Breslau, 1885), 132–133.

187. See Sachs, *Predigten*, I, 249–250; II, 42, 438.

188. Quoted in *Allgemeine Zeitung des Judenthums*, 2:338 (1838).

189. See *Wissenschaftliche Zeitschrift für jüdische Theologie* (ed. Geiger), 1:144–145 (1835), reprinted in *Abraham Geiger's nachgelassene Schriften*, ed. Ludwig Geiger, I, 459–460.

190. *Der Hamburger Tempelstreit, eine Zeitfrage* (Breslau, 1842), reprinted in *Abraham Geiger's nachgelassene Schriften*, I, 113–196; see p. 193.

191. *Abraham Geiger's nachgelassene Schriften*, I, 177, 194. See also Geiger's pamphlet, *Notwendigkeit und Mass einer Reform des jüdischen Gottesdienstes* (Breslau, 1861), reprinted in *nachgelassene Schriften*, I, 203–229, where Geiger says: "Die ästhetische Form und die Predigt können, trotzdem dass ihnen allgemein die erbauende Kraft zuerkannt wird, diesem Übel nicht ganz abhelfen" (pp. 204–205). The *Übel* referred to is the *Verödung* (desolation) of the synagogue.

192. *Abraham Geiger's nachgelassene Schriften*, I, 178.

193. Ibid., I, 178; 69–70. Some of the older preachers had welcomed the distinction between "rabbi" and "preacher." See my article, "Zur Frühgeschichte . . . ," pp. 19–20.

194. See *Wissenschaftliche Zeitschrift für jüdische Theologie*, 5:1–35 (1844).

195. Ibid., pp. 32–33.

196. See the sermon of 1838 reprinted in *Nachgelassene Schriften*, I, 365–366.

197. Ibid., pp. 436, 261.

198. Ibid., p. 439.

199. Ibid., p. 359.

200. See *Wissenschaftliche Zeitschrift für jüdische Theologie*, 5:330ff. (1844).

201. See *Hegel's Vorlesungen über die Philosophie der Religion*, vol. II (Berlin, 1832); 2nd ed. (Berlin, 1840), p. 353.

202. See *Hegel's Vorlesungen*, p. 352. See also Hegel's preface to Hermann Friedrich Wilhelm Hinrich's *Die Religion im inneren Verhältnisse zur Wissenschaft* . . . (Heidelberg, 1822), reprinted in Hegel, *Sämtliche Werke*, Jubilee edition, ed. Glockner, XX (Stuttgart, 1958), 3–28, esp. pp. 19–22.

203. See Philipp [Konrad] Marheineke, *Einleitung in die öffentlichen Vorlesungen über die Bedeutung der Hegelschen Philosophie in der christlichen Theologie* (Berlin, 1842), pp. 53ff.

204. *Abraham Geiger's nachgelassene Schriften*, V (Berlin, 1878), 159. The date of the letter is February 8, 1842.

205. This definition harks back to Moses Mendelssohn's *Jerusalem*. See I, 19 ("Handlungen und Gesinnungen"); I, 27 ("Keine Handlung ohne Gesinnung"); II, 112–115 (*Religionslehren, Geschichtswahrheiten, Gesetze*).

206. *Nachgelassene Schriften*, I, 262. Geiger's estimate of Kantianism is certainly off the mark. His view of Hegelianism is also incorrect, seeing that Hegel insisted on the historicity

of Jesus. It reflects, however, the current theological criticism of Hegel, which Marheineke's treatise (see n. 203) was designed to refute.

207. In his review of Geiger's *Das Judenthum und seine Geschichte*, part I (Breslau, 1864), in *Protestantische Kirchenzeitung*, 1865, no. 10, pp. 225–237.

208. See Geiger, *Das Judenthum und seine Geschichte*, part II (Breslau, 1865), "Anhang," p. 193.

209. *Nachgelassene Schriften*, I, 457–458.

210. *Nachgelassene Schriften*, V, 167 (emphasis supplied).

211. *Nachgelassene Schriften*, I, 357 (emphasis supplied). Many of the reforms advocated by Geiger are meant to promote *Andacht. Nachgelassene Schriften*, I, 142–144, 211.

212. See Ludwig Philippson's remarks in *Allgemeine Zeitung des Judenthums*, Literarisches und homiletisches Beiblatt, vol. I (1838), no. 7, p. 26: "The attacks . . . which are directed against religious Judaism at the present time are . . . no longer of a moral kind but have a dogmatic tendency. Judaism is accused of dogmatic deficiencies concerning . . . , particularly, the reconciliation and mediation [*Versöhnung und Vermittlung*] of human sinfulness. It is, therefore, the present vocation of Jewish homiletics to defend the purity of Jewish dogmatics by elaborating the doctrine of the unmediated relation of man to God as presented in highest perfection . . . by Judaism; . . . [Jewish homiletics] will thereby be able to present Judaism in particular as the union [*Vereinigung*] of faith and the highest reason [*Vernunft*], and thus lead humanity toward reconciliation with God in its purest sense."

213. "Die Religion aber ist das Verhältniss von Geist zu Geist, das Wissen des Geistes vom Geist in seiner Wahrheit . . ." See *Hegel's Vorlesungen über die Philosophie der Religion*, I (Berlin, 1832), 184; 2nd ed. (Berlin, 1840), p. 257.

"Gott, der Geist, kann sich nur dem Geist, der Vernunft, offenbaren." Ibid., I (1832), 189; (1840), 263.

"Der Geist ist für den Geist und zwar nicht nur auf äusserliche, zufällige Weise, sondern er ist nur insofern Geist als er für den Geist ist; diess macht den Begriff des Geistes selbst aus. Oder, um es mehr theologisch auszudrücken, Gott ist Geist wesentlich, insofern er in seiner Gemeinde ist." Ibid., I (1842, not in the 1832 edition), 47.

See also Georg Lasson's edition of Hegel's *Vorlesungen über die Philosphie der Religion*, part II, p. 11 (in Hegel, *Sämtliche Werke*, ed. Lasson, vol. XIII): *Geoffenbarte Religion* "ist Offenbarung Gottes, Offenbarung des Geistes, und der Geist kann sich nur dem Geist offenbaren . . . ; der Geist muss Zeugnis geben dem Geiste. Alle Religion ist in diesem Sinne, dass der Geist Zeugnis zu geben hat, natürlich [sc. natürliche Religion], d.h. sie ist dem Begriffe gemäss, spricht den Geist an."

214. See above, p. 195.

215. See Mannheimer's sermon on "The calling of our children to prophecy in Israel" (1835), published in Kayserling, *Bibliothek*, I, 318.

216. *Siloah*, II, 92, 96.

217. "Hier, wo der Geist zum Geiste spricht, sei Gottes Wort dein Seelenlicht." The inscription appeared on a memorial tablet that recorded also the name of the donor of the pulpit. The present writer quotes from memory. The synagogue (now destroyed) was consecrated by Oberrabbiner Joseph Kahn. The sermon preached by him at the consecration service was published in Trier (1860). See Kayserling, *Bibliothek*, II, 299. No copy being available, it could not be ascertained whether the sermon elaborated the meaning of the inscription on the pulpit.

218. Salomon Formstecher, *Die Religion des Geistes* (Frankfurt am Main, 1841); Samuel Hirsch, *Das System der religiösen Anschauung der Juden und sein Verhältnis zum Heidentum, Christentum und zur absoluten Philosophie. Erster Band: Die Religionsphilosophie der Juden* (Leipzig, 1842); David Einhorn, *Das Princip des Mosaismus* (Leipzig, 1854).

219. For a list of Formstecher's sermonic publications see Kayserling, *Bibliothek*, II, 138. The philosophical content of the two specimens published in Kayserling, pp. 139–152, is extremely meager.

S. Hirsch's sermons in his *Die Messiaslehre der Juden in Kanzelvorträgen: Zur Er-*

bauung denkender Leser (Leipzig, 1843) were intended "as a popular abstract" from his philosophical work, which had appeared a year before (see preface, p. vi). They do, in fact, reflect some of the views propounded in the treatise, e.g., those on the Hegelian topic of "reconciliation" (see pp. 299–319). Einhorn's *Ausgewählte Predigten und Reden* were published by Kaufman Kohler (New York, 1880). For references to the "religion of the spirit" see pp. 113, 120.

220. Emphasis supplied. See Sachs, *Predigten*, I, 174; similarly, p. 244.

221. Quoted in Josef Eschelbacher, "Michael Sachs," *Monatsschrift für Geschichte und Wissenschaft des Judentums*, vol. 52. N. S. 16 (1908), p. 406. A reference in laudatory, though rather empty, terms to Sachs as a rhetorician occurs in Karl August Varnhagen von Ense's *Tagebücher*, 2nd ed., III (Leipzig, 1862), 272, dated December 29, 1845.

222. Adelheid Zunz in a letter dated likewise December 29, 1845, and obviously referring to the same lecture as the one attended by Varnhagen von Ense. See Glatzer, *Leopold and Adelheid Zunz*, pp. 133–134.

223. Julie Fischel in a letter dated March 3, 1846. See *Leopold and Adelheid Zunz*, p. 137. Cf. p. 286.

224. See Sachs's inaugural sermon in Berlin, *Predigten*, I, 178.

225. See *Jüdische Zeitschrift für Wissenschaft und Leben* (ed. Geiger), 6:66–67 (Breslau, 1868).

226. See Samuel Holdheim, *Predigten über die jüdische Religion*, II (Berlin, 1853), 66–67.

227. Ibid.; the passage (*Kohelet Rabba* on Eccles. 9:14–15) is quoted from Zunz, *Die gottesdienstlichen Vorträge der Juden*, p. 345 (2nd ed., p. 358).

228. Holdheim, *Predigten*, II, x–xiii.

229. Ibid., pp. xiv–xv.

230. Ibid., pp. 14–21.

231. Ibid., p. 14.

232. Joel commenced his activities as a teacher at the seminary in 1854 and relinquished them in 1864. See A. Eckstein, *Monatsschrift*, vol. 70. N. S. 34 (1926), p. 320. His lectures in homiletics started in 1858, as attested by Eckstein, *Monatsschrift*, vol. 60, N. S. 24 (1916), p. 81.

233. See Eckstein, vol. 60, p. 81.

234. See Palmer, *Evangelische Homiletik*, p. 14.

235. See Joel, *Festpredigten* (Breslau, 1867), pp. xiv–xv.

236. Ibid., p. xv.

237. Ibid., pp. xiii–xiv.

238. Ibid., p. 59.

239. Ibid., p. 19.

240. Ibid., p. 14.

241. Ibid., p. 86.

242. Ibid., p. 78; see also p. 213.

243. See the passages quoted by Eckstein in *Monatsschrift*, vol. 70, N. S. 34, p. 327.

244. Ibid.

245. Ibid.

246. See *Festpredigten*, pp. 212–213.

247. See Friedrich Daniel Ernst Schleiermacher, *Über die Religion, Reden an die Gebildeten unter ihren Verächtern* (Leipzig, 1911) (following the first edition of 1799), p. 45.

248. *Festpredigten*, p. 201.

249. See Adolf Jellinek, *Predigten*, part II (Vienna, 1863), p. 4.

250. *Predigten*, part I (Vienna, 1862), p. 85. The concern for decorum is already in evidence in Jellinek's early sermons. See his *Zwei Kanzel-Vorträge in der Synagoge zu Ungarisch-Brod* (Leipzig, 1847).

251. See *Predigten*, part I, pp. 93ff. ("Israel's Gesang"); idem, *Reden bei verschiedenen Gelegenheiten*, part I (Vienna, 1874), p. 54. In *Der jüdische Stamm* (Vienna, 1869), pp. 135–136, Jellinek quotes (without reference) Alexander von Humboldt's enthusiastic description of the sublimity of Hebrew nature poetry. The passage mentions *inter alia* the magnificence of "Tempel- und Chorgesängen" among the "Semitic or Aramaic nations" (meaning the Hebrews, as is clear from the context). Jellinek's praise of the choral chant (*Choralgesang*) as characteristic of biblical worship possibly derives from here. The passage occurs in Alexander von Humboldt, *Kosmos, Entwurf einer physichen Weltbeschreibung*

(Stuttgart-Tübingen, 1847), 44ff. Jellinek's admiration for Alexander von Humboldt is expressed in *Predigten*, I, 250–251.

252. *Predigten*, I, 97.

253. *Predigten*, I, 83.

254. Maybaum, *Jüdische Homiletik*, pp. 26–28.

255. Ibid., p. 20.

12 Franz Rosenzweig and Eugen Rosenstock-Huessy: *An Introduction to Their "Letters on Judaism & Christianity"*

The "Letters on Judaism and Christianity" of Franz Rosenzweig and Eugen Rosenstock have rightly been described as one of the most important religious documents of our age.[1] The two correspondents face each other not as official spokesmen of their respective faiths, but as two human beings who are aware both of their separateness as Jew and Christian and their oneness in Adam. They meet, as Rosenstock once put it,[2] "under the open sky." They express but their own views; and it is precisely this informal, personal, and direct character in their meeting that brings out a depth of thought and a frankness of expression that is unparalleled in the long history of Jewish-Christian relations. Unlike the medieval disputations, in which dogma was arrayed against dogma and verse set against verse, this discussion is a true dialog. It is indeed the most perfect example of a human approach to the Jewish-Christian problem. It is also an exemplification of what is called the "existential" attitude to theological problems, in that it breaks down the artificial barrier between *theologumena* and *philosophumena* and considers its subject from an all-round human viewpoint, instead of isolating it.

The present analysis is concerned with the history and background of this important correspondence. It does not enter into an elucidation of the correspondence itself, which is a task that may be reserved for a later opportunity. Everybody who has read these letters will agree that they require an introduction. It is hoped that the present article may serve this purpose and, at the same time, encourage those who are as yet unacquainted with the letters to read and study them.

Franz Rosenzweig and Eugen Rosenstock met for the first time at Leipzig University in 1913. Rosenstock was lecturer in medieval constitutional law, and Rosenzweig, though two years older, was his pupil. He had studied medicine, turned to history and philosophy, written a thesis on *Hegel und der Staat*, and then felt the importance of some training in law. As early as 1911, theology had been added to the subjects to which he was devoting himself "in an unbounded receptivity."

When he met Rosenstock, he found in him not only a jurist and historian but a philosopher as well.[3] Both of them were aware of the discrepancy that existed between the great philosophical heritage of 1800 and the sterility of philosophy in their own generation. Nietzsche had put forward the just claims of the human element in any philosophical approach to the world and history. He had asked for a type of philosopher who was not only a great thinker but a complete human being. The generation of 1910 began to understand how legitimate this claim was. In the years just before and during the Great War, a fundamentally new philosophical approach was gathering strength. The "existential" philosopher was emerging from the barrenness of the schools. The importance of the "existential" factors of personal decision and response was being recognized in determing that generation's philosophy. This soon became clear in theology, to which new depth was being given by Karl Barth. In philosophy, a new irrationalism (Stefan George and his group; Georg Simmel in Germany, Henri Bergson in France) at first obscured the rise of the new "existential" philosophy, but the movement was gaining more and more ground. It expressed itself most notably in the new branches of phenomenology, which sprang from Edmund Husserl's renewal of scholasticism; in Max Scheler's philosophy of values; and, finally, in Martin Heidegger's ontology.

There is evidence that, in some measure, Rosenzweig had worked his way through to an "existential" philosophy even before he met Rosenstock, though the decisive turn toward the "new thinking"[4] was undoubtedly due to Rosenstock's influence. In 1909 Rosenzweig and a circle of friends had met with the purpose of forming a society to save the ripe achievements of the nineteenth century (social progress, the historical approach, nationalism, the scientific attitude) in the twentieth century, so as to possess them no longer as mere objects of a struggle but as elements of a new civilization.[5] The scheme failed; but what Rosenzweig had felt to be the cardinal point of his and his friends' endeavors, namely, that they wanted to realize 1900 as distinctively different from 1800, still remained his guiding star. In a letter to Hans Ehrenberg (September 26, 1910),[6] Rosenzweig emphasized how the twentieth century had departed from the Hegelian view of history. To us, he says, history is no longer something to be contemplated but something to be acted upon. This has, he feels, a vital bearing on theology. Hegel's religious "intellectualism" is no longer ours. Today we emphasize the practical moment, sin, actual history. History can no longer be interpreted as a divine process developed in time and to be contemplated by the onlooker but has to be recognized as the sum total of human actions. It does not present an impersonal process but personal actions, relations, and meetings. Therefore, we refuse to see "God in history" because we do not want to look on history as a picture or as a being that unfolds. We recognize God in every human being of ethical value, but not in the accomplished whole of history; for why should we be in need of a God, if history were godlike, if every deed, once it entered history, became *ipso facto* godlike and justifiable? No, he says, every human deed is liable to become sinful precisely after it has entered history and has become part of it, since through the interrelation of acts in history no act is merely personal but is caught up in an impersonal nexus of cause and effect beyond the control and intention of the doer. For this reason God must redeem man, not through history, but—there is no alternative—through religion. For Hegel and his "school," history was divine theodicy; for us religion is the only true theodicy. Thus Rosenzweig felt that the twentieth century's attack on the nineteenth century's interpretation of history paved the way for a new and deeper understanding of religion.

This new approach to religion had, however, to wait for its actual embodiment in his life and work until he met Rosenstock about three years later. The union of philosophy and theology that was to become the main feature of the "new thinking" could be brought about only by an experience of the reality of religion, not by mere academic reflections. Though some of the sentences quoted could have been written by Kierkegaard, Rosenzweig was still far from a standpoint of faith. The reason must be sought in Rosenzweig's personal situation as a Jew without actual roots in Jewish tradition. He was the son of an old Jewish family that had lost most of its Jewish heritage. True, there was a certain loyalty to the old faith and community, both on his and on his parents' part.[7] But it was of no vital importance to him. And, rather than pretend to be a Jew, he tried to ignore the fact, seeing that, assimilated as he was to German cultural life, his mind had already become Christianized. "We are Christians in every respect," he once expressed himself in an outburst of sincerity; "we live in a Christian state, attend Christian schools, read Christian books, in short, our whole civilization is fundamentally Christian," he wrote in a letter to his parents (November 6, 1909). There was nothing, he felt, that divided him from his Christian friends.[8] But he failed to see that there was a breach within his own being and that he was unable to find his inner form of life until that breach was closed.

The discussions he had with Rosenstock during the summer of 1913 led to a crisis in his life. Not only did Rosenstock share with Rosenzweig a sense of dissatisfaction with contemporary philosophy and a strong tendency toward "existential" philosophy; he seemed actually to personify the new type of philosopher that Rosenzweig was striving so hard, and yet in vain, to become. Rosenstock not only taught but lived his philosophy. The experience of his oneness could not fail to impress Rosenzweig. He was faced with a thinker who was living in accordance with his faith, and this faith was not a naïve return to the old dogma but a reinterpretation of the old faith in a new philosophical language. The "philosophy of speech," which was later to play so great a part in Rosenzweig's own thinking, had already been conceived by Rosenstock, it seems, at the time the two met in Leipzig. According to it, truth is revealed through speech as expressing the intercommunication of one mind with another. It is not the formal truths of logic in their timeless, abstract, systematic character that are really vital and relevant, but rather the truths that are brought out in the relationships of human beings with God and with one another—truths that spring from the presentness of time and yet reach out into the eternal. The I–Thou relationship is the central theme of this philosophy of speech, as against the I–It relationship of traditional philosophy. The truths of revelation are identical with the truths of the I–Thou relationship. The "word" (in the biblical sense) is superior to the logos of philosophy. The "word" springs from meeting and response. It has the character of a dialog, whereas the logos has the nature of a monolog. Rosenzweig was to formulate those ideas and their deeper implications later in his magnum opus—*The Star of Redemption*[9]—and more concisely in his essay on "The New Thinking" (1925). To what extent his philosophy of speech was developed in 1913 is difficult to establish. But its basic character, i.e., the existential attitude, was certainly there.

The discussions between the two reached their climax in a memorable night's conversation on July 7, 1913, which is frequently referred to in the correspondence and forms its permanent background. It was the most decisive and most far-reaching event in Rosenzweig's inner life. It produced a crisis from which, after months of struggle, the new Rosenzweig eventually emerged.

If one puts together the various references to that night's conversation both in the correspondence and in an important letter to Rudolf Ehrenberg, one is able to form a fairly clear picture of how it developed. Rosenstock himself gives a brief account of it in his Preface to the publication of the correspondence.[10] In 1913 Rosenzweig and Rosenstock had opposed each other, not as a Jew and as a Christian, but as "faith in philosophy" against "faith based on revelation." The Christian was confronted with a Jew whose sense of Judaism was not strong enough to face him. He considered his friend's Judaism merely as "a kind of personal idiosyncrasy, or at best as a pious romantic relic of the posthumous influence of a dead great uncle"—a reference to Rosenzweig's great-uncle, Adam Rosenzweig, who had some considerable influence on his nephew—and he felt justified in putting it "in inverted commas."[11] Rosenzweig was forced "to lay bare his own skeleton and to examine his own anatomy."[12] His opponent compelled him to take a stand, and eventually defeated him. Rosenzweig wrote some three months later:

> In that night's conversation Rosenstock pushed me step by step out of the last relativist positions that I still occupied, and forced me to take an absolute standpoint. I was inferior to him from the outset, since I had to recognize for my part too the justice of his attack. If I could then have buttressed my dualism between revelation and the world with a metaphysical dualism between God and the Devil [he meant to say if he could

have split himself into two halves, a religious and a worldly one], I should have been unassailable. But I was prevented from doing so by the first sentence of the Bible. This piece of common ground forced me to face him. This has remained even afterwards, in the weeks that followed, the fixed point of departure. Any form of philosophical relativism is now impossible to me.[13]

The change in Rosenzweig's philosophical outlook can be clearly seen in two letters to Hans Ehrenberg, written in December of the same year.[14] They concern the relationship between faith and reason, revelation and philosophy. What happens in history, he says, is not a struggle between man's faith and man's reason but a struggle between God and man. In world history the absolute powers themselves are *dramatis personae*. Revelation breaks into the world and transforms creation, which is the Alpha of history, into redemption, which is the Omega. Philosophy has a pagan quality. It is an expression of the Alpha, of creation, of pure nature to which God has given freedom—even against Himself. But as revelation comes into the world, it gradually absorbs philosophy, deprives it of its pagan elements, and illuminates it with its own light. The Omega of history will be realized after the element of creation, the world's freedom, has spent itself. Then God, who has allowed the world to be the Alpha, will again be the First and the Last, the Alpha and the Omega.

Rosenzweig believed (cf. the two letters mentioned just above) that the absorption of philosophy into the realm of revelation was not merely a postulate of faith but a historical fact. Medieval scholasticism meant the adoption and transformation of Greek, i.e., pagan philosophy. The reformations of the sixteenth century could not alter the fact that the spiritual world of Europe had already been Christianized; on the contrary, they only confirmed it. Though faith and reason had again been separated, Descartes, Spinoza, and Leibniz were no longer pagans, but they were Christian heretics; and their spiritual descendants, e.g., Kant, Fichte, Schelling, and Hegel, actually returned into the fold of Christianity. Rosenzweig felt that, whatever pagan tendencies may have been left alive in philosophy, they could not have any decisive influence in the post-Hegelian world, because in Hegel's philosophical idealism the Greek, i.e., pagan spirit had spoken its last word. Hegel marked the *finis philosophiae*. "From Thales to Hegel" or "from Ionia to

Jena," as Rosenzweig put it in *The Star of Redemption*, the history of philosophy was identical with the history of philosophical idealism. It was the declared aim of every philosopher to reduce "everything" (God, world, man) to a single principle—to identify everything with one thing. It tried to reduce God and man to the cosmos (in ancient philosophy), man and the world to God (in medieval philosophy), or God and the world to man (in modern philosophy).[15] In Hegel this tendency overreached itself, insofar as he attempted not only to derive everything from the absolute mind but also to comprehend the historical process of philosophical thought as a process of logical necessity. Thus, in Hegel's system the problems of idealistic, i.e., pagan philosophy are finally settled. No further step beyond is possible. After Hegel there can be no more philosophers in the idealistic, i.e., pagan fashion but only philosophers of faith, Christian philosophers. The monologs of the idealistic philosophers have now to be replaced by the dialogs of human beings with faith and common sense.[16] Instead of identifying everything with everything, man has to recognize the distinctiveness and spearateness of the three entities, which are God, man, and the world; but at the same time he has to realize the interrelations that exist between them. Those who in the post-Hegelian period are still trying to philosophize after the old pagan fashion are condemned to sterility. The barrenness of the "schools," about which Rosenzweig had complained before, now seemed to him quite understandable, though not pardonable. The so-called philosophers of the post-Hegelian period he could no longer regard as "philosophers" but merely as professors, doctors. Hegel was the last "philosopher."

But Hegel was not only the last philosopher. He was also "the first of the new Church Fathers," as Rosenzweig would call him.[17] The world *post-Hegel mortuum* had entered upon a period of spiritualized Christianity. The absorption of pagan philosophy by the church had been completed by 1800. "Since 1800 the Greeks are no longer a power (and no longer a burden)."[18] Rosenzweig would later call the new age "the Johannine period" of Christianity, a term he borrowed from Schelling. Schelling had said that if he was to build a new church he would consecrate it to John, because he preached the gospel of the logos.[19] In the past, the church fathers had had to work out the dogma, the "word of self-consciousness." Now the task was a different one. The task was not so much to elaborate what the church wanted to know for itself, i.e., the dogma, but to address itself to the Gentiles. We should interpret Rosenzweig correctly by saying that the task, in his opinion, was not to continue the monolog of dogmatic thought (which was bound up with the need for absorbing pagan philosophy) but to start the dialog of speech, of personal approach, now that the pagan element was already absorbed. There could no longer be any serious conflict between philosophy and faith, since philosophy had found its place within the church.

It appears that Rosenzweig adopted this new philosophy of faith immediately after that night's conversation with Rosenstock. It solved for him the problem of philosophy and faith and enabled Rosenzweig to combine his favorite idea of the contrast between 1800 and 1900 with a new and comprehensive outlook on the history of philosophy and revelation. Rosenzweig the historian and philosopher was merged into Rosenzweig the religious thinker. But his new theory, though it settled the conflict between philosophy and faith, seriously embarrassed his position as a Jew. If it was the function of Christianity to convert the heathen and to transform the Alpha element of creation—the world in its raw state—into the Omega element of redemption—the world as the place of revelation—was there any room for Judaism? Was not the life of Israel throughout the ages one of seclusion, expressing itself primarily in the law, instead of seeking contact with the pagan world of philosophy? Were not Jewish scholasticism in the Middle Ages and Jewish philosophy in modern times an expression only of the periphery of Jewish life, not of its inner concern? How could revelation in this completely inward form hope to conquer the world? At a later stage Rosenzweig recognized the importance of the Jewish form of religious life, not only for Israel, but for the church itself. But at first sight the aloofness of the Jewish people from the world indicated to him a hopeless sterility and a lack of purpose in its existence. He felt that the medieval figures of the church and the synagogue were right in representing the one as holding a scepter and the other with a broken staff and bandages before her eyes. The symbolism of these figures runs through Rosenzweig's letters.

The year 313 (Constantine) had opened for Christianity "the road through the world," the highway of the church militant. That road was the opposite of the one that the year 70 had opened to the Jew. Previously, Rosenzweig had agreed with Eduard Schwartz's theory—which represented the Protestant view—that the year 313 meant "the beginning of a falling away from true Christianity." But now he reversed his opinion. He would no longer begrudge the church its scepter because he saw that the synagogue was holding a broken staff. He would no longer "Judaize" his view of Christianity. And the question forced itself upon him as to whether there was any purpose in the further existence of the synagogue, seeing that in the reality of history the struggle between the pagan world and the message of revelation was being fought out not by Judaism, but by Christianity.[20]

What was Rosenzweig's answer to this disturbing question? His first reaction was an impulse to leave the synagogue and to become a member of the church. "In this world—since I did not, and still do not, recognize anything, outside the world unrelated to what is inside—in this world, then, there did not seem to be any place for Judaism."[21] He was determined to carry his conviction to its final conclusion. He decided to become a Christian. But this resolution was never carried out. In the three months between July and October, 1913, he struggled desperately to find his place. He made a reservation. Before becoming a Christian he wanted to live as a Jew. He felt that he should not enter the church through the intermediary stage of paganism, but as a Jew. This reservation helped him to establish a new and more serious relationship with the world of Judaism, which hitherto he had considered only from the standpoint of the Christian philosopher. Now the deadly earnestness of his crisis forced him to face Judaism as a Jew, and the result was that Judaism conquered him. He wrote to his mother, on October 23: "You will have learned from this letter that I have found the way back which, for almost three months, I had struggled for in vain."[22] And to Rudolf Ehrenberg he wrote a few days later, on October 31:

Dear Rudi:

I have something to tell you which will disturb you, at least for the moment, and which will be incomprehensible to you. After long, and I believe searching, consideration, I have arrived at the point of taking back my resolution. It seems to me no longer necessary and, therefore, in my case, no longer possible. So I am remaining a Jew.[23]

It would be wrong to assume that Rosenzweig's decision to remain a Jew involved a change in the philosophy to which Rosenstock had converted him. The two letters to Hans Ehrenberg, from which we quoted above in outlining his new philosophy of faith, were written in December, 1913, *after* he had decided to remain a Jew. The interesting feature about Rosenzweig's final position, which he reached in October, is the new insight into the compatibility of Judaism and Christianity "within the same realm." What he had worked out for himself with regard to the function of the church militant in the history of the world remained true and valid. But, whereas he had previously failed to see any purpose in the life of the synagogue, because of her broken staff and the bandages before her eyes, he now perceived the meaning of the synagogue as well. He recognized that her stern refutation of the pagan world and her uncompromising attitude constituted the only safeguard for the completion of the work of revelation and of the church herself. The church, taking her road through the world, was always in danger of compromising with the world and its pagan instincts. The conquered might give her their laws. Christianity might be interpreted in the sense of a pagan philosophy. It might become identified either with a myth or with a philosophical system. But the existence of the people of Israel served as a reminder that revelation comes from God not from the natural mind, from the Jews not from the Greeks. In Israel's seclusion from the world, in its priestly way of life, it expresses the essence of revelation in an absolute form, unalloyed by any element of paganism. The synagogue, whose life is ruled by the law, not by a philosophy and not even by a dogma, may be lacking in the power of articulate speech. The synagogue may be unable to convey the contents of revelation to the pagan world. But her very existence is inarticulate speech. She is the "mute admonisher," who reminds the church, whenever she might become entangled in the life of this world, its nations and its empires: "Master, remember the last things." For this reason synagogue and church, though they are exclusive, are actually complementary and call for each other.[24]

Rosenzweig had discovered his identity with the Jewish doctrine. He wrote to Rudolf Ehrenberg:

> You will have noticed already that in my theory I am no longer borrowing from Christianity. . . . I feel myself now in the most important points . . . above all in my deviation, insofar as I have expressed it, namely, in the doctrine of sin, in perfect and unintentional agreement with the Jewish doctrine, whose evidence in Jewish cult and life I had disputed before, but now recognize. As I said before, I am about to interpret to myself the whole system of Jewish doctrine on its own Jewish basis.[25]

Like the explorer of a new continent, he threw himself into the world of Judaism. A fresh vitality took possession of him. But he himself knew too well that he stood only at the beginning. He had found his way back to Judaism, but he was still far from being a Jew in the same sense as Rosenstock was a Christian. He was not yet strong enough to face his opponent again. But he knew the day would come when they would meet once more and that the second meeting would no longer be one between a Christian and a philosopher, but one between a Christian and a Jew. For this meeting he had to prepare himself.

In November, 1913, a month after he had found his way back to Judaism, he made the acquaintance of Hermann Cohen, the great neo-Kantian, who, in his retirement from the professorial chair in Marburg, was lecturing in Berlin. Moved by a certain curiosity, Rosenzweig went to one of his lectures. He held no brief, as we know, for post-Hegelian philosophers and did not expect anything. But he found more than a celebrated professor. He found "a philosopher and a man," a "great soul," a "religious person."[26] He became Cohen's disciple and intimate friend. There are some references to Rosenzweig's reverence for Cohen in the correspondence. They betray a certain reluctance to reveal his true feelings for Cohen. But from other sources we are able to draw a fuller picture of the impression Cohen made on him and the influence he had on his future development.

When Rosenzweig met the old philosopher, a life of fame lay behind Cohen, who was the recognized head and master of a school, the author of a system of philosophy that claimed to comprehend the whole range of human culture. He was a "new Hegel," as Rosenzweig called him,[27] in the sense that he represented the history of philosophy—which to Cohen was identical with the history of "critical idealism"—as a logical process, as the history of human reason. In a trilogy of books, like Kant in his three *Critiques*, Cohen had built up a system of his own. He wanted to crown it with a "psychology of civilization," which was to include the achievements of the nineteenth century. But the "Hegelianism of this neo-Kantian" was not carried to its conclusion. The religious element in Cohen revolted. Throughout his life he had struggled to find religion a place somewhere in the system of culture. Now he began to realize that he had to sacrifice the basic principle of idealism, the absolute sovereignty of the mind, in order to do justice to religion. In his lectures during the winter term of 1913–1914 and in the summer of 1914, he introduced a new category of thought, which he called "correlation" and which expressed, fundamentally, much the same idea as the I–Thou philosophy that Rosenstock and Rosenzweig had evolved. With this new conception he broke down the "magic circle" of idealism in which God and man had been caught as mere functions in a system. Now he perceived them in their separateness and individuality, in their personal existence and their relations to each other. The "pagan" philosopher Cohen had become a theologian or, rather, a philosopher of faith. Rosenzweig, who had denied to the professors of the "schools" the attribute of philosopher, had met in Cohen one whom "without mockery" he would call a philosopher.[28]

But Cohen was not only a philosopher in the new sense that Rosenzweig demanded as the only true form of post-Hegelian philosophy. He was a Jew, and—what must have evoked a deep response on the part of Rosenzweig—he was a Jew who from the "world" had returned to the fold. He had found the "center of his being." Now he wanted to serve his people. In his introduction to Hermann Cohen's *Jüdische Schriften* (1923)—the great memorial to his master—Rosenzweig recorded some of the things that Cohen had said to him in private conversation. They must have struck him deeply, because he himself had just discovered the center of his own life in Judaism. Cohen was pleading at that time for the establishment of a chair for Jewish philosophy at one of the German universities.[29] Rosenzweig was thrilled with the idea. In one of his letters from the war—written at the time of the correspondence—he emphasized its importance for the spiritual renewal of Judaism. He felt that he could give of his best if such a post were offered to him.[30] All his literary plans receded into the background before the deeper concern of his new life: his Judaism.

Yet the question of "Judaism and Christianity" still occupied his mind. The lectures that Cohen held in 1913–1914 gave him a living answer to this problem. He found in Cohen an uncompromising Jew who insisted on the fundamental differences between Judaism and Christianity. Rosenzweig recorded some of the striking utterances made by Cohen in the course of the lectures that his "happy ears were privileged to hear":[31] "God be what He be, but He must be One,"; "On this point we cannot come to an understanding with Christianity"; the unity of God, "the most abstract idea, . . . for whose sake we are killed all the day" (Ps. 44:22); "Balaam's word of the 'people that shall dwell alone' (Num. 23:9), the civilized world cannot comprehend it"; "The whole of Nature, the model of art, is opened up in the Second Commandment—and sealed. This is something for which the world has never forgiven us"; "The Greek spirit, that is, the type of the scientific mind, looks for mediation, as they call it, between God and man. To this Greek charm the Jew Philo and his Logos fell a victim"; "Had Philo not invented the Logos, no Jew would ever have fallen away from God."[32] Sometimes it was only a gesture, a single word, and one could feel the eruptive power of his personality. When Rosenzweig once says that the Jewish attitude "might sometime be expressed in a gesture, but hardly perhaps in words,"[33] Hermann Cohen stands before his mind; and many a passage in these letters[34] could hardly have been written by Rosenzweig without the experience of Hermann Cohen, the fighter and the Jew.

The war broke out. The world was in a fever of excitement. Yet Rosenzweig was not too deeply affected by it. As he confessed in a letter to Hans Ehrenberg, dated October, 1916:

> The war itself has not caused any break in my inner life. In 1913 I had experienced so much that the year 1914 would have had to produce nothing short of the world's final collapse to make any impression on me. . . . Thus I have not experienced the war. . . . I carry my life through this war like Cervantes his poem.[35]

This should not be taken as an indication of apathy but rather of a profound concentration of his mind on the future task of his life, which was to have its center, not in the outside world with its changing events, but in the midst of his people.

Rosenstock he had met again in the summer of 1914, but the subject that had united and divided them was not touched upon. Rosenzweig tried to evade a new discussion; he felt himself not yet mature enough to face his former opponent. Though he was firmly established in his new philosophy and theology, he realized that he had still to grow, and that his life had still to be shaped according to his new insight, before he could meet Rosenstock as an "accomplished fact." And yet, secretly, he was waiting for that final discussion in which he was to meet him as a Jew and secure his recognition as a Jew. It was Rosenstock who broke the silence. During a short stay in Kassel, where he enjoyed the hospitality of Rosenzweig's parents and occupied his friend's room, he wrote to him. The letter started a correspondence in which both their human relationship and the objective problem of the relationship of the two faiths found expression. The two correspondents were then on active service in the army. Some of the letters were written from the trenches and under enemy fire. The correspondence began in May, 1916. In October, Rosenzweig reported to Rudolf Ehrenberg:

> I am having a correspondence with Rosenstock which is not an easy thing for me; we have not yet got over the initial stage, and it proves to be very bad that since that night's conversation in 1913 . . . I have not really spoken to him; as a matter of fact, I could not have done it, because I had to continue the discussion with his ghost of that night.[36]

On December 24 the correspondence had been completed, and Rosenzweig was able to write, again to Rudolf Ehrenberg:

> The real adventure and achievement of the last few months was for me my correspondence with Rosenstock. You will read it one day. You know (or should be able to know) that I expected, dreaded, and postponed the inevitable second discussion with him since November, 1913. It was to be the test of my new life. . . . Now the task is completed.[37]

The correspondence is not only a great document of their renewed friendship, but it was of decisive influence on their future work. It helped them to clarify their ideas and to cast them into their final form. "Without Eugen I would never have written *The Star of Redemption*," Rosenzweig confessed later.[38] There are two things in particular that Rosenzweig owed to this correspondence.

In the first place, it deepened his conception of revelation. The question that had worried him was: Is it possible, and *how* is it possible, to define revelation as distinct and distinguishable from any expression or form of the natural mind? All his endeavors in this respect had resulted in merely historical, not logical, distinctions.[39] His correspondence with Rosenstock gave him an opportunity to ask his friend point blank to explain to him his present idea of the relation between nature and revelation.[40] Rosenstock's answer was: revelation means orientation. After revelation there exists a real Above and Below in the world, and a real Before and Hereafter in time. In the "natural" world and in "natural" time the point where I happen to be is the center of the universe; in the space-time world of revelation the center is fixed, and my movements and changes do not alter it. Rosenzweig felt this was an idea of stupendous simplicity and productivity.[41] Though he did not accept it as a final solution to his problem, it was certainly of great help to him. His own "point of Archimedes," which enabled him to write *The Star of Redemption*, he found a year later, in October, 1917.[42]

There is another point that deserves mentioning. In the correspondence one finds an exposition of Rosenstock's "philosophy in the form of a calendar," as illustrated by the charts of the year. It may strike one as rather queer and arbitrary. But it should be taken simply as the first imaginative suggestion of an idea that he developed with a certain fruitfulness in his *Out of Revolution*.[43] There he tries a way of writing the history of Europe in the light of its festivals, its holidays and holy-days, its celebrations of national revolutions; for a historical event is not a mere event but something taken up out of the mere passage of time into the experience of a people. The calendar may therefore be taken as a symptom of a people's corporate memory, its celebration of the crucial moments in its experience, its sense of what is important or significant. The "present," as a concrete moment in time, must be experienced as an intersection of four "calendars." Rosenstock symbolized it as a cross in which the "present" is the point of intersection, and the four ends represent the course of nature, the course of "secular history," the course of "sacred" (the church's) history, and one's private calendar of inner development.

Rosenzweig seems to have accepted this idea. In his *Star of Re-*

demption the calendars of the synagogue and the church—those "two eternal dial plates under the weekly and annual pointer of ever-renewed Time"[44]—play an integral part. But the relation of the sacred calendar to the courses of nature, history, and man is a different one. Its symbol is not the Cross with its four points, but the Jewish Star of David with its six points formed by the intersection of two triangles, of which God, World, and Man form the apexes of one; Creation, Revelation, and Redemption of the other. The three elements of reality, i.e., God, World, and Man, appear each in three different qualities: God is Creator, Revealer, and Redeemer. Man is a natural being (part of creation); the receiver of Revelation (Priest and Prophet); the agent of Redemption (the holy work of the Saint). The World is Creation (natural law, *civitas mundi*); the place of Revelation (community of the believers); the place of the accomplished Redemption (Messianic Day, *civitas Dei*).

Rosenzweig's influence on Rosenstock can be clearly seen in the chapter on the French Revolution and the emancipation of the Jews in the latter's book *Out of Revolution.*[45] There paganism and Judaism are interpreted as the Alpha and Omega of history:

> God's Alpha was lived by the Gentiles, and God's Omega is embodied in the Jews. . . . The Jews represent the end of human history before its actual end. Without them pagan history would not only have had no goal, but would have gotten nowhere. The pagans represent the eternal new beginnings of history, and without them history would never have acquired any shape or form or beauty or fulfillment or attainment."[46]

Between Jews and pagans stands Christianity as the mediator: "The true Christians can preach the Gospel among the Gentiles. They are the rays sent out from the central fire [i.e., Judaism], which actually transform the world. As coals in the heart of fire, the Jews are prisoners of God."[47] The "periodical persecutions of the Jews" represent a succession of attempts on the part of the Gentiles "to throw off the yoke which joins Alpha and Omega."[48]

In the correspondence, Rosenstock had still refused to recognize in Christianity the "Judaizing of the pagans."[49] The year 1789, which to Rosenzweig signified the final triumph of revelation in the world and the beginning of a new era in history—the dawn of the Johannine age—was considered by Rosenstock in just the reverse sense as the "mightiest outbreak" of the natural, i.e., pagan, mind.[50] Since 1789, he felt, paganism had become dominant even in the churches. He pointed to Adolf von Harnack as the symbol of the paganizing of Christianity, its abandonment of faith in revelation, and its belief in the achievements of the natural mind. Rosenzweig replied that the modern nationalisms of the peoples are not to be confounded with the paganism of the ἔθνη of antiquity. "For nationalism not merely expresses the people's belief that they come *from* God (that, as you rightly say, the pagans also believe), but that they go *to* God." This means "the complete Christianizing of the conception of a people," though "not yet the Christianizing of the peoples themselves." Israel was still the only people in the world in whom revelation was a reality.[51] Rosenstock still disagreed. He felt that modern nationalism was not a Christianizing of the conception of the people but meant that the nations had adopted the idea of the Roman Empire. Modern nationalism was but a rebirth of pagan imperialism.[52]

In *Out of Revolution*, Rosenstock finally accepted Rosenzweig's view that 1789 meant the Christianizing of the idea of nations and thus the triumph of Judaism. The "great idea of humanity as conceived by the French Revolution . . . had discovered man behind men, nature behind nations, Adam behind Shem, Ham and Japhet, and the great identity of all men behind creed, faith, colour and race."[53] Through the act of the emancipation of the Jews, the nations are inoculated with the Jewish promise. "By the addition of the element of Omega, the chosen people of God, the 'Alphaic' nations have acquired one touch of finality and predestination."[54] "Messianism, originally limited to the Jews, later communicated to the heathen by the church, is transferred by the European nationalism born in 1789 to the nations in general, which now enter upon a common race of *messianic nationalism.*"[55] Rosenstock is confident that "the admixture of the Jews, who can never be treated as pagans, secures the nations from backsliding and mistaking mere existence for growth, inheritance for heritage, alpha for omega."[56]

This is clearly Rosenzweig's idea of the Johannine epoch. But Rosenzweig died in 1929, at the last moment when it was still possible to ignore the rising tide of the new paganism, which Rosenstock seems to have forecast in these letters.[57] Rosenstock's faith in the irreversible messianic course of history, "in spite of Hitlerism,"[58] is all the more remarkable. In the light of his theology the latest persecutions of the Jews must be interpreted as another, perhaps final, attempt on the part of the Gentiles to throw off the yoke that joins Alpha and Omega, the first and the last things. In trying to exterminate the Jewish people, the new paganism wants to eradicate the messianic element from history.

Rosenstock felt certain that by the absorption of the Jews the modern nations had become immune against a return to paganism. His confidence in the decisive victory of revelation in 1789 led him to believe that there was no further necessity for the continued existence of Israel as a visible synagogue. He felt that we were living in a new spiritual era in which the functions of Gentiles, Christians, and Jews were no longer invested in a visible race, a visible clergy, and a visible Israel. "In the future the character and the function of a man can no longer be judged by the outward signs of race, creed, or country. He has to choose for himself."[59] The events of recent years are certainly not likely to confirm this view. The nations are far from being transformed into the messianic kingdom that would allow them to disregard the visible manifestations of church and synagogue. They are still in danger of backsliding into paganism. The functions of church and synagogue, as Rosenzweig conceived them, have not come to an end.

NOTES

1. Cf. H. J. Schoeps, *Jüdisch-Christliches Religionsgespräch in 19 Jahrhunderten* (Berlin, 1937), p. 120.
2. In a letter to Miss Dorothy M. Emmet.
3. See Letter No. 2.
4. Cf. Rosenzweig's essay, "Das neue Denken," *Kleinere Schriften* (Berlin, 1937), p. 373.
5. Franz Rosenzweig, *Briefe* (Berlin: Schocken Verlag, 1935), p. 49.
6. *Briefe*, pp. 50, 53.
7. Cf. ibid., pp. 25, 31.
8. Cf. ibid., p. 72.
9. *Der Stern der Erlösung* (Frankfurt, 1921; 3rd ed., Heidelberg, 1954).
10. *Briefe*, pp. 638–39: As translated by Miss Dorothy Emmet:

"This exchange of letters, dating from the third year of the World War, is concerned with the perennial, essential, supra-personal questions of the life of the Jew and the Christian among the peoples of the world, with their 'theological existence today' ['*Theologische Existenz heute*,' the series title of pamphlets issued by Karl Barth]. Thanks to the abnormal tension in people's minds, which isolated them from the rest of the world at that time, the letters are entirely free from any consideration as to whether they would do good or harm.

The 'Jewish question' and the 'Christian question' appear here in a purely introspective form, in a way that is not normally possible because of the nature of the subject.

"Even the two correspondents themselves were only forced to an uncompromising display of their positions after hesitation and to their own surprise. But for that reason the subjective and personal element in the letters should not irritate the reader. Moreover, this element provides the indispensable supply of fuel without which the most matter-of-fact dialogue cannot be kindled. Nor ought the passionate character of the discussion detract at all from its objective truth. The letters themselves mention at some length the thought that only in the extreme necessity of spiritual self-defense is there a chance of learning the truth about the questions that touch one's own life. And Franz Rosenzweig again dealt with this method of thinking several times before his death.

"The two correspondents get into their stride only haltingly. This is explained also by the fact that there was a gap of nearly three years in their exchange of ideas. This was broken after a conversation, which still leaves its echoes in the letters between three people in the summer of 1913, a summer which both correspondents had spent in Leipzig, the one as *Privatdozent*, the other in private study. This conversation too was concerned with questions of faith. But it was not Judaism and Christianity that were then arrayed against each other, but rather faith based on revelation was contrasted with faith in philosophy. From this difference of orientation in that last important conversation, the difficulties in understanding which make themselves felt in the letters are explicable. It was just these difficulties which served to call forth a growing measure of clarity.

"A word must be said about the external occasion which set the correspondence going, because it plays a part at the beginning of the letters. The third participant in the religious discussion of the summer of 1913, Rudolf Ehrenberg, visited Eugen Rosenstock in Kassel, and the latter further utilized his short stay on military business in his friend's home town in order to obtain publication of 'The Original Program of German Idealism,' which Rosenzweig had discovered in Berlin before the War. It was in fact accepted during the War by the Heidelberg Academy of Sciences in its record of Proceedings."

11. See Letter No. 9.
12. See Letter No. 9.
13. *Briefe*, p. 71.
14. Cf. ibid., p. 79.
15. Cf. *Kleinere Schriften*, pp. 377ff.
16. See Letter No. 17.
17. Cf. *Briefe*, p. 81.
18. Ibid., p. 82.
19. Cf. *Kleinere Schriften*, p. 166; *Briefe*, p. 91.
20. *Briefe*, p. 72.
21. Ibid.
22. Ibid., pp. 65–70.
23. Ibid., p. 71 [When writing this essay in 1944, the author was unaware of the important fact disclosed by Rosenzweig's disciple and friend Nahum N. Glatzer in 1952 that Rosenzweig's decision to remain a Jew was ultimately the result of a religious experience and happened with the force of a conversion. The letters to his mother and to R. Ehrenberg were written immediately after he had attended the service of the Day of Atonement, 1913. He "left the service a changed person. What he had thought he could find in the church only—faith that gives one an orientation in the world—he found on that day in a synagogue." See Nahum N. Glatzer, "Franz Rosenzweig: The Story of a Conversion," *Judaism: A Quarterly Journal of Jewish Life and Thought*, Vol. I, No. 1 (January 1952) pp. 70–71. Cf. also Glatzer's book *Franz Rosenzweig, His Life and Thought* (Second, Revised Edition, New York, 1961), p. 25. In the light of this biographical fact Rosenzweig's previous struggles assume the character of a *preparatio Judaica*.]
24. Cf. ibid., p. 73. [See now the author's essay "Franz Rosenzweig on History," in *Between East and West: Essays Dedicated to the Memory of Bela Horovitz*, ed. by Alexander Altmann (London, 1958), pp. 194–214; reprinted in the author's *Studies in Religious Philosophy and Mysticism* (London and Ithaca, N.Y., 1969).]
25. *Briefe*, pp. 75–76.
26. *Kl. Schr.*, pp. 291ff.
27. *Briefe*, p. 305.
28. Letter No. 9; *Kl. Schr.*, p. 291. [For a critical evaluation of Rosenzweig's view of

Cohen, see now the author's essay "Hermann Cohens Begriff der Korrelation," In *Zwei Welten, Siegfried Moses zum Fünfundsiebzigsten Geburtstag*, ed. by Hans Tramer (Tel-Aviv, 1962) pp. 377–99.]

29. *Kleinere Schriften*, p. 323.
30. *Briefe*, p. 92.
31. *Kleinere Schriften*, p. 337.
32. Ibid., pp. 337, 340–41.
33. See Letter No. 9.
34. See Letter No. 11.
35. *Briefe*, p. 123.
36. Ibid., p. 121.
37. Ibid., p. 143.
38. "Das neue Denken" (see n. 4 above).
39. *Kleinere Schriften*, p. 357.
40. *Briefe*, p. 53.
41. *Kleinere Schriften*, p. 359.
42. Cf. ibid., p. 357.
43. New York: William Morrow & Co., 1938.
44. *Kl. Schr.*, p. 392.
45. *Out of Revolution*, pp. 216–17.
46. Ibid., p. 225.
47. Ibid., p. 221.
48. Ibid., p. 226.
49. See Letter No. 12.
50. See Letter No. 12.
51. See Letter No. 15.
52. See Letter No. 16.
53. *Out of Revolution*, p. 235.
54. Ibid., p. 236.
55. Ibid.
56. Ibid.
57. See Letter No. 16.
58. *Out of Revolution*, p. 237.
59. Ibid.

13 Theology in Twentieth-Century German Jewry

The integration of Judaism into the frame of modern culture was the absorbing concern of liberal theology in nineteenth-century German Jewry. "Wissenschaft des Judentums" as a historical science was conceived as the tool for the accomplishment of this end. It was hoped that once one had grasped the development of the Jewish "idea" as a historical process, its essence would emerge in its unadulterated purity, freed from the encumbrances of tradition, and one had no doubt that the "refined" (*geläutert*) type of Judaism thus arrived at would splendidly fit into the world of modern Europe. One failed to see that far from tracing the historical reality of Judaism, one was guided by a preconceived idea of what Judaism ought to be in order to conform to the standards of nineteenth-century religious thought, and in the well-known Hegelian fashion the historical process was seen to culminate and reach its consummation in Abraham Geiger's concept of Reform. In spite of its professed interest in history, Geiger's theology was essentially unhistorical, unromantic, and dominated by the spirit of "Aufklärung." Its reading of Jewish history reflected the motives of his own age, not the spiritual forces that had moulded the Jewish past.

If Geiger and his contemporaries had erred in projecting their own "idea" of Judaism into their reconstruction of history, they were at least guided by a more or less philosophical concept of Judaism. They at least perceived, consciously or otherwise, that without such a perspective and viewpoint, historical research would lose itself in a wilderness. They avoided the pitfalls of historicism by bringing to the study of Jewish history a clear, albeit somewhat arbitrary, conception as to the ultimate goal and nature of Judaism. They did not endeavor to derive a concept of Judaism from a reading of history but read history in the light of their concept. In the Jewish Hegelians of the nineteenth century this tendency is particularly pronounced.

The downfall of the Hegelian metaphysics of history did very much to discredit the type of Jewish theology just described. The naive belief that history manifested the inevitable and triumphant progress of the "Idea" began to wane. The inner connection between "Wissenschaft des Judentums" and the new theology of Judaism as Geiger had conceived it was no longer felt to be self-evident. "Wissenschaft des Judentums" lost its sense of purpose and direction, spending its energies in detailed research with no vision to impart unity to its efforts. And theology, bereft of a philosophical principle to underpin it, ran the danger of a moral breakdown. In this critical situation Hermann Cohen arose, and it is in no small measure due to his influence that twentieth-century Jewish theology in Germany emancipated itself from a sterile historicism and recovered the almost lost domain of the Absolute, of Truth, and faith in the Truth.

Throughout his long and distinguished career as a philosopher, Hermann Cohen had been an ardent defender of the Jewish faith and a champion of the honor of his people. His utterances on the subject of Judaism cover a period of over fifty years, from 1867 to 1918, and are collected in Bruno Strauss's edition in three volumes (1924), prefaced by Franz Rosenzweig's magnificent Introduction. They reflect, at the earlier stages, a philosophy of Judaism still embryonic and lacking in an appreciation of religion as a realm of its own. It took Hermann Cohen some time until he discovered and recognized the specific character, the "Eigenart" as he was to call it later, of religion as such and of Judaism in particular. But even his early writings on the subject of Judaism, however dominated by a sense of the superiority of ethics over religion, helped a great deal to impart to Jewish theology a greater measure of self-respect and a frame of reference within which it could recapture a sense of orientation. Cohen had introduced the idea of God into the very center of his system of ethics in the great work *Die Ethik des reinen Willens* (1904). He was proudly aware of the fact that more than any previous thinker he had established the concept of God as the pinnacle of the ethical system, and theologians could derive a great deal of inspiration from a philosophy constructed in this way. His concept of ethical realization as an "eternal task," and conversely, his interpretation of "eternity" as the ethical perspective, the distant goal, the dimension of a reality other than Nature—all this aroused an enthusiasm and re-kindled faith. It was expressed in a language of high pathos, prophetic rather than academic, and Christian critics did not fail to discover the Jewish note in it.

Indications of Cohen's new trend of thinking were confirmed in his last philosophical work, *Der Begriff der Religion im System der Philosophie* (1915) in which religion is already recognized as possessing a specific character unexpressed by, and inaccessible to, philosophical ethics. The standpoint thus reached is finally elaborated and applied to an interpretation of Judaism in his momentous work, *Die Religion der Vernunft aus den Quellen des Judentums*, which he dedicated to the memory of his father, and which was published after his death in 1919. In his lectures at the "Lehranstalt für die Wissenschaft des Judentums" in Berlin, he had already voiced, with the passionate faith that was his, some of the profound insights expressed in that book, and Franz Rosenzweig was fortunate enough to listen to them. It was Rosenzweig who was later to offer the most incisive and sympathetic interpretation of the significance of Cohen's work and to reveal the novelty of its approach to the younger generation of Jewish theologians.

What was Cohen's concept of the "religion of reason," which he found in the "sources of Judaism"?

Religion and reason, Cohen insists, are not antithetical spheres of the human consciousness but religion itself has a share ("Anteil") in reason. For reason is the "source" of all concepts, the "rock" whence they are hewn, their "organ" and criterion of truth. Since religion too is determined by concepts and not by mere instincts, imagination, or social requirements, it must be understood as flowing from reason. Cohen never loses sight of the bond that connects religion with reason, and is at pains to show how the concepts of religion have their analogies in the concepts of philosophical thinking. True, religion is not philosophy, but its classical expression, the monotheistic faith of Judaism, harbors, already in its earliest literary manifestations an implicit awareness of some of the problems of philosophy in both its theoretical and ethical aspects. Cohen sees a kind of pre-stabilized harmony between religious ideas and philosophical problems, and he is therefore vitally interested in the way in which the medieval Jewish philosophers in particular tried to link Judaism with the Greek philosophical tradition. More than any other modern Jewish thinker, he attached importance to the medieval philosophers of Judaism, "our legitimate theologians," and quotes with warm approval their efforts to derive religious concepts from the principles of scientific reason. Not that he wishes to confound the boundaries between philosophy and religion. No one is more emphatic on the distinction between them. But he is equally determined not to allow an unbridgeable gulf to be fixed between them. No Kierkegaardian "leap" is called for in order to arrive at God from the starting-point of human reason. For since religion shares in reason, the unity of the human consciousness need not be broken or impaired. Religion properly understood is a religion of reason.

On the other hand, religion is a sphere of its own. Cohen carefully distinguishes between the "independence" (*Selbständigkeit*) of ethics and the mere "specificality" (*Eigenart*) of religion. He explains that we have no right to arrogate to religion a complete autonomy that would make it independent of ethics. Religion is still bound to ethics but its specific character is such as to constitute a realm of its own that bursts the confines of ethics without jeopardizing it. The deeper implications of this view are clear. Religion must never violate ethical standards. Its function is to open up fresh areas of experience, not to infringe upon those laid down by ethics.

The fresh insights by which religion enriches ethics and establishes a sphere of its own are twofold. The first is the discovery of man as a "fellow-man" (*Mitmensch*), not only as a specimen of humanity as ethics conceives him. Ethical thinking disregards the individual as such. It is impersonal in its approach, and its organ of expression is the impersonal law. It honors in each man the universal idea of humanity—in itself a great achievement—but it has no concern with the individual person. It views him as a "He," almost as an "It," not as a "Thou." This religion does, and Cohen points out that the experience from which this new orientation flows is the experience of human suffering, especially of poverty and social distress. Cohen shows that philosophical ethics such as found in the Stoics and in Spinoza, tended to belittle or ignore completely the virtue of compassion and of sympathy. It was the Jewish prophetic religion that discovered the human brother in the suffering neighbor and concerned itself with the abolition of social distress as a messianic task. The effect of this religious concept of the "fellow-man" was a deepening of the very concept of God. Whereas in ethics God was conceived merely as the God of humanity, He now became the God of Love, the God of the poor, and prophetic religion spoke in His name when demanding the love of the neighbor.

The other new insight gained by religion concerns the discovery of the human self, the "I" as an individual. Selfhood has here not the meaning it has in Socrates's famous admonition "Know thyself," which Cohen interprets in a theoretical, not ethical sense. Self-knowledge under the aspect of religion has a different meaning. In the consciousness of my sin, I discover my self. Not as a self conditioned by hereditary guilt as in mythology but by my own sin. Thus Ezekiel discovered the individual self as grounded in the consciousness of sin. Again, the concept of God receives a new dimension as a result of this discovery. God is experienced not merely as the God of humanity or as the promulgator of social justice and of love but as my personal Redeemer who forgives my sin and allows me to become reconciled to Him.

Cohen's philosophy of religion does not exhaust itself in the discovery of the two concepts that we have just outlined. It also undertakes to speak of God in terms of "Being" and elucidates the meaning of such theological concepts as creation and revelation. Jewish monotheism teaches the "uniqueness" (*Einzigkeit*) of God, and Cohen explains this term as indicating the absolute otherness of God. He is incomparable, eternal, unchangeable. He is experienced in Moses's theophany as the burning bush, which is never consumed. His Being is distinct from mere existence. No existence is added to His essence. He is not "deus sive natura" as Spinoza would have Him. All nature is transient. Heaven and earth perish but God remains. Nature is as nought compared with the only Being which is God. No Logos can be admitted as a mediator between Him and the world.

Yet God cannot mean a Being unrelated to the world. The very concept of uniqueness implies a relationship. In philosophy, being is conceived as the logical presupposition of becoming. Thus Kant made substance the precondition of causality. In the religion of reason an analogous type of thinking is at work. The unique Being of God has the function of making causality possible. In other words, God is the "Urgrund" of activity. He is the Creator, and creation is contained in the very concept of God as Being. Cohen discusses Maimonides's concept of the omnipotence of God and finds it akin to his own notion of "Ursprung," which plays such an important part in his idealist philosophy. He sternly rejects the idea of creation in the sense of emanation. No such material notion can be admitted since the process of becoming belongs to becoming only, and all emanationist theories of creation are to be repudiated as mythological.

Revelation is interpreted by Cohen as the continuation of God's creative act. It creates man as a moral being, and only means that man's moral reason is rooted in God. Again, Cohen rejects any mythological notion of God communicating with man. We are not dealing with a miracle or, as in pantheism, with an unfolding of God's essence and a kind of revelation of Himself to Himself but with another creation. Cohen uses the brief formula, "Revelation is the creation of reason."

Throughout Cohen's discussion of the fundamental concepts of religion, we meet a term that more than any other has puzzled the interpreters of his philosophy and given rise to some controversy. We are referring to the term "correlation," which seems to imply the positing of God as a transcendent reality and cannot be squared with the idealist method of philosophical construction that is peculiar to Cohen. Franz Rosenzweig held that this concept represents Cohen's radical departure from his idealist standpoint and a recognition of God as a reality facing man rather than an idea conceived by him. Others failed to see any such revolutionary break, and Julius Guttmann expressed the view that, while Cohen did not mean to step out of the self-imposed bounds of his thinking, there was a certain incongruity between his philosophical line of thinking and the metaphysical implications of this new concept of correlation. Cohen himself defines correlation as an expression of the fact that man as a shareholder of reason is created by God. The correlation between God and man, he says, is founded in reason. Or in another place: Reason is the condition by virtue of which God can enter into correlation with man. In the notion of "spirit," more precisely of the "holy spirit," correlation is made intelligible. God is spirit, and man is spirit. Not in the sense of an identity, for

God's spirit is unique. But the spirit connects both partners of the correlation. In the knowledge of God that man achieves, God enters into correlation. It would seem that by and large Cohen still speaks in terms of his idealist philosophy, and does not break the magic circle of his system as Rosenzweig suggested.

Perhaps the most fascinating part of Cohen's great work is the manner in which he discovers the religious concepts of reason in the literary sources of Judaism, especially the Bible, rabbinic Haggadah, and medieval Jewish philosophy. He insists that neither the concept of religion as such nor that of Judaism can be derived from history. He does not fall into the error of historicism and try to arrive at a conception of Judaism by a process of induction. He realizes that the literary sources remain silent unless approached with a definite concept. Nor does he simply identify the religion of reason with Judaism. He declares that the religion of reason is found wherever a nation has reached a cultural level at which science and philosophy are present. But he is convinced that Judaism is the religion in which the essential insights of the religion of reason were first discovered. Judaism has not a monopoly but the primacy in this respect. In the same way in which the Greeks must be considered the creators of a scientific philosophy shared by all mankind, the Jewish people created the religion of reason. Cohen therefore undertakes to illumine its concept by reference to the Jewish classical sources in which they express themselves. In so doing he meets considerable difficulties because monotheism, he acknowledges, grew out of mythical thinking, and bears its unmistakable traces in the earlier strata of biblical literature. Cohen is at pains to show how the biblical authors increasingly stress the spiritual nature of such concepts as creation and revelation, and eventually achieve a level of meaning purged from all mythological reference.

Cohen's reading of Judaism was not altogether unhampered by the method of construction that he applied to his religious concepts, but there can be no doubt that he succeeded in giving a picture of Judaism in which the inwardness of faith was vividly portrayed. No other thinker of the idealist tradition ever attempted such a fusion of the essential spirit of post-Kantian idealist philosophy and Judaism. In his enthusiastic account of Hermann Cohen, Rosenzweig said that the book in which the attempt was made would live on, that it would still be read at a time when the language in which it was written would be understood by scholars only. Unfortunately, interest in it has already waned considerably, and its readers are few and far between today. The problems with which it wrestles are not the problems of the post-idealistic age. But there is enough in Cohen's work to merit a perennial significance.

II

In Leo Baeck we meet a thinker with a cast of mind in many ways different from Cohen's yet bearing the unmistakable traces of Cohen's influence. Cohen himself felt a warm friendship for Baeck, and singled him out as the one on whom his mantle would fall. Indeed, no other Jewish theologian among Cohen's disciples shows a comparable understanding of what Cohen's idea of the "eternal task" means in terms of religious thinking. In Baeck, Cohen's idealism lives on and forms the very center of his being. It is the axis around which his own highly personal thinking revolves, the hidden Self from which as from a fixed and unshakable mid-point all his visions and utterances flow. The singular moral strength that enabled him to remain unperturbed and steadfast in the face of evil stems from the idealist faith that Cohen had planted in his soul. It proved one of the great assets of German Jewry in its darkest hour when Baeck, the thinker, stood at the helm.

Though steeped in the Cohen tradition and molded by it, Baeck's way of thinking derives from yet another source. It received a decisive impulse and direction from Dilthey's *Verstehende Psychologie*, which seeks to enter sympathetically into the patterns of thought that underlie the literary creations of the past. Dilthey's approach was guided by a sense of unity, of "Gestalt," and strove to "understand" rather than causally to "explain" the "vital connection" (*Lebenszusammenhang*) in the elements of the whole, to "re-live" (*nacherleben*) the spiritual struggles of former epochs. His aim was to comprehend, not to sit in judgment. It was psychological rather than philosophical, and being concerned with "meaning" (*Bedeutung*), it stressed the totality of patterns or "structures" (*Strukturen*) rather than isolated elements. Baeck must have felt that it was precisely this kind of approach that was needed in order to do justice to Judaism as an historical entity. He was not satisfied that "Wissenschaft des Judentums," which the nineteenth century had created and which the twentieth had proudly acclaimed as the only method of correctly assessing Judaism, had in fact lived up to its task. He rightly sensed the urgency of the need to see Judaism steady and to see it whole, to approach it with a large and sympathetic vision. His great book *Das Wesen des Judentums* sets out to accomplish this, and succeeds in this aim. It brings to its task an unusual sense for morphological unity, an artistic feeling for "Gestalt." It is determined to "allow Judaism to describe itself" as far as the inevitable intrusion of the subjective element permits it.

Nothing illustrates Baeck's aim more clearly than his stress on the polarity of the Jewish religious experience. There is no Either/Or in it but an oscillation between mysticism and ethics, "Geheimnis" and "Gebot," God's distance and nearness, freedom and strict order, oneness and otherness. Baeck sees in this "tension" the very nature of Judaism and the deepest root of its vitality. God is experienced as the ground of both the mystery and the commandment. The commandment itself bears witness to the mystery. At the same time, Baeck is emphatic as to the primacy of the ethical element in Judaism. With Hermann Cohen, he stresses the fact that Judaism is not merely ethical but that ethics constitutes its very essence. The revelation of God and the revelation of the ethical task are one. For not the nature of God but His Will is revealed. The Jewish concept of religion is free from all admixture of metaphysics or Gnosticism. The prophets, who are the authors of classical Judaism, teach nothing but the ethical aspect of God, and in so doing they have given religion its autonomy. Religion, Baeck agrees with Schleiermacher, is "feeling," sentiment. But he also agrees with Cohen that religion is no religion unless it is ethical. The Jewish religious experience is that of "ethical sentiment." The autonomy of religion that Schleiermacher had claimed is best safeguarded in this combination. Myth is therefore categorically excluded from the Jewish realm. Judaism, Baeck asserts, is the only religion that has produced no mythology proper. For myth is telling us something about the fate of the gods, and hardly anything about the duty of man. Judaism stressed at times the mystery and the wonder, at others the commandment. But mythology was avoided. The path of man remained its essential concern. Wherever the Bible uses mythological images it does so to express the nonmythical, and in Kabbalah too the main concern is the way of man and the doing of God's Will. In spite of minor deviations, Judaism has remained faithful to its essence and has kept a clear direction.

It is obvious that any attempt to describe historical phenomena morphologically is bound to incur a certain amount of formalization that does violence to the fullness of the historical life. Baeck may have idealized Judaism in certain respects and failed to take full cognizance of its more erratic elements, such as we meet in certain strata of Jewish mysticism. He also failed to give due prominence to the halakhic tradition. But, by and large, his portrayal of Judaism shows a balance and penetration unequalled elsewhere. It is poles apart from Kaufmann Kohler's *Grundriss einer systematischen Theologie des Judentums auf geschichtlicher Grundlage* (1910), where in slavish imitation of Protestant accounts the prophetic and priestly elements of Judaism are sharply contrasted, and the "true" Judaism is described as one of "pure inwardness." The difference between Baeck and Kohler marks the distance Jewish Liberalism in Germany had advanced from the position that Geiger held and that still dominated the outlook of American Jewish Reform.

It is not surprising that, following in the Schleiermacher-Dilthey tradition, Baeck deals with the theological concepts of Judaism not dogmatically or in the abstract but as expressions of human experience. He prefers to speak not of God but of the Jewish *faith* in God. He is a psychologist of religion in the deep sense in which Dilthey understood the term "Verstehende Psychologie." In describing faith, he does not expound doctrine but shows how faith arises from a concern with the meaning of life. In discussing revelation, he again does not proceed doctrinally as Kaufmann Kohler still did but deals with the prophetic experience as such. As he puts it, "Not passages are to be interpreted but men are to be understood." This untheological approach leads of necessity to a certain reduction of religious concepts to a humanist level, and is not without danger. It not merely demythologizes but somewhat robs the religious concept of its specific character. Thus the concept of revelation assumes a humanist aspect that is not altogether satisfying and falls below the level that even an idealist like Cohen was able to impart to it. Revelation, Baeck says, is the theological expression of the fact that Judaism possesses a sacred literature and history. He also describes revelation as the recognition of the fact that in the religion of Israel an entirely new idea of God first manifested itself in history, and that this new idea is inexplicable in terms of natural development from lower types of religion. The unique character of this new creation is designated as "revelation," and seeing that it was the "religious genius" of the Prophets and of the people of Israel which accounts for this discovery, revelation may be said to constitute at the same time the "election" of Israel. This view of revelation goes back to Abraham Geiger, and bears an affinity to Franz Overbeck's concept of "Urgeschichte" as the breaking forth of some new vision unaccountable in terms of "development." It does not necessarily abolish the "mystery" of revelation but fails to express it.

When in the early 'thirties the call for an authentic Jewish theology became urgent, Baeck found it necessary to step into the arena of discussion and express his own view of the legitimate possibilities of a Jewish theology. His analysis of the situation that had led to such a claim and the definition of his own concept of a Jewish theology are of extreme interest. They are offered in an essay entitled *Theologie und Geschichte* (1932). It is the crisis of historicism, Baeck suggested, which both in Protestant Christianity and of late also within Judaism had given rise to a desire for a theology. The liberal theology of the historical school culminating in Harnack's account of Christianity had left a spiritual void and called forth the "theocentric theology" of Erich Schaeder, Tillich's doctrine of "Kairos," and above all, Barth's and Gogarten's "Dialectical theology." Judaism too was affected by the crisis of historicism because "Wissenschaft des Judentums" had failed. Judaism had become a matter of research but was no longer a living concern of the thinking Jew. "Because of much history little remained of religion and of the spirit which had manifested itself in the history now studied." Baeck urges a reorientation of "Wissenschaft des Judentums"—a plea already uttered by Ismar Elbogen in 1919—

and calls for a theological rather than purely historical approach to our religious sources. He is concerned with what makes the history of the Jewish people significant and worthwhile, with the spiritual struggle behind the façade of persons and events, and he is confident that, viewed from a large and vital perspective, Judaism will recover its relevance for the modern Jew.

Turning to the project of a Jewish theology, Baeck warns against transferring to Judaism theological concepts that are peculiar to Christianity. In Protestantism, the two elements of revelation and church constitute the nature of theology. The "theologia viatorum" that alone is open to man—as distinct from the archetypal theology of God and the theology of angels and *beati*—is the revelation of the Word of God to the church. It is the "critical reflection upon the Word constituting the Church" and a "function of the Church." Neither of these notions, Baeck insists, has any comparable validity in Judaism. It has been one of the most strongly held convictions of Baeck's—expressed both in his book and in his contributions to the Symposium on the problem of Dogma in Judaism, which was published in the "Monatsschrift" of 1926 and 1927—that Judaism knows no dogmas in the accepted sense of the word. Jewish theology is undogmatic. It can only be a theology of the teachers, not of the church administering the symbols of the faith. Hence Baeck's definition of Jewish theology as a "reflection" (*Besinnung*) not upon the Word of revelation but upon the history and tradition of Judaism. Not the recourse to revelation but the Jewish idea, the eternal task, the way, the future are the concern of a Jewish theology. Baeck is confident that his concept overcomes the pitfalls of both historicism and its opposite, the absence of the historical sense. It avoids historicism by seeking the abiding element, the specific character, the essence and idea of Judaism. And it does full justice to history by discovering this idea in the actual field of history and tradition. For the entirety of Jewish teaching can be found only in the total expanse of Jewish history. Baeck uses the formula: "The teaching of Judaism is its history, and its history is at the same time its teaching."

It will be apparent from this abstract of Baeck's essay how constant his position remained throughout, and how cautious was his approach to the problems of a Jewish theology. He remained firmly entrenched in the liberal position which his *Das Wesen des Judentums* had mapped out. His outline of what a Jewish theology could and should do admirably fits the program he had himself realized.

III

In 1911, Martin Buber published the first three of his "Reden über das Judentum," which were to startle, irritate and inspire his generation, and forced German Jewry to rethink its theology. Cultural Zionism, which until then had spoken only in the measured accents of Ahad Ha-Am's calm philosophy, profoundly critical of the West yet itself lacking in a deep religious faith, now found a new tone, a new message that stirred the imagination and moved the will. The first to respond were members of the Prague Zionist circle, men like Hugo Bergmann, Robert Weltsch, Friedrich Thieberger. But the circle widened, and by 1916 Buber was able to launch a representative literary organ, the monthly *Der Jude*, which united on its platform a great diversity of talents and shades of opinion.

Zionism has been described as the belated flowering of the romantic spirit, which nineteenth-century Jewish rationalism had suppressed. No doubt, a certain romantic element is alive in the Zionist concern with the nation, its history and rebirth. But it would be a serious mistake if we described Buber as a romanticist. Romanticism lives from a sense of the shapeless, infinite to which the world is not "Bild" but "Sinnbild," pointing to an inner life in nature and history beyond the grasp of reason. Symbolic form is therefore the very medium in which romanticism expresses itself. Christianity and the Eastern religions are able to arouse a romantic interest precisely because of this.

Geiger characterized Christianity as the "Mother of Romanticism," and Baeck contrasted Judaism and Christianity as "classical" and "romantic religion" respectively. Buber was not to revoke that judgment. Nor was he a romanticist himself. He was the apostle of the Absolute rather than of the Infinite. He demanded, challenged, proclaimed in prophetic, not in romantic fashion. The moral pathos with which he spoke was in fact antiromantic and stemmed from the same tradition that had inspired Hermann Cohen's concept of the "eternal task." It was the spirit of Jewish prophecy and the messianic outlook that lay at the root of both Cohen's and Buber's philosophy of Judaism.

The question that Buber thrust into the consciousness of his generation was a simple one: What is the meaning (*Sinn*) of Judaism for the Jew of today? How much inner reality does it possess for him? What is its truth not in abstract terms of ideas such as the liberal theology had evolved nor in terms of mere observance such as orthodoxy had proclaimed, but in the sense of true living? To Buber's mind, Judaism is truly found only where men live face to face with the Absolute, with a sense of unconditioned commitment, making God a reality and every act a testimony of faith. He sees in the history of Judaism a line of movements that time and again sought to renew this spirit of unconditional surrender to the Absolute and to express it in forms of communal living. He interprets Jewish history as a conflict between the official, complacent, and timid type of Judaism and the true Jew who is to be found only in the heretics and mystics, the "subterranean currents" of the Jewish tradition, out of favor with the accredited representatives of the Jewish religion. He describes the Rechabites, Essenes, the early Christians, and the Hasidim as specimens of the authentic Jew. The Jewish prophets above all typify for him the mode of existence that we may call Jewish. But where is this Judaism found today? Buber scornfully dismisses Moritz Lazarus's claim that the liberal theology was about to renew the spirit of Jewish prophecy. All it did was to rationalize the faith, simplify the dogma and ease the burden of the ceremonial law. Its "refinement" of Judaism was no act of Reformation in the grand style of a Luther but petty reform. Judaism had lost its meaning and could recover it only by an act of return and inner rebirth, not by a process of development. Buber rejected the notion of "progress" and called for something both more sudden and revolutionary, an inner awakening of the spirit. He felt there was a split in the soul of the modern Jew between the world that surrounded him, the mechanistic type of society of which he was a member, and the substance of his being, his inheritance and the chain of the generations of which he was a part. He saw the Jew uprooted from the deepest springs of his existence, living in a void, and Zionism had for him the meaning of a new beginning. He believed in the healing power of the Land of Israel, and in the creative potency of the Jewish soul.

The theology of Buber's *Reden** reflects much of the spirit of the then current "Lebensphilosophie" of Bergson, Simmel, and others who believed in the creativeness of the *élan vital*, in the truths of intuition, and in a social order realizing true community (*Gemeinschaft*) in the place of mere society (*Gesellschaft*). Buber had not yet evolved a philosophy of his own. He was groping for a new vision but had not yet found it. God then meant to him nothing more than a symbol, an archetype of the soul and its yearning for unity, a projection and externalization of subjective experience. In the preface to his collected eight *Reden* (1923), he found it necessary to reinterpret some of his theological concepts in the light of the "clarification" that, he admitted, he had since been able to achieve. He repudiated the suggestion that his views had fundamentally changed. But as Franz Rosenzweig wrote to him in his famous letter ("Die Bauleute," 1923), Buber's words had a new ring and meant a "conversion" to those whose spokesman Buber had been in the past. God, Buber now explained, was neither a metaphysical idea nor a moral ideal nor a projection nor anything created by man but what Buber meant by this word was—God. True, man could "possess" God only through ideas and images. But these ideas and images are not the work of "free creation"; they are the outcome of man's meeting God, formulae of what happens to man, traces of the mystery. Theophany may change its form but God does not change. In every theophany man has a share, and ideas and images issue from it. But that which reveals itself is God, not an idea or image. Man does not possess God Himself but he meets God Himself.

These were indeed new words, and they were possible because Buber's thinking had undergone a radical change. He had in the

* Martin Buber, in a letter to me dated December 27, 1956, wrote about the present essay: "Zu dem Kapitel über mich wäre zu sagen (und hoffentlich einmal mündlich zu erörten), dass ich mir vor 1916 keine eigentliche Theologie zuzusprechen vermag; ihr Anfang ist fast genau zu datieren. Sie deuten es ja selber an, aber ich würde, wenn ich darüber zu reden hätte, nicht einmal sagen können: 'the theology of Buber's *Reden*'—sie hatten keine." ("As for the chapter dealing with me, it might be said (and, hopefully, discussed one day face to face) that I cannot ascribe to myself any theology proper before 1916; its beginning can be dated with near-accuracy. You hint at it yourself but if I were to make a statement on this subject, I couldn't even say: 'the theology of Buber's *Reden*'—they had none.")

meanwhile found his own philosophy. In 1919, he had written the first draft of his "I and Thou" (*Ich und Du*), and the book was completed in 1922. The theme of this book need not be restated here. It has become a classic of religious existentialism and has exercised a considerable influence on contemporary thought. What interests us here is the fact that Buber was able to apply his philosophy in a most fruitful manner to the interpretation of Judaism. The concept of "meeting"—of "dialog," served as a master key for an understanding of Jewish religious history. Not the subjectivity of "Erlebnis" as such constitutes the core of the Jewish religious experience but the response to happenings that are felt to be the way in which God speaks to us, challenging, castigating and redeeming us. Buber can therefore admit the legitimacy of every kind of literary form in which biblical man gives voice to his experience of meeting, be it didactic, lyrical, or prophetic. The form of narrative in particular is appropriate to the testimony of the mighty acts of God in Jewish history, and myth is an attempt to express in the only adequate language what was experienced in those soul-shaking hours. In historizing myth such as we meet it in the Bible, Buber sees nothing to be explained away but the legitimate expression of true meeting. The criterion of the truth of all forms of religious speech is not its form but the seriousness with which it testifies to the call of God. Religion is true wherever man responds with his whole being to God who is a "Thou," not a mere idea, a metaphysical or neutralized "It."

Buber's new concept of religion enabled him to do justice to what we might call the everyday aspect of religion, which received less than its due in his earlier writings. *Galut*, which he had stigmatized as a period of decline, is no longer rejected as meaningless. There is, he now admits, a "theophany of exile," of God's abiding presence amidst contumely and humiliation. When German Jewry suffered its hour of crushing defeat, in the tragic 'thirties, Buber could act as a great comforter because he had long ago discovered the meaning of this type of theophany. In the addresses of those years, collected in the volume, *Die Stunde und die Erkenntnis* (1937), he spoke with the accents of a preacher and theologian. But he had also become a teacher of Judaism, a scholar and sage. His philosophy of dialog had enabled him to search for new ways of interpreting the religious sources of Judaism, and he had thrown himself into this task. In this, he had the rare fortune of having for his companion no less a man than Franz Rosenzweig.

IV

Franz Rosenzweig's meteorlike appearance on the Jewish horizon was poignantly brief. He made his *début* with his stirring appeal, "Zeit ist's," in 1917, and he died after seven years of suffering from a terrible disease, completely paralyzed, in 1929. Only twelve years were given to him to fulfill his task. But he lived long enough to place his name among the immortals of the Jewish people, and to bring the history of German Jewry to its spiritual climax.

Rosenzweig was a Jew reborn and saved from the brink of baptism, a lost son returning to his Father's home. It was not Zionism that rescued him as it did so many others. It was Judaism that brought him back. The story of his conversion to his ancestral faith has been told more than once, and need not be repeated here. It is the story of a philosopher who found philosophy wanting because it lacked faith, and who founded a new philosophy, a philosophy of faith. He had wrestled with the temptation to become a Christian like some of his best friends, because he saw and admired their attitude of faith. He did not see much religious faith in those who professed to be Jews. When finally he turned to Judaism, he also met the men whom he could regard as Jews in spirit. Hermann Cohen, Martin Buber, and N. A. Nobel were outstanding amongst them.

Rosenzweig's *Der Stern der Erlösung* was written in the fires of an ecstasy that sustains its 532 pages from beginning to end. The spark that set him aglow was his strong conviction that philosophy had reached a phase when it had nothing further to say unless it sought help from theology, and that theology was likewise doomed to sterility unless it called in the assistance of philosophy. Hegel's absolute idealism marked the end of all philosophy "from Ionia to Jena." Having comprehended itself by a reflection of its own history, as Hegel had done, there is nothing left for it to comprehend. No further step in the direction of idealism is possible. Hence the emergence of a highly personal and individualistic type of philosophizing as we meet it in Schopenhauer and Nietzsche, a type that however cannot satisfy. In this situation only an alliance with theology can help. Theology, on the other hand, requires the aid of philosophy. In Schleiermacher and Ritschl it had effected a separation from philosophy that made it "autonomous" but only at a very high price. It had affirmed the total independence of faith from reason only to land itself in a historical theology that was now experiencing the inevitable crisis of historicism. Rosenzweig speaks of a new type of philosopher-theologian, and Hermann Cohen's example is very much in his mind. He refers no doubt to him when he points to "the most determined systematizer amongst the philosophers of the last generation" who "feeds with a whole system the flame of his faith's theology." But in point of fact, the rays of Rosenzweig's *Stern* flow out in directions different from Cohen's. Not the "eternal task" of ethics but the religious experience of revelation stands in the center of his theology.

The central core of the *Stern*, Rosenzweig himself said on two occasions in his *Letters*, is the affirmation of the Name of God as "the Word and Fire of Revelation." It is through revelation, and through it alone, that the other two fundamental concepts of theology, creation and redemption, become real and meaningful. Revelation creates the world and the goal of history. Neither Plato nor Aristotle knew anything about "the whole earth" and "the end of days." These biblical terms are missing from the vocabulary of the philosophers because only revelation transforms the natural, pagan cosmos into the "Kingdom of God," in which existence comes alive and is "on the way" toward redemption. Only in revelation do we experience God, and revelation is therefore the primary religious category. But creation and redemption are equally important. Rosenzweig criticizes the theology of the nineteenth century for having neglected the concept of creation, overemphasizing as it did revelation and redemption. In a sense, both these concepts are rooted in that of creation, notwithstanding the fact that the experience of revelation comes first.

What Rosenzweig means by revelation becomes clear when he compares the mythical world of paganism with the biblical world of the Word, of dialogue, of openness and love. Paganism presents God, world, and man in their mute, closed, unrelated, and unrevealed aspects. It is the world of a mythical Olympus, of a plastic cosmos, of the tragic hero, as Oswald Spengler had depicted the

Apollonian culture. Rosenzweig does not deny that these figures are the elements of our reality, the symbols of the world in which we live. But they represent truth only in an elementary and fragmentary sense. They are the *dramatis personae* but not the drama itself. The world's real drama unfolds only once the isolation of God, world, and man is broken and relationship ensues. Revelation breaks the spell, and makes the true history possible. That history needs time. Truth itself needs time to work itself out, and redemption means nothing but time fulfilled, the Kingdom of God come. In Barth's dialectical theology, eternity cannot fulfil but break time. For Rosenzweig, eternity enters time and fulfils it. It flows from revelation since revelation is not a historical event that happened once but is always renewed and always present. It is a response to God's love and helps to bring about that world of mutual openness that we call the Kingdom of God.

Rosenzweig's *Stern* is a difficult book, and Julius Guttmann has rightly criticized the dogmatic manner in which it posits the three primary realities of God, world, and man. It fails to show the kind of experience that brings them into view, and in constructing their meaning falls back upon the idealist method that he himself had rejected. It is this paradox of an "existentialist"—to use a contemporary term—who dogmatizes that made it difficult to discuss the book and accept its philosophy. But the impression it created was tremendous. Gerhard Scholem summed it up well by an article written in 1931, ten years after its first appearance when a second edition was published. Out of the catastrophe of Idealism, he said, a new theology had arisen which clearly saw that from the idea of man's autonomy, the alpha and omega of liberal theology, there was no way leading to the mysteries of revelation. Little had been published since the *Moreh Nebukhim* and the *Zohar* that presented a greater challenge than this book. Its "mystical theism" had baffled their minds. But a "healing power" had emanated from it.

Rosenzweig himself regarded his *Stern* merely as a prelude to his life's real task, that of living the kind of religious existence that the book had mapped out in its third and final part. The influence that he exerted was not so much due to his book as to his personality and the way in which he applied himself to a closer interpretation of Jewish life and literature. From a theological point of view, the most important of his smaller writings (collected in *Kleinere Schriften*, 1937) are those devoted to the language and literary forms of the Bible. In 1925, he and Buber had begun to cooperate in the grandiose project of a new German translation of the Bible, and in the course of the work felt the need for explaining the principles that guided them in the rendering of the text. The articles written by them on this subject are collected in a book called *Die Schrift und ihre Verdeutschung* (1936). They show the extent to which their philosophy could be made fruitful for an understanding of the Bible.

V

Buber's and Rosenzweig's essays on the Bible show a remarkable unity of purpose. There is hardly a dividing line between the two thinkers, and the theology underlying their approach to the Bible is almost identical. Buber acknowledged Rosenzweig's great merit of having made the concepts of creation, revelation, and redemption the key words of biblical theology. Both felt the need to awaken in their contemporaries a sense of faith in the truths of the Bible, and both understood that the faith required was not of the dogmatic kind but rather an attitude of openness, an inner readiness to be touched by the biblical word, to allow it to speak to us and reveal what had been revealed to him who spoke it first. To both, the Bible was the record and testimony of meeting and dialog. Rosenzweig suggested that none of the biblical statements about God, including the most scurrilous and anthropomorphic, could be regarded as beyond the range of modern man's experience. For wherever a man calls, God's "ear" listens. Wherever a man puts his hand out in supplication, God's "hand" can take hold of it. Wherever he seeks God or flees from Him, God will "come down" to meet him or face him at the end of his flight. All anthropomorphisms of the Bible can be shown to be but statements about meeting. God is never "described." He is only attested from an experience. Herein lies the human element of the Bible, its relevance for us, and this is why, as Margarete Susman put it, the Bible can mean something to us today as at any time. Buber and Rosenzweig greatly helped German Jewry to approach the Bible from an attitude of faith.

They made at the same time a lasting contribution to biblical scholarship. Biblical studies had been more or less in the hands of Protestant scholars, and both Buber and Rosenzweig acknowledged the debt Jewry owed them. But it was an anomalous position from the Jewish point of view, and the need for a Jewish biblical exegesis was apparent. Benno Jacob, the eminent biblical scholar, had shown the way, and Buber and Rosenzweig were following it. Buber's *Königtum Gottes* (1932) was the first major fruit of an I–Thou theology allied to a method of literary analysis that was oriented toward an understanding of religious experience. Buber and Rosenzweig did not repudiate biblical criticism, but they were able to see unity where the critics found only a mosaic of sources. The unity of the Bible meant to them more than a unity of authorship of this or that book. The unity they perceived was the unity of an organism in which everything is related to one another. As Rosenzweig put it, the Bible wants to be read in such a way that one passage evokes all the others in which a similar term, a similar theme is expressed. Only the synopsis of the total ground yields a valid theology. Not Chapter i or Chapter ii of *Genesis* gives us the biblical view of creation but both together. Whoever the Redactor of the Torah was, he is our Teacher, Rabbenu as Rosenzweig would read the symbol R by which the critics denoted the final editor. Rosenzweig expressed regret at the fact that Jewish orthodoxy could not see eye to eye with this view of the Bible, which avoided both the Scylla of unbridled criticism and the Charybdis of a fundamentalism that was unacceptable to the historical consciousness of modern man.

VI

The theological attitude that Buber and Rosenzweig represented made its impact felt in the way Judaism came to be studied in the 'thirties. The purely historical orientation that had dominated in the past had already been overcome by Cohen and Baeck. But an element of idealist construction, of idealization, had obtruded itself that was not entirely convincing. Nor did it always tally with the facts that historical research was bringing to light. Buber's and Rosenzweig's approach was both more empirical and historical. Its influence can be felt in such scholarly works as Nahum N. Glatzer's *Untersuchungen zur Geschichtslehre der Tannaiten* (1933), Abraham Heschel's *Die Prophetie* (1936), Elias Bickermann's *Der Gott der Makkabäer* (1937), and in the concept of Jewish history that Fritz Baer evolved.

But the 'thirties also led to fresh attempts at assessing the spiritual situation in which German Jewry found itself. In 1933, Max Wiener published his *Jüdische Religion im Zeitalter der Emanzipation*, a close and penetrating analysis of nineteenth-century Jewish theology in Germany. Of great interest were Ignaz Maybaum's articles and books. Maybaum expressed a deep sense of anxiety over the process of secularization that had undermined the spiritual structure of Judaism. He saw both in Liberalism and political Zionism manifestations of the same phenomenon. The national liberalism of the Zionist faith no less than the individual liberalism of the nineteenth century robbed the Jewish people of its sacred history. Their programs were mere ideologies, secularized versions of the authentic religious teachings, and tended to give way to what was even worse, the myth and magic of the youth movements, their songs and dances, which obliterated the primacy of the family and the reverence for parents and teachers. Maybaum clearly saw the dangers that threatened both the world at large and Judaism in particular. He was not satisfied to consider theology in the abstract but felt the urge to diagnose the spiritual ills of the time and employ the insights of theology—Rosenzweig's theology in the main—for their cure.

The period was indeed one of bewilderment and unrest. It was the time when Karl Jaspers wrote his *Die geistige Situation der Zeit* in which he portrayed the growing uneasiness and alienation of modern man. In 1931, Martin Heidegger had published his *Sein und Zeit*, the most authentic and compelling document of secularized man, bereft of the sense of eternity and interpreting existence as *Sein zum Tode*. In this atmosphere, Buber's and Rosenzweig's theology of dialog seemed to be too optimistic to those who could not help seeing the world under the aspect of a demonic self-deification and could expect salvation only from a radical return, a sense of crisis and judgment. Hans Joachim Schoeps expressed this mood of despair in his *Jüdischer Glaube in dieser Zeit* (1932). He shared Maybaum's reading of the situation but was far more radical in his theology and introduced a fully fledged

Barthianism, only slightly modified to suit the Jewish requirements. Revelation was no longer, as in Rosenzweig, distinct from redemption but in itself a redemptive act, the promise of salvation that God held out to sinful man. This concept of revelation, though occasionally found in rabbinic and kabbalistic thought, is not characteristic of Judaism. In Schoeps it has a decidedly Christian flavor. Nor can it be said that Schoeps's emphasis on the Sinaitic Revelation, though *prima facie* confirming the central Jewish dogma, shows much understanding of the theological significance of the "gift of Torah." In the manner of dialectical theology, Schoeps speaks of the paradox of our possessing and yet not possessing of God's Word. Revelation is not the gracious act of a gift as it is in rabbinic thought nor an ever-renewed meeting as it is described by Buber and Rosenzweig but a paradox and is uneasily hovering in an historical void. It is interesting to note that though professing great admiration for Rosenzweig, Schoeps evaded a discussion of his theology as well as Buber's. The force of Schoeps's position lay in its negation of man-centered idealism. Once the centricity of man was abandoned as was the case in Buber and Rosenzweig, the theology of crisis lost much of its pungency. German Jewry felt on the whole spiritually much safer in the company of Buber and of Rosenzweig than in that of Karl Barth and his Jewish disciple.

VII

Our survey of Jewish theology in twentieth-century German Jewry has so far been confined to liberal Judaism. The orthodox scene shows a different picture. In Liberalism, the problem of a Jewish theology arose from the fact that the meaning of Judaism had to be found within the framework of contemporary thought. It had to fit the situation in which the modern mind found itself as a result of the changes wrought in philosophical and historical thinking. It became entangled in idealism and historicism, and had to disentangle itself from the crises in which it was caught. It was time-bound, groping for the truth. In Cohen, Buber, and Rosenzweig, it owed its birth to the insights of a general philosophy. It stemmed from a larger whole, and could allow Judaism to run the gamut of other truths. In orthodoxy, the position was different. Here not certainty was sought but certitude. And the certitude of faith was not in danger. Historicism was not allowed to touch the citadel of belief. "Wissenschaft des Judentums," to be true, had prominent representatives in German-Jewish orthodoxy. Men like David Hoffmann, Abraham Berliner, Jacob Barth, and others were adornments of Jewish learning. But their historical studies did not bring them into conflict with their faith. Orthodoxy was by its very nature bound by tradition, and biblical criticism could evoke only contempt or indignant rejection. Hoffmann's learned and skillful rebuttal of Wellhausen was more in the nature of apologetics than of modern scholarship, no matter how justified were his strictures in details. The fundamental attitude of Jewish orthodoxy had been well defined by S. R. Hirsch, the great opponent of Geiger in the nineteenth century. Judaism was not to be brought into line with modern philosophy but to be explained from within itself. How strongly Hirsch's principles were felt to be still valid can be seen from Joseph Wohlgemuth's lecture on "S. R. Hirsch und das gesetzestreue Judentum" (1927).

It would be wrong, however, to infer from this general attitude of orthodoxy that there was an absence of interest in the progress of thought outside the orthodox camp. Both the members of the Frankfurt circle of the more rigorous Hirsch type and those belonging to the Berlin group round the *Hildesheimer Rabbinerseminar* showed a great amount of sensitiveness to the stirrings of the period. Zionism considerably changed their outlook, and Friedrich Thieberger has rightly pointed out how much Isaak Breuer, Hirsch's gifted grandson, profited from it. Nor did the currents of general thought leave orthodox thinkers unaffected. Joseph Wohlgemuth, the indefatigable editor of the monthly *Jeschurun*, was not only an able exponent of Judaism and its defender against the misrepresentation of it by Protestant theologians but also tried to utilize philosophical trends for a deepening of Jewish religious thought. His study of *Teshubah*, which is based on Max Scheler, is a case in point. Oskar Wolfsberg's use of Driesch's "philosophy of organism" and Breuer's attempt to interpret the concept of creation in Kantian terms are further examples. But it has to be borne in mind that all these efforts arose not so much from a genuinely philosophical impulse as from a desire to fortify the faithful. They provided intellectual embellishments of the faith rather than new philosophical approaches. Perhaps N. A. Nobel was the only true philosopher amongst German-Jewish orthodoxy. A disciple of H. Cohen and teacher and friend of Rosenzweig, he understood the problem of religion in the modern world, and sought new paths in a direction of Jewish mysticism. He thus formed a link with some of the finest spirits of the liberal camp, and Leo Baeck's moving tribute to him bears witness to this fact.

The great importance of German-Jewish orthodoxy lay in the loyalty with which it treasured the unabridged tradition and in this way preserved the substance of historic Judaism in an age of mounting secularization. It did so without withdrawing into a cultural Ghetto, and thus proved the possibility of combining strict adherence to traditional Judaism with a living concern in general culture. Unfortunately, it had lost touch with the more profound strata of the Jewish tradition, which are found in Kabbalah and Hasidism—Scholem spoke with justice of its "Kabbalah-Angst"—and also failed to establish a vital contact with medieval Jewish philosophy. But these were minor deficiencies compared with the important function it fulfilled.

VIII

The gropings for a Jewish theology expressing the vital concerns of a reawakened German Jewry in an authoritative and comprehensive statement remained unfulfilled. The cruel stop that history put to the realization of any such hopes was one of the tragic facts in which Jewish history abounds. But at least a plan emerged at the last hour that may be recorded for future historical reference. In the 'thirties, Martin Buber convened a meeting of Jewish theologians at the office of the "Reichsvertretung" at which he submitted a scheme for the joint production of a book to be entitled *Beiträge zu einer jüdischen Theologie*. The present writer has a vivid recollection of the discussion that took place, and has fortunately still in his possession the "Table of Contents" that was submitted on that occasion. It is reproduced below with Professor Buber's kind permission. From it a clear picture emerges as to the state of Jewish theological thinking at that grave hour of Jewish history, and of the problems that were then uppermost in our minds. There was, in the first place, the question of the relationship between religion and state, a question that bears eloquent testimony to the disquiet aroused by Nazi totalitarianism. Then there was the problem of Messianism *versus* the ideology of progress, which is linked with the problem of religion and culture. Dialectical theology had played havoc with the liberal concept of religion as one of the elements of culture. It had expressed the view that the crisis of modern man resulted from the absoluteness with which he had invested culture. In the place of man-made culture it put the Word of God. This radical questioning of culture constituted a challenge to Jewish theology, both liberal and orthodox. A sense of "Kulturfreudigkeit" and belief in the religious value of human culture had been deeply ingrained in Jewish thinking. Hence the urge to examine from a Jewish point of view the question posed by dialectical theology.

The second part of the program concerned the "elements" of the Jewish tradition, its history, its double aspect of teaching and law, and the rôle it assigns to authority. In dealing with the Bible, it rightly distinguishes between the historical aspect that biblical scholarship investigates, and the perennial meaning of the message of the Bible. The themes of prayer, sin, atonement, and death conclude the central part.

The last section was to describe the "paths" of Judaism. It envisaged a discussion of the sects and trends in Jewry, the methods of Jewish education, the question of "theology as a profession" and the part Judaism could play in solving the spiritual problems of the age. Unfortunately, this ambitious program was not carried out. Events beyond control interfered. But the plan still stands, and waits for its implementation:

BEITRÄGE ZU EINER JÜDISCHEN THEOLOGIE

I. ABGRENZUNGEN

1. Das Problem der Macht.
   Von den Ansprüchen des Staates, der Absolutheitsanspruch in Staat und Kirche.
   Das Verhältnis des Judentums zum Staat und zum Anspruch der Absolutheit.
2. Messianismus und Gesellschaftsvervollkommnung.

3. Religion und Kultur.
   Echte und falsche Universalität.
   Die Mission.

Exkurs A: Das Judentum und die dialektische Theologie.

II. ELEMENTE

1. Geschichte und Tradition.
2. Lehre und Gesetz mit besonderer Behandlung des Autoritätsproblems.
3. Die Bedeutung der Bibel.
   (*a*) Bibelwissenschaft.
   (*b*) Bibellehre.
4. Das Gebet.
5. Sünde und Versöhnung.
6. Die Anschauung vom Tode.

Exkurs B: Der Systembegriff der jüdischen Theologie.

III. WEGE

1. Sekten und Richtungen.
2. Die Formen der Unterweisung und die Methoden der Erziehung.
3. Theologie als Beruf.
4. Der Anteil des religiösen Judentums an den Gegenwartsaufgaben.

14 Leo Baeck and the Jewish Mystical Tradition

The story is told that shortly before Hermann Cohen died, some of his friends voiced to him their grief at the prospect of German Jewry losing its most honored spokesman; and that thereupon Cohen comforted them with these words: "Be of good cheer; when I go, Leo Baeck will still be with you."[1] This utterance proved to be prophetic to a degree that Cohen himself could not have foreseen. Like Elisha of old, Baeck received a "double portion" of his master's spirit. Upon him fell the mantle of both spiritual and political leadership in German Jewry's darkest hour, and he became the symbol of its legacy. Among its religious leaders and thinkers, Leo Baeck stood out as one destined to show the way. Unlike Cohen, Buber, and Rosenzweig, he did not have to come from the periphery to the center; from the start he had his very being at the center of Judaism, rooted as he was in the great tradition of enlightened rabbinic Judaism. It was with pride in this tradition that he chose for his epitaph the simple words "mi-geza‘ rabbanim," "of rabbinic stock," and throughout his life his all-consuming love was Judaism. The literary work he produced consisted in inexhaustible variations of this one theme. In paying homage to his memory we reinforce our own allegiance to the classical Jewish heritage.

It bespeaks the depth of Baeck's commitment to Judaism that he, a liberal rabbi, felt increasingly drawn toward an area in the Jewish tradition that had suffered almost total eclipse in the period of emancipation. I am referring to the Jewish mystical tradition, once a powerful and bold force in Jewry, but in the nineteenth and early twentieth century hardly known any more to the Jews in the West and treated with scant respect, to put it mildly, by most Jewish scholars. Today the situation is markedly changed. Thanks to the unbiased vision and devoted labors of Gershom Scholem, Kabbala has gained its rightful place in modern Jewish studies. It should be remembered, however, that Leo Baeck discovered the significance of the mystical element in Judaism even before Scholem's tremendous achievement compelled a new appraisal. Baeck's scholarly work lay, above all, in midrashic literature. His research in the field of Jewish mysticism commands respect, but his chief merit lies in his effort as a theologian to integrate an awareness of our mystical tradition—at least of some of its strata—into the very fabric of modern Jewish thought. It is here that Baeck the thinker comes into his own, and that his interpretation of Kabbala is significant in the context of Jewish intellectual history in our time. No other Jewish theologian among his contemporaries—liberal or orthodox—has a comparable achievement to his credit.

Baeck opened himself to the world of Kabbala only after much initial reluctance. In his Berlin doctoral dissertation of 1895,[2] he spoke of the kabbalistic teaching in the seventeenth century as a "mental delusion" (*Irrwahn*) then widespread among the Jews.[3] Heinrich Graetz, whose student he had been during his years in Breslau, had used far more outspoken epithets in denouncing Kabbala. Baeck's attitude had hardly changed when ten years later, in 1905, he published "The Essence of Judaism,"[4] the book that established his fame. Opposition to all mysticism, including its Jewish variety, is evident throughout the first edition of the work. The reason for it has to be seen not merely in the then common Jewish stance but also in the particular purpose of the book, the vindication of Judaism before the bar of reason and ethics. It seemed imperative to present Judaism as a religion of reason, unencumbered by dogmatism, exclusiveness and, above all, mysticism; features that liberal Protestant theologians of the time were anxious to eradicate from Christianity.[5] One has to remember that just then, around the turn of the century, German Protestant theology was dominated by the school of Albrecht Benjamin Ritschl, which rejected the mystically inclined theology of Schleiermacher as a relic of romanticism, and the Hegelian type of thinking as too metaphysical. It pleaded for a return to Kant's view of religion as a nonmystical, nonmetaphysical, purely practical, i.e., ethical concern.[6] This outlook greatly appealed to Leo Baeck, who had come under the influence of Hermann Cohen and, it seems, also of a Dutch thinker, Rauwenhoff, a follower of Kant and Pfleiderer, who had stressed the moral aspect of religion and had warned against the danger of mysticism.[7]

While Baeck was in sympathy with the theological trend of the period, he abhorred the intellectual anti-Semitism that pervaded Protestant theology in Germany. In Protestant circles the view had gained ground that Christianity had nothing in common with either the Old Testament or postbiblical Judaism; a doctrine that had its roots in the Socinian denigration of the Old Testament.[8] It had achieved prominence in Schleiermacher's description of Judaism as "dead," a mere "imperishable mummy," and a "sad legacy."[9] Fresh utterance had just been given to it in Adolf Harnack's celebrated lectures on "The Essence of Christianity," which presented Pharisaic Judaism in utter gloom. According to Harnack it was only in Jesus's gospel that morality and religion had become one.[10] Leo Baeck rose to the challenge in a masterly review-article in which he chided Harnack for having projected an idealized modern concept of religion upon the historical Jesus, who had been far more in accord with his native environment than Harnack had chosen to admit. Harnack the historian had been ousted by Harnack the apologist.[11] In his book "The Essence of Judaism," which was his full-scale counterattack, Baeck no longer engaged in direct polemic but offered a portrayal of historical Judaism as the religion of ethical monotheism *par excellence*. Considering the intellectual climate of the time, one is not surprised to find that in this presentation of Judaism the mystical features of the Jewish tradition did not receive their due.

A few quotations will illustrate the attitude that Baeck took in the first edition of the book. He says of Judaism that having received its direction from the "practical, moral character" of the teachings of the prophets, it "is thereby withdrawn from all mysticism and esoteric practice."[12] Put differently, it was an important achievement of prophecy that "it conceived religion purely as religion and kept it free from all alien matter, from all admixture, be it natural philosophy, metaphysics or mysticism."[13] "Even the most sublime truth comprises no secret (*Geheimnis*) and no mysticism, except for the depth that appertains to all things Divine and related to the soul."[14] It follows that "within Judaism no scope is offered for a division between the initiated and the profane, between believers of the first and those of the second grade." For a division of this kind presupposes an exclusiveness resulting from certain extraordinary mystical experiences. Esoteric circles were indeed formed in Buddhism, the Greek mystery cults, Roman Catholicism, Protestant Pietism and, Baeck added, "also in certain places within Judaism into which the un-Jewish entity mysticism (*der unjüdische Mystizismus*) succeeded in penetrating in both ancient and more modern times."[15] This remark is further elaborated in a subsequent passage that reads: "The longing for the soul's dark mysteries of the faith, for the divine bliss of ecstasy and solitude stirred also within Judaism, particularly in times of extreme anguish. The history of Jewish mysticism tells of many attempts that sought to fulfill this desire." As examples Baeck cites the fraternities of the Essenes and the "cloistered festive gatherings" (*Feiertagsklöster*) of the Hasidim.[16]

How did Baeck explain the intrusion into Judaism of what he considered an alien, non-Jewish entity? One of his favorite answers to this question suggests that it was the harshness of historical reality at certain times in Jewish history that gave rise to mystical yearnings; that Jewish mysticism was largely a product of deep anxiety; and that it flourished when people felt the need for escape into the realms beyond. This theory, which has been rejected by Scholem,[17] appears throughout Baeck's writings.[18] Baeck explained Kabbala also as a natural reaction to excessive intellectualism at certain periods when either philosophic or halakhic concerns threatened to stifle the emotional life. Somewhat similarly Scholem characterized the motivation that led Moses de Leon to the writing of the *Zohar* as an endeavor to "stem the tide of rationalism."[19] This second line of thought likewise occurs repeatedly in Baeck's writings.[20]

In the first edition of Baeck's book, which shows a definitely antimystical bias, the attempts at explaining Jewish mysticism certainly imply that mysticism is not by itself part and parcel of the essence of Judaism. In fact, the point is made that within Judaism mystical movements were but transient phenomena of relatively short duration. Baeck understood the essence of Judaism to have remained constant, not to be subject to transformation. The curve of the essence fluctuated between high and low points but the essence never changed. In Judaism development meant a process of rebirth, regeneration, not of mutation or *Gestaltwandel*. Baeck's concept of essence therefore involves primarily the idea of a norm, and only to a lesser degree the notion of a sum total of historical phenomena.[21] The high points on the trajectory represent the normative essence. According to Baeck's early view Jewish mysticism may be said to be still within the essence of Judaism if by this term we mean to designate the total curve, although in the strict, normative sense of the term it is not, since it shows Judaism at its nadir. We shall see that in a later period Baeck revised this judgment and allocated to Kabbala its rightful place within the normative essence of Judaism. What he refused to acknowledge even then was the "Jewishness" of *all* forms of Kabbala, including its more bizarre manifestations. The normative viewpoint militated against such recognition. There was a limit to what may be said to belong to Judaism. It is here that Scholem made a radical break with the very concept of the "essence of Judaism."

We may note that Baeck reserved his strongest critique for the Protestant form of mysticism known as Pietism. The "inward feeling" that is so highly valued in Protestant Pietism, he said, often amounts to nothing but unbridled indulgance in self-adulation and religious coquetry. With biting sarcasm he added: "Pharisaism in the unhistorical sense in which this term has come to be used is something specifically Protestant."[22] He repeatedly attacked Schleiermacher, who had extolled the "feeling of absolute dependence," and the sense of humility as the essence of religion and thereby, in Baeck's judgment, had made religion conterminous with romanticism and mysticism. Humility, according to Baeck, was indeed an indispensable element of religion,[23] but its authentic motivation was trust, not dependence, and it had to be matched by a man's consciousness of his freedom and responsibility. Schleiermacher's concept of religion suffered from a serious flaw that could be traced to his faulty relationship to the Old Testament.[24] Baeck, a man of great gentleness, was of strong fiber. Attack rather than apologetic was his method of countering the theological antisemitism in Germany. The superb documentation of his fighting spirit is his great essay "Romantic Religion" (1922), which was inspired not so much by purely theological viewpoints as by his acute awareness that moral stamina was sadly missing in many German theologians. In his opinion their ready subservience to power could be traced to the romanticism inherent in Pauline Christianity.[25]

A marked change in Baeck's attitude to Jewish mysticism appears for the first time in an essay of his that bears the title "The Parties in Contemporary Judaism in Relation to their Historical Antecedents."[26] By 1911, when this article was published, the intellectual outlook in Germany had somewhat changed. A certain recoil from the rationalism of the Ritschl school had set in, and mysticism had become a force. A new trend toward mystical inwardness expressed itself in the poetry of Liliencron and Dehmel, in the neoromanticism of Hugo von Hofmannsthal and Maurice Maeterlinck, in Stefan George and, above all, in Rainer Maria Rilke, whose *Stundenbuch* (1906) reflects the anguished odyssey of a secular mystic.[27] The monistic movement had given birth to the nature mysticism of Bruno Wille, Julius Hart, and Wilhelm Bölsche. Redemption from individuality, absorption in the "living All," *Entwerdung* and *Entsinkung ins Wesenlose* were the slogans indicating the direction of the new mysticism, which found a deep echo in the young Martin Buber.[28] The theologians could not afford to ignore this tendency, and mysticism became an issue also for the philosophers. Windelband rejected the new trend in his essay "Mystik unserer Zeit" (1910).[29] An article dealing with "Mysticism and Protestantism" appeared in the very same issue of *Religion und Geisteskultur*[30] in which Baeck's aforementioned essay was published in 1911.[31]

Unlike Buber, Baeck was by no means enamored with the mystics' effort to transcend individuality by submerging it in total being. He remained utterly opposed to the mystical quest for evanescence, *Entwerdung*, which he considered to be a flight from moral responsibility.[32] What did change in Baeck was his specific view of *Jewish* mysticism. How did this change come about? It seems that the emergence of the new trend had caused him to take a closer look at the mystical tradition in Judaism, and that, much to his surprise, he found it to differ from all other forms of mysticism.[33] He admitted that Jewish mystics shared with all the rest some undefined yearning for the immediacy and presence of the Divine.[34] Yet while everywhere outside Judaism the goal of the mystical experience was mystical union, the merging of the human and the Divine, Jewish mysticism bore certain features that precluded such union. What rendered Jewish mysticism immune against the quest for union; what set it apart as a mysticism *sui generis* was precisely its Jewish, i.e., ethical, character. Baeck's essay of 1911 testifies to this new evaluation of the Jewish mystical tradition.

Having differentiated between Jewish mysticism and what henceforth he called "mere mysticism," Baeck could now in all honesty present the Jewish mystical tradition as part and parcel of historical, authentic Judaism; as one of the three major trends that compose postbiblical Jewish religious history, namely, the talmudic, philosophical, and mystical. "The characteristic note of Judaism," he pointed out in the essay, "is prominent even in the third of the medieval trends, i.e., in the mystical one, for it too bears the impress of ethics." This discovery was a major breakthrough. Once Baeck had legitimized Jewish mysticism he could acknowledge its significance in Jewish history: "The place which mysticism occupies within Judaism," he said, "is enormous; its history extends over more than one millenium, and the variety of its manifestations is stupendous."[35] Baeck clearly sought to impress his non-Jewish readers with the vast scope given to mysticism in the Jewish tradition. He remarked that if Jewish intellectual history was a *terra incognita* to the world at large, Jewish mysticism was the least known part of it.[36] The eagerness with which he tried to fill this lacuna in common knowledge was no doubt prompted by his awareness that in the new climate of opinion the existence of a strong mystical component in Judaism was likely to be considered an asset.

Baeck's positive assessment of Kabbala rested on his belief to have discovered the specifically Jewish features that set it apart from all other forms of mysticism. We mentioned briefly that in his view Jewish mysticism was ethically oriented. What evidence did he adduce in support of this broad claim? The essay of 1911 provides an answer. It points out that all trends of Jewish mysticism agree in one respect: When the Jewish mystic speaks of God he means God's Will. The powers that operate in the world are "powers of will, moral potencies, ethical energies." "The moral order is the basic law of the world. Hereby this mysticism avoided the danger . . . of the ethical command becoming diluted in its force, and of piety degenerating into total absorption (*wesenlose Versenkung in Gott*) and mere sentiment of dependence. In the prominence given to commandment and duty mysticism shows here its Jewish character."[37] Baeck considered the kabbalistic doctrine of the *Sefirot* as an expression of ethical monotheism. In a subsequent essay he amplified this view:[38]

> Between the earth and God are worlds, the ten spheres that emanate from his creative Will. They are the cosmos, worlds of a spiritual and ethical nature, realities of the good, energies of perfection, spheres of wisdom, understanding, justice, love, mercy, greatness, exaltedness. They continually mediate between Creator and creature, in them fullness flows from fullness. Man is able to elevate himself toward them on the ladder of ascent if he opens himself to the good, the Divine commandment. Through pious deeds and devotion he can become part of them and live in this higher world, close to God, and be himself a source of power in this realm of creativity. It all depends on his decision and action. He may ascend or descend. For below him is the "reverse side" of the universe, and through sin he goes down to it, to this power of negativity, nonbeing, destruction, unreality that is but a "shell" enveloping and oppressing. Thus here too the old position of the ethical is maintained.

This moralistic interpretation of the Sefirotic realm and its demonic counterpart is a good example of the way in which Baeck tried to harmonize Kabbala and normative Judaism.

He stands on surer ground in a lecture delivered at Berlin University in 1927. Its subject was "Origin and Beginnings of Jewish Mysticism," and its main thesis proclaimed:[39] "This mysticism wants to make the ethical man also into a cosmic being." We meet this phrase again in a number of reformulations.[40] What it intends to convey is the following: Man, a creature bound to earth by his natural ties and moral duties, assumes cosmic significance if he lives up to his ethical task. The moral act is not a purely human affair. It represents a creative force that extends into infinity and bears on the fate of the Divine. Man is raised to a cosmic level. As Baeck explained it in yet another essay:[41] "The history of the *saddikim*, the pious and just, is the true history of the world. It is the history of God as it were. For without man who is wholehearted with God and thereby unified in himself there is, as it were, no God on earth." Baeck added a psychological nuance to his formula of the ethical as reaching into the cosmic:[42] Being assigned a circumscribed place in the here and now, and experiencing the daily round of strictly defined duties as too narrow a type of existence, the Jew felt the urge to transcend the earthly and soar into the cosmic and infinite. Thus from the very confines of the ethical, Jewish mysticism arose as a yearning for larger horizons. The mystic remained anchored in the commandment. He did not strive for mystical union, which would have obliterated the commandment, but he saw the supernal realms ready to receive the impact of human action. God remained the personal God, creator of heaven and earth, the God of justice and love; but man became a cosmic being. Thus the Jewish note in Kabbala is unmistakable.

Baeck found this "grandiose cosmic optimism" prominently displayed in the *Sefer Bahir*,[43] a book since shown to reflect strong Gnostic influence.[44] In Baeck's view it presents an "ethical cosmic system" and thereby expresses the essential character of Jewish mysticism. He stressed the Jewish element also in the *Sefer Yeṣira*, the other important mystical text to which he devoted painstaking research.[45] From among the many significant themes in Kabbalistic literature, Baeck singled out that of the Sabbath as of central concern in all phases of Jewish mysticism.[46] In a happy phrase he described the Sabbath as "the mystical time" or "the mystical day," and he suggested that without the specifically mystical quality of this day the Jew might have lost his sense of the mystery and his power of spiritual rebirth.[47] It is clear from these references—to which many more could be added—that Baeck had become fully alive to the importance of the mystical tradition in Judaism.

The second, much enlarged edition of *The Essence of Judaism*, which appeared in 1922,[48] reflects this new orientation in the many deletions and additions of the text. All earlier statements about the incompatibility of Judaism and mysticism are eliminated,[49] and appreciative references are introduced. The supremacy of the ethical is said to have retained its validity in the Jewish mystical tradition, and the *Sefirot* are described as moral potencies.[50] Jewish philosophy and mysticism are said to be closely related to each other,[51] and the intimate liaison between Jewish mysticism and rabbinic Haggada is noted.[52] On the other hand, Baeck maintained his disapproval of the luxuriant imagery by which the Jewish mystics had expressed their eschatological notions about heaven and hell, and the messianic age.[53] He obviously excluded these features from the normative essence of Judaism. However, the revised edition contained far more than the changes mentioned. The basic structure of the work had been recast in the light of the new attitude to Jewish mysticism.

It has been said that all effort to understand aims at reducing the many to the one. The one essence that manifests itself in the many historical forms of Judaism Baeck now defines in the formula "mystery and commandment" (*Geheimnis und Gebot*). Judaism, the ever-recurrent and ever-self-renewing pattern of the Jew's response to reality, is seen as the awareness of a polarity and tension between the mystery, the hidden ground of being, the inscrutable and wondrous on the one hand, and the clear ethical command, the categorical imperative on the other. These two aspects of the ultimate—that which is and that which ought to be—the Jew experiences not as two distinct and separate spheres but as entailing each other and, at the same time, as creating a tension to be overcome and yet not allowed to vanish. In response to this polarity man has to preserve a balance. He must neither submerge himself in the mystery nor become a mere keeper of the law. He must remain conscious of both the mystery and the commandment. For the commandment proceeds from the ultimate ground of being, and the mystery issues forth in the unconditional "thou shalt."[54] Never before had the "mystery" been visualized in such fruitful polarity to the ethical. Goethe had advised man to "be content to explore the explorable" and "to revere the inexplorable in silence." The conflict that he sought to solve was the one between reason and intuition.[55] The world, nature, life was to him the great mystery speaking in symbols: "Und drängt nicht alles nach Haupt und Herz dir und webt in ewigem Geheimnis unsichtbar sichtbar neben dir?" Baeck was not "content to revere the inexplorable in silence." Only the union of mystery and commandment created the whole man.

The twenties of this century were an exceedingly creative period in Baeck's life. It was then that his most important essays were written, including those on Jewish mysticism and others that were delivered as lectures at the Darmstadt "School of Wisdom" under the chairmanship of Count Hermann Keyserling, the noted essayist.[56] The three Darmstadt lectures presented Baeck's most compelling philosophical statements bearing on Judaism. The first elaborated the concept of "Geheimnis und Gebot," and made it evident that this formula derived from the impact that the discovery of Jewish mysticism had produced on Baeck's thinking. In Judaism, he declared, the polarity of mystery and commandment precluded any opposition between mysticism and ethics. Jewish ethics was imbued with mysticism, and vice versa. In medieval Hebrew terminology, he pointed out, the same word signified both ethical sentiment and mystical contemplation. He was referring, of course, to the word *kavvana* ("intention"), which denotes devotion, inwardness as well as mystical contemplation.[57] Baeck obviously assumed a correlation to obtain between mysticism and the mystery.[58] The second Darmstadt lecture dealt with polarity and tension.[59] It showed the contrast between two fundamentally disparate types of civilization: The Greek mind was essentially contemplative, fixed upon timeless perfection, whereas biblical man experienced the tension between the infinite ground of his being and the infinite task to be accomplished in perfecting the world. The Greek adoration of the completed, rounded off, perfected, be it an idea or a piece of art, lives on in Christian romanticism. The biblical spirit manifests itself wherever man wrestles with God and strives to shape reality in the image of the Divine Will. The future, Baeck proclaimed, belongs to the biblical spirit, for that which is perfect in a static sense belongs to the past, the "perfect" tense. Such was the impression created by Baeck's lecture that Count Keyserling, in his concluding remarks, extolled it in rather startling terms: The lecture, he said, was possibly the most important event in the whole history of Judaism since the death of Jesus, for it had for the first time shown what was truly positive in Judaism, and it had done this from a rostrum visible to all.[60] Keyserling was obviously no great expert in Jewish history but the sincerity of his tribute to Baeck cannot be doubted. The third lecture discussed authentic religiosity as expressed in the capacity for rebirth.[61]

In his Darmstadt lectures Baeck refrained from making distinct reference to Jewish mystical sources. It may well be that he imposed this limitation upon himself because the atmosphere at the "School of Wisdom" was overcharged with mysticism and even with a penchant for the occult sciences.[62] Hence, we suggest, he preferred to quote from the classical documents of Judaism, from Bible and rabbinic literature. Yet he did feel the need to explain to the non-Jewish world the character of the Jewish mystical tradition as he saw it. In 1923 he published in the periodical *Die Tat* an essay on "The Significance of Jewish Mysticism for Our Time," and in 1928 he discussed the theme "Mysticism within Judaism" in the *Süddeutsche Monatshefte.*[63] He stressed the importance of the "active" mysticism of the Jewish tradition in contrast to current mystical trends that advocated quietism, moral passivity, and sentimental retreat into oneself. The "old Jewish mysticism," he said, had a message for our time; it was identical with what Edvard Lehmann, the Danish historian of religion, had postulated as the ideal, desirable "new mysticism." Baeck, who rarely quoted modern authors, in this instance referred to Lehmann and in his name cited one single sentence:[64] "God no longer wants his faithful one to claim identity with Him; He desires that in his fear of God he remain himself." This phrase, which Baeck deemed worthy of quotation, can be found in the context of an allegory told by Lehmann at the end of his book *Mysticism in Paganism and Christianity*. The passage from which Baeck took the sentence deserves to be quoted in full:[65]

> There is a small oriental poem about a youth who went to visit his beloved at night and knocked at her door. To her question who was outside he replied: "It is me." She did not open her door. So he went out into solitude, and when he returned to her door and she asked again who was outside, he answered: "It is you." Then she let him in.
>
> This is, in short, the history of mysticism, yet not the whole story, for there is a sequel. A thousand years later the lonely man came and knocked at the door of Divinity. When asked who he was, he answered, as he had learned to say: "It is you." But the door was not opened. So he went out into the world and labored and served his neighbor. And when he returned and knocked at the door and was asked who he was, he replied: "It is me." Now the door opened. For God had changed his mind. He no longer wants his faithful one to claim identity with Him: He desires that in his fear of God he remain himself.

With this story we could conclude our lecture. For it highlights Baeck's view of Jewish mysticism as a type of its own, as averse to mystical union and imbued with practical piety and the fear of God.[66] Yet our story too has a sequel. Baeck's literary activity continued during the fateful thirties that placed such immense burdens on his shoulders. In addition to important contributions to other areas of Jewish religious history[67] he managed to complete his *Sefer Yesira* studies,[68] and his analysis of the *Sefer Bahir* was probably also a product of those years.[69] Then followed the aweful caesura of 1941 to 1944. Yet his literary activity did not cease even in the concentration camp of Theresienstadt, where he stayed from 1943 to 1944. The work that emerged from the darkness of that period—the two volumes of *This People: Jewish Existence*—is a *confessio Judaica* in which Jewish mysticism is given far greater prominence than was the case in *The Essence of Judaism*, the classical document of the earlier period of tranquility.

Baeck was greatly fascinated by the difference in character between Sefardim and Ashkenazim, particularly so far as it expressed itself in Sefardic and Ashkenazic mysticism. In volume II of *This People*, he formulated the difference:[70] Mystery of the Divine is what the *Sefardim* sought to contemplate. The *commandment* given to man formed the main topic of the Ashkenazim. Sefardim and Ashkenazim together represent the mysticism of this people. They complement each other like mystery and commandment.[71] This picture is somewhat too neat and tidy, and it does not entirely correspond to historical reality. There was much metaphysical speculation in the German Hasidim of the Middle Ages, and there was a great deal of ethical concern in the Mussar books of the Sefardic mystics. Yet in a basic sense Baeck had the right intuition. Personally he seems to have been more attracted to the Ashkenazic type of mysticism, which he considered to have been less speculative and more ethically motivated. He was particularly impressed with eighteenth-century Hasidism. He characterized it as a mysticism of charismatic figures, of profound devotion in prayer and—what is today a point of debate—of messianic expectation.[72] In his interpretation of Hasidism, Baeck was obviously much influenced by Martin Buber's writings[73] but his view of the particular Ashkenazic quality of both medieval and latter-day Hasidism was strictly his own.[74]

In *This People*, the concept of "essence" is replaced by that of "existence."[75] The Jewish religious tradition appears no longer as a mere phenomenon in the history of ideas but as the very expression of this people's uniqueness. Baeck speaks of "this philosophy," "this poetry," "this mysticism," "this religion,"[76] the demonstrative adjective "this" designating the unique, singular character of "this people." Previously he had pointed out the uniqueness of ethical monotheism as something that broke into the world with the revolutionary force of an entirely new idea and thereby constituted a "revelation." Now he describes the historical appearance of "this people" as something unique, as *ein Einmaliges*. Of all nations Israel alone sees its own particular origin in the ground and origin of *all* being, as having come forth from the "beyond"—*ein Volk aus der Bahn des Jenseits*—as rooted in the Ultimate. No wonder, Baeck remarked, it is considered "rootless" by those whose sole concern is with the earthly.[77] This nation's existence is therefore metaphysical in nature, and all its significant creations bear witness to this fact.

Only the Jewish people, Baeck points out, has the peculiar gift, the special genius for embracing the mystery and the commandment in one single glance; to experience the metaphysical as an imperative, as "the commanding mystery" (*das gebietende Geheimnis*).[78] There is poetic creativity at work in picturing the commandment as emerging from the beyond. Bible, Midrash, Talmud, and Kabbala speak in terms of poetry about the commandment, the law, the covenant. "This poetry" looks beyond the earthly and limited. It reaches out into the mystery. It therefore differs from myth, for myth, according to Baeck's definition, remains bound to the earthly, which it magnifies but never transcends.[79] Yet this people's power of imagination is imbued with the ethical, and this "ethical imagination" creates the poetry of faith, of prayer, of customs and practices.[80] More than ever before Baeck now envisioned the manifold manifestations of the Jewish spirit as so many expressions of a special poetic gift that connects heaven and earth.

This meant that mystical imagery had won Baeck's full approval as a legitimate form of religious language. Thus, the biblical "And God saw that it was good" he called " the old simile in the creation story" (*das alte Schöpfungsgleichnis*); it expressed an idea, he said, that is also conveyed in the "late mystical simile" of the "Divine sparks in all living beings."[81] The old Bible and the Lurianic new Kabbala use different imagery but mean the same thing. The changes of imagery testify to the creative power by which "this people" renews its vision from period to period and thereby renews itself. The poetic genius of Israel is, one might say, a function of its existence.[82] Seen from this perspective, Jewish mysticism is a manifestation of Israel's regenerative power.

A final remark. One of the main reasons for the breakdown of Jewish mysticism in the modern age was the powerful tendency to deny Jewish uniqueness, the "metaphysical" difference between the Jew and his neighbor.[83] Kabbala had gone to rather bizarre lengths in asserting this metaphysical difference and had thereby raised invisible barriers in addition to the visible walls of the ghetto. In his endeavor to tear down those walls, the modern Jew first demolished the kabbalistic fences. He no longer wished to believe in any essential otherness of the Jew. Leo Baeck's *This People* reverts to the old mystical understanding of Jewish existence. It reaffirms the uniqueness of the Jewish people in metaphysical terms. He had always seen the Jew as "the great nonconformist in history,"[84] as a visionary of the messianic goal destined to hold his own against the entire world, if necessary. This, however, he had visualized merely as a commitment to an idea. In *This People* he anchored Jewish otherness in the very character of Israel as a people "from beyond," as "a people of metaphysical existence." His intensive preoccupation with the world of the Midrash—his primary field of research—had no doubt prepared him for his growing appreciation of Jewish mysticism. The experience of the holocaust, far from forcing upon him a new theology, simply reinforced his belief in the unique character of Israel as "a nation that dwelleth alone." While he was still in Berlin, at the time of the most horrendous defamation of Jewish honor known in history and at a moment when the fiendish plot of genocide was taking shape, he began to write *This People* as an impassionate account of the raison d'être of Jewish existence throughout the ages. In the twelfth century Jehuda Ha-Levi wrote his famous book *Kuzari* and subtitled it "In Defense of the Despised Religion." That book is the most moving document of faith in the destiny of Israel produced in the Middle Ages. Leo Baeck did in our time what the philosopher-poet did in his. *This People* reveals him at the height of his power and in close affinity to Jewish mystical thinking.

NOTES

1. Baeck himself told me this story in 1953.
2. Leo Baeck, *Spinozas erste Einwirkungen auf Deutschland. Inaugural-Dissertation Berlin 1895* (Berlin, 1895).
3. Op. cit., p. 70f.
4. Leo Baeck, *Das Wesen des Judentums* (Berlin, 1905).
5. All of these phenomena were referred to by Baeck and declared to be alien to Judaism; see op. cit., pp. 2f.; 29–31; and passim.
6. Cf. Karl Barth, *Protestant Thought: From Rousseau to Ritschl* (New York, 1959), pp. 390ff.

7. D.L.W.E. Rauwenhoff, *Religionsphilosophie* (tr. and ed. by J. R. Hanne), 2nd ed. (Braunschweig, 1894), pp. 117, 143. Baeck's indebtedness to Rauwenhoff deserves to be further investigated. It is clear from the references given in *Wesen des Judentums*, 1st ed., pp. 162f. that Baeck followed the Dutch philosopher in several important respects, viz., in seeing religious faith as based on value judgments; in regarding the ethical monotheism of the prophets of Israel as a radical innovation, a view Rauwenhoff himself took from A. Kuenen, *Volksreligion und Weltreligion* (Berlin, 1883); in claiming for the discovery of ethical monotheism the term "revelation." See Rauwenhoff, op. cit., p. 154 and Baeck, op. cit., p. 40. Further points of contact are "faith in ourselves" (R., p. 231; B., p. 93ff.); the function of poetry in religion (R., p. 564; B., 88, 90).

8. Cf. Leo Strauss, *Spinoza's Critique of Religion* (New York, 1965), p. 65ff., 278.

9. Friedrich Schleiermacher, *On Religion: Speeches to its Cultured Despisers* (tr. by John Oman) (New York, 1958), p. 238.

10. Adolf Harnack, *Das Wesen des Christentums* (Leipzig, 1900); 1908 edition, p. 47.

11. Leo Baeck, "Harnack's Vorlesungen über das Wesen des Christenthums," *MGWJ*, 45 N.F. 9 (1901), pp. 97–120; see especially pp. 99–105.

12. *Das Wesen des Judentums*, 1st ed., p. 21–22.

13. Op. cit., p. 23.

14. Op. cit., p. 28–29.

15. Op. cit., p. 29.

16. Op. cit., p. 30.

17. Gershom G. Scholem, *Major Trends in Jewish Mysticism*, Revised Edition (New York, 1946), p. 23.

18. See Baeck, *Das Wesen des Judentums*, 1st ed., p. 30; 3rd ed., pp. 44, 273; "Die Parteien im gegenwärtigen Judentum in ihrer geschichtlichen Grundlage," *Religion und Geisteskultur*, ed. Th. Steinmann, V (1911), p. 76; *Dieses Volk: Jüdische Existenz* (Frankfurt am Main, 1955), p. 81; II (1957), p. 197.

19. Scholem, op. cit., p. 203.

20. Baeck, *Das Wesen des Judentums*, 1st ed., p. 153; 3rd ed., pp. 49, 299; "Die Parteien . . . ," p. 76f.

21. See Hans Liebeschütz, *Von Georg Simmel zu Franz Rosenzweig* (Tübingen, 1970), p. 95. The way in which Baeck understood "essence" both in a normative and total *Gestalt* sense reflects Ernst Troeltsch's discussion of the methodological problems raised by Harnack's *The Essence of Christianity*. See Troeltsch, *Gesammelte Schriften*, II (Tübingen 1913), pp. 368–451, reproducing the article from *Die Christliche Welt*, 1903.

22. Baeck, *Das Wesen des Judentums*, 1st ed., p. 35; 3rd ed., p. 52.

23. Op. cit., 1st ed., p. 71f., 78f.; 3rd ed., pp. 121–126 and passim.

24. Op. cit., 1st ed., p. 80; 3rd ed., p. 135, 139; "Romantische Religion," *Aus drei Jahrtausenden* (Tübingen, 1958), pp. 44, 54, 94, 96.

25. Cf. Liebeschütz, op. cit., p. 80.

26. See above, n. 18. Kurt Wilhelm, "Leo Baeck and Jewish Mysticism," *Judaism*, II (Spring 1962), pp. 123–130 first drew attention to this essay.

27. See the survey of the new trend in the article "Neue Mystik" in *Religion in Geschichte und Gegenwart*, 2nd ed., IV (1930), 355–360; Hans-Rudolf Müller, *Rainer Maria Rilke als Mystiker* (Berlin, 1935). Evelyn Underhill's *Mysticism* appeared in 1911.

28. See the analysis of Martin Buber's early mystical phase in Paul R. Mendes-Flohr, *Von der Mystik zum Dialog* (Königstein Ts., 1979), pp. 55–110.

29. Cf. W. Windelband, *Präludien*, 5th ed. (1915), I, pp. 290–299; quoted by Erich Przywara, *Religionsphilosophische Schriften*, II (Einsiedeln, 1962), p. 342f.

30. Gustav Lasch, "Mystik und Protestantismus," *Religion und Geisteskultur*, V (1911), pp. 34–52.

31. See above, n. 18. Lasch sought to show the incompatibility of mysticism and Protestantism, a view which also characterizes the antimystical stance of dialectical theology; cf., e.g., Emil Brunner, *Die Mystik und das Wort* (Tübingen, 1924).

32. See Baeck, "Die Parteien . . . ," p. 77; *Wege im Judentum* (Berlin, 1933), pp. 96–99.

33. Baeck seems to have been an avid student of all forms of mysticism. He knew P. D. Chantepie de La Saussaye's *Lehrbuch der Religionsgeschichte* (Tübingen, 1889; 3rd ed. 1905); see *Das Wesen des Judentums*, 1st ed., p. 162f.; he quoted from Edvard Lehmann's

Mystik in Heidentum und Christentum; see p. 304. In 1954 he recommended to me Sergius Bulgakow's *The Eastern Church*, a book that has an instructive chapter on eastern mysticism. Reading Baeck's succinct characterization of mystical types in his essay on the significance of Jewish mysticism (1923) gives one a vivid impression of his command of the field; see *Wege im Judentum*, pp. 96–97.

34. For Baeck's view of mysticism as a longing for immediate contact, see his lecture on the origin of Jewish mysticism (1927) in *Aus Drei Jahrtausenden*, pp. 246f.; the essay on "Jewish Mysticism," *JJS*, 2.1 (1950), p. 3; *Dieses Volk*, I, p. 81; II, p. 165, 227.

35. "Die Parteien . . . ," p. 76.

36. Ibid.

37. "Die Parteien . . . ," p. 77. The voluntaristic aspect of the Divine is indeed of supreme importance in many trends of Jewish mystical theology but by no means in all; see the references to "Will of God" and *Maḥshabha* in G. Scholem, *Ursprung und Anfänge der Kabbala* (Berlin, 1962), Index, pp. 428; 434.

38. "Die Mystik im Judentum" (1928), *Wege im Judentum*, p. 93. We quote the passage in a slightly abbreviated form.

39. *Aus Drei Jahrtausenden*, p. 247f.

40. See below in the text and *RGG*, 2nd ed., IV (1930), 340.

41. *Wege im Judentum*, p. 98f.

42. *Wege im Judentum*, p. 90f.

43. See Baeck's essay "Ssefer Ha-Bahir," which was first published in the 1938 edition of *Aus Drei Jahrtausenden*; republished in the 1958 edition, pp. 272–289. See particularly pp. 287–9.

44. Cf. Gershom Scholem, *Ursprung und Anfänge der Kabbala*, pp. 59–85.

45. See *MGWJ*, 70 N.F. 34 (1926), pp. 370–6; 78, N.F. 42 (1934), pp. 448–55; republished in *Aus Drei Jahrtausenden*, pp. 256–271. Baeck attributed some of the most intriguing concepts of the *Sefer Yeṣira* to the influence of the Athenian Neoplatonist Proclus (d. 485 C.E.), a thesis mentioned by him already in his Berlin lecture of 1925–26 and reiterated in his article on "Jüdische Mystik" in *RGG*, 2nd ed., IV, (1930), 340. Scholem, in his article on "Kabbala" in *EJ*, IX (1932), 108f., 644, disagrees with Baeck's view (see also *Major Trends*, p. 368, n. 128 and *Ursprung und Anfänge der Kabbala*, p. 44). Baeck seems to have remained convinced, however, that his theory was correct; see *JJS*, 2.1 (1950), p. 10; *Dieses Volk* II, p. 78f.

46. For nonmystical characterizations of the Sabbath by Baeck, see *Das Wesen des Judentums*, 3rd ed., p. 159 and passim; "Das Judentum," in Carl Clemen (ed.), *Religionen der Erde* (Munich, 1927; 2nd ed., 1949), p. 284.

47. *Wege im Judentum*, p. 94, 100f.; *RGG*, 2nd ed., IV (1930), 340; *JJS*, 2.1 (1950), p. 16.

48. Leo Baeck, *Das Wesen des Judentums*, Zweite neu bearbeitete Auflage (Frankfurt a. Main, 1922), 308 pp. The third edition (from which we quote here) appeared in 1923 and has 327pp. The following editions (4th–8th) remained unchanged; see Theodore Wiener, "The Writings of Leo Baeck: A Bibliography," *Studies in Bibliography and Booklore, I* (June, 1954): 3, p. 109.

49. Cf. 1st ed., pp. 22, 28–29 with 3rd ed., pp. 33, 40–41; and 1st ed., p. 30 with 3rd ed. p. 44. Cf. Ernst Simon, *Brücken: Gesammelte Aufsätze* (Heidelberg, 1965), p. 368f.

50. 3rd ed., p. 54.

51. 3rd ed., pp. 100, 143.

52. 3rd ed., pp. 97, 134.

53. Cf. 1st ed., pp. 110, 142 with 3rd ed., pp. 204, 274.

54. 3rd ed., pp. 86, 90, 99, 101, 131, 135, 169, 174, 202, 250, 254f., 256. For a discussion of the concept of "mystery and commandment," see Albert H. Friedlander, *Leo Baeck: Teacher of Theresienstadt* (New York, Chicago, San Francisco, 1968), pp. 157–159, 166–170, 173, 184–185; K. H. Miskotte, *Het Wezen der Joodsche Religie* (Amsterdam [1932]), pp. 118, 124, 134, 137f. The latter discusses Baeck's *Wesensschau* on pp. 87–142. His book was brought to my attention by Baeck himself.

55. See Walther Gerlach, "Goethe as a scientist," *TLS*, August 3, 1973, 907f.

56. The lectures were published in Count Keyserling's annual *Der Leuchter* in the 1921–1922, 1923 and 1925 volumes, and they are reprinted in *Wege im Judentum*, pp. 9–67.

57. *Wege im Judentum*, p. 37f.; in *Das Wesen des Judentums*, 1st ed., p. 107, 3rd ed., p. 196 the Hebrew term was said to denote both *Gesinnung* and *Andacht* (sentiment and devotion), no mention being made of mystical contemplation. Cf. Hermann Cohen, *Die Religion der Vernunft aus den Quellen des Judentums* (Leipzig, 1919), pp. 413f., 439. Baeck's designation of the nonmystical meaning of the term as "ethical" agrees with Cohen's.

58. Cf. Leo Baeck, "Theologie und Geschichte," in *Aus Drei Jahrtensenden*, p. 38, where "mysticism and ethics" is juxtaposed with "mystery and commandment" (*die Verborgenheit und die Forderung*), which implies that mysticism corresponds to the mystery.

59. Its original title was "Die Spannung im Menschen und der fertige Mensch" (Der Leuchter, IV, 1923, 117–141); in *Wege im Judentum* (pp. 9–32) changed into "Vollendung und Spannung."

60. *Der Leuchter: Jahrbuch der Schule der Weisheit*, ed. Count Hermann Keyserling, IV (Darmstadt, 1923), p. 203.

61. "Tod und Wiedergeburt," *Wege im Judentum*, pp. 49–71; see p. 60.

62. Count Hermann Keyserling was coauthor jointly with Count Kuno Hardenberg and Carl Happich of *Das Okkulte* (Darmstadt, 1923). He recommended the writings of Georg Beyer, S.J. who did not attach religious significance to occult practices (p. 26f., n. 1), but considered it imperative for science to take occult phenomena seriously. Keyserling was particularly impressed by Rudolf Steiner. Baeck wrote an article "Okkultismus und Religion" (*Jüdisch-liberale Zeitung*, 5:11, March 13, 1925) in which he took a stand similar to Beyer's but argued in his own characteristic way: Religion demands reverence for the mystery. Occult knowledge does not constitute religion. Genuine piety respects every new discovery but has its own domain, namely, the ethical life.

63. Leo Baeck, "Bedeutung der jüdischen Mystik für unsere Zeit," *Die Tat*, 15 (1923), 340–344; reprinted in *Wege im Judentum*, pp. 96–102; "Die Mystik im Judentum," *Süddeutsche Monatshefte*, 26 (1928), pp. 38–49; reprinted in *Wege im Judentum*, pp. 90–95.

64. *Wege im Judentum*, p. 99.

65. Edvard Lehmann, *Mystik in Heidentum und Christentum*, tr. Anna Grundtvig, Aus Natur und Geisteswelt No. 217, 2nd ed. (Leipzig and Berlin, 1918), p. 144.

66. In his essay "Theologie und Geschichte" (*Aus Drei Jahrtausenden*, p. 31), Baeck suggested that Ernst Troeltsch's "mystical" philosophy of history was reminiscent of "certain motifs and creations of Jewish mysticism." He mentioned as one of those motifs Troeltsch's concept of "an essential and individual identity of the finite spirits and the infinite Spirit, by virtue of which the historical and the normative, the real and that which ought to be realized are unified." Baeck's vague remark makes it difficult to determine which kabbalistic concept he had in mind. On no account can it be assumed that he attributed to Jewish mysticism the notion of *unio mystica*.

67. See Theodore Wiener, op. cit., nos. 155, 159, 213, 252, 259, 260, 260a, 276.

68. See above, n. 45.

69. See above, n. 43.

70. *Dieses Volk*, II, p. 163.

71. Op. cit., II, p. 165.

72. Op. cit., II, pp. 233–239. See, however, Gershom Scholem, *The Messianic Idea in Judaism* (New York, 1971), pp. 176–202.

73. See Leo Baeck, article "Chassidismus" in *RGG*, 2nd ed., I (1927), 1493f.

74. See *Dieses Volk*, II, pp. 235, 238f.

75. Baeck's turning toward a theology of existence is already noticeable in a lecture on "*Existenz des Juden*" delivered at the Berlin *Lehrhaus* in June, 1935 (see *Gemeindeblatt der jüdischen Gemeinde zu Berlin*, June 16, 1935, p. 2): The existence of the Jew was always imperiled; and it could be lived only in obedience to God. Hence Jewish thinking has invariably been what is nowadays called "existential thinking"—one that involves (*einbezieht*) man himself in his thinking. It does not merely look on but forms life by fulfilling the commandments. It makes a total demand on every Jew. It is existence before God, not in God.—One may regard this lecture as the nucleus of *This People*.

76. *Dieses Volk*, I, pp. 27, 119, 122; II, p. 237.

77. *Dieses Volk*, I, pp. 11, 12, 14.

78. Op. cit., I, pp. 13, 121, 131.

79. Op. cit., I, pp. 27–28, 78–79, 83. For a previous definition of myth, see *Das Wesen des Judentums*, 3rd ed., pp. 92f.

80. *Dieses Volk*, I, pp. 24, 118f.; II, p. 25. Baeck spoke of the "inner unity" of Halakha and Haggada, and he pointed out the deep significance of the fact that Jewish philosophers, mystics and poets were often also Halakhists of high rank; see *Dieses Volk*, II, p. 83f. Baeck did not elaborate, however, on the mystical concept of Torah nor did he discuss the mystical "reasons of the commandments" (*ta'amey ha-misvot*).

81. Op. cit., I, p. 104.

82. Op. cit., II, p. 16f.

83. For a similar use of the qualitative term "metaphysical" in this particular context, see Jacob Katz, *Exclusiveness and Tolerance* (Oxford, 1961), p. 139; see also pp. 136–142, where the doctrine of Rabbi Judah Löb of Prague is analyzed.

84. See Baeck, *Das Wesen des Judentums*, 3rd ed., p. 292.

Acknowledgments

The Gnostic Background of the Rabbinic Adam Legends. A revised reprint from *The Jewish Quarterly Review*, N.S. 25.4 (1945): 371–391.

Creation and Emanation in Isaac Israeli: A Reappraisal. Reprinted by permission of the publishers from *Studies in Medieval Jewish History and Literature*, edited by Isadore Twersky. Cambridge, Mass.: Harvard University Press. Copyright © 1979 by the President and Fellows of Harvard College, 1–15.

Free Will and Predestination in Saadia, Baḥya, and Maimonides. Reprinted from S. D. Goitein (ed.), *Religion in a Religious Age*. Proceedings of the Regional Conference held at the University of California Los Angeles and Brandeis University in April, 1973 (Cambridge, Mass., 1974), 25–51.

Maimonides's "Four Perfections." Revised reprint from M. J. Kister et al. (ed.), *Israel Oriental Studies*, II (1972): 15–24. The volume is dedicated to the Memory of S. M. Stern.

Maimonides and Thomas Aquinas: Natural or Divine Prophecy? Reprinted from *AJS Review* (ed. by Frank Talmage), III (1978): 1–19.

Ars Rhetorica as Reflected in Some Jewish Figures of the Italian Renaissance. Paper delivered at the Harvard Jewish Center International Colloquium (1980): Jewish Thought in the Sixteenth Century.

Moses Mendelssohn's Proofs for the Existence of God. Reprinted from Cécile Lowenthal-Hensel (ed.), *Mendelssohn Studien* II (Berlin 1975), 9–29. Copyright 1975 by Duncker & Humblot, Berlin.

Moses Mendelssohn on Miracles. Reprinted, with the omission of the last section, from *Hommage À Georges Vajda, Études d'histoire et de pensée juives*, éditées par Gérard Nahon et Charles Touati (Louvain 1980), 463–477.

The Philosophical Roots of Mendelssohn's Plea for Emancipation. Reprinted from *Jewish Social Studies*, XXXVI, Nos. 3–4 (July–October 1974): 191–202.

Moses Mendelssohn on Excommunication: The Ecclesiastical Law Background. Reprinted from *Studies in the History of Jewish Society in the Middle Ages and in the Modern Period. Presented to Professor Jacob Katz on His Seventy-Fifth Birthday by His Students and Friends* (ed. by E. Etkes and Y. Salmon), (Jerusalem 1980), 41–61 (English Section).

The New Style of Preaching in Nineteenth-Century German Jewry. Reprinted by permission of the publishers from *Studies in Nineteenth Century Jewish Intellectual History*, edited by Alexander Altmann. Cambridge, Mass.: Harvard University Press. Copyright © 1964 by the President and Fellows of Harvard College, 65–116.

Franz Rosenzweig and Eugen Rosenstock-Huessy: An Introduction to Their "Letters on Judaism and Christianity." Reprinted from Eugen Rosenstock-Huessy (ed.), *Judaism Despite Christianity* (University, Alabama, 1969), 26–48, which itself is a reprint, with minor revisions, from *The Journal of Religion* XXIV (October, 1944): 259–270. Copyright © 1944 by the University of Chicago Press.

Theology in Twentieth-Century German Jewry. Reprinted from *Leo Baeck Institute Year Book* I (London, 1956), 193–213.

Leo Baeck and the Jewish Mystical Tradition. Reprinted from *Leo Baeck Memorial Lecture 17: In Tribute to Leo Baeck (1873–1956) on the Occasion of the 100th Anniversary of His Birthday.* (New York, 1973). Copyright © 1973 by Leo Baeck Institute, Inc.

Index of Names

Index of Subjects

LIBRARY OF CONGRESS CATALOGING IN PUBLICATION DATA

Altmann, Alexander, 1906–
Essays in Jewish intellectual history.

Includes bibliographical references and indexes.
1. Judaism—History—Addresses, essays, lectures.
2. Philosophy, Jewish—Addresses, essays, lectures.
3. Philosophy, Medieval—Addresses, essays, lectures. 4. Mendelssohn, Moses, 1729–1786—Addresses, essays, lectures. 5. Judaism—Germany—Addresses, essays, lectures. I. Title.
II. Title: Jewish intellectual history.
BM45.A45 296 80-54471
ISBN 0-87451-192-5 AACR2